PENGUIN BOOKS

THINK LIKE A CAT

Renowned feline behaviorist Pam Johnson-Bennett is the award-winning author of five books on cat behavior, including *Psycho Kitty* and *Twisted Whiskers*. Her first book was inducted into the *Cat Fancy* magazine Hall of Fame as one of the best books on cats ever published. Self-taught, she began her career when her own problem cat was labeled "hopeless" by the vet. Pam educated herself on animal psychology in order to save her cat's life. After successfully treating her own cat, as well as hundreds of other so-called "hopeless" pets, she became a veterinary technician while continuing to build her behavior consultation practice.

Considered one of this country's leading experts on cat behavior, Pam runs a private vet-referred counseling practice in Tennessee. She also writes a monthly behavior column for *Cats* magazine and is the cat expert at ivillage.com. Pam is a popular guest on national TV and radio as well as being a contributing expert to all of the leading cat publications.

Pam lives in Nashville with her husband and three cats.

Think Like a Cat

How to Raise a Well-Adjusted Cat— Not a Sour Puss

PAM JOHNSON-BENNETT

Feline Behaviorist

PENGUIN BOOKS

PENGUIN BOOKS
Published by the Penguin Group
Penguin Group (USA) Inc., 375 Hudson Street, New York, New York 10014, U.S.A.
Penguin Books Ltd, 80 Strand, London WC2R 0RL, England
Penguin Books Australia Ltd, 250 Camberwell Road, Camberwell, Victoria 3124, Australia
Penguin Books Canada Ltd, 10 Alcorn Avenue, Toronto, Ontario, Canada M4V 3B2
Penguin Books India (P) Ltd, 11 Community Centre, Panchsheel Park, New Delhi – 110 017, India
Penguin Books (N.Z.) Ltd, Cnr Rosedale and Airborne Roads, Albany, Auckland, New Zealand
Penguin Books (South Africa) (Pty) Ltd, 24 Sturdee Avenue,
Rosebank, Johannesburg 2196, South Africa

Penguin Books Ltd, Registered Offices: 80 Strand, London WC2R 0RL, England

First published in Penguin Books 2000

20 19 18

Copyright © Pam Johnson-Bennett, 2000
All rights reserved

LIBRARY OF CONGRESS CATALOGING IN PUBLICATION DATA
Johnson-Bennett, Pam, 1954–
Think like a cat: how to raise a well-adjusted cat—not a sour
puss / Pam Johnson-Bennett.
p.   cm.
Includes bibliographical references and index.
ISBN 0 14 02.8854 6
1. Cats—Training.   2. Cats—Behavior.   3. Cats—Psychology.
I. Title.
SF446.5.J656   2000
636.8′0835—dc21   99–31324

Printed in the United States of America
Set in Bodoni Book
Designed by Jessica Shatan

To the two greatest men I've ever known:
my husband, Scott Bennett,
and my late father, Albert Johnson

and to my beautiful mother and sister . . .
we'll always be Daddy's girls

Acknowledgments

After years of working with cats, their owners, veterinarians, and so many people in the animal-care field, I've been lucky to learn something from everyone (two-legged and, most especially, four-legged). Being able to witness on a daily basis, the love and commitment that owners and cats have for each other has been such a privilege. I'm even grateful to all of the owners who initially viewed me with skepticism (and believe me, there were many) and to the cats who did their very best to run me off. In the beginning, some of them almost did. Challenges became opportunities to grow. Boy, have I had plenty of opportunities!

The veterinarians I've had the privilege of working with over the years have been exceptionally generous with their time and knowledge. Vets are truly the unsung heroes for our pets. They deal with patients who are less than cooperative and who often prefer to take a bite out of the very doctor saving their lives. I'm impressed at the lightning fast reflexes some doctors have developed and the patience they show toward even the most fractious cat.

Thank you to my editor, Wendy Wolf (a very patient woman), and my new family at Penguin Books.

Thanks to Joe Ed Conn, DVM, for valuable input and wisdom on the medical section of this book and for true devotion to providing the best veterinary care.

Special thanks to my agent, Linda Roghaar, for guidance.

And to the remarkable Ellen Jones Pryor, for doing so many things for me it would take a book in itself just to list them.

Steve Dale, who I'm so lucky to be able to call my friend. Thanks for watching over me.

Cat kisses to Ginger Barnett, for support and friendship.

I've also been lucky in becoming a member of a wonderful family through marriage. Thank you to the Bennetts for welcoming me into their hearts. If knowing that their only son was marrying a *cat shrink* caused them to raise an eyebrow, they've never let it show.

My love and amazement go to my precious fur family: Mary Margaret, Beatrice, Olive, Annabelle, and Albie.

Finally, to the ever-present spirit of my greatest feline teacher, Ethel, who has taught me many of the most valuable lessons in life: love unconditionally, express your true feelings, respect others' territory, protect the family, get enough sleep, and always keep an eye open for mice.

Contents

Introduction

I've written this book so that a new cat owner can have the tools to start providing what a cat needs right away. I don't want you to waste a minute misunderstanding what your cat is trying to communicate, or damaging the relationship by using old, ineffective training methods. The title of this book truly describes the way I approach training. By understanding your cat's motivations, needs, and communication, you can so easily enjoy a close, wonderful relationship. Even if you're not a cat novice, I'll bet there are many ways you could improve your relationship. Perhaps you've been dealing with a behavior problem and have long since resigned yourself to just accepting it. This book may offer solutions that you didn't think were possible. I want to change the way you look at your cat. I also want to change the way you look at your cat's environment. Instead of seeing it from the vantage point of, say, a height of five-foot-seven (give or take an inch or two), I want you to look through your cat's eyes. What does the world look like when you're ten inches off the ground?

This book will enable you to solve problems by focusing on the good behavior you do want rather than the bad behavior you don't want. Shifting your approach from negative to positive puts you in the mind-set of being a successful problem-solver as opposed to a frustrated pet owner. It becomes an easy and logical progression: Think about the behavior you want from your cat and the route necessary to get him there. I'll guide you through it every step of the way.

My introduction to cats came as it does for many people—accidentally. Growing up in a family of dog lovers. I thought dogs were the greatest pets in the world and cats were, well, *cats*. I believed all the myths I'd heard about them and while I certainly found them to be beautiful, I'd just as soon have a dog.

Then, one Christmas Eve many years ago, my life became forever changed. I was spending the holidays at my parents' Long Island home. It was bitter cold and snowy and I was doing some last-minute shopping. I passed a teenage girl standing in front of a church. On the steps beside her was a cardboard box. A handmade sign read FREE KITTENS. Surely this girl wouldn't have kittens outside on a day like this, I thought. I peered over the top of the box, and there inside were indeed two tiny kittens. With just a towel lining the box, the kittens were huddled together, trying to stay warm.

Furious at the lack of compassion and responsibility of this teenager (and the parents who most likely sent her out to do this), I offered to take the kittens, opened my jacket and placed them inside my sweater. They felt like two little ice cubes. I doubted they'd even live long enough for me to get them home.

In the car, I turned up the heat full blast and hurried home (quite sure that when I arrived, my parents would probably be less than thrilled at the unexpected addition to their holiday celebration). Luckily, my family's love and compassion for any animals in need outweighed any hint of disapproval concerning what I'd impulsively done.

The quiet Christmas holiday we'd planned became a mad dash of specific responsibilities. My mother began to search for the long-lost heating pad while my father made a makeshift litter pan from a cardboard box. My sister and I were busy in the kitchen handling the job of feeding the kittens, who were able to eat solid food. (We didn't know it at the time, but they were six weeks old.)

Once warm and with full tummies, the little kittens curled up in the winter coat I'd tossed on the floor when I'd burst into the house. We all stood around watching as they settled in. Even my parents' two dogs quietly watched the sleeping kittens. As my mother's Christmas cookie dough sat unbaked on the kitchen counter and the gifts I'd bought that day sat unwrapped in the trunk of the car, two tiny, cold, malnourished, flea-infested, frightened, dirty, unhealthy kittens did something remarkable . . . they *survived*.

Those two kittens survived despite having been taken away from their mother much too young, being exposed to extremely cold temperatures, and getting adopted by someone who knew nothing about cats.

Having these two lives totally dependent upon me made me aware of how little I knew about cats and that what I did know wasn't even accurate. Lucy and Ethel (not very original names, I admit) endured my well-meaning but often fumbling attempts at care with such grace, tolerance, and love.

Cats were supposed to be aloof, so why were these two so sweet and affectionate? Cats are known for being untrainable, so why was it so easy for me to teach them to behave so well? If cats are independent, then why were these two becoming my constant companions? I began to realize that the people who think negatively toward cats do that because they don't *know* them. To know them truly is to love them.

Lucy died at the age of three of a congenital heart condition—ironically, on Christmas Day. Ethel, who had the same congenital defect, lived much longer before finally succumbing. Those two cats not only brought such love and happiness into my life, they also inspired me to embark on a career that I (and certainly my family) never could have imagined.

If you are a longtime cat owner, there will certainly be basic information in this book that will seem old hat to you, but I urge you not to rush past subjects you may think don't apply to your situation. While you may not need to learn how to pick out a veterinarian or how to set up a litter box, by looking at your cat's life through his eyes and employing a *think like a cat* approach, you'll solve behavior problems, prevent potential ones, and avoid owner pitfalls. (Yes, even experienced owners often can't see the feline forest for the trees.)

If you're about to become a cat owner for the first time, congratulations. You are soon to enter into a relationship in which you are unconditionally loved, endlessly forgiven for your mistakes, never judged, and constantly entertained. A cat can make the stresses of your day disappear just by curling up in your lap at night. When you've been working too hard, a cat will walk across your papers to let you know it's time for a break. A cat will show his gratitude for the simplest act, such as scratching him under the chin, by serenading you with his deep, rich purr. A cat will still adore you on those days when you look your worst. A cat is a patient listener, even when you're telling a story for the third time. A cat is the most dependable alarm clock you'll ever have. A cat will show you how to enjoy life.

A cat chooses the company he keeps.

Think
Like a
Cat

The Cat of Your Dreams

Will You be a Match Made in Heaven or The Odd Couple?

Cats aren't shirts that you buy at the store and then return if they don't fit. Nor are they a pair of shoes you give away or toss out when you've outgrown them. While these comparisons may seem ridiculously obvious to you, the sad fact is that too many cat owners actually do view their cats that way. As a result, countless cats end up relinquished to shelters or just abandoned because they didn't meet their owners' expectations of "the perfect cat."

Why do you want a cat? Taking the time to examine your desires honestly can help ensure a lifetime of love.

Choosing to become a cat owner is, of course, an emotional decision. It's also choosing to take on a serious responsibility because the cat's health and welfare will be completely dependent on you. If your impression of cat ownership involves filling up a food bowl and putting a litter box in the extra bathroom, then both you and your cat will soon become very unhappy. Although a cat may *seem* to be a lower maintenance pet than a dog, you must be prepared to meet his emotional, medical, and physical needs.

Being a cat owner also involves a financial commitment which some people aren't prepared for. Cats or kittens acquired for free need the same veterinary and nutritional care as the purebred you paid top dollar for: the initial vaccinations and neuter or spay surgery, then yearly vaccinations for the rest of his life. He'll also undoubtedly need periodic medical care for unexpected ailments or injuries, and veterinary care isn't cheap.

Over the years I've seen many incredibly close cat/owner relationships. I've also seen cats and owners who seem to be just co-existing in the same house with no emotional bond. Many times, that's the result of the owner having had the wrong expectations about cats from the start. You have an opportunity now, with this book, to create a close cat/human bond. Even if you already have a cat (maybe you've had him for years), you can create a closer relationship—and that's the key, it *is* a *relationship*.

Rumors, Innuendoes, and Lies

Some of the comments I've heard over the years are:

Cats steal the breath from babies.

You must get rid of your cat if you're pregnant.

Litter boxes always stink.

Cats ruin the furniture.

If those were true, why would *anybody* ever want a cat? Unfortunately, people continue to pass along this inaccurate and unfair information. The result? Many people who might have become cat owners get scared off. It's the cats who suffer as they continue to be charged with crimes of which they aren't guilty. Let's take a closer look at some of the common misconceptions so that you can learn fact from fiction and go ahead with plans to share your life with a cat.

Cats are aloof. We've all heard that! In fact, if most people had to describe cats in one word, *aloof* would be it. And, if you mention *aloof*, you might as well throw in *independent* as well. I believe these descriptions come from inappropriately trying to compare cats to dogs. It's the old apples and oranges comparison. The dog is a pack animal. He hunts in a pack and his whole social structure is built on the pack mentality. A cat, on the other hand, is a sociable animal but not the pack animal that a dog is. His social structure is built upon his sense of territory. Don't misunderstand me: Cats can and do live happily together, but unlike dogs, their primary focus isn't to establish a pack.

Part of the reason cats may appear aloof is that they are predators (and take in their entire environment). Sometimes the cat may sit on your lap, enjoying your affectionate stroking, but there are times when he'd prefer just sitting nearby, relaxed yet ready should any prey come on the scene. Cats are stimulated by even the slightest movement, which might indicate potential prey.

Cats by nature are not generally *contact* animals the way dogs are. With their pack mentality, dogs encounter a great deal of close physical contact with each other. In the wild, an adult cat's physical contact with another cat may be generally limited to mating or fighting. This isn't to say that your cat won't enjoy being petted or held, just that some cats need a larger personal space than others and if you respect that, you'll be able to build trust and eventually increase his level of comfort. How they were socialized as kittens and whether they were gently handled by humans also plays a role in how large a personal space they require later. Much of how your individual cat's personality develops and whether he becomes friendly and sociable versus timid and unfriendly depends on you.

This book will teach you how to understand his language and communicate with him so you two can develop a strong, loving bond. If you expect him to do all of the work then you'll end up with, *yes,* an aloof, independent cat.

The bottom line: Stop comparing your cat to a dog, and suddenly you'll start noticing his uniquely wonderful traits.

Cats can't be trained. False! Once again, you just have to stop thinking DOG and start thinking CAT. My approach to training is based on positive reinforcement. If I want my cat to stop doing something, I direct him to something better. My *think like a cat* method involves understanding why he's behaving the way he does so I can meet his needs in an acceptable way. This training method is easier and more effective than continually reprimanding your cat for doing things that are instinctually natural to him (such as scratching). So throw out all of those old ideas you've had about how cats can't be trained. It's easier than you think. Actually, I'll let you in on a little secret: I think it's easier to train a cat than a dog.

Cats are dangerous if you're pregnant and *cats steal the breath from babies.* I really hate these. First of all, if you're pregnant, there *are* precautions you should take concerning the litter box. The box could be a serious health risk to your unborn baby, but it doesn't mean the cat should be tossed out. To get the accurate story, refer to the medical appendix in the back of this book. As for that stupid myth about cats stealing the breath from babies, it's not true, yet it continues to resurface year after year. My theory on this is that long ago, before SIDS (sudden infant death syndrome) was identified, cats were blamed for the unexpected death of sleeping babies.

Litter boxes always stink. Well, actually a litter box will stink IF YOU DON'T CLEAN IT!!! As long as you maintain an adequate cleaning schedule, no one will ever have to hold his nose to enter your home.

Cats ruin the furniture. Oops, you got me again. There's some truth to this statement but only if you neglect to provide him with a scratching post. Now I know some of you reading this are thinking, *Well, my neighbor has a scratching post and the cat* still *ruins the furniture.* My answer to that? Wrong post. Chapter 9 will teach you how to get it right the first time.

So now that we've cleared that up and you're standing on the threshold of cat ownership, let's go get the cat, right? Uh, not quite yet. You have many decisions to make. Do you want a kitten or a cat? Male or female? Will the cat be an indoor or outdoor cat? Where should you get the cat? Pet store? Breeder? The next-door neighbor?

A Kitten or a Cat?

Kittens are cute. I mean really, really cute. Whenever I bring a kitten on television with me, just about every crew member has to come by for a closer look. Kittens are definitely smile magnets, but before you fall in love with that adorable little bundle of fur, take the time to understand what'll be required of you as the owner of a kitten.

You need to kitten-proof your home if you decide on a youngster. You have to patrol for dangling electrical cords, dangerous cleansers, poisons, etc. (Even if you decide on an adult cat you'll have to safeguard him from these things as well, but kittens seem bound and determined to get into trouble.) Basically, you have to know where your kitten is at all times to prevent him from hurting himself. Kitten-proofing a home isn't that difficult, but for some people it's not possible. For instance, an artist friend of mine lives in a one-bedroom apartment. She wanted the companionship of a feline but knew that getting a kitten would surely result in spilled paint. Not only would that be messy, but it would cause a serious health risk to a curious little kitty. The artist chose to adopt an adult cat who had a quiet personality. Aside from one incident when the cat accidentally walked across Sonia's palette and left a trail of fuschia paw prints on the carpet, they have a very compatible relationship.

A family with young children should reconsider the idea of a young kitten and opt for an older one (at least six months old). Kittens are very fragile and can easily be injured by exuberant young children. An older cat can still be injured, but he is better able to escape from a child's grasp.

If you or anyone in your family is unsure of his footing, a kitten zooming underfoot through the house could create a danger.

Consider how much *time* you have to devote to a kitten. They require more supervision and can't be left alone as long as an adult cat.

If you adopt a kitten, it affords you the opportunity to have a greater effect on shaping his personality than you would have on an adult cat. By exposing him to a variety of situations, you stand a good chance of raising a cat who is comfortable around strangers, not afraid of unfamiliar surroundings, adapted to travel, etc.

So why would you want to miss all the fun and get a grown-up? One of the best reasons to choose an adult cat is that you know just what you're getting. Physically, it's all there for you: body type and color/ length of coat. You can also get a good sense of his temperament— whether he's active, nervous, docile, sociable, very vocal, quiet, etc. Because all kittens tend to be fuzzy little race cars, you don't know which ones will actually stay that way and which ones will calm down. If you want to be sure of a specific temperament or personality, go for an adult cat.

One thing to keep in mind though is that a shelter cat may initially appear very timid or defensive in that stressful environment. Once he becomes acclimated to your home and family, he may begin to blossom. On the other hand, a cat at the shelter may have been relinquished by the previous owner because he had behavior problems. It doesn't mean the problem isn't workable, but you have to be prepared to address whatever situation does arise. I'll discuss shelter adoptions later in this chapter.

An adult cat doesn't need the seemingly constant supervision that a kitten does. This is great for people who don't have the time to be following a kitten all around the house day and night.

If you truly have the love and a desire to share your life with a cat, adopting an adult could literally save his life. Whether kittens are brought to shelters, found in alleys, or given away outside of grocery stores, they stand a better chance of being adopted than the adult cats. By taking that four-year-old tabby, you'll be saving him from a life behind bars or worse, death.

Financially, an adult cat is often less expensive than a kitten. Kittens require a series of vaccinations and at six months of age, there's the cost of neutering or spaying. Adopting an adult cat from another family or from a shelter often means the cat is up-to-date on vaccinations and, in some cases, already altered.

The He or She Dilemma

This is another area where myths and rumors seem to run wild. If you know someone who has only had male cats, they'll be able to rattle off all of the great qualities of a male and numerous shortcomings of females. They'll tell you how much smarter and outgoing males are. Longtime owners of females will quickly dispute that and add how territorial males are.

Here's the truth. Once a cat is altered, it doesn't matter if you choose a male or a female. Hormones are what drive undesirable behavior such as a spraying male or a yowling female in heat. Simply by having the cat spayed or neutered, you can control that. Left intact (unaltered), I don't care whether you choose a male or female, you'll be one unhappy (and that's putting it mildly) cat owner. Intact males are territorial and they will spray. If allowed outdoors, they'll roam and get into countless fights that could lead to death. Intact females, when in heat (which happens several times a year), call relentlessly in search of a male and will try to sneak outdoors every chance they get. Altered cats make much better companions. They won't spend their lives in frustration, and you won't spend your life pulling your hair out.

Purebred (aka Pedigreed) Cats

Although most cat owners choose nonpedigreed cats (or else those cats choose them), you may have your heart set on a purebred.

Lovers of purebred cats will argue that there are hundreds of reasons to go that route versus mixed-breed, but I'm going to assume you're a novice in the cat world, and focus on what I feel would be of the most importance to a new cat owner.

When considering a purebred, make certain you're aware of any potential genetic health concerns prone to that particular breed. Two familiar ones are the respiratory problems associated with the short-nosed Persians and the potential skeletal problems associated with the Manx. Do your homework before deciding on a purebred. Read breed-specific books and check cat registry Web sites. Talk to your vet, breeders, and owners of the breed you're considering. Visit cat shows in your area to get a closer look. Talk with the breeders who are there to show their cats. To find out what cat shows are in your area, check out the listings in the various cat magazines or visit the cat registry Web sites.

In the dog world you find big dogs, bigger dogs, small dogs, even smaller dogs, hunting dogs, herding dogs, sporting dogs, guard dogs, longhaired, shorthaired, no-haired, vocal dogs, and quiet dogs. Such variety! In the cat world, the greatest variety exists mainly within the purebreds. Let's take size, for example: If you want a very large cat, you'd probably be interested in the Maine Coon Cat. If an athletic cat is more to your liking, there are several breeds to choose from, for example, the Abyssinian. So, if you like specific physical traits or a certain personality type, purebreds can be more predictable. This could be an important factor in your decision-making process. Within the world of purebreds, you will find cats with folded ears, bobbed tails, no tails, kinked fur, no fur, or colors that could only exist in nature; cats who are talkers or couch potatoes.

Some breeds require special attention that you may not have the time, desire, or ability to provide. For example, several of the long-haired breeds—such as Persians and Himalayans—require daily brushing or their hair will mat. Do you have the time required to care properly for this kind of cat?

Finally there's money. A purebred will cost you. Some are much more expensive than others, but be prepared to pay.

The Long and Short of It: Hair Length

No question about it, a beautifully groomed longhaired cat is a head-turner. Cats such as Persians have the feline world's equivalent of Hollywood glamour. We watch them on TV as they recline on their pillows in their diamond collars, eating out of stemmed crystal glasses. Truly glamorous, dahling! That's probably why Persians are one of the most popular breeds. We see them and fall in love, unaware of the "behind the scenes" work that goes into maintaining that glorious coat.

The coats of many longhaired cats will mat if not brushed daily. That silky coat can get into a knot faster than you can say "creme rinse." Aside from the unsightly look of matted fur, mats can create health risks if left unattended because they can prevent air from reaching the skin. Fleas can also seek refuge under mats. As mats tighten they pull on the skin and make walking painful. The nails of the cat can get stuck in the mats as he attempts to scratch. I've seen neglected Persians who have ripped holes in their skins in an attempt to scratch beneath the mat. If you love the look of a silky longhaired cat, give serious thought to the maintenance.

Not all longhaired cats are prone to matting. Even if you choose a not-matting cat, be aware that all longhaired breeds will still require more frequent brushing. The Maine Coon and Norwegian Forest Cat, for example, have thick, long hair that doesn't mat. Maintenance is still required, though, to keep this coat looking lustrous.

Longhaired cats, whether they mat or not, occasionally need special assistance concerning their personal hygiene. Their long fur can now and then catch and trap pieces of feces. If a longhaired cat develops diarrhea, the cleanup is much more involved than with a shorthaired cat.

Hair balls. You've heard of them. You've maybe even seen them. Although any cat regardless of coat length can have them (depending on how frequently they self-groom), long haired cats experience more than their share. A good grooming schedule by you and a regular dose of hair ball prevention paste (available from your vet) will help, but if you aren't able to maintain the cat's coat, you'll be subjecting him to certain hair balls. For more on grooming, refer to chapter 12.

Some breeds are more fragile than others. The Sphinx, for example—which is a practically hairless cat—requires warmer temperatures and therefore wouldn't be a good choice for someone who prefers keeping the thermostat set low.

Magnificent Mixed Breeds

Some of the most loved, spoiled, cared for, doted on, cherished cats are the ones who don't come with a pedigree. They're the ones we find lost by the roadside, at our back door, in the neighbor's garage, in the barn, the local shelter, brought home by our children or shivering in the parking lot. So many are in need of our rescue. Really, I believe many more actually rescue *us*.

Unless you're already set on a specific breed, are planning to enter your cat in shows (and actually, there are several mixed-breed shows), or embarking on a breeding career (something I strongly advise against), you should consider a mixed breed.

What is a *mixed* breed? It refers to the product of the random matings of different or mixed breeds of cats. Sometimes you may see a trace of an identifiable breed (for instance, the cat may have a sleek oriental body and be very vocal) but usually, the years of random matings create cats whose histories are mysteries.

Mixed breed cats come in all shapes, sizes, and colors. From a personality standpoint, you may not get the predictability that you often have with purebreds, but in general, what you will get is a hearty, adaptable cat.

Where to Find Your New Cat

Now that you're sure you want to share your life with a cat, let's examine the many sources out there for acquiring your new companion— whether a kitten, adult, purebred, mixed, longhaired, shorthaired, male, or female.

As I'm sure you're well aware, cats aren't in short supply. You could probably open up your back door and literally find one hanging out in the yard. I live on three acres, and almost every morning I spot a different cat crossing through the field.

While a great many people come across the cat of their dreams through rescue efforts, that method isn't for everyone. The injured or starving cat you pick up from the roadside or the one you rescue from the shelter's death row may or may not turn out to be the friendly, trusting, well-socialized animal you'd hoped for. I'm certainly all for anyone who gives a cat a second chance at life, but you should make sure you know what you're getting into. I want you and your cat to spend many, many happy years together.

A note of caution: When you begin your search, I recommend that you not bring your children along. Your first visits to shelters, breeders, etc., need to be strictly to evaluate the facilities. I've seen too many owners coming home their first day out with a kitten they weren't prepared for because the children fell in love. Oh, and by the way, children aren't the only ones who suffer from the inability to walk out of a pet store or shelter empty-handed—we adults wrote the book on that one!

SHELTERS—FINDING YOUR DIAMOND IN THE ROUGH

Walking into a shelter is a very emotional experience for an animal lover. Walking out *empty-handed* is very difficult for an animal lover. Be prepared—you can't save all the animals. It's very tough to go from one cage to the next, staring into the eyes of the cats in need of homes. As much as you may want to take the neediest of the cats into your arms forever, be sure you know what it'll require. Making an impulsive decision you aren't ready for could end up being wrong for you and for the cat.

There are many shelters around the country, ranging from public animal control facilities to nonprofit private organizations. In your search, you'll find well-run facilities and you'll come across horrible jailhouses.

Chances are very slim that you'll be able to come across a purebred cat at a shelter but it does happen (most likely the more popular Persian or Siamese). If you're looking for a kitten, they go fast—everyone wants kittens, especially around Christmas. But if you're open to the idea of an adult cat, you'll find many ages, colors, and personalities.

Although most shelters are staffed by caring people who try their hardest to house the cats in as comforting of an environment as possible, considering how stressful shelter life is, don't expect the cats to be on their best behavior. Very often these cats are in emotional shock. Many have been abandoned by their owners, lost, homeless, or injured. Suddenly they're put in a cage, away from anything even remotely familiar from life as they knew it and they're terrified. Even though your heart's in the right place and you plan on giving a cat the best home in the world, initially he may not act very appreciative. Some cats who've been relinquished to the shelter by a family due to a behavior problem will pose an extra challenge to you. Very often, though, a cat adopted from the shelter eventually puts his past behind him and ends up being the love of your life. Some of the smartest, prettiest, most sociable, tolerant cats I've seen came from shelters.

Nowadays shelter staffs work with cats when they're first brought in to help them become adoptable. Years ago, when pets were brought to most shelters they'd be tossed into a cage or dog-run and remain there until they were either adopted or put to death. Luckily, more and more shelters have volunteers who come in daily to interact with the pets, offering comfort, affection, and playtime.

Before you decide to go to the shelter adoption route, inspect the facility, ask questions, and be completely informed regarding their policies (for instance, many shelters have rules stating that the adopted cat must be kept indoors). Some even require an in-home visit first to make sure *you* are suitable.

CAT RESCUE GROUPS

If you'd like to provide a home for a kitty in need through a local rescue agency, keep in mind that as with shelter-adopted cats, you'll very likely be dealing with a traumatized animal. These cats need a stable, peaceful, secure home and an owner with an abundance of patience and love.

Many of the cats rescued will not have had the advantage of having been socialized to humans during kittenhood. This is an important thing to consider if you absolutely want a cat who will sit in your lap and view life in a carefree way. A cat who has been rescued may need quite a bit of time before daring to trust. When it happens, though, it's amazing to watch as the cat begins to lower his guard and let you in. The times I've experienced it will stay in my heart forever.

BREEDERS—THE GOOD, THE BAD, AND THE BOTTOM OF THE BARREL

If you truly have your heart set on a purebred, your best source will be a breeder. A *good* breeder isn't so easy to find, though. As with any other business, when money is involved, ethics can get lost on the way to the bank.

A Good Breeder

- is very knowledgeable about the breed
- welcomes any questions you may have
- competes in cat shows
- offers references
- welcomes inspections of her cattery
- lets you see the parents of the kittens
- has all registration papers
- requires the buyer to spay or neuter the cat
- has documentation of health exams and vaccinations
- doesn't sell any kitten less than twelve weeks old
- prohibits declawing
- specifies in the contract that the cat must be kept indoors
- doesn't pressure you to buy
- displays a genuine love for the breed
- screens *you* to make sure her kitten goes to a good home
- offers a refund and not just a replacement kitten
- requires the kitten be returned if you can't keep him

Good breeders are dedicated to maintaining the integrity of their breed. They lovingly keep a very clean, healthy cattery and are extremely knowledgeable about cat health, nutrition, and behavior. They should know about any congenital problems that their breed is prone to and how to avoid them. Good breeders welcome questions and inspections of their catteries.

To begin your search for a good breeder, start by attending the cat shows in your area. Even if the nearest one is a bit of a drive, it's worth it. Good breeders *show* their cats. It's a good opportunity for you to talk with several breeders. Unless they're getting their cat ready to be judged, they should be more than happy to answer any questions you have.

Raised underfoot is a phrase you'll hear very often when talking to breeders. That means the kittens have been handled and socialized by humans as opposed to being locked away in cages. Beware, though, anyone can claim that their kittens were raised underfoot; it's up to you to decide if they're truthful. Visit the cattery; ask questions; carefully observe and handle the kittens. Remember, a *registered* kitten means he comes with an official-looking piece of paper. It doesn't guarantee that he's a well-adjusted kitten.

PET STORES

Don't be a sucker. Kittens in pet stores are way overpriced, under-socialized, and most likely the result of someone's breeding boo-boo. Don't support the unethical business of purchasing kittens from pet stores.

A good breeder would never sell a kitten to a pet store. Just because you have the cash or can flash a credit card doesn't make you the right owner for the purebred. Anyone who would sell a cat based on who can fork over the cash fastest isn't someone you should even think about buying from in the first place.

Some pet supply stores have changed their policies and refuse to sell kittens and puppies because of the vast number of unethical breeders. I applaud them and show my support by purchasing my pet supplies there.

BUYING BY PHOTOGRAPH

Whether your dealing with a breeder or a private owner, don't agree to purchase a cat you haven't seen. Some breeders who live out of your area will agree to sell cats long-distance. They send you a photograph and the first time you actually get to meet your cat is when you pick him up at the airport. My word on this practice? DON'T.

If the breeder of the specific breed you want lives far away (and this usually is the case if you're interested in a rare breed) and you absolutely have to have this kitten, then get on a plane and go see him, evaluate the facilities and then if all seems right, take the kitten back with you.

NEWSPAPER ADS

Be cautious. Just because a kitten is advertised for free and the description sounds perfect doesn't necessarily mean things are as advertised.

Treat the owners as you would a breeder by asking questions. How was the kitten or cat raised? In the case of older cats, ask why they're needing to find another home. The reason may be stated in the ad, but ask for more specific details.

Check out the home carefully. Don't let the owners meet you at the mailbox with the kitten in their arms. You want to see where he was raised and if possible, see the mother cat.

If the owners are trying to place a cat who has behavior problems and you still want to adopt him, find out *everything* and I mean *everything* you can. Not only what the problem is but where, when, and how it happens. What methods did they use to correct the problem? The behavior problem may be a result of something going on in that household and might be solved just by removing the cat. Just make sure you've received full disclosure and that you're prepared to be patient through the cat's adjustment period.

Sometimes adult cats are put up for adoption because there have been changes in the family. For example, the owner may have passed away and the relatives are trying to place the cat. If you know the reason why the cat is being placed, you can be better prepared to help him through the changes.

An adult cat from a previous home often makes a wonderful companion as long as you have the time and patience to help him. Cats who have lost their owners, have been abused or suddenly shunned (because of something such as rejection by an owner's new spouse), are confused, scared, and in crisis. With your love, though, they stand a chance at a wonderful life.

If it's a kitten advertised in the paper, and the ad states that initial vaccinations have been given, don't just take a stranger's word for it. Ask to see written proof in the form of a vet receipt. Don't be satisfied by one of those little "My Pet's Record" folders where the vaccinations are checked off and the date entered. Anyone with a pen can write in those booklets. Find out who the vet is, and call for verification if the owners have no written proof.

If the owner has the mother cat, find out if she is up-to-date on vaccinations and has been tested negative for *feline leukemia* and *feline immunodeficiency virus*.

Another big question that should be on your mind is *why* did this owner allow the cat to become pregnant? Are they backyard breeders who thought they could make a little money by mating their purebred with some friend's male purebred? By purchasing a kitten from such people, you only encourage them to continue this practice. If you think you'll be getting a valuable purebred at a bargain, you're sadly mistaken. What you may actually be doing is paying a high price for a low-quality cat with genetic defects.

I'm also upset about the people who don't alter their mixed-breed cats and then when the cat has a litter, put an ad in the paper, knowing that people are always looking for kittens and they'll be able to get those four or five little *problems* off their hands.

GETTING A KITTEN OR CAT
FROM YOUR FRIEND OR NEIGHBOR

Refer to the previous section on "Newspaper Ads" because the same "do's and don'ts" apply. They may be fabulous gardeners or conscientious neighbors but problematic cat owners. Ask the right questions.

CHECK OUT THE PEOPLE,
NOT JUST THE CATS

Summon up every intuitive ability you have, and while you're asking questions of the people who have raised the kitten or cat, make sure you're comfortable with their answers. As an animal behaviorist, I've learned that when I ask a question of many owners, they'll often give me the answer they think I want to hear rather than the truth. I've had to sharpen my skill at separating fact from fiction. For instance, if anything an owner, breeder, pet-store owner, or shelter worker says doesn't coincide with what you're seeing, then your antenna should go up. Ask questions and get whatever history is available on the kitten.

WHEN THE CAT CHOOSES YOU

I'll bet that if you took a poll among cat owners, an overwhelming number of them would tell you that they hadn't been looking for a cat, hadn't planned on one, and maybe didn't even care much for cats—the feline love of their lives just walked in. More often than not, it's the cats who choose us, whether they show up at our doorstep, on the roadside as we take our morning run, or huddled on the warm hood of our car on a cold winter night. This is the way almost all of my cats have come into my life.

If a cat appears at your door, before deciding to become his owner, make sure he doesn't belong to anyone else. Obviously check for a collar or any other form of identification. Some owners have microchips implanted under the cat's skin. These chips are then read by a special hand-held scanner. Many shelters and vets now have these scanners. Check with your local shelter and the vets in your area in case someone has been searching for a lost cat. Search the newspaper under *Lost Pets* and also place an ad yourself. Don't tell everything about the cat though so you'll be able to tell who the true owner is. For example, if the cat has a white spot on his back right foot, or is missing a canine tooth, these are the kinds of facts that only the true owner would know.

Before keeping the cat who has chosen you, he'll need to be tested for deadly diseases such as feline leukemia and feline immunodeficiency virus. If the tests come back negative, he should be vaccinated and dewormed.

If the cat who chooses you is *feral* (a domesticated cat who has reverted back to the wild) as opposed to being a *stray* (a cat someone once owned and socialized but has since been on his own for whatever reason), then the process of becoming his owner is more complicated. A feral cat hasn't been handled or socialized through contact with humans. These cats can remain mistrustful and distant. They also may not integrate well into households where there are existing cats.

When It's Time to Choose

Now you see that *where* and *how* a kitten is raised has a huge impact on whether he'll be a sociable, friendly member of your family or the invisible ball of fur who spends his days hiding beneath your bed, avoiding humans every chance he gets. Whether you're choosing a shelter, breeder, or private home, don't go into the situation seeing only an adorable little kitten and closing your eyes to the environment in which he has been raised.

PICK OF THE LITTER

Rule number one: Don't let anyone sell or give you a kitten taken away from his mother before the kitten is twelve weeks of age. Kittens need to be with their mother and also their littermates until that time. This is the time they're still learning from each other. The playing and posturing kittens do with each other is actually preparing them for adulthood. They're learning valuable social skills. Kittens taken away from their littermates too early often have difficulty integrating into multicat households later. They don't have appropriate *play* skills and can have trouble bonding with companion pets.

A kitten taken away from his mother before she has had time to gradually wean him can become a wool sucker (or earlobe sucker, finger sucker, shoelace sucker—the list is endless).

Rule number two: A kitten who wasn't properly socialized will have trouble bonding to humans. The crucial socialization period is between three to seven weeks. It's at this time that frequent, gentle handling by humans help kittens learn to trust and become comfortable around us scary-looking giants.

Observe the mother cat if possible, and ask questions concerning the kind of care she gives her kittens. How is the mother cared for? What kind of physical condition is she in? If she looks thin and unhealthy, then the quality and quantity of the milk she provided her kittens could be compromised.

With five adorable kittens staring at you, how do you choose just one? It's hard. Your head is calmly saying, "We agreed that we'd get only one kitten," but your heart is saying, "They're so cute, WE WANT THEM ALL!" Stop and think. Five kittens means five times the veterinary and food expenses, five times more care and attention needed, and five kittens grow into five cats. It can be overwhelming.

If you don't have any other cats already at home though, I would strongly recommend that you do consider taking *two* kittens. Adopting or purchasing two kittens will be a very rewarding experience. They'll continue to learn from each other as they grow, they'll have companionship (because you can't always be around) and from a behavioral standpoint, it's a heck of a lot easier to bring two kittens into a household now than to just get one and decide after he's an adult that he needs a buddy. Adult cats are territorial and introducing a second cat can be very tricky. I can't even count how many owners of adult cats have told me how they wished they'd adopted a second kitten when they had the chance.

FINDING YOUR FELINE SOULMATE

If there's a litter of kittens, try to see them all. Even if you know in advance that you want a female and the owners tell you that there's only one in the litter, look at each kitten anyway. Why would I want you to look at the males when you're sure you want a girl? Observing the litter as a whole can help you sort out personality types. You may want a female kitten but maybe you don't want a wild one and by watching the whole group you'll get a sense of where she fits in. You may find a male cat who seems playful and confident but not as revved up.

Although you may be tempted to "rescue" the so-called *runt* of the litter, realize that the kittens who are on the far ends of the scale (i.e., very aggressive or very timid) may develop behavioral problems. I'm not saying that only perfect kittens should be adopted, just that you have to

CatwiseClue

If you're at a pet store, shelter, or in a situation where you don't have the opportunity to observe the litter (the kittens may already have been separated), then **TAKE YOUR TIME** when evaluating whether the kitten you're looking at is right for you. It's a decision you'll both have to live with for a long time.

be aware of your expectations and your limiting factors. For example, if you have children at home who are expecting the best little kitten in the world, then bringing them a very frightened kitten who hides at the slightest sound or movement will be disastrous for both your family and the kitten.

Many people choose kittens on looks alone. They've always wanted a black cat or maybe it's the orange tabby look that melts their heart. Well, while looks are certainly nice, take a moment to think back over relationships you've had in your life. How successful have your relationships been that were based on looks alone? Would you choose a partner to spend the rest of your life with just because he or she is attractive? If you answered "yes," then I want you to take this book, close it, hold it up next to your head, and give yourself a good whack. Shame on you.

Now, let's get back to work. Remember, the cat you choose will, with luck and care, be in your family for ten to twenty-three years (maybe even more). Physical appearance is only a part of what makes up a cat. Now you can go get an ice pack for that lump on your head.

TESTING YOUR POTENTIAL KITTEN'S TEMPERAMENT

Find out if the kittens have just eaten before attempting to judge personalities and activity levels, because everyone will most likely be sleepy after a meal.

- Notice who is playful, confident, and friendly.

- Get down on the floor and let the kitten (or kittens) get used to you. How does he react? Does he panic and hide? Does he hiss at you? Basically, he should be comfortable and unafraid.

- Tempt the kitten with anything that will elicit a play response (a feather will do). He should express interest in it, pouncing on it and batting it around and in general, if he causes you to giggle with his antics, he gets an A+.

- After he's enjoyed a good playtime and has settled down (remember, kittens seem to have bursts of energy), try gently holding him. He shouldn't hiss, spit, or attempt to bite or scratch. And, while kittens in general don't tend to want to sit still long enough to be held for any length of time, he should be accepting of handling. A kitten who hasn't been well socialized to humans will do everything in his power to get out of your grasp. A little squirming is fine, but biting, fear, and aggression are not.

THE PHYSICAL ONCE-OVER

While a kitten may not want to stay still long enough for you to do a thorough exam, you should check him out physically (your vet ought to examine him as well) before you make your decision. Once again, I'm not saying you should reject a kitten if you see fleas or he has ear mites, but *be aware* of what you're getting into. If the kitten is ill, you'll be going back and forth to the veterinarian. Can you handle the possible expense? You also don't want to fall in love with a kitten who won't survive. BE INFORMED.

- *Skin and coat*. A healthy kitten has a soft coat with no bald patches or broken hairs (which could indicate ringworm). Sniff the kitten's fur—it should smell clean. If the coat is greasy, rough, dry, or has an odor, it could mean parasites, improper care, or an underlying disease. (Most kittens and puppies are born with worms and will get dewormed several times in early kittenhood.)

  The skin should look clean, without any scabs or rashes. Look for signs of fleas or flea dirt (flea excrement—little black specks). Don't reject a kitten just because he has fleas, but a badly infested kitten may be anemic from the loss of blood caused by the parasites.

- *Body*. When you pick the kitten up, he shouldn't feel fat or skinny. If you can feel his ribs, that's okay. If you can *see* his ribs then he's too thin. His belly shouldn't feel hard or swollen. If he has a *potbellied* look, then there's a good chance he has worms.

- *Eyes*. They should be clear and free of any film or discharge (either watery, milky, or greenish). There should be no sign of squinting and the third eyelid (which is a protective membrane that unfolds to cover the eye) shouldn't be visible. The normal position for the third eyelid is to remain folded in the inner corner of the eye.

- **Ears**. They should look clean inside. Head shaking or the appearance of gritty brownish/black exudate indicates a strong probability of ear mites. While not a reason to reject a kitten, be aware that he'll require medication for about three weeks (which is the life cycle of the ear mite).

- **Mouth**. The gums should be pink, not red and not pale. Teeth should be white. Look for signs of periodontal disease (red, inflamed gums, tartar buildup, loose teeth, foul breath) in adult cats. Ask about the kitten or cat's diet and appetite. Make sure a kitten is able to eat solid food.

- **Tail**. To be more precise, it's what's *under* the tail that you're going to check. The kitten or cat's tail area should be clean, with no signs of discharge or diarrhea.

Be realistic when evaluating the kitten or cat. Don't reject him just because he may have something such as tapeworms (which also means he has fleas), but be cautious of multiple or potentially serious problems.

DOCUMENTATION, GUARANTEES, AND PAPERWORK

If you're purchasing from a breeder or pet store, read every word of the contract and guarantee. Question anything you don't understand. It should be written in the guarantee that when you take the cat to be examined by the vet, if he is determined to be unhealthy, you can return him. I know it sounds cold, almost as if you're buying a washing machine and not a living creature, but keep in mind that some people spend thousands of dollars for certain breeds of cats and there are some breeders, owners, and pet stores who will knowingly sell you an unhealthy pet then refuse to refund your money.

If it's written in the guarantee that should the kitten be deemed unhealthy by the vet you can choose another cat, but not a refund, insist on having that changed. None of the remaining kittens may be what you want. The option should be yours to decide if you want to take your business elsewhere rather than being locked into taking the "best of the worst."

THE "SPECIAL NEEDS" KITTY

Not everyone looks for the perfect kitty. Some are drawn to the kitten or cat no one else wants. Cats with physical disabilities very often turn out to be the most amazing companions—some should even be applauded for being kitty role models, so to speak. But sadly, some don't do well. If you have it in you to give a kitten or cat a second chance at life, consult your vet to discuss what you can expect in terms of care required and long-term prognosis.

If you decide that you do want to adopt and nurse an ill kitten or cat back to health, make sure you're prepared for the time, expense, and possible heartbreak should your best efforts fail. Bringing a sick cat home to a household where there are existing cats will also mean isolating him to keep everyone safe. Think everything through carefully before committing to the welfare of a cat with special needs.

2
Head to Toe

A Guided Tour of Your Cat and the Ways He Communicates

Take the time to go on a little tour of your cat's body. He's not just a cute little ball of fur who chases mice and sleeps in the sun. A cat's body is perfectly built for hunting, with every piece of equipment performing intricate, well-timed functions. And what about those meows? Do they really mean anything? Cats communicate with their voice, body language, and by leaving their scent. Becoming familiar with your cat's language can unlock the mysteries of behavior problems and cat/owner misunderstandings.

Let's start with some basic information on the internal/external workings of a cat:

TEMPERATURE

It ranges from 101.5 to 102.5°F. Under stress, the cat's temperature can rise (for example, while being examined by the vet), so depending on the circumstances, a temperature of 102.5°F. would be considered normal.

HEART

The cat's heart averages from around 120 to 240 beats per minute. The number of beats will increase in times of stress, fear, excitement, or physical activity. A fever can also cause an increase in the number of beats.

RESPIRATORY RATE

About 20 to 30 breaths per minute is the average for a resting cat. Humans average about half of that.

BLOOD

There are three blood types: *A*, *B*, and *AB*. The *AB* type is very rare.

THE EYES

Cats have binocular vision, which means an image is seen by both eyes at the same time. This provides the cat with excellent depth perception.

Light that enters the eye through the pupil is focused onto the retina. Bright light causes the muscles in the iris to contract the pupil vertically.

A cat's retina, compared to a human's, is made up of a larger number of rods (the light sensors), which enable them to see in almost total darkness. People mistakenly assume that cats can see when it's totally dark, which isn't the case. They can, however, see in conditions we consider total darkness. There are a smaller number of cones (the color sensors) in the cat's eye than in the human's, so while it has been determined that they can recognize some color, just how they interpret it is a mystery. Dusk and dawn are the times most cats hunt, so color vision would be of less importance than the ability to detect the slightest movement from potential prey. I imagine that in the evening the color differences between a chipmunk and a mouse wouldn't matter much to a hungry cat.

Cats have a layer of cells beneath the retina called the *tapetum lucidum*. These act as a mirror and reflect light back onto the retina, which allows the cat to use all available light. You've seen this glowlike effect as your car's headlights are reflected in the eyes of nocturnal animals.

Cats have a third eyelid known as the *nictitating membrane*. This pale pink membrane normally rests at the inner corner of the eye. If protection of the eye is needed, it will unfold and cover the surface.

Kittens are blind at birth and then as their poorly focusing eyes develop, they are very sensitive to light. Kittens also are born with blue eyes. Their true eye color will develop several weeks later.

Cat's eyes come in several colors, the most common being green or gold. White cats with blue eyes suffer from congenital deafness. Frequently, odd-eyed cats have the deafness on the side with the blue eye.

Your cat's eyes can help indicate what he's feeling. The pupils dilate when a cat is stimulated, surprised, or fearful. Constricted pupils can indicate tension or potential aggression.

Avoiding eye contact is one method a submissive cat uses to try to prevent a violent confrontation with another cat. An aggressive cat will make direct eye contact.

THE EARS

Because cats prefer to hunt in dusk, their sense of hearing is as important as their sight or smell. A good predator has to be able to detect the faintest rustling in the grass. A cat's hearing range is better than a human's or even that of a dog. Their hearing is so sensitive that cats can distinguish from dozens of feet away between two similar sounds in close proximity to each other.

The *pinna* is the flap of the ear that is shaped like a cone. It collects sound waves, funneling them to the inner ear. The many muscles in the pinnae are what allow the cat to rotate his ears in a wide arc, enabling him to locate the source of sounds accurately.

Your cat's ears are also valuable mood indicators. Ears flattened sideways and down reflect irritation or possible submission. An anxious cat may twitch his ears. When the ears face forward, it often indicates alertness. During a fight (or in anticipation of one), the ears are rotated back and flattened to prevent them from being damaged by an opponent's claws or teeth.

THE NOSE

A well-developed sense of smell is vital for survival in the cat world. It enables the cat to identify territories, relays specific information about the opposite sex, informs him of the presence of potential enemies, and alerts him to prey. It also directly influences his appetite. A cat who cannot smell will become anorexic.

The inside of the cat's nose is lined with a mucous membrane that traps foreign particles and bacteria in an effort to prevent them from entering the body. The mucous membrane also warms and moisturizes inhaled air before it continues on through the respiratory tract.

Some cats have to work harder than others when it comes to breathing due to the differences in muzzle shapes. Flat-nosed breeds, such as Persians, have a compromised breathing ability due to the distorted shape of their compact nose. Their sense of smell may be compromised as well.

Cats also have an extra scent "analyzer" that plays a specific role in identifying sex-related odors in urine (see "The Mouth").

THE MOUTH

Kittens get their temporary teeth at four weeks of age. The permanent teeth are usually in by six months. There are thirty teeth in total. The two canine teeth are used for severing the spinal cord of prey and delivering the killing bite. The six incisors located in the front of the mouth in both the upper and lower jaws are for tearing off small bits of meat and also to pluck feathers. The premolars and molars cut off larger pieces of flesh from the prey. Cats don't chew or grind these pieces, but rather, they're swallowed whole.

The cat's tongue is covered with tiny backward-facing barbs (papillae) which are used for grooming and also to remove meat from the bones of prey. Cats drink water by curling the outer edges of their tongue inward to create a spoon.

Cats use their tongue very efficiently to keep their coats well groomed. Grooming serves a behavioral function as well. In a stressful situation a cat may groom himself to displace the tension he feels. You may notice this if your cat is sitting at the window watching a bird outside. When the bird flies off, the cat may begin a round of self grooming to defuse the energy he was storing and the frustration he feels.

Located in the roof of the mouth is a scent organ known as the Jacobson's organ (or vomeronasal organ), with ducts leading into both the mouth and nose. The cat inhales, opens his mouth, and curls his upper lip. The odor is then picked up on his tongue. It's almost a cross between smelling and tasting. He then moves the tongue toward the roof of the mouth with the collected odor, passing it to the Jacobson's organ. While performing this scent analysis, the cat's lips are pulled back in a sort of grimace (called a *flehmen reaction*). This behavior is most commonly performed by males reacting to the urine or pheromones of females in heat.

THE WHISKERS

Whiskers (*vibrassae*) are used as a sensory device, relaying messages to the brain. Whiskers are located on the upper lip, cheeks, above the eyes, and on the forelegs. The whiskers on the upper lip are in four rows. The upper whiskers which extend beyond the head, also help guide a cat through total darkness. Whiskers on the forelegs are used to sense any movement of prey trapped under the cat's front paws.

Whiskers play an important role in feline body language as well. Whiskers that are forward facing and spread out usually indicate that the cat is alert and ready for action. The whiskers of a relaxed cat are positioned sideways and not as fanned out. Fear is communicated by the whiskers being tightly spaced and flattened back against the face.

THE NAILS

Cats have five toes each on the forefoot and four on each hind foot. The fifth toe on the inside of the forefoot is known as the dewclaw and doesn't come in contact with the ground. Some cats, referred to as *polydactyls,* have extra toes.

When a cat scratches on a tree or scratching post, the outer sheath of the nail is removed. This allows the new growth to come through. If you look at the base of where your cat normally scratches, you'll probably find the little discarded crescent shaped sheaths.

Unlike dogs, the nails on the cat's forefeet don't wear down because they remain sheathed until needed.

THE TAIL

The tail, which is part of the spine, is used for balance and serves an important role in communication. An upright tail when the cat is standing or walking lets you know he's alert. It's also the position used in greeting. A relaxed cat's tail is horizontal or somewhat down. When your cat flicks his upright tail at you, it's usually meant as a greeting. In most cases, the message he's sending is "Hi, I've missed you. When's dinner?" A lashing or thumping tail reflects irritation. If you're petting your cat when this happens, it's a very good idea to back off. When a cat is resting, an occasional twitching or sweeping motion of the tail is his way of saying he's relaxed but still alert. A frightened cat will puff out the hairs on his tail (*piloerection*) so it looks more than twice its size. A tail in an inverted "U" shape indicates that the cat is fearful and

Relating the Feline Aging Process to Ours

Just about everyone is familiar with that age-old saying about how a dog ages seven years for every one of our human years. Applying that principe to cats is inaccurate (and it isn't even entirely accurate for dogs as well). As you can see from the following chart, the differences vary from year to year.

With dogs, life expectancy can vary based on breed. Large dogs have shorter life spans than the smaller breeds. With cats, breed doesn't affect life expectancy as much as lifestyle does. An indoor cat who is well cared for stands a much better chance of living to a ripe old age than an outdoor cat who only sees the vet for emergencies.

CAT'S AGE	IN HUMAN YEARS
1 month	6–8 months
3 months	4 years
6 months	10 years
8 months	15 years
1 year	18 years
2 years	24 years
4 years	35 years
6 years	42 years
8 years	50 years
10 years	60 years
12 years	70 years
14 years	80 years
16 years	84 years

potentially defensively aggressive. A submissive cat will tuck his tail between his legs, trying to be as small and invisible as possible.

VOCAL COMMUNICATION

Cats use vocal communication along with marking and body language to relay *distance-reducing* or *distance-increasing* messages.

Cat owners become very familiar with the subtle (and some not so subtle) nuances of their cat's vocabulary. Almost every owner can identify "help," "treat," "open the door," "I'm in pain," "play with me," "leave me alone," or "you're late with my dinner." If I've been very busy and haven't played enough with my cats, Olive has an unmistakable sound that means, "This is your last chance. Play with me *now* or I'll knock something over . . . something *breakable!*" I've learned from past experience and numerous shattered treasures that she's not kidding.

A cat's vocal repertoire is quite extensive. It ranges from soft contented murmurs (such as a purr) and vowel pattern sounds (various meows) to strained intensity sounds (demands and cries). There's no such thing as a simple "meow." Here are some examples of the cat's vocabulary.

Purr

It's the most charismatic and endearing sound that a cat makes. How the purr is actually produced remained a mystery for a long time. Experts had various theories but recent studies seem to indicate that it's generated by the sudden change in air pressure as the glottis opens and closes through contractions of the laryngeal muscles.

Initially, the purr is produced by the queen as a way to communicate with her kittens. They feel the vibrations of the purr, which enables them to locate her.

Although we as owners are most familiar with the purring our cats do during times of contentment or nursing, they may also purr in a variety of other, less expected situations. Veterinarians have witnessed cats who purr during times of extreme pain. The general theory being that purring is the cat's attempt at reducing stress. When a cat is close to death is also a time that purring can occur. This is perhaps a result of a euphoria felt as death is near. This experience has also been reported in terminally ill human patients.

Acknowledgment Response

A short murmur issued by a cat who is either answering to his name or recognizing something positive he is about to get (such as a treat).

Call

Used by females to signal readiness to mate ("Come on over, big boy!") and by males to coax the females ("Hey, good lookin'!"). Tomcats may also call out as an announcement to other males that he's ready to fight if necessary ("This town ain't big enough for the both of us!").

The call is also issued to owners by cats who feel they've had to wait an unreasonably long time for something, such as dinner or being let outside.

Grunt

Produced mostly by newborn kittens.

Chirp

A soft trill-like sound used as a greeting.

Chatter

Produced by the highly aroused cat as he sits at the window watching a bird or any potential prey.

Demand

The feline version of begging.

Complaint

No self-respecting cat would be caught without a well-tuned *complaint* in his repertoire.

Bewilderment Cry

A loud call expressing confusion. Older cats may issue a bewilderment "yowl" when disoriented. This often happens at night when everyone has gone to bed and he's walking around the dark house.

Mating Call

The estrous female gives out a two-syllable call. The male's call resembles *"mowl."* These nightly sounds are what elicit slipper throwing, water squirting, and various four-letter words from sleep-deprived humans.

Hiss/Spit

Hissing, used as a defensive sound, is created by the mouth being open, lips pulled back, and forcing out a burst of air through an arched tongue. Because it sounds almost snakelike, the cat uses the hiss to try and bluff an attacker into backing off.

Spitting often accompanies the hiss. It's produced in reaction to being taken by surprise or threatened. A menacingly quick slap to the ground with a paw adds to the drama of spitting.

The hiss is used as a defensive warning, with the creator of the sound most likely hoping that this vocalization and accompanying body posture will deter potential violence. Aggression will likely follow should the danger persist.

Growl

A steady, low-pitched warning sound. Just as the cat tries to appear larger and more threatening by piloerection, the deep growl may also be an attempt to seem bigger to the enemy. My dog quickly learned to tip-toe around a growling cat.

Snarl

A short but intense aggressive sound usually produced during fighting.

Pain Shriek

Most commonly associated with the female as she cries out after copulation. The male's penis has tiny barbs on it that most likely hurt her as he withdraws.

The Silent Meow

It is exactly that, *silent*. The mouth opens but no sound comes out. It seems to be the visual version of meow. The first time I witnessed one of my cats doing this, I was working at my desk. My cat Ethel jumped up and sat delicately perched on the corner. I was very engrossed in work, and she seemed to sense that it wouldn't be wise to disturb me. I just happened to glance over at her. We made eye contact and she opened her mouth as if to meow but no sound came out. It was as if she knew she shouldn't bother me but she couldn't help herself, so she showed only enough restraint to contain the vocal part of her request. Needless to say, the endearing effect it had on me was more powerful than any vocalization she could've done. My work was put on hold.

An owner becomes putty in the paws of the silent meower. The gesture's purpose in cat-to-cat communication is a mystery. But it works—and it still melts my heart each and every time.

Marking Communication

Cats have scent glands that produce chemicals called *pheromones*. These scent glands are found on the forehead, around the mouth, the paw pads and anus. The cat's use of scent marking is elaborate and highly developed. For example, secretions from a female's scent glands provide the tomcat with information concerning her hormonal condition.

To help you get an idea of a cat's emotional state during specific marking behaviors, picture your cat in profile. The pheromones produced from the front end (facial rubbing) have a calming effect on the cat. They're usually reserved for marking in the cat's inner nest territory. The pheromones that come from the back end (urine spraying) are produced during excitation or anxiety.

The glands located between the cat's toes secrete a scent whenever he scratches on objects such as a tree or a scratching post. This activity provides an olfactory territory mark in addition to the visual.

Another gland involved in feline communication is located at the tip of the tail. This rather mysterious sebaceous gland is more active in intact males. Occasionally, the gland can become overactive and then the tail gets a greasy look. This condition is commonly referred to as *stud tail.*

Cats also use scents as a way of recognizing and communicating with each other. Two familiar cats will recognize each other by engaging in front end and back end sniffing.

URINE MARKING

The pheromones in urine are the least subtle way for a cat to mark his territory. Unneutered males are very territorial and tend to establish their ownership by spraying this strong-smelling urine. (Having your cat neutered before he gets in the habit is very wise.) The perimeters of the turf are sprayed as are paths and crossings. Let there be no doubt whose territory you are about to enter. The cat who is about to spray turns his back to the object, and you very often will notice his tail twitching. When a cat sprays (as opposed to engaging in normal urination), the urine is sent out at a high level to make it convenient for another cat's nose to catch the scent. Spraying, as opposed to urinating a small puddle on the ground, also allows the cat to cover a wider area.

Outdoors, urine spraying by an intact male is also used to entice females.

Spraying is a more efficient method of marking than urination since it's sprayed at nose level.

For cats in the wild, the marking with urine tells another cat who has claimed this property and how long ago it was marked. If you allow your cat outdoors, you may notice that he goes around checking the area to make sure all his territorial claims are intact.

There are also scent glands around the cat's anus so he can mark his feces with his own scent. A dominant cat may defecate in a conspicuous area on a trail or pathway and leave his feces uncovered. In multicat households, I've seen litter scratched into a mound in the box, with a displayed feces crowning the top—a point graphically made.

RUBBING

Using the scent glands located on the head and around the mouth, the cat will frequently rub on certain protruding objects in his territory. Doorways, table legs, your legs, chairs, bedposts, and lamp shades are popular rubbing sites. Depositing facial pheromones on objects within the cat's territory appears to be comforting. Whereas the scent marking done with spraying usually indicates a perceived threat, rubbing reflects a positive emotion.

Rubbing is a friendly social behavior, and many cats who live together will allorub (mutual rubbing) and allogroom (mutual grooming) quite often. Cats in the same home will often rub each other in passing as a way to reinforce a familiar "family" scent. Your cat will even come over and rub his head against your face (this behavior is called *bunting*) in a gesture of family acceptance and love. He'll rub along your chin and nose, engaging in the bunting behavior that began as a kitten when he'd rub around his mother's head seeking to nurse. Very often, purring will accompany the rubbing behavior. If the cat's emotion becomes intense, he opens his mouth slightly, exposing more of his lips. Some cats get so carried away that they even drool.

The next time your cat jumps onto the bed and seems to butt you in the face with the top of his head, don't get irritated, realize the loving compliment he just paid you.

SCRATCHING

In addition to marking and nail conditioning, scratching helps a cat to stretch the muscles of his back and provides an emotional release. Scratching behavior is covered in depth later in this book.

Body Postures

By using all of his height and creating piloerection (standing on end) of fur, a cat will attempt to appear larger and more threatening.

In contrast, the submissive cat crouches low to the ground, flattens his ears, tucks in his tail, and attempts to look as small and nonthreatening as possible. A cat on his back, exposing his underside is *not* being submissive (as compared to the dog's familiar submissive posture). Rather, he is preparing for full battle. Rolling onto his back, he can then make full use of his natural weapons by exposing the claws on all four feet as well as using his teeth. It's his ultimate defensive aggressive posture. An interesting side note to this posture is that in relaxation, your cat may roll over onto his back and stretch, exposing his underside and looking as if he wants his belly scratched. If you've ever obliged, that may explain why your hand then became a pin cushion. Even though his posture originated out of relaxation, you triggered his defensive aggression response. As a sexual behavior, a female may roll over onto her back in courtship. It's interesting that one posture can have several meanings, depending on the circumstances.

When one cat encounters another and they've engaged in a scent investigation through back and front end sniffing, allorubbing may occur. If the two cats meeting are unfamiliar with each other, some serious posturing will go on while they check each other out. In the case of intact males, it's not uncommon to give and receive slashes to the face and neck. Tomcats develop thick cheek pads on each side of their face specifically to lessen damage done by an attacker's unsheathed claws.

Years ago, it was believed that cats were asocial creatures who lived solitary lives. We now know that cats do form friendships and can exist in cat communities (especially around a common food source). Within this community, there will most likely be dominant cats who claim little patches of territory. There are also the more submissive cats who try to keep the peace by taking up as little space as possible. If you think of the rungs of a ladder and each cat in the community representing a rung, life goes relatively smoothly as long as everyone knows their place. The trouble occurs when someone tries to jump to the next rung. And of course when a female goes into heat the rules change completely as males of varying dominance fight each other to mate with her.

By learning to read your cat's body language, you may improve your relationship with him. Understanding what he's communicating can help prevent potential aggression and can enable you to interpret his mood. For example, during a tense standoff in a multicat household, you may be able to tell who is being *offensively* aggressive by the body posture and the constricted pupils. Or, knowing that your cat's tail lashing back and forth while you pet him means that he's becoming irritated might enable you to stop before you get scratched or bitten.

A BRIEF GUIDE TO BODY POSTURES

These are only general descriptions. When determining a cat's posture, take into consideration the environment he's in. Your cat may show only some of the characteristics of a certain posture. Observe your cat in various situations (such as during play, rest, at the vet) to become familiar with his postures.

FRIENDLY

- ears pointed slightly forward
- whiskers pointed sideways (relaxed)
- whiskers fanned out, pointed forward (alert)
- smooth hair coat
- vertical tail
- head bunting
- vocal murmur of acknowledgment
- nose-to-nose touching

PLAYFUL

- ears pricked forward
- dilated pupils
- various tail positions
- fanned out, forward-facing whiskers
- stalking movements
- occasional chattering

FEARFUL

- dilated pupils
- hair coat may be raised along back and tail
- tail may lash or be tucked close to the body
- whiskers pulled back along face

- flattened ears pointing down and back

- crouched body, often facing sideways to opponent

- hissing, growling, or spitting

OFFENSIVE AGGRESSION

- direct stare with constricted pupils

- fanned out, forward-facing whiskers

- lips curled into a snarl

- piloerection of hair along shoulders and tail

- forward-facing body with hindquarters raised (ready to pounce)

- tail down

DEFENSIVE AGGRESSION

- dilated pupils

- ears flattened, facing down and back

- whiskers pulled back along face

- arched back

- piloerection of hair coat

- tail held either up and over the back or low to the ground or inverted "U" position

- facing opponent sideways

- mouth held open

- hissing, growling, or spitting

- slapping the ground in front of him with front paw

- rolling onto his back to fight if there's no means of escape

SUBMISSIVE

- dilated pupils, avoids direct eye contact

- ears held flat

- smooth hair coat

- tail down, close to the body

- crouched position with head held down

- may issue a "silent meow"

Now that you have more insight into your cat's methods of communication, are there times you can remember in the past when you may have misread a signal? I have encountered hundreds of clients who for years thought that their cats' wagging tails meant they were happy. It would continually be a shock when the owners got bitten or scratched because they hadn't understood the initial warning signs.

Whenever I do behavior seminars and people come up to greet me, as I'm shaking hands I always look down at theirs. Every time I see a hand with several scratches, I think, *There's an owner who isn't listening to what the cat is trying to tell him!*

3

Watch Out for That Hot Tin Roof

Creating a Safe Home for Your Unstoppable Kitten

Tragically, many times we learn lessons too late. It isn't until the kitten gets burned at the stove or swallows some thread that we rearrange things in our home. Don't think that just because you put the crystal vase up on a shelf, that a curious, adventurous kitten won't find a way to get up there and knock it over.

Before you bring the kitten home and everyone gets caught up in the excitement is the time to go through your home and create a safe environment.

Especially if it is a kitten you are bringing home, you'll need to go inch by inch through the house, because their energy, curiosity, and lack of experience will cause them to try some potentially dangerous stunts. If it's an adult cat you're bringing in, you'll still need to "cat-proof," but it's the relentlessly curious kitten who will have to depend on you to keep her out of trouble.

Later in this chapter, I'll discuss how to bring your kitten or cat into the house and create a room for her so she can begin to adjust to her new life. For now though, you have some preventative kitten-proofing to do.

A House Is a Dangerous Thing

When you bring a new pet home you have two immediate safety concerns: protecting your *pet* and protecting your *house*.

Even though the kitten may be a tiny little thing, there's very little out of her reach. To get a proper perspective on how a kitten views our world, get on your hands and knees and crawl around a little. Come on, don't be embarrassed—no one's looking. Do you notice how your perspective changes? Look at how the dangling electrical cords that you, as an upright human never notice, are now in plain view? And look at that sewing basket by the chair—from here it's a basket of yarn, thread, and other things that a kitten could hardly resist. Now, bear with me a little longer and go from being on your hands and knees to lying flat on your stomach. Now look around. The perspective changes again (and now you're truly *kitten height*). What do you see? Perhaps you notice the aspirin tablet that you lost last night and couldn't find when it rolled under a chair. Oh, and there's a needle on the carpet next to the sewing basket. And there's that jelly bean that your daughter dropped yesterday. Perhaps you even notice how there's enough space behind the refrigerator for a kitten to get stuck. And look at those dustballs rolling around—uh-oh, better get the vacuum cleaner out.

The next exercise I want you to do is to look up, way up, from your current position on the floor. If someone walks in on you, just tell them you're doing your yoga exercises. From this position, you'll be able to see how a little kitten could find many ways to climb to where all the interesting stuff is. After she scales the back of the couch, what's waiting for her on the end table? Is an ashtray full of cigarette butts sitting there? Once she climbs the curtain, will she reach an open window without a screen?

We have a lot of work to do!

ELECTRICAL CORDS & PHONE CORDS

Three main dangers exist here: 1) the risk of electrical burns should your kitten chew through the cords; 2) the chance of her pulling something (such as a lamp or an iron) over on top of herself; and 3) the possibility that she could get tangled up in a cord (such as a tightly curled phone cord).

Try to avoid having dangling cords and especially the mass of cords that are often around stereo equipment and computers. Hide cords as best you can by tucking them out of sight and out of reach. You can find commercial cord-containers in the baby supply department and also the computer supply area of stores. They come in several configurations. You can make them yourself if you prefer with plastic tubing available at your local home improvement center. Make a slit lengthwise along one side and push the cords through. Some home improvement stores sell cord containers that run along the baseboard, and in addition to keeping your kitten safe, they make that ugly jumble of cords disappear. At the very least, run cords along the baseboard and secure them to the wall with metal clips. Any exposed part of the cords should be coated with a bitter tasting anti-chew substance such as Bitter Apple (available at pet supply stores). On a regular basis, go around the house and check any cords for signs of toothmarks or damage.

A company called Safe Living/Smart Products makes a three-outlet pet-proof power cord with an electronic sensor that monitors electrical flow. Any break in the flow causes it to shut off automatically. The product is available through mail order (see Resource Guide). My advice is to have these throughout your home.

The danger of a kitten tugging on a cord and having whatever is on the other end—an iron, for instance—topple over on her, is a real one. If you're using a small appliance, don't leave it unattended. Be sure to secure the cords of other electrical objects such as lamps, so kitty can't pull them.

To prevent your kitten from sticking her paw in an electrical outlet, use outlet covers (found in the baby department of most stores).

To keep your kitten away from the curly cord attached to the handset of the phone, switch from a long cord to a short one. If you really need to move around as you talk on the phone, use a retractable cord (available in office supply and hardware stores) or switch to a cordless phone.

STRINGS AND THINGS

A cat has backward-facing barbs on her tongue (that's what creates the sandpaper feel when she licks you) so if she eats certain objects she has to swallow them because she will be unable to dislodge them. String objects in particular pose a danger. You may see lots of cute pictures of kittens playing with balls of yarn, spools of thread, or Christmas tinsel, but in real life these things can cause very serious injury. The same holds true for string, ribbon, and rubber bands.

It's ironic that it can be nearly impossible to give your cat a pill should medicating be necessary, yet that same cat happily swallows the most unlikely objects such as earrings, coins, pills not intended for her, or pieces of toys, among many other seemingly unappetizing objects. As you go around your house, if an object looks small enough to swallow or like something a kitten might bat around with her paw, put it away.

PREVENT DISAPPEARING ACTS

As part of her ongoing investigation, a kitten will inevitably find and try to get into the smallest, narrowest spot in the house—the space behind the refrigerator or the inside of a shoe in the closet, for instance. Block access to dangerous areas and use child-proof locks on cabinets that don't have secure latches. If you've taken in an adult cat who feels stressed in the new environment, she may look for a hiding place in order to feel safer. If the places she chooses are not dangerous, let her stay there so she has some quiet time to de-stress. But before you bring her home, reduce the possibility of her discovering unsafe hiding places.

Always check on the whereabouts of your kitten when opening and closing drawers and doors. Closets are a popular hangout for kittens and cats. If you plan on allowing your kitten to sleep or play in a closet, fix the door so it won't close all the way and shut her in. Whenever you go into any closet, always check and re-check before closing the door. Kittens have often been accidentally locked in closets for an entire day because their owner didn't notice them before she closed the closet door and then left for work.

Boxes, bags, and even piles of laundry can also be great hiding places, so check to be sure your kitten isn't in one before throwing a box away or putting a pile of laundry in the washer.

Kittens can climb inside of an open drawer before you're even aware of it so close any drawer as soon as you're through, but check inside it first. Kittens can easily be trapped *behind* the drawer as well, and you could injure her when you close the drawer.

Another thing to remember is that you'll have to change any pre-cat owner habits you may have had. If you used to stand at the front door, holding it open as you waved good-bye to your school-bound children, you'll now have to wave from behind the safety of the closed storm door.

Later in this chapter, we'll go room to room and work on specific kitten-proofing methods.

INNOCENT-LOOKING POISONS

A surprising number of household items are poisonous to cats—from the detergents and cleansers you store under your sink to the mothballs in your closet. It's not enough just to be careful that lids are tight, you also must be sure the cabinet doors are securely latched so there's no chance of your kitten finding her way to the danger. Even if the cap is tightly on the bottle, any drips that have run down the outside can be harmful should the kitten lick them or rub up against the bottle. For a list of household poisons, refer to chapter 18.

Many plants are poisonous to cats, causing reactions from being irritating to outright deadly. Keep poisonous plants out of kitty's reach. Trim hanging plants so they aren't a temptation and spray the leaves with an anti-chew spray made especially for plants, such as Bitter Apple (available at pet supply stores). It doesn't harm the plants, and its bitter taste will discourage your kitten from munching on the leaves. A list of poisonous plants can be found in chapter 18.

Your medications and vitamins pose a serious danger to your kitten. Acetaminophen (such as Tylenol) is so toxic that just one pill can be fatal. Don't leave any medications around because your kitten could be tempted to play with it and wind up ingesting something deadly.

Antifreeze is toxic to animals, and just a small amount can be deadly. The added danger of this chemical is that it has a sweet taste, which can attract a cat. A few companies manufacture less toxic products now. Check with your local auto supply store. These products are also available through mail order.

WINDOWS

Many people are under the assumption that cats have perfect balance, and even if they fall, always land on their feet. While they do have the ability to right their body while falling, if the distance is too short they won't have time, and if they fall from a higher distance, the impact will cause serious injury to their legs and chest. A fall from a high window will kill a cat no matter how she lands. Do you think the ability to land on your feet would make much difference in a ten-story fall?

All windows should have sturdy well-fitting screens that can't be pushed out. An unscreened window opened just a crack can still be wiggled through by a determined cat chasing a fly or curious to get at the sights and smells of the outside.

Don't make the very tragic mistake of assuming your placid cat

> **CatwiseClue**
>
> When you spray Bitter Apple on your plants, take the plants outdoors or cover the floor with newspaper or a towel to avoid getting the spray all over everything. Be sure to wash your hands as soon as you've finished because you definitely don't want to taste this stuff either.

understands how high up she is and will just sit on the window sill sunning herself. It only takes her attention being diverted by a passing bird or insect for her to lean too far out and lose her balance.

Cords from window blinds and drapes can also be very dangerous. A cat can get tangled in them and possibly end up hanging herself. Secure all cords by rolling them up and tucking them out of reach.

ROOM-BY-ROOM

The Kitchen

This is a dangerous room that looks so deceptively innocent. Everywhere you turn, there's something that could potentially cause harm to your pet. Let's start with the appliances:

A kitten who is able to get up onto the counter (and it doesn't take long before she'll be big enough to make it in one easy leap) could walk across a hot stove. Enticing food aromas make that danger even more likely.

When cooking at the stove, keep a squirt bottle handy in case your cat shows any sign of attempting to jump. Because of the immediate danger should she land on a hot burner, be on your guard if she's in the kitchen with you. From her point of view, all she knows is that there are tempting smells coming from the area. She won't realize until it's too late that the surface is hot. Use burner covers if needed after removing the food from the stove.

I've seen curious kittens crawl up into the refrigerator without the owners even being aware of it. Before closing the door, always check for the possibility that your kitten is hiding behind the mayonnaise jar.

To keep your kitten from getting behind the refrigerator, tape a piece of cardboard across the space blocking the way.

Oh, the delicious smells that come up from the garbage disposal. Keep it clean and empty—never allow food to sit in the disposal, which creates a dangerous temptation. Routinely running fresh lemon slices through the disposal will help keep it clean and provide a citrus scent which isn't appealing to cats. As an added safety feature, keep a drain-stopper over the opening.

Check before you close the dishwasher door to be sure a sneaky kitten hasn't crawled in when you were loading it and not looking.

Cats very often don't know what food is good for them. As far as they're concerned, the world is just one big buffet. Some foods can be deadly (these include chocolate as well as chicken bones) and some spicy or rich food can cause illness. Keep food in containers and never leave tempting food unsupervised. Use covered garbage cans in your kitchen or secure the can in a cabinet with a child-proof latch. After meals, don't leave dangerous foods (such as chicken bones) in the garbage—take the bag to the outside trash can.

Even the kitchen sponges or paper towels you use to clean food spills can be harmful. A kitten may ingest pieces of the sponge, mistaking it for food.

Glasses and other breakable items can be knocked to the floor and shatter when a cat jumps on the counter. I think it's a must that from the beginning you establish boundaries for where your kitten may and may not venture. The kitchen counter should always be off-limits. For training tips, refer to chapter 7.

Rodent or insect poisons, traps and baits you may have placed in certain areas of the kitchen might not be as out of kitty's reach as you think. Be very careful about which products you use and where you place them. If you're having a pest problem, consult a professional exterminator and your vet for information on the best products to use.

Sharp utensils that contain food residue may cause injury if left out. A dirty steak knife or the big one used to carve the Thanksgiving turkey can injure a cat's tongue should she attempt to lick the tasty juices clinging to the sharp edge. The same holds true for the sharp-pronged corn-on-the-cob holders, toothpicks, skewers, etc.

Speaking of toothpicks, don't ever leave them on the counter because of the danger of your cat chewing on them. Store them in a closed container in the cabinet. If you're testing a cake for doneness by using a toothpick, don't leave it out before or after you use it.

The Bathroom

Get in the habit of keeping the toilet lid closed. A kitten attempting to jump onto the seat and not expecting an opening there can easily slip and fall right in. An adult cat may be able to jump out but a kitten is unable to and will most likely drown. Or if you use an automatic toilet disinfectant, its chemicals will harm even an adult. She'll groom herself and ingest the toxic substance. Keeping the lid down will also prevent pets from drinking the water. I strongly advise against using the automatic bowl disinfectants just because of the risk to pets (even if you leave a note over the toilet to remind all family members and guests, someone might still neglect to close the lid). Keeping a closed toilet will also prevent the things your kitten knocks off the tank from falling into the bowl.

Hair dryers, curling irons, electric rollers, and electric razors shouldn't be left on the counters. Should the kitten pull the dangling cords, there is a risk that the appliance would come down on her.

Not only medications but also makeup, nail polish, polish remover, and perfume are all toxic so keep these tightly capped if you leave them on counters.

The wastebasket in the bathroom should have a snap-on lid or should be kept in a cabinet. Dangerous things such as dental floss, discarded razor blades, and disposable razors can lurk in there.

Keep all bathroom cleansers put away in cabinets (make sure that your clever cat can't open the doors).

The Living Room

Take a cat's eye view of your furniture. Is there anything that could potentially be a danger to your kitten? Rocking chairs are notorious for landing on cat tails and paws. If you have a recliner, it poses a very serious risk to your cat should you forget to be sure she isn't underneath before attempting to raise or lower the footrest.

If you have a fireplace, you'll need a very sturdy screen to keep your kitten out of danger. Don't ever leave the kitten unsupervised in the room when you have a fire going.

Cats love warm places, so check before closing any doors to an entertainment cabinet to be sure your kitty isn't curled up on top of the TV or VCR.

The Bedroom

As I've said, be careful not to lock the cat in the closet and check before closing any drawers. An added danger in some closets and some drawers are mothballs. Just the fumes from mothballs can cause serious liver damage to a cat, so don't put them in any closet or drawer that your kitty might have access to.

Be careful about small jewelry items. Make sure they are put away in a box or drawer so your kitten won't swallow it or bat it to the floor. (This will also keep your diamond earrings out of the heating vent.)

Many cats, especially frightened ones, will claw at the material underneath the box-spring part of a mattress. Once they make a hole, they can crawl up inside and it feels safe. To prevent this, slide a fitted sheet over the bottom of the box spring.

The Laundry Room

When I worked at an animal hospital, we had several clients who tragically failed to check the clothes dryer before closing the door. They were unaware that their kittens had crawled inside. The thought of how horribly those kittens died continues to haunt me. I check my washer and dryer without fail before I close the door and turn the machine on. I don't just look, I also feel around. When I'm unloading the laundry, I check again before closing the door to make sure none of my cats are trapped in the empty machine.

If your laundry room has a door, close it when you are doing laundry to keep your kitten out of there. This is one very important reason why I don't really like having the litter box located in the laundry room.

When you do your ironing, don't leave the iron and ironing board unsupervised. Should your kitten try to jump up on it, the board and the iron could topple over onto her. As soon as you've finished, unplug the iron, wrap the cord around the base, and put it in a safe place to cool.

If your family normally leaves dirty clothes in a pile or even in a laundry basket, there's a good chance the kitten will discover it to be a great place for a nap. Don't just toss the pile into the washer or even the hamper without first checking. Having the kitten around could be a good excuse to ask your family to be a little neater. Ask them to toss their dirty duds in the hamper and always make sure to close the lid immediately.

Detergents and bleaches should be safely put away out of the kitten's reach.

The Home Office

As I write this, there is one cat on my lap, another on the chair next to me, and my dog is asleep under my desk. I couldn't imagine not having at least one cat near me whenever I'm in my office, but cats aren't always compatible with computers so you have to take precautions to protect not only your pet but your equipment as well.

What with the computer, printer, fax, phone, copier, lamps, and whatever else you have that plugs in, you usually wind up with a big mess of cords behind your desk. Refer to the section on "electrical cords" earlier in this chapter to learn how to keep them safely away from kitty.

Don't leave your computer keyboard exposed and unattended or you'll come back to a screen full of *Z*s or *Q*s, courtesy of kitty's dancing paws. A keyboard drawer is a great idea. Keep the mouse hidden out of reach as well.

If you use a paper shredder, take precautions to make sure your kitten isn't in the vicinity. The moving parts of any of your office machines can be dangerous, so watch your kitten carefully.

To reduce the amount of cat hair that will inevitably find its way into your equipment, you may want to invest in plastic covers to put over them when they're not in use or you can keep them in cabinets.

Make sure all small items, such as thumbtacks, push pins, rubber bands, paper clips, etc., are in covered containers or in drawers.

If your cat consistently attempts chewing on rubber bands that are wrapped around piles of papers or even loves to nibble on the paper itself, set up a few dummy papers coated with an anti-chew product. Lay out a few treated papers and even coat any rubber bands that are wrapped around the pages. Set these out every time you're at the desk working so your cat gets the consistent message that this stuff tastes awful. Don't leave the rubber bands out if you're not right there to supervise, though.

When I was setting up my home office, one lesson I learned early on was to put my answering machine where my cats were least likely to step on it. Albie stepped on the *outgoing announcement* button once and erased my recording and replaced it with a well-timed "meow." While I thought that was so sweet and clever of him, I was less pleased a few days later when he stepped on the *erase* button and wiped out all of my incoming messages.

The Children's Room

Pacifiers shouldn't be left lying around where they could easily be chewed.

Modeling clay, small toys, or any game pieces that could be swallowed should be put away when your children are finished playing with them. I know that getting children to pick up their toys can be an unpleasant battle, but the consequences of not doing it can be worse—such as having to take your kitten in for emergency surgery to remove a blockage.

Look around—balloons, ribbons, strings, etc., *anything* that looks tempting or dangerous needs to be put away.

The Basement, Attic, and Garage

These are the three most dangerous areas of your home and three areas where your kitten shouldn't ever be allowed to go.

When you need to go into the attic, I urge you first to close the kitten in another room. A dark, interesting attic can be irresistible to a kitten. Contact with insulation can cause breathing difficulty and skin irritation. And should you shut the door without realizing that your kitten has hidden in the attic, exposure to the extreme temperatures could result in her death.

Basements and garages also hold lots of danger in the form of stored paints, cleaning agents, pesticides, antifreeze, etc. There are also sharp-edged tools and other equipment that can cause injury to the curious kitten.

If you park your car in the garage, on cold days a cat might crawl up into the engine, seeking warmth and end up getting killed when you start the motor. Antifreeze that leaks from your car and sits on the garage floor is also a deadly danger for your cat.

An automatic garage door can kill a cat should she be attempting to get in or out while the door is closing. Nowadays, garage doors come with sensors that prevent them from closing if something is in the path, but older models may not have that safety feature.

Because of all the potentially deadly hazards in basements and garages, I don't feel that your kitten should ever be near them. You have a big enough job making sure you create a safe *indoor* environment— why take unnecessary risks by exposing her to these additional hazards?

Balconies

A cat shouldn't ever be allowed on a balcony. Railings don't offer much protection for a cat who can slip underneath or through the bars. All it takes is for your cat to get distracted by one bird or a flying insect, and a tragedy could result. Don't mistakenly believe that *supervision* will keep her safe. Should a passing bird entice your cat, her instinct to leap after her prey will cause her to go over the railing long before you can grab her.

If you're still under the assumption that cats always land on their feet, refer back to the section on "Windows."

It's a Jungle Out There—Outdoor Life

I don't think the outdoors is any place for a cat. There are too many dangers and a little eight-pound cat is no match for cars, trucks, large dogs, mean people, disease, and other very real hazards. Your cat stands a much greater chance of living a longer life if you confine her indoors. Everything she needs is inside your home. As you read through this book you'll learn how to create all the best that the outdoors has to offer without exposing her to any of the dangers.

Even though my indoor cats may still get sick or injured, I take great comfort in knowing that they won't get hit by cars, attacked by dogs, poisoned and abused by cruel people, or get into fights with other cats. Every night when I go to sleep I know my cats are safe.

If you're going to allow your cat access to the outdoors, you'll have to be very careful about the fertilizers, weed killers, and pesticides you use on your lawn. Secure all outdoor trash-can lids with bungee cords to prevent a cat from rummaging through the garbage.

Leaks from the bottom of cars, such as antifreeze, are deadly.

In the winter, the salt used to melt ice can burn the pads of a cat's paws and burn her mouth when she grooms her paws. You will have to use a pet-safe ice-melting product. Check with your local pet supply store.

Finally, although you may take great pains to assure your cat's safety when she's in your yard, should she wander onto the neighbor's property, you have no idea what hazards she may face.

Collars and Identification

Even if you never plan on allowing your cat outdoors, she should wear ID. Indoor cats can accidentally get outside, and one gray-striped tabby running through yards looks like all the others from your neighbors' point of view. Identification can mean the difference between getting her back or losing her forever.

Identification tags are available at your local pet supply store or through mail order. You can choose metal or plastic. Many companies offer plastic in neon colors, which make them extremely visible. Reflective tags are also available. Most people engrave the cat's name, owner's name, phone number on the tag, and—if there's room—an address. For an outdoor cat that's fine, but for an indoor cat, I recommend a few changes. My indoor cats' tags read as follows:

INDOOR CAT
I'M LOST
IF FOUND, CALL
(my name)
(my phone number)

In my yard I come across many cats wearing tags with their names and their owners' name and number. So many times I've called the owner only to be told that the cat is allowed to roam and isn't lost. So how do you tell the lost cats? From the vital information on the tag. My cat's names on the tags aren't as important as the information that they're *indoor* cats.

When you shop for a collar, choose a *breakaway*. This type of collar has an elastic insert so there is no chance that your cat will strangle herself should she get caught on a tree branch.

When you fit the collar around your cat's neck, be careful that it's not too tight. You should be able to get two fingers underneath. If you are fitting a kitten, keep in mind that she's constantly growing and you must frequently check her collar. Don't let a day go by without testing the fit.

To get your cat used to the idea of wearing a collar, put it on her, then distract her with playtime or feed her dinner. While she may scratch and paw at it initially, if you focus her attention elsewhere, she'll become comfortable enough. If she continues to struggle, take it off and try again at the next mealtime. Until you're sure she's used to the collar, don't leave it on her when you're not around to supervise.

Other forms of identification are available to pet owners. You can have a microchip that can be read by a hand-held scanner implanted just under the cat's skin. The downside to this is that not every vet or shelter has the various scanners and certainly, the neighbor who may find your cat doesn't. Check with your vet and local humane shelter to see if they are equipped. I personally think that a visible ID tag is the best way for your neighbor or someone driving along a road to immediately contact you. The microchip is a great backup, though, in case the collar gets hung up on a branch. If you really want your kitty protected, use both methods.

Catwise Clue

Don't weigh your cat's neck down with all kinds of bells, thinking that that's going to warn away any birds. I'm convinced that a cat with the disadvantage of the bells is forced to become even stealthier and faster at the hunt.

Always Keep a Current "Lost Cat" Picture

In addition to identification on your kitty, always have at least one clear picture to use in case the unthinkable happens and she gets lost. As she grows and changes, take a few good shots in which her face and markings are clearly visible. As a pet owner, I certainly have loads and loads of pictures but in a crisis, I don't want to have to go searching through a stack for the right one. I have my "lost cat" and "lost dog" pictures in an envelope clearly marked so no time will be wasted should that disaster ever occur. For tips on how to find your lost cat, see chapter 14.

Your Cat Isn't the Only One Who Needs Protection

Your son has a pet lizard or your daughter has a gerbil. Maybe you have a bird or perhaps you love fish tanks. How do you train the cat to leave the bird alone? You don't. Cats are predators and birds are natural prey, so keep the cat away. While your kitten may seem to get along well with your parakeet, don't take chances. Keep these pets in separate locations in the house—*always*.

Bringing Kitty Home

Whether you're bringing home a tiny little kitten weighing in at less than one pound or a full-grown Maine Coon at a whopping eighteen pounds, you need a *carrier*. If you already have a cat at home, don't use the same carrier for the new kitty. Refer to chapter 14 for the types of carriers and how to transport a cat safely.

Why do you have to bring her in a carrier? Because this is a *big*, I mean *really big* step in the cat's life. She's leaving what she knows for something totally unfamiliar. Even if her previous life was bad, she has no idea what's ahead for her. The carrier will keep her safe during the trip to your house and provide her with a little hiding place.

Place a towel in the bottom of the carrier for warmth and also to absorb any messes. I also always bring an extra towel so I can replace that one should it get soiled.

Because this is such a big step for a little cat (and for little you), if you can arrange it, the best time to bring her home is at the start of a weekend or when you can take a day or two off.

If you haven't taken your kitten to the vet yet, make sure it's done in the next few days. If you already have cats at home, the kitten MUST be taken to the vet to be tested for feline leukemia virus (FeLV) and immunodeficiency virus (FIV), given a physical, and vaccinated before she is exposed to your current cats or vice versa. The last thing you want to do is bring an unhealthy kitten home. Even if your cats are up-to-date on their shots, no vaccine is 100 percent foolproof.

HAVE A KITTY SUITE READY

The whole family is excited, even the dog is eagerly wagging his tail in anticipation of the new cat's arrival. In your sweetest voice, explain to them that for the time being, the cat will need a small space of her own and time to adjust to her new surroundings. As you watch your family's smiles fade and the dog's tail droop, remember—you're doing the right thing.

So why am I being such a meanie and not allowing you to let the cat run free about the house, especially since you've already taken the time to kitten-proof it? Because I don't want to overwhelm her. She's a small cat and it's a big house. Imagine if I whisked you off and dropped you in the middle of a large, unfamiliar city. I then tell you that you have to find your way around the entire city right away. You'd probably get lost, overwhelmed, frustrated, scared, and your initial impression of this strange place might be negative. Basically, that's what you'd be doing to your cat if you give her the run of the place—you'd be dropping her in a strange city (a foreign one, no less).

Much of a cat's sense of security centers around her territory, so allow your cat to begin acquainting herself with her new home a little at a time. This is crucial for a kitten because she won't know where any of her necessities are.

If you're bringing an adult cat into the house, this is a big change in her life and you must make her feel safe. Safety for her comes in the form of a little sanctuary place. When you set up the kitty suite, place the litter box on one side of the room and the food/water bowls on the other. It's important to keep a good distance between them because cats don't eat in the same area they use for elimination.

Place her in the room but leave her in the carrier. Open the door to the carrier and let her come out in her own time. A kitten will most likely eagerly charge right out, but an adult may not be sure of herself right away. Even after she has stepped out of the carrier, leave it in the corner of the room as an extra hiding place for your cat.

She may hide under the bed for two days but that's okay. The fact that she *can* hide will make her feel better. After you've closed the door and left her alone is when she can begin to investigate the room around her. Inch by inch is how she may expand her comfort zone, in quiet, in private, and without a bunch of eyes watching her every move.

No matter what kind of room you've chosen as your kitty's sanctuary room, make sure that she has plenty of hiding places there. Don't put her in an empty room where she'll feel totally exposed and threatened. If it's not a room with furniture, place boxes lined with towels around. One trick I do is to cut a doorway into the side of a box with a lid or a box placed upside down to make a little cardboard cave.

Create a comfortable and cozy bed area for your new kitty. You can either purchase a pet bed at the store or line a box with some old clothes. I prefer to line a box with a couple of sweatshirts that I've worn so the cat gets used to my scent.

If you're bringing in a kitten at a cold time of year, her room should be warm enough and draft-free.

If you're bringing your new cat into a household of existing cats, oh boy. A sanctuary room set up for her is absolutely necessary or the fur will fly! How to introduce a new cat to your other pets is covered in chapter 11.

If your new cat is an adult, one very helpful way you can increase her comfort level is through *facial pheromone* placement. Facial *what?* It sounds like a mouthful, I know, but stick with me because you're going to like it. If you need to refresh your memory about pheromones, go back to chapter 2.

Pheromones, those chemicals produced by the cat and released through scent glands, contain information about the cat, which is why she deposits them along objects in her territory to mark it. Marking behavior also enables her to leave information about herself for other cats who may pass by. The facially produced pheromones have a calming effect as opposed to those on the other end of the cat (i.e., spraying). They are connected with anxiety and excitation. We don't want to encourage those anxiety-related pheromones, but we do want to encourage the comforting, calming ones that will help your cat adjust and feel more at home.

To aid you in this, there's a product available called Feliway. It contains synthetic feline facial pheromones. If you spray it on prominent objects in her sanctuary room that would naturally lend themselves to facial rubbing by a cat, it will have a calming effect. For instance, she wouldn't rub her face along a flat wall but she might do it at a corner of a desk, table legs, chair legs, etc. Once your cat is allowed access to the rest of the house, use Feliway on prominent objects throughout. (In veterinary clinics, the staff can spray cages with Feliway to help ease the cat's stress during hospitalization.)

Feliway should be sprayed four inches away from the object and eight inches up from the ground (that's the average cat's nose height). One squirt in each spot once or twice a day for about a month will greatly aid your cat in accepting her new home. Where you notice her engaging in facial rubbing you no longer have to spray Feliway there. Spray only objects. Never spray the cat, and don't saturate anything—one squirt is all that's needed.

Feliway was created to help with urine spray-marking behavior problems. The idea behind it is that cats don't spray where they do facial rubbing. The calming effect of the product may help in all anxiety-related situations. It is available through veterinarians and pet supply stores and comes with instructions. Don't throw the instructions away—read them completely because the product must be used correctly to be effective. For more information on Feliway refer to chapter 8, which discusses its use in correcting urine spray-marking problems.

How much interaction should you initially have with your new cat? Each case is a bit different. If you have brought home a kitten, you'll need to give her plenty of time and attention because she'll be anxious to bond with you. If the new arrival is an adult cat, you'll have to use your judgment and base it on her emotional state. If she acts threatened, back off and give her some time by herself. Introduce yourself slowly.

How will you know when it's time to spring your new cat from kitty jail? If she's a kitten, you can do it as soon as you're sure she has the routine down: eating, drinking, using the litter box. An adult cat may take longer. What you should look for is for her to resume normal activities: i.e., eating, drinking water, using the litter box, and seeming more secure. If she's still hiding in the back of the closet, buried beneath a pile of shoes, she's not ready. If you already have cats in the house, the new cat will need to stay in the room for a while so you can do a gradual introduction (see chapter 11).

Your main concern for a kitten is to make sure she stays safe and has enough time and privacy to eat, sleep, and use the litter box. Everyone is going to want to hold her and play with her, but she's still a fragile baby and needs your watchful eye.

When you do decide to open the door, let her investigate the house a little at a time. To help an adult cat feel more comfortable, spray Feliway on prominent objects. The calming effect of the facial phero-mones can make a difference in how quickly she adjusts. You don't need to use Feliway for a kitten.

How do you introduce your new adult cat to your family? *S-l-o-w-l-y*. She could easily feel overwhelmed. I come from a very small family, and when I think back to the first time I met my husband's large family (four sisters and lots of nieces and nephews) I remember I was over-whelmed. Do your cat a big favor and let her have all the personal space she needs. Don't rush anything. After all, you're going to have many years together, so start things off right.

Your children may have a difficult time with understanding the importance of the kitty's need for a sanctuary room. They may be anx-ious to have the kitty sleep in bed with them. Use your judgment, based on the kitty's age, level of comfort, and any other specifics of your situa-tion. Make sure the cat absolutely knows where her litter box is and routinely uses it before trusting her in other rooms. A kitten doesn't have training perfected yet and could have an accident on your child's bed because she may not remember where the box is.

Taking in a Stray Cat

Be prepared—this is a slow process. Taking in a cat whose history is unknown means you have to give her a wide comfort zone and work slowly on building trust.

Just because you've rescued this skinny, hungry, cold, and lonely cat, don't expect her to instantly recognize her sudden good fortune and be appreciative of her new comfort. Depending upon how much contact she has had with humans (if any at all), she may never become the lov-ing, sociable, happy cat you want. She could always remain timid, unpredictable, impossible to handle, or even aggressive.

First on your list with a stray is a trip to the vet. The cat must be tested and vaccinated. If she's healthy enough at the time, make plans to have her altered as well. She should be checked for parasites and if there's so much as one flea on her, take care of that right away so you won't be bringing the little pests home to your other pets.

At home, she should be kept in one room, just as you would when bringing in any new kitty. Make certain there are plenty of hiding places in the room because she'll need the security of being able to have cover as she gets her bearings. If the room doesn't have enough hiding places, bring in a bunch of boxes (all sizes) and scatter them around the room. Place them on their sides so she'll have a cover over her head. Another great way to create a hiding place and yet allow her to move around is to buy a few soft-sided cat tunnels (available in pet supply stores and through mail order). You can also make a tunnel by cutting the bottoms out of several boxes, then laying them on their sides. Create a snake-like pattern that maybe leads from the litter box to the cat tree. That way, she'll feel secure enough to get to her litter box and maybe venture over to the tree without feeling exposed.

Spray Feliway on the corners of the boxes and on the corners of any furniture twice a day, which will help promote a calming effect. Don't spray near the litter box, though. Also, to help the cat begin to get comfortable with your scent, line some of the boxes with T-shirts or sweatshirts that you've worn.

One of the best ways to start building a relationship with a stray cat is through food. Even if she doesn't yet feel secure enough to eat in your presence (which she probably won't), *you* be the source of the food supply.

At night, leave just a small night-light on for the cat. Don't leave a regular light on because she'll feel more comfortable moving around in darkness. By having a night-light on, you'll be able to enter the room and be aware of where she is in case she tries to bolt out the door, without having to switch on a bright light.

Begin to start spending time in the room by just sitting on the floor. Don't try to approach the cat. Let her have total control as to what pace this should move. When you sit on the floor, quietly talk to her so she gets used to the sound of your voice. Your body language and voice should convey a message of being casual, calm, and totally nonthreatening.

After a few times of just going in to visit, bring in some special food that the cat will hopefully find irresistible. If she's starving and goes for anything, try handfeeding her dry food. In the beginning, just place the kibble a safe enough distance away from you. If she responds, you can move it a little closer. The same goes for canned food or treats. Each time you feed her, place the food a fraction of an inch closer to you.

Watch her comfort level, though, if she gets nervous, you need to go back a few steps. Remember: Go slowly. Don't rush the trust-building process. Let her dictate the pace. If she does seems comfortable and willing to come close, try feeding her right from your hand. Don't make any sudden moves and don't attempt to reach out and pet her.

In between mealtimes, bring in an interactive toy (a fishing pole design) and casually move it around. Don't go in her direction because she'll be frightened. Just nonchalantly move it to catch her interest. She may or may not feel bold enough to go after it, but at least you'll be getting her interest. If she does go after the toy, be careful not to bring it too close to you. Work up to that point slowly. After a few play sessions you can let the toy go close to you or even right over you. Don't let it rest on you though because you certainly don't want the cat scratching your legs.

After mealtime or playtime, lay down on the carpet and remain motionless for a while. This may be the time the cat feels brave enough to begin checking you out. When I did this with Olive, I often ended up falling asleep. When I awoke, I'd find her curled up on my legs or across my chest, fast asleep. We had bonded. One day I awoke and found her nuzzled up next to my face. It had been a slow trust-building process, but that day I saw the light at the end of the tunnel. After one month of hiding, fear, hissing, growling, and total mistrust, she was beginning to let me in. I cried. The moment was short-lived though because my crying scared her and she bolted for cover. I still had much to learn.

Have a Safe Holiday

Holidays can be stressful for everyone. For cats, though, it's an especially confusing time because their whole world can be turned upside down. There are often many strangers coming into the house, and the cat may be overlooked by the busy owner. Using your *think like a cat* mentality, try to look at the events from your kitty's point of view. An owner's guests may be viewed as intruders by the cat as they attempt to pick up and hold her. Usual playtime rituals may get forgotten as the cat follows the owner around waiting for the appearance of a favorite toy. Unfamiliar kids are running around the house. There's way too much noise, and kitty can't find a safe place to sleep so she hides under the bed. Doesn't sound much like a happy holiday to me. Then there's the food. Why eat that boring old cat food when there's a feast spread out on the kitchen counter?

Aside from the general holiday dangers, each special day can hold specific dangers, such as:

CHRISTMAS

For some cats, Christmas, with its decorations, must seem as if they've stepped into the feline version of Disneyland. For others, Christmas holds no particular interest. To be safe, even if your cat does not seem to express any interest in the goings-on of the holiday, don't take chances. Use safe decorations and avoid hazardous temptation.

First, there's the tree. I know many owners who spend lots of time and money decorating their beautiful tree, only to find it later that evening lying across the carpet. Don't be fooled—your six-pound cat can knock a six-foot tree right over. Use a heavy, sturdy base so the tree won't be top heavy. Choose a tree that's wide at the bottom, rather than tall and narrow. You can even install a hook in the wall and attach fishing line from it to the tree. If you have a picture on the wall behind the tree, take it down and use that hook so there won't be a new hole after Christmas when you take down the tree and replace the picture.

Get your cat used to the tree before you put decorations on it. Leave the bare tree up for at least a day, so you can see how your cat is reacting. If she starts chewing the needles, use a bitter anti-chew spray for plants. If she attempts to climb the tree, give her a squirt of plain water from a spray bottle.

If you have a live tree, you have to be careful to keep your cat away from the water in the reservoir. The pine sap that comes off the tree and ends up in the water is toxic to cats. So are any life-extender chemicals you might add. Cover the exposed part of the reservoir with netting so you can water easily but your cat can't get to it to drink.

Now let's decorate the tree. Start with the lights. Coat each strand with a bitter anti-chew spray to discourage your kitty from munching on the cords. Put the lights deep in the tree near the trunk as opposed to resting them on the edges of the branches. It's also a good idea to stay away from twinkling lights which could attract your kitten. To keep the cord that goes from the tree to the outlet safe, slide it through an empty paper towel tube. No one will see it behind the tree. Plug your tree lights into the Safe Living Electronic Smart Cord (see the section on "Electrical Cords" earlier in this chapter).

Tinsel is dangerous—deadly in fact, should a cat swallow a piece. Don't use it at all—*ever!* Don't think you can keep it out of your kitten's reach by placing it on the top of the tree because some inevitably comes off. Besides, the way it moves and glitters can tempt a kitten to climb the tree in an attempt to reach it. Also, because it's so light, some comes off the tree almost every time someone passes. Your tree will look great without it. I haven't used tinsel in years and to tell you the truth, I don't miss having to pick up those pieces that were forever floating down.

The ornaments you choose should, of course, be cat-proof. If you have breakable ones, the best place for them is back in their boxes. That said, if you really want the fragile ones on the tree, place them higher up, out of your cat's reach. The ornaments on the lower third of the tree shouldn't have any sharp or breakable pieces, ribbon, string or anything that could be dangerous.

Ornament hooks can be hazardous too, not just for the cat but for children as well. I once stepped on one that was sticking up out of the carpet pile. Trust me, it hurt. Instead of hooks, find safer ways to attach your ornaments. I've always used the twist ties that come with trash bags. If you use green ones, they're invisible and they actually fasten the ornament to the tree more securely than hooks.

The gifts you so lovingly wrap and place under the tree need to be cat-safe too. Ribbons are not only the biggest hazard but unfortunately, the most tempting accessories. Keep your gift wrapping simple. Use a plain bow on top rather than the thin curling ribbon or long tendrils of easily chewed strands. If there are gifts you want to wrap elaborately with lots of flowing ribbon, keep them put away until it's time for them to be opened. And, speaking of opening gifts, that's the time when an unnoticed kitten can get into trouble. Your family is busy tearing open packages and no one notices that the kitten grabbed the ribbon that was tossed on the floor. Another major potentially dangerous time is when you gather up the discarded wrapping paper and boxes to toss in the outside trash. A kitten could easily be buried in there. If your kitty isn't in sight, go through every piece of paper and every box before tossing it away.

Be careful about such seasonal plants as poinsettias, holly, and mistletoe. Some are toxic and all cause intestinal problems. Keep them out of your cat's reach. Another very serious threat to your cat's safety is the many holiday candles. Don't leave any candles unattended. A cat's tail can easily come in contact with the flame or a cat can knock over the whole candle.

Now we come to my favorite part of Christmas—the food. The rule here for your cat is simple: Keep her away from it. The rich foods we eat during the holidays will cause your cat digestive upsets. Also be very careful of things such as turkey bones, which if your cat gets hold of, can cause her to choke or suffer serious intestinal injury. Don't leave the turkey sitting out on the counter if no one's in the room. When you discard the turkey carcass, wrap it securely in a heavy trash bag and put it in the outside trash container right away.

Don't leave chocolate candies, cookies, alcohol, or anything out. Chocolate is deadly to cats.

Another problem cats face at Christmas is the sudden invasion of strange faces. Without warning, they burst into the house (that's how it'll seem to your cat). The cat is pursued by unfamiliar children, denied access to certain favorite spots (such as the guest room) and is all but forgotten by her usually attentive owner. House guests can let your cat outside, step on her, or just downright frighten her. If you're having a house full of guests for the day, provide your cat with a sanctuary—perhaps in your bedroom or some other area where guest traffic won't be allowed. Put her litter box in there, along with some water (and food if you feed free-choice). When I do this for my cats, I put on some soothing classical music and engage them in some interactive play. That way, they're ready for a nap while I go and attend to my guests.

A word of caution, with all the partying, shopping, visiting, and other hectic activity at holiday time, don't neglect kitty. Cats are creatures of habit and rely on the comforting familiarity of their normal activities. Don't neglect regular playtime schedules, grooming, feeding, and other routines.

THANKSGIVING

Food, food, and more food. Everywhere you look there's food. The turkey, stuffing, creamed onions, candied yams, wine, pumpkin pie—all of it needs to be kept away from the cat. Read the previous section on "Christmas" for why it's important to keep kitty away from this stuff.

If your cat is on a diet or seems to become possessed in the presence of people food, for her sake, don't give in and let her have snacks. You won't be doing her any favor, and you risk endangering her health.

HALLOWEEN

This is the most frightening day of the year if you own a cat. There are people in this world who seek out cats on this day to hurt, torture, and even kill. Protect your cat by not allowing her outdoors at all, starting at least a day or two before Halloween. Even cats who are exclusively outdoor cats (which none should be) must be kept inside to be safe. All cats are at risk but black cats are at the most risk. Many humane shelters won't adopt black cats out to anyone during the month of October. If you're trying to find a home for your cat or a litter of kittens, don't do it close to Halloween and don't give away or sell any black cats during the entire month.

Your front door will be opened repeatedly so keep your cat in another room, away from the hectic activity. With her litter box, food, and water, she can spend a quiet evening listening to music or being with another family member. If she's frightened of the doorbell, having her at the far end of the house with someone in the family will help keep her more relaxed.

Keep all candy out of the cat's reach. Chocolate, as you surely must know by now, is lethal to cats.

One more thing to watch out for, is not to let the cat be frightened by costumed children. Sometimes children dressed as monsters or ghosts get so excited that they go around attempting to scare other family members or pets. Keep an eye on your cat.

FOURTH OF JULY

Even I find it hard when the neighborhood kids shoot off firecrackers all night long. I must be getting old because I find myself preferring the quieter holidays.

This is not a good day or night for a cat to be outdoors. The noise of the firecrackers can be very frightening. And, as with Halloween, there are some people who take sick pleasure in frightening or hurting animals and might throw firecrackers at your cat. Even if a firecracker isn't thrown directly at the animal, the noise can cause her to bolt in panic and she could run right into the road—and an oncoming car.

Keep your cat indoors and play music or turn on the TV. Engage in a play session, and everyone will get through this safely.

BIRTHDAYS

Balloons, ribbons, and lighted candles are the three major safety hazards. If you're having a birthday party, kitty will also have to contend with noise-makers, lots of activity, and the possibility of getting stepped on, grabbed, or petted without her consent. Find a safe room for your cat to wait out the party.

Birthday cake, candy, and any other goodies should also be kept out of the cat's reach. If you're hosting a children's party, there's a very good chance that some cake or candy will end up on the floor, so it's best to do your cleanup before allowing the cat back into the general part of the house.

"Save Our Pet"

Despite all your precautions, emergencies and unexpected situations do arise—and you may not even be home to help your cat. Having a visible sign to alert authorities that there's a pet (or pets) inside your house can give you peace of mind if you're away from home should an emergency, such as a house fire, occur. Many companies make window or door stickers for this very purpose. Or you can get a sign on a post to stick in the ground. Putting the sign near the front of the yard, away from the house will make it easily visible for authorities, rescue workers, or neighbors.

Make sure there's a place on the sign for you to indicate what kind of pet you have and how many. Zoo West (see list of suppliers) makes a sturdy post-mounted PET ALERT sign.

What If Something Happens to *You*?

I know, it's weird, it's not something any of us like to think about. Unfortunately, though, it may happen. What if you have to be hospitalized? What if you are no longer able to care for your cat? If you live alone, this is a very important consideration and one worth being well prepared for. In chapter 17, which is primarily about coping with the loss of a cat, there is a section on page 310 on how to make sure your cat is provided for in your will.

4

The Doctor Is In

The Other Most Important Person in Your Cat's Life and How to Tell if Your Cat is Sick

No matter where you got your cat, he's going to need veterinary care. Whether purchased or rescued, he'll need to be monitored throughout his life.

Your relationship with your vet is more than just a yearly visit for vaccinations. Together, you and the vet are responsible for keeping your cat healthy. The vet will depend on you to notice changes in your cat and bring them to his/her attention immediately. Your observations of your cat will be valuable information for the vet.

Beginning the Search

STEP ONE

Take some time to think about what qualities you're looking for in a vet and what services matter most to you. Would you prefer a large, multi-doctor practice or a small one-doctor clinic? Do you want a vet whose practice is limited to cats? There are several vets around the country

What Your Vet Can Provide

- preventative medical care throughout the life of your cat
- nutritional guidance
- answers to basic care/training questions
- emergency medical care (maybe through an emergency clinic)
- access to information on groundbreaking medical care
- information regarding other pet-related services (such as pet-sitters)
- lost and found resources
- bathing/grooming services (optional)
- boarding services (optional)
- emotional support during a feline health crisis
- long-term care of ongoing medical conditions

who are board-certified feline specialists. Find out if one practices in your area.

You'll want to know if the vet provides after-hours care or if there is an animal emergency clinic in your area. Cats have a knack of getting sick on holidays or after everyone has closed up for the night, so having emergency care available is a must.

You may prefer a vet who owns cats. Although that shouldn't keep you away from any vet, you may feel you can relate better to a cat owner.

Do you want a young doctor recently out of vet school or an older one? Younger vets are up-to-date on the latest techniques, but older vets have had years of experience. It depends on your preference.

Finally, although it won't have any effect on ability, you may have a preference concerning gender.

STEP TWO

Ask friends and neighbors you think take particularly good care of their pets for their recommendations. Don't just ask for names, ask your friends what specifically they like or don't like about their vet.

If you're new to an area, you can check the listings in the yellow pages of the phone book or call your local veterinary medical association for recommendations.

STEP THREE

Once you've accumulated some names, narrow down the list to the two or three who seem to be the most likely candidates. If a friend gave you a name of a great vet who's on the other side of town, that may rule him/her out.

Next, you'll need to visit the clinic to view the facilities and meet the veterinarian. I suggest that you call ahead to let them know you're coming so someone will be available to give you a tour. When you get to the clinic, begin your assessment from the moment you walk in the door. How does the clinic smell? Does it look clean? The receptionist who greets you should be friendly and knowledgeable. As you take your tour of the hospital, pay attention to how the staff interact with each other. Happy people are usually more pleasant. I've toured hospitals in which I've heard bickering between technicians and even foul language being used toward the animals. Keep your eyes and ears open. As you walk past the cages, notice how they are kept. Are they clean and are messes taken care of as soon as possible? One thing I always check for is if the surgery patients are given towels or blankets to keep them warm or if they're just left to shiver on the few sheets of newspaper that line the bottom of the cage.

When you meet the veterinarian, keep in mind that he or she may be very busy with patients (another reason why it's always a good idea to call ahead) and won't have time for a long chat. Within a few minutes you should, however, get an idea of how well he or she communicates and if you feel comfortable.

Your relationship with your veterinarian is very important, as you're both responsible for the health of your cat. If after the first few times you visit the vet with your kitten you don't feel comfortable, change vets. Just ask for a copy of your cat's records and go somewhere else. Don't stick with a vet you're not happy with, but before making the decision to switch, think about whether or not your expectations are unrealistic. For example, some clients call the vet several times a day and expect to be put through immediately, not taking into consideration that the vet may be in surgery or with another patient. If you feel that your expectations are realistic, however, and you've either talked with the vet or given the staff an opportunity to correct things, then just move on.

Transporting Your Kitten to the Vet

Even though he's just a tiny little thing right now and is easy to hold in your arms (although some kittens can be nearly impossible to contain when they don't want to be held), he'll feel more secure in a carrier. Having him in a carrier also eliminates the chance that he could suddenly become frightened and leap right out of your arms. Begin getting him acquainted with the carrier at an early age. It'll be much easier now than later. It will also protect him in the waiting room, where other patients may not necessarily be as polite as he is. For all of the specifics on carriers, see chapter 14.

What to Expect on Your Kitten's First Vet Visit

No matter where you got your kitten and no matter what you were told about how healthy he is, he must be taken to the veterinarian. If you already have other cats at home, the kitten *must* be taken to the vet before you expose your cats to him.

When you bring your kitten in, you should also bring along a sample of his feces so the vet can test it for internal parasites. Try to collect the freshest sample. If your kitten defecates in the morning but your appointment isn't until later in the day, wrap the sample in a plastic bag and put it in the refrigerator. Write yourself a note and leave it on the front door so you won't leave for the vet without taking the sample. If the kitten doesn't cooperate by providing you with a sample, don't panic—the vet can get one from him in the office (though it's much less traumatic for him if he volunteers one peacefully at home in his litter box).

If the kitten hasn't been tested for feline leukemia virus (FeLV) and feline immunodeficiency virus (FIV), or if there's any question regarding the reliability of any previous tests, he should be tested. This involves taking a very small blood sample (for more information on FeLV and FIV, refer to the medical appendix). This is usually done by a technician before the veterinarian examines the kitten.

While the blood and stool tests are being completed in the lab, the veterinarian enters and begins the kitten's physical exam. The kitten will have already been weighed and had his temperature taken by a technician. The vet begins at the kitty's head and works his or her way to the tip of the tail. The vet will check inside the ears with an otoscope (a conical light). If ear mites are suspected, the vet will swab a sample of exudate from the ears for microscopic examination. Next, the kitten's eyes and nose will be checked for any signs of discharge. The vet will open the mouth and make sure all looks normal in there as well.

The doctor will run his or her hands along the kitten's body, feeling for anything out of the ordinary, then he or she will use a stethoscope to listen to the kitten's heart and lungs.

Your veterinarian will also go over the vaccination schedule needed and cover the basics of kitten nutrition, flea control, grooming, and training. This is your time to ask any questions. Make certain you understand all of the vet's instructions.

Your kitten will then begin to receive his vaccinations. You will have to bring him back for a return visit in three to four weeks, so he can get the next series. Your vet will instruct you on how many visits will be needed and which vaccines should be administered, based upon your kitty's age and risk factors.

Some vaccines, depending on the type and the manufacturer, are combined. Some are even administered intranasally rather than via injection. Your vet will explain specifically about each vaccine as it is being drawn up for administration. The vet should also explain any potential side effects, what to watch for (such as breathing difficulty) and how your kitten may react over the next twenty-four hours.

If internal parasites were detected from the stool sample, your kitten will be given a de-wormer. Depending on the type of de-wormer, a second dose may be administered on the kitten's return visit. If ear mites were found, you'll be given medication to administer. Refer to the medical appendix for more information on ear mites.

During your first visit with the vet is the time to get a demonstration on how to trim your kitten's nails. If there's anything else you feel unsure about, such as how to give any prescribed medication, how much to feed, how to groom your kitten, ask it now. Have your vet explain anything you're not sure about. Your vet's main concern is starting you and your kitten off right.

Vaccine Risk

Some cat owners now hesitate about yearly vaccinations because in recent years, there have been reports of cancerous tumors appearing

General Kitten Vaccine Schedule

Your veterinarian will tailor your kitten's specific vaccine requirements according to his risk factors, but here's a general guideline:

SIX TO EIGHT WEEKS OF AGE

- feline rhinotracheitis-calicivirus-panleukopenia vaccine #1
- chlamydia vaccine #1 (optional—sometimes combined in above-mentioned vaccine)
- stool check for internal parasites—deworming done if needed

TWELVE WEEKS OF AGE

- feline rhinotracheitis-calicivirus-panleukopenia vaccine #2
- chlamydia vaccine #2

- feline leukemia vaccine #1
- second de-worming (if necessary)

SIXTEEN WEEKS OF AGE

- feline leukemia vaccine #2
- rabies vaccine
- feline infectious peritonitis vaccine #1 (a highly controversial vaccine usually only recommended in catteries or multicat households)

TWENTY WEEKS OF AGE

- feline infectious peritonitis vaccine #2

ANNUALLY

- all vaccines are boostered
- a fecal exam for indoor cats (every six months for cats who go outdoors), you can just drop a sample off at the vet

at vaccination sites. The disease, vaccine-associated feline sarcoma, unfortunately has resulted in the death of cats.

Many vets are now giving vaccinations in specific locations and noting it on the cat's record so they can track which vaccines may be responsible for the cancer.

Is it worth the risk to vaccinate your cat? I feel that the risk of cancer is low compared to the risks associated with *not* vaccinating. To learn more about the diseases your cat could acquire if not vaccinated, refer to the medical appendix.

You should discuss any concerns you may have about vaccine-associated feline sarcoma with your vet.

Some Common Diagnostic Procedures

RADIOGRAPHS
Radiographs (X rays) taken of your cat are the same as the ones they take of humans and used for the same diagnoses of fractures, obstructions, tumors, malformations, etc. Cats are usually tolerant of the procedure, but if yours is in pain (because of a fracture or injury), he'll be sedated beforehand.

BLOOD TESTS
There are numerous tests performed on the blood to help diagnose a vast array of disorders. Blood tests can help determine how well a particular organ is functioning, if there's a disease present, the number of red and white cells, etc. Some tests can be performed at the vet's office but many are sent to an outside diagnostic lab for processing.

If only a small amount of blood is needed, it can be drawn from the vein in the cat's foreleg. Larger amounts of blood are drawn from the jugular vein in the neck.

ULTRASOUND
Ultrasound uses soundwaves to create a picture of the cat's internal organs. It's a painless and noninvasive procedure and can provide the veterinarian with valuable information concerning the shape, size, and condition of particular organs.

ELECTROCARDIOGRAM
Contact leads are attached to the cat's skin so the ECG machine can record the heart's electrical functions to determine any abnormalities. It's not painful, and cats are usually very tolerant of the procedure.

URINALYSIS
Urine samples are used to help determine the presence of urinary tract disorders, diabetes, or kidney disease.

A urine sample can be obtained by your vet using a needle and syringe (cystocentesis). The needle is injected into the bladder, and the urine is drawn up into the syringe. Urine can also be collected through catheterization, manual expression of the bladder (done under sedation), or "clean catch" (using a container to collect the urine as the cat

CatwiseClue
To prevent your kitten from associating the vet's office only with pain and fear, bring him in periodically for "hello" visits, when he'll just be petted and greeted by the staff.

voids). Nonabsorbent litters are also used to collect urine samples at home.

BIOPSY

A sample of tissue is taken and sent to a diagnostic lab for analysis. Biopsies are used to identify growths, determine if a growth is benign (noncancerous) or malignant (cancerous) and also to confirm that all of the cancer has been removed (this is done by examination of the edges of the tumor).

FECAL EXAMINATION

The color, consistency, and odor of the cat's feces tell the vet a lot about his health. The vet or technician will check a fecal sample to make sure it looks normal and check for signs of blood or mucous.

As a routine part of the examination, a small sample is also mixed with a special solution and examined under the microscope in order to check for signs of parasites (this is usually limited to cats who are allowed outdoors).

Which Way to the Emergency Clinic?

If there's an animal emergency clinic in your town, it's wise to be familiar with its location before an emergency hits. That way you won't be driving unfamiliar streets in the middle of the night with a sick or injured cat, making wrong turns and having to ask for directions.

When Should Your Kitten Be Spayed or Neutered?

These two terms refer to the sterilization procedure—*spaying* for females and *neutering* for males.

Some shelters perform the procedures on kittens as young as eight weeks. It is a much debated topic as to whether there are negative aspects to early sterilization.

The most common time to spay a female is before she goes into her first heat—at about six months of age. Males are usually neutered somewhere between six to eight months old.

If you're unsure about whether to have your kitty altered, let me assure you the benefits of doing so go beyond helping to cut down on pet overpopulation. There are far more behavior problems with intact pets than with altered ones. Intact cats are more territorial, tend to roam and fight, and if you haven't already experienced the scent of tomcat urine, be prepared, because intact males spray. From a medical standpoint, intact cats are more at risk of certain cancers than altered pets. If you have any questions, discuss it with your vet.

Health Insurance for Your Cat

Money. It can be the deciding factor for whether a pet lives or dies. When you first get a kitten, the last thing you want to think about is what horrendous diseases, injuries, or disorders this very healthy animal could be subject to down the road.

Huge strides are continually being made in veterinary medicine. Unfortunately though, the breakthrough procedure that could now save your cat's life may be unaffordable for you.

I urge you to purchase veterinary health insurance. It could not only save you money, but tremendous heartbreak as well.

Check with your veterinarian concerning the plans available in your state. In addition to traditional insurance, there are special membership clubs in which you receive discounts off services from participating vets.

Refer to the resource guide for more information on insurance companies, then do your homework to see which one is right for you.

How Do You Know If Your Cat Is Sick?

Your cat depends on you for his health and comfort. Cats don't really have nine lives, so it's up to you and your vet to be responsible about his health and welfare.

Become familiar with your cat's normal routine. Notice how much water he usually drinks. This will be important information because an increase or decrease in water consumption can be a sympton of certain diseases. Are you familiar with your cat's litter box habits? If so, you may be able to detect diarrhea, constipation, and urinary tract problems early. Become familiar with his usual volume of urine or feces, as well as its color.

Signs to Watch For

- change in appearance of coat: dull, dry, sparse, bald patches, greasy-looking

- change in normal grooming behavior

- inflamed or irritated skin: any change in normal color or texture

- change in usual behavior: cat who doesn't play anymore, is lethargic, hides, is nervous, aggressive, irritable

- change in eating habits: increased/decreased appetite, weight change, difficulty eating

- increased or decreased water consumption

- vomiting: frequency, food vs. liquids, color, volume

- change in urination: urinating outside of litter box, more frequent urination, straining, blood-tinged urine, inability to urinate (this is an absolute emegency), crying during urination, change in urine odor

- change in bowels: eliminating outside of litter box, diarrhea, constipation, mucous-coated stool, unusual color, blood in stool, unusually foul-smelling stool, volume of stool produced

- weakness

- limping or pain

- excessive vocalization, crying, howling

- fever or low body temperature

- sneezing

- coughing

- change in eyes: discharge, film, appearance of nictitating membrane, squinting, enlargement or reduction of pupil size in one or both eyes, pawing at eyes

- discharge from nose (note color and consistency)

- discharge from ears, appearance of exudate, pawing at eyes, head shaking

- swelling on any part of the body

- shivering

- lumps on or below the skin surface

- lesions or bruises

- change in breathing: rapid, shallow, labored

- change in appearance of gums: swelling, paleness, blue or gray color, bright red color

- bad breath

- excessive drooling

- strange odor

- neurological changes: seizures, tremors, palsy, etc.

A regular grooming schedule gives you the opportunity to examine your cat's body so you'll know the norm that will aid in the early detection of lumps, sores, external parasites, bald patches, rashes, etc. Check your cat's ears, eyes, teeth, under his tail, genitals, stomach, and even the pads of his paws on a regular basis.

Cats are experts at hiding the fact that they don't feel well. Sometimes you'll have to rely on the slightest change in his behavior.

When you talk to your vet, provide the following information:

- a description of the problem

- how long the cat has had the problem

- the frequency of the problem

For example, don't just say, "My cat is vomiting." The vet needs to know what the vomitus consists of: food? liquid? what color? Did the vomiting start today? Last night? How often is it happening? Does the cat vomit immediately after meals? Has he thrown up five times today in the space of an hour? An accurate description by the owner provides valuable diagnostic clues to the veterinarian.

How to Take Your Cat's Temperature

Taking your cat's temperature may seem close to impossible, but if you do it gently and calmly, both you and your cat will survive the procedure unscathed. You may never need to take your cat's temperature, but the situation could arise so it's helpful to know the easiest procedure. If your cat gets very agitated during a vet visit, the vet may suggest that you take the temperature at home if the cat is calm.

A cat's temperature is taken rectally, using a *rectal* thermometer. *Don't* use an *oral* thermometer. The cat's natural reflex is to bite down, which will break the thermometer and cause severe injury.

If possible, have someone assist you by holding the cat. If your cat is difficult to handle, you'll definitely need an extra pair of hands. Even the most good-natured cat can react quite violently to a thermometer, so if help is offered, take it!

If you are using a standard mercury thermometer, shake it until the mercury registers 96° F. or less. If you are using a digital thermometer, follow the packaged instructions. Lubricate the tip with K-Y or petroleum jelly.

Place the cat on a table or counter so you won't have to crouch on the floor. Raise the cat's tail with one hand and gently insert the thermometer one inch into the anal canal. Hold it in place for two minutes. If you have trouble inserting the thermometer, lightly scratch or pet your cat at the base of his tail as this sometimes causes a relaxation of the rectal muscles. The thermometer may also slide in more easily if you gently twist it. Be patient and use *gentle* pressure. Try to keep the cat as calm as possible because if he gets too anxious, it may give you an inaccurate readout.

When you remove the thermometer, wipe it clean with a tissue, read the temperature, then clean the thermometer with alcohol before placing it back in its case.

A cat's normal temperature ranges from 101.5° F. to 102.5° F, depending on the circumstances. For example, if your cat is under stress, his temperature will most likely register on the high side.

There are also instant-read digital thermometers that are inserted just inside the ear. This may be the least stressful way for you to take your cat's temperature. Check with your vet about using one of these. I've found some brands to sometimes be less accurate than the rectal thermometers, but if your cat refuses to let you have access to his hindquarters, you at least have another option.

How to Take Your Cat's Pulse

Feel the inside of the hind leg where it meets the groin for the *femoral artery*. You can do this with your cat in a standing position. Press your fingers on the artery until you feel the pulse. Count the number of pulsations you feel within a fifteen-second period. Multiply that by four to get the pulse count per minute. The normal rate for an adult cat is 160 to 180 beats per minute. A kitten's pulse is much higher (usually around 200).

Respiratory Rate

Observe the movement of the cat's chest or abdomen. Counting the number of movements that take place in sixty seconds will give you the respiratory rate.

Don't attempt this if the cat is excited or hot, because the rate will be abnormally high.

The average respiratory rate for a cat at rest is about 20 to 30 breaths per minute.

Rapid breathing can indicate pain, shock, dehydration, or disease. Panting is normal if your cat has engaged in strenuous physical activity.

Panting that appears labored or if the cat seems restless can indicate a serious medical condition such as heatstroke.

Medicating Your Cat

PILLS

Not an easy task to be sure. Some owners would prefer having their teeth drilled by the dentist to giving a pill to their cat. You and your cat can quickly become wrestling opponents as he squirms and wiggles and you turn into a contortionist, trying to unclamp his steel-trap jaws. I witnessed some of the most horrified expressions I've ever seen on a person's face when I worked in an animal hospital and they were in response to the vet telling the owner, "Give your cat one of these pills every day."

You may think that the easiest way to pill a cat is to hide it in food but there are several reasons not to do that. First, some pills are coated to protect the contents from being destroyed by stomach acid before they can be absorbed in the intestines. Also, some pills have a strange smell or a bitter taste and your cat may refuse to eat the foods they are in. Besides, cats are *very* adept at detecting a trick and will look at you with such disgust for underestimating their intelligence. If you really believe that your cat will fall for a pill hidden in your special concoction of cream cheese and sardines, check with your veterinarian first, to be sure it won't destroy the pill's effectiveness.

Some cats will take pills more easily if they have been disguised in a hair ball prevention paste or Nutrical paste.

To me, the best approach is subtlety and speed—with a lot of emphasis on the latter. Don't make a big production out of it because the more fuss you create, the more worried your cat will be. Just be organized and choose your *timing* carefully. For instance, if your cat is more receptive to handling when he's sleepy, then that's the time to pop the pill.

The procedure: You may prefer to place the cat on a counter so you don't have to crouch down. Put the palm of your hand over the top of the cat's head. Tilt the head up *slightly.* Open his mouth by applying gentle pressure with your thumb on one side and middle finger on the other against the area behind the canine teeth (they're the ones that look like daggers but don't let that thought intimidate you). Hold the pill between

CatwiseClue

Many tablets can be made into a liquid by a compounding pharmacist. If your cat handles liquids better than pills, your vet should be able to recommend a compounding pharmacist.

the thumb and index finger of your free hand, and with the middle finger, press the lower jaw open. Drop the pill on the back of the tongue. Coating the pill with butter will make it easier to swallow (but sometimes harder to release from your fingers). Let go of the cat's mouth so he can swallow but keep hold of him so he doesn't escape and spit the pill out. Don't clamp his mouth shut or he won't be able to swallow. You can gently massage the throat in a downward motion to help ease the pill down.

After you have administered the pill, observe your cat to make sure it went down and he doesn't spit it out. If his tongue comes out to lick his nose or mouth, that's a sure sign that the pill has been swallowed. If the cat begins coughing, it means the pill is lodged in the windpipe. Release your hold on him so he can cough it up. If it doesn't come up, grasp your cat by his hips and turn him upside down to dislodge the pill.

An alternate pilling position is to first kneel on the floor, then sit back on your heels with your legs open in a "v" position. Place the cat between your legs, facing away from you. This way, if he tries to back away, he has nowhere to go.

If you find you can't pill with your fingers or if your cat bites, you can buy a plastic pill gun from your veterinarian or pet supply store. The pill is grasped on the end of the syringe by plastic fingers. When you push the plunger, the pill gets deposited onto the tongue. I find pill guns more difficult than just using my fingers, but what's important is getting the pill in the cat without being bitten, so use whatever method works for you.

If your cat squirms and scratches, try wrapping him in a towel. If he's very difficult to handle, enlist the aid of an assistant, although it's sometimes hard to find a volunteer willing to help pill the family cat.

LIQUID MEDICATION

You'll need a plastic dropper or syringe. Don't use a glass dropper because it could break if your cat bites down. Don't use a spoon because it always spills and you won't get the accurate amount into your cat. Also, using a spoon for liquids that are thick and sticky presents a greater risk of your getting it all over your cat's fur.

The easiest way to administer liquids is into the cheek pouch (the space between the cheek and the molars). Put the cat on a table or counter, measure the correct amount of liquid into the dropper and place it in the cat's cheek pouch. Administer in small amounts, allowing the cat to swallow each time. If you try to dispense too much liquid at once, you risk having him inhale the medicine. He may also just let most of it dribble out of his mouth. Keep the cat calm so he doesn't panic and aspirate the liquid. If someone can assist, he or she can gently hold and stroke the cat while you administer the medication.

If you find it impossible to get liquid medication into your cat, ask your vet whether the liquid can be mixed with food. If it can, use a strong-tasting food to disguise the taste. Don't use a large amount of food because your cat may not eat it all, and so get an inadequate dose of medicine.

POWDERS

Powders can usually be mixed with moist food. If the powder has an unpleasant taste, mix with a strong-tasting food. Ask your veterinarian about the preferred method of administration.

INJECTIONS

There are some medical conditions (such as diabetes) that require that the cat receive injections. If the condition is ongoing, you will most likely have to learn to administer these injections yourself. Should this need arise, your vet will give you instructions as well as demonstrations for the correct procedure.

Depending on the medicine, injections are given either subcutaneously (under the skin) or in the muscle. The injections you would most likely have to administer would be subcutaneous.

OINTMENTS/CREAMS

The easiest way to apply these may be to sit in a chair with the cat in your lap. Begin by first stroking to relax him and then stroke on the ointment. Continue to stroke the cat and try to keep him on your lap (but don't force him) so the ointment has time to be absorbed and the amount of medicine he'll lick off once he gets down is decreased. You may find that the cat will fall asleep on your lap and then the medicine gets to do its work without any feline interference. If your cat doesn't enjoy sitting on your lap, distract him with interactive playtime or a meal to give the medicine more time to absorb.

If licking is sabotaging the healing process, ask your vet about using an Elizabethan collar. This collar, which resembles a lamp shade, fits around the neck and will prevent your cat from turning his head to lick off the medicine.

EYE MEDICINE

Place the cat on a counter, or you can sit with him in your lap or in the "v" position previously described above.

Administering ointment: Make sure your hands are clean and thoroughly rinsed of soap. Tilt your cat's head slightly upward with one hand. Rest the hand holding the tube against your cat's cheek so you won't poke him in the eye if he should make a sudden move. Gently pull the lower lid down and apply the amount in a strip along the lid. Be careful not to touch the eye with the applicator. There's no need to rub the eyelid which could cause irritation. The ointment will automatically spread as the cat blinks.

Administering drops: Tilt the cat's head upward. The hand holding the dropper should rest against the cat's cheek to prevent injury in the case of a sudden movement. Drop the prescribed amount into the eye, being careful not to touch the eye itself with the applicator. Let go of the cat to allow him to close his eyes.

Never put any drops into your cat's eyes unless they have been prescribed by your vet.

EAR MEDICATION

Ear medications work best in clean ears so gently swab the ears with a cotton pad or tissue. Your vet will instruct you on whether to use an ear cleansing solution.

Place the cat on the counter, on your lap, or in the "v" position. Be sure your hands are clean, then hold the ear; and steady the cat's head. Don't hold the tip of the ear, hold it at the base, or fold the tip back. Be gentle, because if the ear needs medication, it may also be irritated and sensitive. Put the prescribed amount of medication into the ear. Hold onto the cat's head gently to keep him from shaking his head immediately. This gives the medication time to travel down the ear canal. If the ear isn't irritated, you can gently massage the base to distribute the medication. If the medication is for ear mites, don't massage because the ear is already very irritated.

One tip: Don't wear your best clothes when administering ear medication because your cat won't realize that his head shaking (which all cats do after you put medicine in their ears) will splatter the antibiotic ointment all over your favorite shirt.

Nursing an Ill Cat

Taking care of an ill cat at home is a big responsibility. Although your cat may prefer the comfort of his own familiar surroundings over the unfamiliarity of being in a hospital, make sure you are confident about your abilities and comfortable with all of the instructions given to you by the vet. If you have any questions or are unsure about a particular procedure, ask for a demonstration before attempting to do something on your own.

THE ROOM

The cat should be placed in a peaceful, quiet room. This is especially important in busy households where there are children or other pets.

The room should be warm enough and free of drafts so the cat doesn't get chilled. If you have an air purifier, this is a perfect time to use it.

Set up a low-sided litter box near the cat so he won't have far to walk. If he's unable to get up, you may have to assist him by placing him in the box and providing support.

THE BED

Provide a comfortable bed, covered in towels so you can keep it clean in case he has accidents. Keep the bed clean and dry and change the towels as often as needed. Orthopedic beds are available at pet supply stores. These beds allow for air circulation and can make a cat much more comfortable. If you can't find one, you can buy the "egg crate" foam bed covering in just about any discount or linen store. Cut a good-sized piece and cover with towels.

If your cat seems chilled, you can wrap a hot water bottle in a towel and place it nearby or use a towel-wrapped heating pad set on the lowest setting. Be very careful with these because it's easy for them to burn your cat. Always cover the surface with a towel, never set the thermostat above the lowest setting, and monitor your cat frequently.

FOOD

Your cat may not have much of an appetite. He may prefer several smaller meals. Just make sure he's getting enough nutrition. If he's not on a special diet you might have success using a strong-smelling food. Or try warming it slightly. If he's unable to keep food down, your vet may recommend a bland prescription food or baby food. If the cat refuses to eat, your vet may instruct you to force-feed. The best way to do this is with a plastic syringe and a very smooth, liquid-type food, such as Hill's Prescription A/D. This food is easily syringed and is very palatable. Feed small amounts so you don't cause your cat to gag or vomit. Ask your vet how much to feed and how often, based on your cat's specific needs.

If your cat isn't drinking enough water, your veterinarian may instruct you to administer it orally with a syringe. Since a cat can easily aspirate water into his lungs, mix the water with a little cat food to give it just enough flavor so he'll be able to taste something. Giving water by syringe can be very dangerous, so do it in small amounts, giving him adequate time to swallow and rest. Don't give water by syringe unless specifically instructed to do so by your vet. Often, as long as the cat will eat canned food, the high water content of that diet will be adequate.

GROOMING

An ill cat often isn't up to maintaining his normally high standards of hygiene. If he vomits or is being force-fed, has diarrhea or urinates in his bed, his coat and skin will need extra attention.

If you're force-feeding him, there's a good chance that a significant amount of food will spill onto his chin and down his neck. To reduce the mess, put a small towel over his chest to create a bib to keep his coat clean. Use a warm, moist washcloth to clean his face immediately after you've finished feeding. Don't allow food or medicine to dry on his fur.

If your cat has urinated on himself or has diarrhea, clean him up immediately to prevent the skin from being scalded by urine or irritated by diarrhea. If the cat has chronic urinary or bowel problems, the hair around the anus and genitals may need to be clipped short to help make cleaning easier.

Gently brush your ailing cat regularly to keep his skin and coat healthy. If you have a longhaired cat, you'll have to brush a little every day to prevent mats. If your cat can't move, be sure and turn him occasionally to allow circulation to the skin and prevent sores from developing.

LONELINESS AND DEPRESSION

Keep your little patient's spirits up by spending time with him. If he doesn't enjoy being petted or touched, you can sit with him, providing comfort just by your presence. Spend an hour reading a book or the newspaper in the room with your cat.

When I worked in an animal hospital, one of the most important recovery aids for the animals was being comforted and touched as they lay scared, confused, and hurting in their cages, I petted heads, scratched under chins, and kissed noses. I held the ones who wanted it and for those who viewed me with suspicion, I tried to comfort with a soothing tone of voice.

If other pets or family members provide a sense of comfort for the patient, then allow them to have access to him. But keep everyone calm and quiet. If there is any tension in your multipet household or if your other pets become nervous or aggressive around the sick cat, keep him separated from the family while he recovers. The patient doesn't need any additional stress.

Hospitalization and Surgery (What to Expect)

The following descriptions of anesthesia and surgical procedures are very general guidelines. Every veterinarian has different protocols, based on patient age, surgery to be performed, length of procedure, even personal preference.

In most cases a pre-surgery evaluation will be conducted. This evaluation involves diagnostic tests to make sure there are no underlying conditions that could pose an added risk to your anesthetized cat. Generally, the tests may include a physical exam, ECG, complete blood workup, and radiographs. Pre-anesthetic lab work helps to evaluate such things as kidney and liver function. This doesn't guarantee anesthesia will be safe, but it can help screen for underlying problems that could interfere with the anesthesia or surgical recovery.

THE NIGHT BEFORE

The cat will need an empty stomach on the morning of the surgery, so you'll be instructed to withhold food after midnight. Generally, water shouldn't be withheld though. Check with your vet for more specific instructions, especially if your cat is very young or geriatric.

If your cat is on medication, in most cases you'll continue to give him his usual P.M. dosage but always check with your vet to be sure and to find out if you should administer his A.M. dose the morning of the surgery.

HOSPITAL ADMISSION

You'll bring your cat to the hospital first thing in the morning. At that time you'll be given consent forms to read and sign. The consent forms confirm that you give permission for the doctor to administer an anesthetic to your cat and perform the scheduled procedure.

Some hospitals have a section on the consent form regarding additional pain medication. Because it could be an added expense, they may require your permission to administer any additional medication. Be sure you give your permission for this because many cats (like many people) have varying thresholds of pain. You want your cat to be as comfortable as possible.

PRE-MED

Once your cat has been admitted, he'll be examined by the vet and may be given his "pre-med." This is an injection which will contain one or more mild sedatives to help him relax. These sedatives not only relieve some of your cat's anxiety but serve to reduce the amount of general anesthetic needed.

ANESTHESIA

After the pre-med has taken effect, your cat will be brought to the surgical prep area. A small strip of hair on the foreleg will be clipped and the leg will be cleaned. An anesthetic will be injected into the vein of the leg. Immediately, the cat will begin to become unconscious.

An endotracheal tube is then placed in the cat's windpipe. Once it's in place, it's connected by another tube to the anesthesia machine. The anesthetic, along with oxygen, keeps your cat at the correct degree of unconsciousness. The level of anesthetic is monitored, as well as your cat's vital signs, during the entire procedure.

SURGICAL PREP

The area of the cat's body to be operated on will be prepared for surgery. The surgical assistant will clip the hair and clean the skin with a surgical antibacterial scrub.

In the meantime, the veterinarian prepares him/herself by scrubbing with a surgical antibacterial soap. He/she will wear a sterile surgical gown, mask, cap, eye protection, and, of course, gloves. Surgical assistants will prepare themselves the same way.

SURGERY

A sterile surgical pack which contains the instruments needed for the procedure is opened. Additional equipment, if and as needed, will also be opened from sterile packs.

Before beginning the procedure, the vet or assistant will cover the cat with a sterile surgical drape. This drape has an opening positioned over the site where the incision will be made.

POST-OP RECOVERY

After the cat is disconnected from the anesthesia machine, he is taken to the recovery area. Here, he's monitored by the staff until he wakes. Because the body temperature lowers under an anesthetic, the cat will be placed on a towel or pad and often has a towel placed over him as well to keep him as warm and comfortable as possible.

Additional pain medication is administered if needed.

HOSPITAL DISCHARGE

Depending upon the surgery, you may be able to pick up your cat later the same day or the following morning. Don't be in too much of a rush to bring your cat home, though, if the vet recommends that he remain hospitalized overnight. The first twenty-four hours after surgery are when any potential complications could arise. Follow your vet's suggestions. If you want to visit your cat, ask your vet if he or she feels that would be all right.

You'll be given instructions for at-home care. You'll also be told when to return for a follow-up examination or to have the sutures removed.

Follow all instructions to the letter and remember, even though your cat may want to go back to his normal routine, *you* have to make sure he has adequate rest and recovery time. If he has sutures, check them regularly to be sure that he hasn't chewed on them. Watch for signs of drainage, swelling, or infections. Call your vet right away if something doesn't look right.

A cat recovering from surgery needs plenty of rest and shouldn't go outdoors. If he's on medication (especially pain medication), his reflexes may be sluggish, so be careful that he doesn't attempt to do something such as try to jump to a place from which he might fall and injure himself. Keep him in a safe area and be sure he gets all the prescribed medication as directed by your veterinarian.

Before you leave the vet's office, be certain that you're comfortable with whatever medicating procedures you'll need to perform. If you're unsure of things, you may tend to be nervous during administration and your cat will pick up on this. If you're calm and confident it will help your kitty stay calm. If there is any administration of medication or at-home nursing care that you feel unable to take care of, inquire about at-home visits by one of the vet's staff. Very often a technician will make a house call. The most important thing is your cat's recovery, so don't be shy about asking for help if you don't feel you can handle it by yourself.

5
House Rules

Basic Training

Training. What a misunderstood word. For many owners, the very word conjures up an image of a behavioral tug-of-war between owner and pet. I want you to rethink your definition of the word *training* to include your responsibility to understand what your cat is actually telling you as far as her needs are concerned. Also, training means communicating to your cat in a language she understands. Stop looking at her as a pet in need of training and get inside her head. How can you combine your training expectations as an owner with her daily needs as a cat? Get on her level physically, emotionally, and mentally in order to map out an effective training plan.

Training a cat correctly not only makes her a pleasure to be around, but you'll also realize that you *can* have nice furniture and not worry about it being damaged. You won't have to battle constantly with your cat to make her stay off the counter and you'll know that she'll come whenever you call her.

There are some people who think cats come pre-trained, meaning they will already know how to use the litter box, will know not to scratch the furniture, and will be able to be let outside without fear that they'll wander off. I feel sorry for those owners, but I especially feel sorry for those cats, who are the ones that end up abandoned, at the shelter, or dead.

In order to successfully train a cat, you have to understand how a cat communicates and the difference between normal cat behavior and cat *misbehavior.* This is where getting on her level and seeing things as she does will offer valuable insight. For instance, if your cat is scratching the furniture, although it may make you angry, for her it's a very normal behavior. Because scratching is inherent to her, you can spend your days yelling at your cat and chasing her around the house, but she'll never understand why she's being punished. All you'll have accomplished is to make your cat afraid of you. The better way to train her is to understand that scratching is *natural* and provide her with an acceptable scratching surface, i.e., a good scratching post or pad.

Too many times we confuse training with discipline, punishment, or dominance. So, after attempting to set our cats straight about who's boss, we come to the conclusion that they're just untrainable. They are if we try to use the same training methods for cats that we do for dogs. As I've explained before, a dog is a pack animal hardwired either to be the leader of the pack or to follow the leader (which you hope is you). The cat is a solitary hunter. She doesn't understand *pack mentality.* While your dog is sitting at your feet, anxiously watching you for signals, your cat is sitting next to you, keeping an eye on her territory and watching for potential prey. Trying to use the same method to train both species can only lead to failure and frustration. If you want to succeed in training your cat, you must *think like a cat.* Learn her language instead of insisting that she learn yours.

In order to train your cat you will have to use three basic approaches:

positive reinforcement

remote control

redirection

Positive reinforcement means giving treats or praise for correct behaviors. It's the fun part of training for both cats and owners.

Remote control training means setting up deterrents or using something such as a squirt bottle to teach your cat to avoid certain behavior (such as jumping up on a counter). Remote control is the only so-called "negative" type of training you should use. Never try punishment, it's not only inhumane, it is also an extremely ineffective training technique. A remote control method for something such as jumping onto a forbidden area simply makes the cat dislike being on that surface—a quick squirt of water on the fanny comes out of nowhere, as far as she's concerned; she doesn't associate it with you hiding around the corner. Punishment, such as spanking, will only make the cat fear you.

Redirection should be used whenever you deny your cat access to something she wants. For example, if you don't want your cat to scratch the furniture and you've set up remote control deterrents such as double-sided tape along the back of the couch, you must then *redirect* her natural scratching instinct toward an acceptable surface such as a scratching post.

If your old ideas of training involved spanking your cat, rubbing her nose in her messes, denying food, or yelling, throw them out. I don't want you to become one of those pet owners who is forever screaming at the cat or having kitty running away in fear of you. I want you and your cat to live happily together, and for everyone in the family to have his or her needs met. It will be much easier to start your cat off with the correct training methods than to try and correct already-established misbehaviors.

The Litter Box

The use or non-use of the litter box can make or break a cat/owner relationship. Too many owners are under the assumption that the cat will automatically use the box no matter what—even if we never clean it, put it in the wrong place, or buy a brand of litter that the cat finds objectionable.

In order to avoid litter box problems, you have to understand what's important to a cat when it comes to this part of her life. Your "Litter Box Survival Guide" can be found in chapter 8.

The Dreaded Scratching Dilemma

No, you don't have to declaw your cat. No, your furniture doesn't have to end up shredded—but yes, you *do* have to have a scratching post.

Not all posts are created equal, though. Once again, it comes down to what *we think* our cats need versus what *they know* they need. In chapter 9, I'll show you how to save your furniture and create a scratching post that'll actually get used! What a concept.

Teaching Your Cat to Respond to Her Name

A perfect place to start. I have three rules about this, though. They are:

Rule #1: Pick an easily recognizable (for her) name for your kitten. Long names such as "Cinderella's Prince Charming, Frederick the Fabulous" aren't a good idea. I didn't make that name up. I know a cat with that name, and he wouldn't answer when his owner called. It wasn't until I suggested that the owner simply refer to him as "Fred" that he began to respond when she called to him.

Rule #2: Don't use ten different nicknames for your kitten and expect her to respond to them. Stick to one name so she learns to make the association.

Rule #3: Never call your kitty's name in anger. If you call her by her name and then proceed to punish her, she'll never want to come to you again (and after reading this chapter, you'll know *never* to punish your cat anyway).

Begin teaching your cat to associate positive things with her name. While you're petting her, repeat her name over and over in a soothing, quiet, friendly voice. As you're preparing her dinner, call her name. Hand-feed her a little before you fill her bowl. Say her name repeatedly as you give her a kibble. After a few repetitions of this exercise, put her food in the bowl and let her eat. Don't overdo the sessions. Keep them short and positive.

In between meals, take a few pieces of kibble or break up a couple of cat treats and practice calling her name (in your sweetest, most loving voice) a few times a day. When she comes, give her a kibble. As she gets the knack of it, call her from farther away. Again, don't overdo. It's better to have three short sessions during the day rather than one long one. In no time, she'll respond to her name because she knows there's a reward at the end. Work up to calling her from another room. When she has learned her name, you can cut out some of the treats. When she comes to you, praise her, play with her, or pet her. Still continue to give a food reward now and then until you're positive she has it down. Even when you cease giving treats, the message she should receive is that no matter what, something good awaits her.

Teaching your cat to come when called is a valuable safety feature if you let her outdoors, or if you need to locate her to make sure she isn't locked somewhere in the house. Because my cats respond to their names I have another way to redirect them away from doing something. They associate their names with positive things. If I see that they're getting testy with each other and I'm not able to reach my interactive toys in time, I lovingly call out their names. The tension is eased immediately as their mind-set switches from agitation to anticipation. I then give them a treat (usually by tossing the treats in different directions to keep the cats farther away from each other) or offer something pleasant and they completely forget why they were getting edgy with one another. Keep in mind, though, this works for low-level tension and won't necessarily work for high-intensity aggression because a cat's focus won't shift that quickly. Handling aggression is covered in chapter 7.

Once your cat has learned to respond to her name, don't forget Rule #3: Never call her in anger. Also, don't trick her by calling her name in order to put her in the carrier, especially if it's still a source of anxiety.

How to Pick Up and Handle Your Cat

When your cat becomes an adult, it will be very valuable if you had spent the time to get her used to being picked up and handled when she was a kitten. Everyone wants a cat whom they can pick up, hold, pet, medicate, and groom without ending up looking like a slasher victim. Starting early is the key. Hold your kitten with two hands, no matter how small she is, to give her a feeling of security. No kitten wants to be carried around with her middle squeezed and her legs dangling in the air.

Get your kitten comfortable with being handled by incorporating gentle touch manipulations into your petting sessions. Place the kitten on your lap and gently handle each paw. Run your fingers down her leg, hold her paw briefly and then very gently expose her little claws, touching the top of each one. This helps her to become comfortable with having her paws handled so you'll be able to trim her nails later. Gently touch her ears and look inside. Pet her as you do that and talk soothingly. This exercise prepares her for future ear cleaning and any necessary medicating.

Stroke your kitty along the sides of her mouth (she'll actually enjoy that) and under her chin (she'll really enjoy that). Then gently slide your finger inside her lips and massage her gums. This prepares her for having her teeth brushed. Go back to rubbing her under the chin and down her back, then return to her mouth. Carefully open it by placing one hand over the top of her head and gently supporting her upper jaw while you pull down on the lower jaw with the finger of your other hand. That's all, make it quick, then let her close her mouth. Go back to petting, then engage in a play session. If you do these exercises on a regular basis, your kitten will grow up to be a cat who is comfortable with touch.

If you have an adult cat who isn't used to being held, you'll have to go very slowly so that she will never feel confined or trapped. You may first need to get her comfortable with being petted once or twice, then gradually work up to using slower strokes so your hand stays in contact with her body for longer periods.

When you pick up your cat, always use two hands. Don't grab her by the scruff of the neck and carry her with her hind legs dangling and never scoop her up with one hand around her middle so she feels as if her chest is being crushed.

The proper way to pick up a cat is by putting one hand on her chest, just behind her front legs and use the other hand to cradle her hindquarters and hind legs. Bring her in close to you so that she can lean against your chest. Her front paws can rest on your forearm. This method allows her to feel supported, yet not trapped.

When you put your cat down, do so *gently*. Don't let her leap out of your arms. You don't want to train her that the only way she can get out of your grasp is to struggle and jump for her life. Let her down *before* she struggles and she won't associate being held with confinement. Your responsibility as an owner is to stay very aware, sense the moment she's getting restless—and immediately place her back down. Initially, you may only be able to hold your cat for a few seconds, but as she gradually realizes that being held is not such a terrible thing, she'll relax in your arms.

Don't try to hold your cat in your arms on her back like a baby. She'll feel trapped because it's not a natural position for her.

Make sure your cat sees you before you attempt to pick her up. If you startle her by coming up from behind, not only will that make her grow more nervous about being touched but it could also cause you to get scratched.

Determining Boundaries

You'll never have a well-trained cat if you aren't consistent about what she's allowed to do and where she's allowed to do it. You'll just create confusion and frustration if one family member lets her on the bed but another one doesn't. Is she going to be allowed on kitchen counters? The dining-room table? Only when there's no food on it? Well, how is she supposed to know the difference?

Sit down with everyone in the family and go over what the boundaries are to be. It's not fair to your cat if you're inconsistent, because she'll end up in trouble for things that are truly *your* fault.

Who's Been Sleeping in My Bed?

Are you someone who would enjoy curling up in bed with a cat at your feet? Do you look forward to sharing your pillow with your cat and haven't the least concern for shedding hairs? Or do you want your bedroom to be strictly off-limits at night? Be consistent right from the beginning about where your cat will sleep, because it'll be harder to change the rule later.

If you want a kitten to share your bed, no problem. I promise she'd like nothing better than to snuggle up with you and enjoy the warmth and companionship. It's one of the most tender ways for kittens and their owners to bond. If you've adopted an adult cat, she may or may not choose to sleep on your bed. Depending upon her personality and comfort level, she may prefer to stay in the main part of the house or find her own private place to sleep. Some owners, in an attempt to entice a cat to sleep on the bed will bring her in and close the bedroom door (allowing for litter box access in there) in the hope that she'll learn to like it there. If you bring her into the bedroom and she doesn't want to sleep on the bed, there may not be another place in the room where she feels comfortable. If you do decide to go this route, at least place a cat tree in the bedroom. I prefer to let the cat find her own spot.

When you buy a cat bed, keep in mind that in general, cats prefer elevated places for sleeping and lounging. If you put a cat bed on the floor in the corner it may be doomed to being forever unused (or used only by your dog). Observe the places, fabrics and elevations your cat goes to and that will help you create the most comfortable spot for her. Once again, understanding the differences in the way dogs and cats think will easily guide you to success. A dog will usually willingly sleep on the little bed you fixed up for him in the corner. It becomes his den. That same arrangement for a cat will fail because it doesn't meet her safety requirements. Use your cat's eye view to find solutions.

If you'd prefer to not have the cat in bed with you, then you have two options: close your bedroom door or close your cat up in a separate room during the night. If you put her in a separate room, make sure it's one she likes being in which has lots of sleeping place options. If there's room, put a cat tree in with her. Install one of the window perches made especially for cats (available at pet supply stores) so she'll have something to keep her occupied during the long night. She is a nocturnal creature, after all. Carefully scrutinize the room to be sure it doesn't appear to be a kitty prison. Create a cozy bed with one of your worn sweatshirts. Wrap a hot-water bottle in a towel so she'll have something warm to curl up against. This is a situation in which adopting *two* kittens works well. If you don't want the kitten in bed with you, they'll have each other to cuddle and play with instead of being lonely.

If your cat scratches on the carpet under the door in an attempt to dig her way out, play with her right before you both go to bed, offer her some food (divide her normal daily amount so you aren't overfeeding) and leave an activity toy out (see chapter 6).

Remember to look through your kitty's eyes as you set up her sleeping area. Respect her nocturnal nature, and you won't have to listen to cries of frustration. You can both get a good night's rest.

Ho Hum, Just Another Boring Day

Much so-called "misbehavior" can just be the result of a cat needing something to do, and there are some cats who do require more stimulation than others.

Start your kitty off right by making sure she has enough in her environment to keep her interested. A kitten can be fascinated by the piece of lint that falls from your clothing, but as she grows it may take more thought on your part to maintain her interest. Set up one or two window perches or put a cat tree by the window. A window that overlooks outdoor bird activity is especially interesting. Maintain a regular schedule of interactive playtime (see chapter 6) and rotate your cat's solo toys to keep them from becoming boring. Consider getting a second cat if your work or social schedule leaves your kitty home alone all day and then much of the evening.

When you walk in the door at the end of the day, remember that your cat has been alone for hours and will be looking forward to interacting with you. A good balance of stimulation and attention from you will help her become a happy, sociable, well-behaved cat.

A Place of Her Own

Throughout this book, you'll notice that I refer to cat trees. A cat tree consists of two or three (sometimes even more) perches that sit on top of posts of varying lengths. The posts can be bare wood or covered with bark or rope. They serve many purposes. Cat trees provide comfortable window viewing, serve as sturdy scratching posts and their elevation allow the cat to feel more secure. Multi-tiered trees enable two or more cats to enjoy bird watching without having to crowd each other. One of the most important functions of a cat tree, though, is that it's truly the cat's furniture and will only have her scent as opposed to other pieces of furniture such as chairs and sofas that will contain unfamiliar scents of guests.

My cats use their cat trees during the day for playing, scratching, bird watching, and sleeping. Because they're on my furniture less, it cuts down on the amount of cat hair on the couch. A cat tree in the corner of the living room can be enough of a security blanket for a shy or tentative cat to stay in the room with the family instead of going off somewhere.

Don't Raise a Scaredy-cat

Kittenhood is the time to start desensitizing your cat by gently exposing her to a variety of potentially scary objects and situations in everyday life. This will help her as she grows up to be unafraid of ordinary things such as the vacuum cleaner or unfamiliar people.

Get your kitten used to potentially scary sounds such as the vacuum or the hair dryer by first running one in another room while you play with her or offer her treats. If she isn't bothered by the faraway sound, you can bring it a little closer. You can then try setting a hair dryer on *low* and run it in the same room. Continue to play with the kitten. Every time you dry your hair, have the kitten in the room with you. Have a toy in there to distract her or offer pieces of kibble. The reason you want her to become comfortable with the hair dryer is that you may at some point need to bathe and dry her and for many cats, the noise is the most frightening part.

The sound of the vacuum cleaner was what sent my cats under the beds, into the closet, and to hang from the ceiling fixture. So I began their desensitization by running the vacuum in a distant closed room. The sound was far enough away that it wasn't too unsettling. I then used *redirection* methods by either playing with my cats or feeding them while the vacuum was making its noise. Every day I moved the vacuum cleaner a little closer but still in a closed room, and ran it while engaging my cats in something positive. When I finally brought the vacuum cleaner out into the largest open area of the house, I placed a blanket and several cushions over and around it to muffle the sound. While my cats were initially startled when I first turned it on, they soon got used to it. Albie still views the vacuum cleaner as something to be cautious of and prefers to remain either on his cat tree or in a chair when I run it, but at least he doesn't bolt in terror and fear for his life.

You can turn all the scary aspects of life into things your kitten barely even notices with gradual introduction and desensitization. Take your kitten for short car rides (in her carrier) on a regular basis so that her first trip as an adult won't be traumatic. Reward her when you come home, with a treat, her dinner, or playtime so that she associates the adventure with positive experiences.

My friend, Steve Dale, who writes the syndicated column "My Pet World," took his kitten everywhere. Ricky very often went to work with Steve as well as to the bank and even the dry cleaner. Ricky was taken to neighbors' homes so he would become comfortable with people in unfamiliar surroundings. All the while, Steve kept rewarding Ricky and always made each step gradual so the kitten would be comfortable. As a result, Ricky is one of the most sociable, well-adjusted adult cats I've ever met.

Introduce your cat to grooming when she's a kitten. Although as a kitten she may not have any mats to worry about or even very much hair, getting her used to the feel of the brush, the nail trimmers, and being handled will make both of your lives so much easier as she grows.

A common behavior problem that develops in single-owner homes is that the cat becomes so used to the sound, touch, and movements of the one person, that when just one guest comes over, the cat panics. Imagine the cat's terror should the owner get married (especially if children and other pets are part of the package). Early, gentle exposure to a variety of situations will help your kitten grow up well adjusted rather than a cat nobody every sees or worse, the kind your friends label as "The Attack Cat."

A note of caution, though: The object of these exercises is to desensitize your kitten gradually. If she shows fear, you've gone too far too fast. Always proceed at a slower pace than you think is required. Your two most important tools for raising a well-adjusted cat are *love* and *patience*. We usually get the *love* part down right away, it's that *patience* aspect to being a pet owner that we often have to work harder on.

Leash Training

I don't think that outdoors is a safe place for a little cat to roam freely. If you want your cat to experience the good aspects of the outside world, then do it in a safe way by leash training. Even if you never plan on taking your kitty outdoors, leash training is valuable. That way, if you do travel with her, when you take her out of her carrier, you have added control.

Not every cat is a good candidate for leash training. A timid, nervous cat may find more security in the unchanging world of her indoor environment. All the unpredictable noises, smells, and sights of the outdoors could fuel her nervousness. A cat who gets very upset while looking out the window at the mere sight of another cat in her territory, might become even more agitated if she's outside and confronted with the scents of unfamiliar cats.

You may also be setting yourself up for a cat who starts demanding to be let outdoors or who decides she doesn't need to wait for permission and attempts escape. Another negative is that outdoors your cat will be at risk for getting fleas, ticks, and contagious diseases.

Now that I've told you the negatives, it's only fair that I give you the positive side of leash training. For a cat who requires a great deal of stimulation, going outdoors in a safe way can be just the right adventure for her. On a beautiful day it can also be a way for you and your cat to spend time together outdoors.

Leash training a cat doesn't mean going for a brisk walk. The way you walk with your dog will in no way resemble the way you'll walk with your cat. First of all, you'll need to confine your walking to your own yard. It'll be much safer because there's less of a chance of running into other animals. Should your cat become upset or if you drop the leash, she'll be in more familiar territory in your own yard and you won't have far to go if you have to pick her up and carry her inside. She may also be less inclined to panic because she'll be in familiar surroundings. Another reason to stay within your own yard is that you don't want to teach her that it's okay to roam beyond her own territory. That way, should she ever get out of the house, she may be more inclined to stay closer to home.

HOW TO LEASH TRAIN

The right equipment comes first. You'll need to purchase a lightweight leash. Don't get a chain or a heavy leather leash—you're not walking a Rottweiler. The lighter the leash the better, because it'll be more comfortable for both of you and it'll take less time for your cat to get used to it. You'll also need a cat harness rather than a regular collar. Your leashed cat will pull out of a collar. Choose a harness with closures at both the neck and chest. This will be more comfortable for the cat if she pulls on the leash because it won't tighten around her neck. This harness is known as an "H" type. I prefer the "H" type over the "figure 8" style because the "8" harness tightens at the neck when pulled. When on the cat, the "H" harness resembles a sideways-facing letter H. When you put tension on the leash, the cat will feel an even tug on her torso that won't cause discomfort. The "figure 8" type has two loops, resembling the number 8. One loop goes around the neck and the other goes around the chest, just behind the front legs. When you pull on the leash, the tension becomes uneven as the top loop tightens at the neck.

Make sure your cat's vaccinations are up-to-date before exposing her to the outdoors. She'll also need an identification tag just in case she escapes from you. Also, if it's flea season, be sure she's protected (see chapter 13).

Start leash and harness training indoors for the first few weeks. The first time you put the harness on your cat just be casual about it, then give her a treat, feed her, or distract her with playtime. Mealtime usually works best. Leave the harness on for about fifteen minutes to half an hour. Repeat the procedure before the next meal. If your cat is normally fed free-choice, use treats or playtime to divert her attention away from the harness. When I was leash-training Olive, I used her absolute all-time favorite food—yogurt. Whenever she seemed to be bothered by the strange contraption around her, I put a drop of yogurt on her lips. That immediately made her tolerate the experience much more cheerfully. If your cat struggles too much as you try to put the harness on, don't attempt to buckle it; just get the harness on her and then immediately distract her.

As your cat gets more comfortable, put the harness on her for longer periods during the day and always provide a positive diversion should she begin to resist it. Don't leave it on her when you're not there to supervise because she could get herself tangled up in it should she become impatient about having to wear it.

In week two, introduce the leash. Attach it to the harness but don't tug on it. She first has to get used to the idea of being connected to something. If the leash is light enough, let your kitty drag it behind her while you provide positive diversion. Be careful that she doesn't get the leash caught on anything. Once she's comfortable with this new attachment, you'll begin the next phase of training.

Very important warning: don't tug on the leash at this point or your mild mannered cat will turn into a thrashing, growling, fur-covered chain saw. The way to introduce her to walking on a leash is through good old-fashioned bribery. Have a supply of treats or kibble in your pocket. With the leash loosely in your hand, take a step out in front of her. Hold a treat out at her eye level. As she walks toward the treat, say, "Let's walk." Give her the treat and then take another step forward, holding another treat. As she moves, again say, "Let's walk." Continue this several times so she becomes used to walking with you. Gradually introduce a very slight tug as you step forward. Don't pull or yank the leash. It should be a tug that's barely detectable. Make sure you give the treat to her as she's moving forward so she'll know that it's the *walk* she's being rewarded for. She will need time to stop and eat the treat, though, so don't expect her to stay in motion all the time.

When your cat is comfortable with this exercise, begin walking around the house. Don't attempt to go outdoors with your cat until she's totally comfortable with walking on the leash. She shouldn't struggle when you put any tension on it. Be prepared for this to take two to three weeks.

When you go outdoors, stick close to the house and don't stay out too long. This is a new experience for your cat and it'll be overwhelming. Carry a towel with you so that if she becomes very upset, you can pick her up by wrapping the towel around her. This way you won't get injured.

Your cat is a curious predator with a strong sense of territory, so walking with a leash will be a new experience for you too. Be prepared for her to stop every few seconds to smell something interesting, watch a butterfly, follow the trail of an insect, or just lounge in the sun. If you try to pull her along, you'll only scare her and defeat your purpose. Let her investigate things but carry your treats with you and continue to use the "let's walk" request occasionally.

As you walk, keep on the alert for potential dangers such as a dog walking by or even kids on bikes. The first few times out, you won't know how she's going to react to sudden noises or the appearance of other animals (even a squirrel could spook her). If you see a dog or another cat approaching, casually scoop up your cat and go back into the house. Don't try to introduce your cat to the neighbor's poodle.

When going out and coming in for leash walking, *carry* your cat through the door. Don't let her walk in and out because you don't want her to get the idea that she can walk out whenever there's an open door. Carry her out and then place her on the porch or the yard. When the walk is over, carry her back inside and put her down on the carpet on the far side of the room to take her harness off. Remember, no activity should take place at the front door.

When I take my cats out, I don't use the front door. I have a back door that connects the laundry room to the garage. My cats don't associate the front door with the outside, so there is never an escape attempt there. If one of my cats did try to bolt through the laundry room he'd only get as far as the garage, not outside. If you have a similar setup, even though it may not be as convenient for you, it'll be safer. You don't want your cat waiting by the front door for the opportunity to escape.

A Couple of Basic Tricks to Amaze Your Friends

I know you're probably not going to believe this, but you can actually teach your cat to do tricks. Where many owners fail when attempting to teach their cats to do tricks is that they use praise as a reward, just as they do with dogs. Cats don't respond to praise as well as dogs do. For cats, food is a much better motivating factor, so have your supply of treats or kibble handy. Training sessions should be brief, a few minutes a day.

Training should be fun. Always keep that in mind when you are attempting to teach a cat tricks.

Teaching "sit" is easiest of all. Face your cat and hold a treat in front of her. Saying, "Sit," slowly move the treat just slightly up and over her nose. As her head follows the treat, her back end will naturally go into a sit. Immediately give her the treat. As soon as her little fanny touches the ground she should have the treat in her mouth so she makes the association. If she backs up instead of sitting or tries to stand on her hind legs to reach it, then you're holding the treat too high. If you're holding it at the right height, just above and behind her nose and she isn't sitting, give her some help by gently guiding her back end down with your other hand. Don't push or be forceful. If your cat bats or grabs at the treat with her paw, repeat the exercise.

"Down" is another easy trick for a cat. This trick is best done on a table (make sure it's a table that your cat is allowed on so you don't send a mixed training message). Have her sit and then with the treat in your fingers, move your hand down until it touches the table, and then slowly out away from her. As you do this, say, "Down." As soon as she goes into the down position, reward her. If she isn't going into a down position and, instead, just leans forward or gets up, gently place your other hand on her rear when she's in the sit position as you move the treat down and away. If you move the treat too fast, the cat *will* get up, so go slowly.

Don't push on your cat's shoulders or yank on her front legs to get her to comply. With dogs, owners will take the front legs and pull them forward to put the dog in a down position. This absolutely will not work with a cat. She will back away from you and might even panic. Reward her each time she lies down, however briefly and whether or not she received assistance from you. If you go slowly, she'll eventually lie down as she begins making the connection. If she's just not getting it, let her go and try again tomorrow. If you frustrate her or she becomes impatient, she'll never respond to your training requests.

6

Fast Forward . . . Stop . . . Rewind . . . Play

Playtime Techniques Used for Behavior Modification

I know, I know, you're scratching your head while looking at this chapter title and thinking, *Why would cats even need instructions on how to play?* Well, actually they don't—*you* need them. Do you make any of the following common mistakes playing with your cat:

- play with her in the same way you would play with a dog, for example: wrestle with her (something that shouldn't even be done with a dog, yet many owners do)?

- assume that if you just supply the toys, the cat will play by herself, whenever she wants to?

- play with your cat now and then whenever you have time—once a week? once a month?

By *thinking like a cat*, you will view playtime as more than just fun and games—it's a powerful behavior modification tool, and it can help raise a confident, sociable, well-behaved kitten. If your cat is an adult, playing with her can help correct behavior problems, ease stress or depression, help her lose weight, and improve her overall health. In general, cats sleep about sixteen to eighteen hours a day. If your cat has extended that to twenty-four hours, a regular play schedule will help her re-establish a more normal sleep pattern. Play can also accelerate acceptance of a new cat into a multicat household. If you want to strengthen the bond you share with your cat, playtime can be almost magical.

Defining Play

Cats engage in two forms of play: *social* play and *object* (or solo) play. Social play involves another cat, pet, or a human. With a young kitten, social play begins with her littermates. This type of play behavior helps the kitten develop motor coordination and gives her the opportunity to bond with her companions. Kittens take turns playing the aggressor as they learn about their own and each other's abilities.

Object play also builds and strengthens a kitten's motor coordination as well as teaching her about her environment. What might appear to you to be just an amusing game of a kitten chasing a toy around the house is actually a vital educational process. She's learning about different surfaces (floor, carpet, grass, gravel, slippery, rough, etc.), how each feels, and how they affect her movements. She's also learning about her emerging ability to climb and what objects are safe to land on. Much to everyone's dismay, she will also discover what objects aren't for kitten landings.

Littermates will play socially more before twelve weeks of age, when their sense of territory begins to develop. After twelve weeks, social play sessions become shorter and sometimes end with a little genuine aggression. Object play becomes the main focus as kittens mature.

Successful, frequent playtime helps build confidence. I know you may be wondering if this sounds silly, *confidence for a cat?* It makes a lot of sense when you think about it. Cats being predators, are attracted by movement, especially if that movement resembles the behavior of prey. If an outdoor cat had to depend on hunting for food but was afraid of and distracted by every leaf that fell from a tree or the sound of a distant car horn, she'd soon starve. The cat who spies her prey, makes a quick assessment of her surroundings to make sure *she's* not in danger, and then focuses in on her hunt, eats. She begins to strengthen both her *air hunting* skills (for flying prey) and *ground hunting* skills (for rodents, insects, and other creepy crawlies). Each success also builds her confidence and she learns how to modify her technique, depending on whether she's hunting a bird, mouse, snake, or butterfly. The more she hunts, the more athletic she becomes as her muscles get exercise and her reflexes quicken.

When I go on consultations, one of the first things I ask about is the cat's playtime routine. Many owners will show me the cat's basket of toys but often can't recall actually seeing the cat play with any of them recently. When an owner says he does play with his cat, I always ask for a demonstration. After years of doing consultations and working with cats and owners, I realized that many people don't know *how* to play with their cats. The worst is, too many cats—troubled by stress, boredom, obesity, or other problems—eventually give up on playing.

Interactive Play

While your new kitten may seem to have the whole play routine down to a fine art: Zooming ninety miles an hour around the house in pursuit of a dust ball (something in ample supply at my house), *your* participation is still greatly needed. That's where *interactive* play comes in.

Interactive play is so powerful throughout a cat's entire life—from the day you bring her home as a kitten to her golden years as the geriatric queen of the house. If you're just starting out with a kitten, establishing an interactive playtime schedule will help develop the bond you share, will teach her what *is* and *isn't* acceptable to bite, and will help avoid many future potential behavior problems. If you have an adult cat, especially a troubled one, interactive playtime can redirect her negative behavior toward something positive and help correct many problems.

Interactive play involves *you* participating in the game with your kitten or cat, using a fishing-pole type toy. Now, you may already feel that you engage in lots of playtime with your kitty, but what toys do you use? Your hands? Little furry mice? Unfortunately, many owners use the most readily available toys—their *fingers*—to play with their kitten. While it may not be bad now, as your kitten grows, a bite from her adult teeth *will* hurt. You're also sending a very bad message to the kitten when you use your fingers as toys—you're telling her that it's okay to bite skin. Never encourage biting, not even in play. If you start a kitten off correctly, you'll avoid having to retrain her once she has grown.

Okay, so maybe you've never allowed your cat to bite your fingers but you use those furry little mice or a light spongy ball for playtime. What's wrong with that? First, it puts your fingers and the toy too close so you stand a greater chance of being accidentally scratched or bitten by an excited kitty. Also, you can't control the movements of the toy very well. Fishing-pole type toys give you greater control and you can create a more prey-like movement.

The concept of an interactive toy is simple: pole, string, and a toy target dangling on the end. What I love about these toys is that you can make the toy move as prey naturally would. If you're going to *think like a cat,* you have to understand how they react to prey. The problem with all of the cute little toys that are strewn about the house is that they're essentially dead prey. In order to play with them, the cat must work as both prey and predator. She has to bat at the toy to make it move. Once it slides a little on the floor it dies again and remains lifeless unless the cat pushes it back into motion. An interactive toy lets you create the movement so the cat can just enjoy being a predator.

There are many interactive toys on the market. Some are pretty basic and others are very elaborate. When shopping for one, again, use your *think like a cat* approach. Look at the toy and imagine what kind of prey it resembles and how your cat, based on her personality, would react to it. Because cats are opportunistic hunters, which means they hunt whatever is available, look for several different types of interactive toys. Try to cover the various types of prey such as: birds, mice, insects, snakes. Your cat will be more interested if you vary the toys, because she'll never know just which prey to expect.

Several interactive toys have feathers on the end to make them resemble birds. My all-time favorite is called Da Bird, available in most pet supply stores. This fishing-pole type toy has a swivel device at the end of the string where the feathers are connected. As you wave the toy through the air, the feathers spin around, so it looks and sounds like a bird in flight. Cats go crazy for it. This toy will make even the most sedentary cat dust off her hunting skills.

For simulating the movements of a cricket or a fly, nothing beats the Cat Dancer. The toy consists of a wire with a little rolled up cardboard target on the end (it's very durable, don't let the idea of it being cardboard discourage you). If you just move it subtly, the Cat Dancer darts and moves as unpredictably as a fly does. This toy makes your cat use her concentration skills and best reflexes.

The Cat Charmer, made by the company that created the Cat Dancer, is my pick as the best snake toy. It's made of durable fabric firmly attached to the pole and can withstand the most determined kitty attacks.

The Kitty Tease is an interactive toy made of a small piece of denim dangling from the string attached to a pole. I like this toy because the denim makes it a soft, quiet toy. For little kittens or timid cats, the small quiet denim target isn't too intimidating and she can grasp it easily in her paws. Even though the toy doesn't actually look like a mouse, I use it as one during interactive play.

A unique toy called Quickdraw McPaw is a wonderful interactive toy for cats who aren't able to get around, perhaps because of arthritis or other age-related problems. The toy consists of a long flexible plastic tube. There's a wire inside that has a little feather toy at the end. If you hold the hook at the top of the tube with your finger, you can make the feather appear and disappear. If your cat is hiding under the bed, too intimidated to come out and play with the other interactive toys, you can put the end of this tube under the bed and she can play without leaving her comfort zone. I think every cat who is caged in a boarding facility should have one of these toys. Also, if you have young children who want to play with the cat and you're afraid they may accidentally poke her in the eye with the fishing pole toy, Quickdraw McPaw is a very safe way for them to interact with her.

These are just a few of the many interactive toys out there. You may find one that fits your cat's personality or play skill even better. Before buying it, though, make sure it matches your cat's play skill, emotional state, and physical size. A shy, timid cat would be overwhelmed by a large toy that made lots of noise, and a cat who lives to air hunt may not find the slithery movements of the Cat Charmer intense enough.

For more information on the above-mentioned toys, refer to the resource guide.

Bubble Blowing and Laser Glowing

A popular game is to blow bubbles and let your cat run around after them. Some cats absolutely love this. My only problem is that she

Why Your Kitten Needs Interactive Play

- helps her bond with her new family
- helps coordination and muscle tone
- helps her become comfortable with her environment
- reduces fear

- helps teach her what is and isn't acceptable to bite or scratch
- prevents damage to items in your home
- reduces tension in multicat households due to addition of the new kitten
- eases discomfort after a traumatic episode (for example, loud noises)

doesn't actually get to capture anything. The bubbles always pop and she's left with nothing. If your cat enjoys this game, make sure she gets a treat at the end of it or make it a preliminary to an interactive game. Don't make bubble blowing your cat's only game. If you have children who enjoy blowing bubbles for the cat, instruct them not to blow the bubbles at her, especially at her face.

Laser toys for cats are very popular as well. I think their success is based on the fact that they require minimal movement from the owners. You can sit in your chair, watch TV, and point the laser all over the room. As with the bubbles, I don't like the fact that the cat never actually gets to capture anything. If you use the laser toy, don't make it your cat's only plaything and be sure to reward your cat with a treat or another toy afterward.

How to Use Interactive Toys

First, imagine your living room or den is about to be transformed into a hunting ground. The sofa, chairs, and tables will now become trees, bushes, rocks, and other things that the cat can hide behind. If you have a big, open space, scatter some pillows, cushions, or even an open paper bag to provide additional *cover* for your little predator.

A common mistake made by well-meaning owners is to play with their cat by dangling the toy in front of her. The cat bats at the toy repeatedly. She sits up and appears to almost *box* the toy. Although this play method may look amusing and seem as if she's having fun, it isn't a natural form of cat playing/hunting. Remember that playtime is supposed to be a make-believe hunt. What self-respecting prey would hover in front of the cat and hang around to be repeatedly batted? The cat ends up just using reflexes instead of using her best tool—her brain. Cats don't chase to exhaustion (the way dogs do), they silently stalk and ambush when they've gotten close enough. In the wild, a cat uses every rock, tree, and bush for cover as she inches closer to her prey (that's where your sofa, chairs, table, and cushions come in). Therefore much of her efficient hunting technique involves *patience*, *planning*, and *precision*. Play with your cat in a way that's natural and satisfying to her. Use your toy to simulate the way prey would truly move in a real hunt: It would get the heck out of there and run for cover. Move *away* from the cat, not *toward* her. Guide the toy over to a hiding place and then entice your cat by letting it just peek out.

Because the purpose of the game is for the cat to have fun, not to frustrate her, don't frantically wave the toy around at the speed of light, out of reach. Let her have many successes. If she grasps it in her paws, let her savor the victory and then gently try to get it away.

Think of the natural intensity curve of a real hunt. When you work out, you have a *warm-up*, the *intense exercise*, and then the *cool-down*. Your playtime should provide this as well. Don't play like crazy with your cat, ripping around having a grand time, and then, discovering it's time to leave for work, suddenly end the game. If she hasn't had enough opportunities to capture and kill her prey, she'll be left frustrated. A cool-down will leave her satisfied and content. To cool kitty down, begin to move the prey as if it's becoming injured and allow the cat to capture it. (Okay, I know that in the real world the bird very often gets away, but with you as the producer/director of this hunt, you can let your cat win every time.) That's how you inspire confidence in the cat, by allowing her to be the Mighty Hunter. So, when you feel it's time to end the game, begin to let your prey slow down.

When your cat has achieved her great capture, reward her by either serving her dinner or giving her a treat—the *hunt* and then the *feast*. You're going to have one happy kitty!

When to Play

For play sessions to be most effective and have long-term positive effects, they should be a part of your daily schedule. I'd recommend a

> ## Catwise Caution
> Always put all interactive toys away in a closet, out of kitty's reach when the game is over, so she won't chew on the stringed parts.

Interactive Playtime Tips

- If you're using a birdlike interactive toy, remember to incorporate frequent landings into the game. Birds don't fly all the time, they also walk. This gives your cat time to plan.

- Frequent freezes in action, with the prey staying absolutely still (as if in terror) can be very exciting. This is the time that the cat thinks and plans her next move.

- Don't forget sound effects. I'm not talking about bird chirps or rodent squeaks, but the little sounds of the Cat Dancer slightly tapping on the floor or the subtle sound of the Cat Charmer sliding on the carpet as it goes around the corner.

- Vary the speed of your movements—everything shouldn't be fast. Just barely quivering the toy will drive your kitty wild!

- You're not conducting a kitty marathon here, so don't exhaust your cat. Her sides shouldn't be heaving and she shouldn't be gasping for breath. If you get her too worked up, she won't have the opportunity to plan and stalk. Remember, this exercise should be as much mental as physical.

- Whenever she gets the toy in her mouth or paws, allow your cat to savor each victory for a few seconds.

- Reward her with a treat (or serve dinner) after the game. She caught her prey; well done!

minimum of two fifteen-minute sessions a day for adult cats, but three would be even better. I can hear you now: "Where am I going to find an extra half hour a day?" If you can't fit in a half hour a day for your cat, you maybe shouldn't be a cat owner. This little creature's whole world revolves around you. Surely you can squeeze in some time to bond with her. It's amazing how, if you really try, you can become very adept at doing two things at once. Combine watching television in the evening with a playtime. Use those fifteen minutes while dinner's in the oven to squeeze in a play session.

Unless you're using specific play sessions to work out behavior problems (see section later in this chapter), I'd recommend that the first session be in the morning before you leave for work, because after you go, your kitty will be sleeping on and off for the entire day. The second session would then be in the evening. A third session right before bedtime will help with a cat who tends to keep you up at night with her nocturnal activities.

A kitten may require more play sessions during the day but of shorter duration. She may play like a little maniac for five minutes and then go off to sleep. A kitten needs playtime, but she also needs frequent little naps. Don't exhaust her.

Schedule your play sessions to coincide with your particular kitten or cat's active times. Don't wake her up to play (especially a kitten) unless you're dealing with a depressed or sedentary cat who sleeps twenty-four hours a day.

Interactive Playtime in Multicat Households

A cat has to focus completely on her prey and plan her attack. Two or more cats stalking the same toy will be distracted by each other. Also, the more dominant cat will take charge, leaving the more submissive one sitting on the sidelines. That certainly isn't much fun for her.

Interactive playtime should provide pleasure and confidence, so make sure each cat has her own toy. Your goal isn't achieved if they simultaneously pounce on a toy and one cat crashes into the other. That will result in hisses, swats, and somebody running away in fear. But you can avoid that problem. Either take one cat at a time into another area of the house and conduct an individual play session or hold a fishing pole toy in each hand. It's tricky at first but you get used to it. The secret of working two toys at once is to keep the cats far enough apart so they avoid crashing into each other. With two toys you are obviously not going to be as adept at imitating precise preylike movements, but it's better than nothing. Or you could enlist another family member to help. Unlike when it's time to medicate the cat, you can usually find a willing assistant for play sessions.

If you have more than two cats, you'll have to arrange individual play sessions to be sure that everyone gets his or her turn. You can still do group sessions using two toys (obviously the cats will have to take turns) but you have to be very aware of who might be backing away from the game. Make sure everyone gets a shot and don't allow two cats who maybe aren't on the best of terms to find themselves eye to eye. If you are going to do individual sessions, leave the radio or TV on to create background noise for your other cats. The electronic noise will cover the familiar sound of the interactive toy off in the distance.

After a group play session, provide everyone with a treat for a job well done. Then go lie down and put a cold cloth over your eyes.

Interactive Play for Behavior Modification

Because a cat is first and foremost a hunter, you can use an interactive toy to switch her focus from something negative to something positive. Here's a common example: Your cat hides whenever she hears a strange noise. You look under the bed and find two eyes staring at you in terror. By getting out one of your interactive toys and just *casually* moving it around the room, you get your cat's attention focused on it. She may not come out from under the bed right away, but she'll at least give the toy some of her attention. Your casual attitude sends a signal to her that all is okay in the house. The wrong thing to do would've been, after the cat dove in terror under the bed, to reach down and pull her out so you could hold her. The last thing she'd need is to be clutched in your arms. First of all, she'd feel confined (cats hate that) and second, she'd pick up the message from you that whatever the noise was, it must've been something as bad as she thought. Casual playtime, on the other hand, allows her to keep the comforting option of remaining under the bed, but helping her realize she doesn't need to.

Cats, like children, require two very specific emotional things from us to let them feel loved and secure. Affection is one. Humans and animals both benefit from being held and provided with a reassuring physical connection. What parent doesn't enjoy holding her child, and what cat owner doesn't cherish any opportunity to hold or pet her cat? The other side of that reassuring behavior though, is that parents (and also cat owners), must allow their children to gain confidence by letting them accomplish things on their own. If you're a parent, I'm sure you've watched your child trying to do something new or maybe even a little scary (such as going down a slide for the first time). Instead of confirming her fears by clutching her in your arms and agreeing that the slide is a big, scary thing, you explain to her how much fun it is. You reassure her that you'll be at the bottom to catch her but that she's going to love it. Your reassurance, calm voice, and light manner (maybe you even go down the slide yourself) calm her fears. When she does finally go down the slide, you are waiting at the bottom, and she immediately forgets the fears she had and wants to do it again! Casual interactive playtime with your troubled cat works the same way. Your impulse may be to hold your cat when she reacts to something scary but that'll only convince her that she was right to be frightened. (You may even get scratched in the process as the cat struggles to get free.) By sparking the predator in her by dangling a toy, she'll become more confident.

Use toys to counteract any negative situation. Play sessions can help with two cats who don't get along by distracting them from focusing so intensely on each other. As soon as you see the tension building, pull out a couple of toys. The cats become distracted by the toys. As they each play (remember, use *two* toys so they don't have to share), they begin to associate fun playtime with being together. They get used to being in the same room without it having to be tense.

Interactive toys can also be used to help combat several behavioral or emotional problems, such as re-igniting a depressed cat's spark for life. Interactive sessions can also help a cat become more comfortable in a new home. Cats who tend to be aggressive benefit from this sort of play because they can take their aggression out on the toy instead of their owners or other pets.

If your cat hates your new spouse, have your husband or wife engage in an interactive play session. This will help build trust at a distance to the cat (and the spouse) to feel safe. Through play, the cat begins associating the spouse with positive things.

If your male cat is spraying in a certain room, conduct a play session right in that area to help change his association with that room. He's marking that room because he considers it the perimeter of his territory. By playing there, it becomes his nest area. Cats don't eliminate where they eat, sleep, or raise their young. For more on spraying, refer to chapter 8.

If you are expecting a new baby, interactive playtime helps the cat adjust to the frightening changes. Try playing a tape of baby cries during play sessions to help kitty remain relaxed and comfortable around the noise.

When you're dealing with a timid cat, provide many opportunities for *cover*. For example, if you're playing in a wide open room with all the furniture close to the walls, the timid cat might be too nervous to step out into the open and expose herself. Placing boxes, bags, cushions, and pillows in the middle of the room create hiding places and thus security for her. Once she ventures out and eventually starts playing, she'll become more at ease. If you'd prefer, you can purchase several soft-sided cat tunnels that can be connected to one another. Several of these, placed around a room can be enough to help make a timid cat feel invisible enough to attempt to hunt.

Why Your Adult Cat Needs Interactive Play

- strengthens the bond you share
- provides exercise for overweight or sedentary cats
- eases tension in multicat households
- helps diffuse aggression
- provides beneficial stimulation for depressed cats
- builds confidence in shy or nervous cats
- encourages a normal, healthy appetite
- reduces fear
- corrects inappropriate biting and scratching
- accelerates acceptance of new family members
- eases reactions to traumatic events
- eases discomfort of a new environment
- builds trust
- builds confidence
- allows you to interact with an unpredictable cat without risk of injury

Interactive play sessions, by appealing to a cat's natural instincts, can change her focus and behavior. As you go through this book, you'll find I've indicated many situations in which sessions would be beneficial.

Catnip

Not enough owners understand the value of catnip nor how to use it correctly.

Catnip is a minty herb that contains a substance known as *nepatalactone*. It's this substance that causes a pleasure-release in the brain, and cats to react to it with ecstasy. They rub, roll, play, lick, jump, munch, and basically act as if they're going through second kittenhood. Very often cats will eat catnip (it's safe), but the pleasure-inducing effect is actually only achieved by smelling the herb. The effects, which last about fifteen minutes, are completely harmless and nonaddictive, and after those fifteen minutes of ecstasy and zany fun, cats are relaxed and ready for a nap.

Catnip can be used to help everyone get past a stressful situation, it can jump-start a play session or just light a fire (figuratively speaking) underneath a sedentary kitty. It's one of the perks of being a cat—that is, being able to enjoy such a joy-inducing substance without any side effects, repercussions, or danger.

Here's what many owners don't know about catnip: If you leave catnip or catnip-filled toys out for your cat all of the time, she can become immune to its effects. I explain that to my clients whenever I enter their homes and see dozens of catnip-filled toys. I think, how sad for the kitties that without knowing it, their owners may be ruining this feline pleasure. Limit catnip to once a week. You can always add an extra session now and then if needed, for instance, after a visit to the vet, or other stressful event.

Buy good quality catnip. I prefer to buy loose, dried catnip instead of all the catnip-filled toys because unless I'm familiar with the toy manufacturer, I don't know whether the catnip is of good quality. Some manufacturers don't even use real catnip. Check the label on loose catnip to make sure only *leaves* and *blossoms* are used. Lower quality catnip contains *stems* which do nothing but fill up the package. Dried stems are also very hard and sharp so if your cat enjoys eating catnip (which most do), she could hurt herself. Stay away from supermarket brands. Better quality catnip can be found in pet supply stores and cat specialty shops.

My favorite way to use catnip is to put some in the tip of a sock, knot the end and let my cats jump on it, kick it, and roll all over it. You can also give your cat loose catnip. Just sprinkle some on the floor or on a paper plate and watch her do somersaults. To release the aromatic oil rub the catnip between your hands before you sprinkle it on the floor. If the catnip is in a sock, rub the sock between your hands to release the full potency.

Keep unused catnip tightly sealed in an airtight container, out of kitty's reach. I'd also recommend that instead of buying all of those catnip-filled toys, buy a few furry mice toys and drop them in the catnip container. When you pull one out after it's been "marinating," it'll have acquired the real scent of top quality, potent catnip.

GROWING YOUR OWN

You can grow your own catnip plant. If you plant it outdoors though, I warn you, word will spread within the feline community and you'll soon have every cat in the neighborhood visiting your garden. Catnip spreads so you'll have to keep it pruned to prevent it from taking over your garden. Find a safe place to grow it outdoors (good luck) or grow the plant

CatwiseClue

If you have a large quantity of catnip, storing it in the freezer in several small airtight containers will prolong its freshness. All you have to do is take out one little packet and allow it to come to room temperature before giving it to your cat.

indoors in a sunny window. Packets of catnip seeds are available at garden centers and many discount stores. Planting and growing instructions will be on the packet. To ensure peak potency, don't allow the plant to flower or you'll end up with skinny branches. Keep nipping those flower buds. To harvest and dry catnip, cut the branches, tie them in bunches and hang them upside down in a dry, dark place. Once the herb has dried (the leaves will look shriveled), carefully sort the leaves into an airtight container and discard all stems. You don't want to release the potent oil until it's time to use the herb so don't crumble or crush the catnip.

UNEXPECTED REACTIONS

Not every cat reacts to catnip. There is actually an inherited catnip response gene that some cats don't have (it's been estimated that one out of every three cats lack this gene). So if your kitty seems unimpressed, don't worry, there's nothing wrong with her. Kittens don't respond to catnip, so don't attempt to entice yours until she's at least six months old. Kittens don't need anything to encourage their playfulness, they have enough natural energy.

If you have a male cat in a multicat household, the first time you give him catnip, do so away from the other cats. There are some males who actually display an aggressive behavior while under the influence of catnip. You also never want to give it to any cat (male or female) who is showing aggression because catnip can cause them to lose inhibitions, which may escalate the behavior.

Activity Toys

One of the reasons cats become overweight is because they have no activity but eating. They sleep, walk a few steps to their food bowl, eat, and then go back to sleep until it's time to eat again. They don't have to hunt for their food—heck, they don't have to do *anything* for their food.

Lack of activity because of insufficient stimulation also contributes to a cat feeling bored and depressed. A cat whose owner works long hours or has little time for interaction can lose her spark. An interactive toy is the best way to guarantee that your cat gets enough stimulation, but what if you're never home to do it? Or, what if you'd like a way to supplement your interactive sessions?

Activity toys can help in both of the above situations as well as many others. The concept behind an activity toy is they allow the cat to work for food—the way nature intended. I'm not talking about her having to work for her actual meals, those will be provided as usual—I'm referring to little extra treats or pieces of kibble. Activity toys are very popular behavior modification tools for dogs who suffer separation anxiety. Owners place several toys around the house, each with a biscuit in it and the dog discovers and works on them over the course of the day. They work well for cats also. The way an activity toy works is that you place several treats or pieces of her regular dry food inside a hollow ball that has an opening on one end. As the cat rolls the ball, a treat falls out. She soon learns that when she moves the toy just right, she gets a food reward. This keeps busy an overweight cat who is on scheduled meals and provides her with a little treat. It stimulates a bored or depressed cat to think and focus, with the positive result for her of a reward. I love toys that require a cat to *think*. Keeping your cat occupied with a "thinking" activity can help avoid potential behavior problems.

Activity toys that I like are Play-n-Squeak, Play-n-Treat, Zig-n-Zag, Push-n-Roll, and Kitty Kong. The best activity toy around, Play-n-Treat is a ball that you fill with pieces of dry kibble or small treats. As the cat rolls the ball, pieces of kibble fall out. This is an absolutely wonderful toy. Another toy, Kitty Kong, was not created to be an activity toy but that's how I prefer using it. Kitty Kong is a plastic mouse-shaped toy with an opening on the back end. The toy comes packaged with special nonshreddable, catnip-treated paper that you put in the open end. You can still use it as a catnip toy but I prefer to use it as a food-related activity toy by putting a drop of cream cheese just inside the edge (don't use the paper and the cream cheese at the same time). This can introduce a sedentary cat to the concept of working for food. As she gets the idea you can then switch to Play-n-Treat. An activity toy placed out for your cat while you're gone can give her fun and a rewarding task to accomplish during the day.

Nonfood-related activity toys such as Play-n-Squeak, Zig-n-Zag, and Push-n-Roll are also wonderful. Play-n-Squeak is a catnip-filled furry mouse that emits an irresistible series of chirping sounds (by way of a lifetime battery inside) whenever it's touched. My cats continue to remain fascinated by it. The Zig-n-Zag ball has a nonmotorized tension mechanism inside that makes the ball move unpredictably as the cat rolls it along. Push-n-Roll is a "Y" shaped open tunnel track with two

Catwise Caution

If you have a dog who shares space with your cat, don't use these activity toys. They're small enough for a dog to swallow (and the enticing food will tempt him).

balls inside for your cat to reach in and bat around. I like this toy because it's so light your cat can activate the balls just by rubbing up against the toy or touching it with her paw. You can make your own activity toy that your cat might enjoy with a couple of Ping-Pong balls in an empty tissue box. Place a couple of these around the house for her to discover during the day.

Other Toys for Solo Playtime

Besides interactive and the specially targeted activity toys, your cat will enjoy other kinds for solo play sessions. As I've said before, don't provide her with an overflowing basket of toys. They'll just gather dust. Rotate a few toys in and out every couple of days to keep them interesting for your cat. The furry mouse that reappears after three days and terrifies you when you step on it in the middle of the night will seem brand-new again to your kitty.

As I mentioned previously in this chapter, solo toys are essentially dead prey and your cat has to do the work to make them come to life, so choose lightweight toys. That way, the slightest touch of your cat's paw will cause movement.

Standard kitty toy equipment should include a couple of furry mice. Choose small, lightweight ones. A toy that's too large can inhibit your cat. She'll be more attracted to something she knows she can conquer.

Ping-Pong balls are great, especially if you have areas of bare floor. If you have a large cat who tries to carry the Ping-Pong ball in her mouth, only let her have them when you can supervise. There is an extremely remote danger that she might puncture the ball with her canine teeth and perhaps be unable to dislodge it.

The Kitty Hoots Crackler is a catnip-filled soft toy that makes a crackling cellophane paper sound when it is touched or stepped on. Cats are attracted to the crackling paper, and this is a safe way to provide it. Plain cellophane wrap or the wrapping on cigarette packs is extremely dangerous. Cellophane, if swallowed, can cause serious damage because during the digestive process it becomes sharp, resembling glass. The Kitty Hoots Crackler allows your cat to play safely with something crackly. The toy comes in several shapes such as frogs and moths.

In the pet supply store, you can find packages of soft tiny balls. Some have crackling paper sounds, some are just very lightweight. I like them because they're soft and the cat can carry them around easily. If your cat is inclined to swallow things she shouldn't, choose larger toys instead of the tiny balls.

Homemade Toys

Here are some things you can find around your house that make great toys:

The plastic ring from milk or juice containers probably tops the list as the all-time best cat toy. The next time you buy a container of juice, instead of tossing the ring in the trash, toss it on the floor. I know many cats who prefer the plastic container rings over all other toys, even the most expensive.

Opened paper bags are unbeatable for diving into and leaping out of repeatedly. Never use a plastic bag—it can cause suffocation. If the bag has handles, cut them off because a cat can get caught up and maybe strangled in them. Fold a cuff of about an inch around the top to help keep the bag from collapsing. Lay the open bag on its side and toss a Ping-Pong ball in there, then STAND BACK!

Plastic drinking straws are lightweight and easy for your cat to bat around. Try tossing one in the opened paper bag.

Save those boxes. Just remove all packing material, staples, or anything else that could be dangerous and then let your cat enjoy. Actually, your cat most likely claimed the box only seconds after you removed the contents. Don't use boxes if your cat likes to chew on them.

Mom told you never to play with your food, but I'm sure even *she'd* enjoy the sight of a kitten batting around a green bean or a grape.

A champagne cork is also fun as long as your cat doesn't chew it to pieces. Just supervise.

The next time you're loading film in your camera to take pictures of your adorable kitten or cat, don't throw away the plastic container—let your cat have it.

Another great thing about homemade toys is that if your cat loses any of them to the great Toy Magnet located under your refrigerator, bed or sofa, they're easily replaceable. My vacuum cleaner bag always contains a number of grapes, green beans, brussels sprouts, and drinking straws.

Dangerous Toys

Ribbons, strings, yarn, rubber bands, and dental floss may seem like fun things for cats to play with, but they're extremely dangerous if swallowed. With all of the safe toys available, don't take a chance with any of these.

Any stringed toy, even an interactive one, should be used only when you are present. Put it away, out of the cat's reach, when the game is over.

Plastic bags should be kept away from your kitty because of the risk of suffocation.

Don't tie any stringed toy to a doorknob, because your cat could easily get tangled up in it.

Aluminum foil is dangerous if swallowed. Don't start the practice of wadding up aluminum foil into a ball. Some owners create aluminum foil balls from foil that had been wrapped around food, so there is an irresistible smell on the ball. That's just asking for trouble because it'll be hard for the cat to resist chewing off pieces of the foil.

How to Tell If Your Cats Are Playing or Fighting

Sometimes it's hard to tell the difference, but here are a few general guidelines:

- When cats are *playing,* one or both may hiss once or twice, but if they hiss several times, they're more likely engaged in a *fight.*

- Cats who *play* together usually take turns in the offensive and defensive postures. When they are *fighting,* there's usually no role reversal—one cat remains offensively aggressive and the other becomes defensive.

- There should be no yowling or screaming in *play.*

- No cat gets hurt during *play* (unless it's accidental). *Fighting* cats may give or receive a scratch or bite wound.

- When *play* is over, the cats should act normal and don't avoid each other. After a *fight,* one or both of the cats often stay out of the other's way or appear afraid of each other.

- If two cats who are not normally friendly to each other appear to be engaged in *play*, be careful. There's a good chance that it's actually a *fight*. If you're in doubt, distract them with a positive noise, such as the opening of a can of cat food, the shaking of the box of treats, etc. Keep it positive though. If they were really *playing*, you don't want to discourage their blossoming friendship.

Misunderstood Intentions

In multicat households, one cat may misread another's playful intentions because each cat was socialized differently. A kitten who was taken away from her littermates too early and didn't engage in social play behavior may be more comfortable with object play. When your other cat, who may be very socially playful, comes over to the kitten, communicating an invitation to play, the kitten may interpret it as a threatening gesture. That's when you need to step in with an interactive group play session to help both of them.

Or if you're raising a litter of kittens, be aware if any of the males play too aggressively. That could cause the females to react by not responding favorably to any play invitation.

Keep Your Camera Loaded

I always keep a loaded camera within easy reach because even after almost sixteen years, Albie will strike poses I want captured forever.

You don't have to have expensive equipment or be a professional photographer to take great pictures of your cat. Almost everything a cat does is photogenic. A few basics and patience will allow you to capture both posed and action shots.

If you're a novice, you can purchase one of the inexpensive autofocus cameras that are basically "point and shoot." If you really want to make things easy, just get a disposable camera in which the film is already loaded and ready to go. That way you won't even have to deal with making sure you have batteries or film.

If you're confused about what type of film to buy, a basic guideline is 400-speed for indoor photos and 100-speed if you're shooting outdoors in sunny weather.

ACTION SHOTS

Your kitten will be more than happy to provide you with many of these. What you have to be careful about, though, is a poorly timed shot, which can result in a blurry photo of a ball of fur. These usually come when you try to grab the camera and center your moving cat in the picture too quickly. To avoid this, while your kitten is playing, watch her through the camera's viewfinder until you have a steady hand.

Try to be aware of your background so the picture doesn't look too busy or the kitten doesn't blend in so much she disappears. For instance, you're photographing your calico kitten playing with a toy on a patterned multicolored rug. The pattern of the carpet will compete with the cat's coat and the toy will also disappear against the busy background.

Try putting a toy in a basket, then patiently waiting nearby with your camera. Your kitten diving in and out of the basket for the toy will make a great shot.

POSED SHOTS

It's best to start with a relaxed kitten, so don't decide that you want a still shot when your kitty's revved up to play.

If you want to try for a more formal shot with a solid background, you can use a sheet or buy rolled paper at an art supply store. Choose a color that will highlight your cat's coat color. If you want to highlight the cat's eyes, choose that same color for your background.

Your cat probably won't want to just sit in front of the background. Placing a basket or a decorative pillow near her will provide her with a little more security. If you're photographing a kitten, set your props up in front of the background. If you're using a basket with a toy in it, when she starts playing in the basket, make an enticing sound. That millisecond when she pops her head out of the basket and looks in your direction is the moment to snap the picture. Don't overdo the sound— you're not trying for a look of terror.

To photograph an adult cat more formally, avoid a straight-on pose. Stand a little to the side so your cat's body will show and she won't look like just a head with legs. Entice her with a toy or a sound and you'll get her ears to prick forward and eyes to look alert. If you want her focus off to the side, dangle a peacock feather to your right or left. Don't make the feather movements too exciting or your cat will run right toward you in anticipation of playtime. You might want to use a tripod to keep the camera steady so you'll have one hand free. If you use an assistant, make sure it's someone your cat is comfortable with.

To avoid the alien eye glow that often appears in pictures, don't shoot directly at the cat's eye level—be a little above.

Don't try too hard for avant-garde camera angles, or you may wind up with a photo of a cat who looks very out of proportion.

BE PATIENT

Don't ever force your cat to sit still while you frustratingly try to pose her. Your best photos will most likely be the candid shots anyway. If you want to attempt a posed shot, do it when your cat isn't in play mode. After she has eaten and is relaxed is the best time. If things aren't working, let her go. Leave the background set up, your camera nearby, and before you know it, you'll find your kitty stretched out right where you want her.

7

Sour Puss

Solving Common Behavior Problems, Serious Problems, and the Ones You're Too Embarrassed to Tell Anyone About

How Do Behavior Problems Begin?

We ask so much of our cats. We leave them alone all day with nothing to do, thrust unwanted companions on them, lay down ever-changing rules, and force them to adjust their nocturnal nature to coincide with our more convenient daytime schedule. We love the convenience of not having to walk cats but then insist that they use a litter box that often falls way below their standard of cleanliness. We're positive that the motivation behind their furniture scratching is willful destruction, because there's a scratching post somewhere in the house—oh yeah, it's in the laundry room (so what if that's also where the dog sleeps). We spank our cats and then don't understand why they become defensive. We yell at them and then act surprised when they no longer want to be around us. We rub their noses in their messes because somebody some-where told us that's the way to train a pet. We punish our cats when we come home from work at night for something they did earlier in the day—it doesn't matter that the cat is now peacefully sleeping in his bed—he'll *know* why he's being yelled at. We play with our cats when it's convenient but push them away if they playfully bat at the newspaper we're trying to read. We treat our cats as children, adults, friends, enemies, confidants, even dogs—but not often enough as *cats*. Finally, we think our cats should *know better*, when in reality, *we're* the ones who should.

Okay, so by now you get the idea that I believe owners create most of the behavior problems in cats. There are certainly other factors contributing to behavior disorders such as medical conditions or lack of socialization, because the cat had no human contact early in his life. But, for the most part, the owner messes things up.

Your relationship with your cat is just that—a *relationship*. As with any relationship, you have to communicate with each other and understand one another's needs. People too often take on the responsibility of becoming cat owners, then expect the cat to do all of the work, suppress his natural behaviors, and understand what the heck is being told to him in a language he can't possibly make out.

You know by now that I truly believe it's your responsibility as a cat owner to educate yourself about this beautiful creature you've chosen to spend your life with. Learn to interpret what your cat is communicating, what his needs are as a cat and finally, if you hope to solve a behavior problem, learn to understand his behavior. Many of the behaviors we label as "bad" are actually normal in the cat's world. So how do you correct a so-called "bad" behavior? You understand and work with the motivation behind the behavior. It's only when you look at the behavior from your cat's point of view that you'll be able to find solutions, because then you'll both be speaking the same language. If you continue to see the situation only from your point of view, you'll misread the problem and cause frustration for both of you. Your misreading of a cat's motivation and inability to understand what he's communicating is most often why he lands a one-way ride to the local pound. Behavior problems kill more cats than any disease ever will.

So what triggers behavior problems? For some cats, the cause can be as seemingly minor as a change in routine. A cat is a creature of habit, so when his daily rituals are disturbed, it can cause stress. Boredom can also cause problems as the cat searches for something, anything to do. If a cat feels his territory is being threatened, that can spark a behavioral change. There are also numerous medical conditions that can lead to behavioral problems. Improper early socialization, abuse, inappropriate punishment—the list could go on and on. The point is, it's up to you to identify the motivation for or cause of the behavior you don't want.

A wonderful thing happens when you stop looking at your world through your eyes and start seeing it from your cat's view—not only do you stand an excellent chance of solving the current behavior problem, but you'll probably be able to head off future ones as well.

Here are the common training mistakes made by owners:

- *misreading motivation*

- *inconsistency*

- *unfair changes* (for example, now that you've bought a new couch, the cat is punished when he attempts to get into his usual spot)

- punishment

- *reinforcing unwanted behavior* (for example, your cat meows at five A.M., so to quiet him you go to the kitchen and put food in his bowl)

Changing Undesirable Behavior

Behavior problems fall into two general categories: normal training problems (scratching furniture, jumping on counters, aggression toward a new cat, etc.) and the kind of behavior problems that your vet should look at before you attempt to solve them.

If you're attempting to change a long-standing problem, stop whatever it is you've been doing in the past, because it obviously hasn't worked so far. Don't force your cat to do or *not* do something. Don't go head-to-head with your cat in a battle of wills. Step back, take a deep breath, make yourself a cup of tea, and I'll help you plan out a new strategy. Oh yeah, grab a couple of chocolate chip cookies—I think better on a full stomach.

As you go through this chapter, keep in mind the following *think like a cat* perspective:

- Determine the motivation or cause.

- Make whatever environmental changes are necessary.

- Redirect the behavior toward something positive.

Litter Box Problems

This is such a complex subject that it needs a chapter all its own. Refer to chapter 8.

Destructive Scratching

Another big one. See chapter 9.

Destructive Chewing

WOOL CHEWING

If you're not familiar with this behavior, it's exactly what it sounds like. Although you can't imagine why a sweater or blanket would seem appetizing, wool chewing cats can turn a pair of socks into swiss cheese in a matter of minutes.

The theory about wool chewing is that some cats crave fiber, and some breeds appear to have a higher need than others. Siamese cats, for example, are often wool chewers.

To solve this problem, first remove all temptation. That means no more tossing your socks on the floor or leaving the bed unmade. If you have a blanket on the bed, make sure there's a comforter or bedspread over it. Keep sweater drawers closed and don't store any sweaters on open closet shelves that a cat can get to.

If you're feeding your cat canned food, make the switch to dry. You may even need to feed free-choice (leaving it out for the cat to nibble when he wants it). If you're already feeding dry food, talk to your vet about changing to a higher fiber formula. If your cat absolutely refuses to eat dry food, increase the fiber content of his canned meals by adding either a half-teaspoon of canned pumpkin or half a teaspoon of bran. Start slowly, though, and add just a few flakes at a time. Work up to a half-teaspoon.

Grow some kitty greens for your cat (see section on "Plant Attack"). Make sure there's always a supply of kitty greens, so your cat won't go looking for an afternoon snack in the form of your daughter's brand-new wool sweater.

WOOL SUCKING

Not the same behavior as wool chewing, wool *sucking* is believed to be the result of abrupt or early weaning. The kitten continues the nursing behavior on clothing, shoelaces, owners' fingers or earlobes, even shirt buttons. Some cats will suck their own flanks, tips of their tails, or paws.

Most kittens eventually grow out of this behavior. The best way to stop him is to distract him. When he begins to suckle, gently disengage him and then pet or play with him. One of my cats was an earlobe sucker as a kitten. I'd be falling asleep when there'd be this disconcerting slurping sound in my ear. I began keeping a feather under my pillow and when my kitten began walking up toward my head, I'd distract her with a little playtime. Then she'd fall asleep, and in time, her earlobe sucking days were behind her.

PLANT ATTACK

If you haven't already removed the dangerous plants (for the list, see chapter 18) and sprayed the remaining ones with a bitter anti-chew plant spray, you'd better get going.

Many cats enjoy munching on greenery, and you can provide a safe alternative by purchasing one of the many kitty grass kits available in pet supply stores or through mail order. Keep it in a convenient location. Your cat will prefer this grass over your nasty-tasting ferns. Follow the setup directions, water as indicated, and in no time you'll have lush greenery that's safe for your cat's afternoon snack. The only thing I don't like about many of the kits is that they come in lightweight containers. If your cat pulls on the grass with his teeth instead of just munching, the container moves around. I usually transfer the contents to a heavier pot such as a terra cotta one. You can even make your own kitty greens by sprinkling seeds in a pot of soil. Buy seeds that have not been treated and use sterilized potting soil. Cover lightly with a $\frac{1}{4}$-inch layer of soil, water well, and allow to drain. Mist daily with a plant sprayer so you don't disrupt the tiny seeds. Keep the pot in a dark, warm place until you see the little green heads peek out of the soil, then place it in a sunny location. As soon as the grass is tall enough, place it in a location convenient to your cat.

SELF-CHEWING AND GROOMING

Some cats groom excessively to the point of creating thinning hair or actual bald spots. A few cats not only groom but begin chewing on themselves to the point of creating sores.

Speak to your vet to make sure there isn't an underlying medical condition causing the problem. Even simple fleas can cause a cat to chew himself raw.

If it turns out that the problem is behavioral, you must identify the trigger. The chewing is not the main problem—it's a symptom. Whatever is causing the cat to feel so stressed is the problem. It could be anything from a change in your work schedule to the addition of another pet, the death of a companion—*anything* can cause this behavior. The stress and nervousness build up to such a point that the cat must do *something* to relieve his anxiety. The medical term for this behavior is *psychogenic alopecia*.

Provide as much stability, consistency, and distraction for your cat as possible. Make sure his environment is as stress-free as you can. If the dog barks at him or relentlessly pursues him to play, make sure he has access to a safe area where he can get away from other household pets. Make sure his meals are on time—never late—so that he doesn't have to wait and worry. The area in which he eats should be stress-free. When you place his food bowl on the floor, if you notice that he is constantly looking around, frequently stopping to check out his surroundings, then you should move his feeding station to what feels to him to be a more secure spot. Try feeding him on top of a cat tree or in a quieter room.

As much as you want to hold and cuddle him, he needs to feel in control of his environment, so interactive playtime should be a regular part of his daily schedule. Two or three a day will not only dispel his tension, they'll build up his kitty confidence. Leave activity toys out when you're not at home. Make sure he has enough distractions when you're not around. A cat tree in the window so he can watch the birds will help him pass the time.

Keep your schedule as consistent as possible for him. He needs stability and the reassurance of his loving owner.

If you're not sure about the quality of his diet, discuss any possible changes with your vet. Your cat needs a high-quality food to help him stay healthy during times of stress.

Don't be in a hurry to put your cat on anti-anxiety medication. Wait and see if you've identified the source and done something helpful about it. If the cat doesn't respond or the situation worsens, talk with your vet about consulting a behaviorist.

Trash Can Invaders

There are some cats who, no matter what you feed them, insist on using the self-serve buffet found in the kitchen trash can. Your cat may dine on the most expensive cat food money can buy and then later that evening rummage through the banana peels and coffee filters to lick the aluminum foil you used to cover the roast.

I could suggest you try booby traps and elaborate deterrents, but why not just make it easy on everyone and buy a trash can with a lid? Better yet, keep the trash can in a cabinet. The more you booby-trap the can, the more trouble it becomes for you to throw something in it. I keep a can under the sink. This works out much better than the large one that used to stand next to the refrigerator—not only because the cats can't reach it, but because this one is smaller, it gets emptied more often, which keeps the kitchen cleaner.

Excessive Vocalization

If you have a Siamese or other oriental breed known for being talkative, then you might as well skip over this section because he's not going to change. Siamese cats love to provide running narratives on their daily activities and aren't shy about voicing opinions. Know this and accept it.

Other cats may become vocal for many reasons. Mostly it's a surefire way of getting your attention. When the less subtle method of staring you down, walking back and forth across your newspaper, or sitting on your chest doesn't do the trick, nonstop meows usually work. The odds are that because he is born with patience, determination, and unrelenting persistence, you'll eventually cave in and give him what he wants. It may take five minutes of meowing, but he now knows that as long as he doesn't give up, you'll give in. Whether it's to be let outside, fed, or petted, *he* knows that *you* know the only way to quiet him is to surrender. Of course, once you give in, you've just shown him that his meowing has successfully trained you. How do you change this behavior? Ignore his vocal demands. Don't reward negative behavior. Even if you can hold out for twenty minutes and then in desperation, you finally get up and put some food in his bowl—he'll remember that persistent meowing works. It took an inordinate amount of time, but it worked.

So, don't give in. Put headphones on, read aloud, just don't cave in. Instead of rewarding his negative behavior, when you notice your cat may be about to enter into his meowing phase, redirect him with an interactive toy *before* he starts up. If you're unable to do an interactive session, have an activity toy such as Play-n-Treat around. The key to retraining the behavior is to redirect him *before* he actually starts vocalizing. Otherwise you're right back at square one again. I prefer doing an interactive session because I can make sure he has gotten a good dose of mental and physical activity. Then when the game is over, I can feed him or let him take a well-deserved nap.

One reason your cat may be meowing is because he isn't sufficiently stimulated. Make sure you're engaging in daily interactive sessions.

An older cat may yowl at night after everyone has gone to bed. As he walks through the darkened house, his declining senses may cause him to become disoriented. Have him checked by the vet to make sure he's not in pain. When you hear your older cat yowling in the night, call out to him so he can find you. If it begins to happen on a regular basis or if he really seems to be getting more disoriented, confine him to your room at night.

The Fearful Cat

Cats hate change and prefer the security of their familiar territory. It's only natural then that new people, places, or things may cause them to be fearful. One common situation a cat may fear is having strangers come into the house. As soon as the doorbell rings, he may take off for the farthest closet. Here's an exercise you can do: Ask a friend to come over (make sure it's not someone your cat already hates). Have him or her sit in the living room while you go into the room where your cat is hiding. With total nonchalance, sit down on the floor and casually conduct an interactive playtime (key word: *casually*). Don't try to entice your hiding cat out, just lightly play with a toy, gently moving it around a small area of the room. Use your voice in a calm, comforting way. The effect is for your cat to start picking up the signal from you that this is no big deal. So what if there's a guest in the house—who cares? *You* want to play with your cat. If you're relaxed and make no attempts to force your cat out of his comfort zone, he'll relax too. He may not actually play or even venture out of the closet the first few times, but he will begin to relax.

After several minutes with your cat, leave him alone. But instead of going back to your guest, sit on the floor in the hallway. Engage in a quiet conversation with the guest but dangle the toy gently to get your cat's attention. You can also offer cat treats. Although your cat may not come out of the room, he may risk leaving the closet. He may even come as far as the hallway. If he'll play, engage in a session but don't try to take it any farther into the living room. Have your guest leave, then reward your cat. Ask your friend to return again the next day and repeat the same exercise. Keep up these visits, and move inch by inch closer to the living room. Eventually your cat should be calm enough that you can sit in the living room and he will make an appearance (however brief). If he can be distracted with playtime, let your guest conduct a game with him. The guest must remain in his or her seat, though, so as not to frighten the cat. Remember to give your friend a treat too (like lunch) for being such a good sport!

This slow and steady way helps a cat get over whatever frightens him. Conduct light play sessions. Let your cat dictate the pace, though. If he only wants to come as far as the hallway, then be content with that for now. Eventually, as he sees there's no threat, he'll inch closer. Your behavior throughout should be casual and relaxed. Very often, in an attempt to comfort a cat, the owner tries to hold the struggling pet. The owner's voice also often sounds worried, and the cat interprets this as

Helping the Fearful Cat

- Don't force him to be in the room with you.
- Make sure he has access to a hiding place.
- Let him determine how close he wants to get.
- Use gentle interactive playtime or treats for distraction.
- Keep your tone of voice soothing.
- Take several deep breaths to relax yourself.
- Introduce changes in a cat's life gradually.

Big-Time Causes of Stress

- death in the family
- marriage
- new baby
- divorce
- a move to a new house
- renovations
- natural disasters
- house fires
- abuse
- neglect
- loneliness
- illness or injury

confirmation that there really *is* something to fear. He needs to know there's a secure place for him besides the back of the closet.

Is Your Cat Stressing Out?

Any cat in a stressful situation long enough can change from being healthy and sociable to nervous and fearful.

What does a cat have to become stressed about? Don't they just sleep, eat, and play the day away? I wish life for cats did just involve sleeping, eating, and playing, but unfortunately they encounter many things that can have an impact. We often forget how much security a cat finds in familiarity. Therefore, any change—however trivial we consider it—can be very upsetting for kitty.

First, let's think about the things that would stress *us*. A death in the family, a divorce, a move to a new home, a move to a new city, illness, a natural disaster, even getting married can be stressful (after all, a wedding wouldn't be a wedding without a truckload of stress). These affect your cat as well. Plus, he gets a double whammy because for him it comes out of the blue. One day he's sleeping in his favorite spot and the next thing he knows, everything's being boxed up around him. A few days later he's whisked off to a new place.

Okay, so you're not surprised that those things could stress your cat. What you may not realize though is that seemingly little and insignificant things can cause stress as well. Some cats resent *any* change. Here are some situations we might overlook in terms of how they affect a cat:

Causes of Stress Owners Often Overlook

- dirty litter box
- change in litter type
- change in food
- food and litter in close proximity
- litter box in a noisy location
- children
- holidays
- travel
- change in your work schedule
- boarding
- buying new furniture or rearranging
- new carpet
- addition of another pet
- ongoing appearance of another cat in the yard
- not having access to hiding places
- ongoing loud noises
- rough or improper handling
- punishment

In order to help a stressed-out cat, you must recognize the cause of the stress and if possible, eliminate or modify it. The best method, if you know something potentially stressful is coming up, is to prepare your cat gradually for it. Whether it's a small thing such as a change in food or a big, big one such as a move to a new house, *prepare* him ahead of time. Introduce changes gradually. For example, when you want to change the cat's food, mix a little of the new food into the current diet and increase the amount of the new food over the course of a week. If the change is a move to a new house you should pack in stages, keep calm, and when you get to the new home, put your cat in one room. Let him get his bearings gradually (see chapter 14). The bigger the change, the more prep time needed. When there is an unexpected crisis, such as a death in the family (human, feline, or canine), realize that your cat is experiencing the same emotions as you. Provide lots of playtime, keep his schedule as normal as possible and monitor his eating and litter-box habits. At these times he needs as much consistency and normalcy from you as possible.

Because playtime puts cats in a more confident frame of mind, I use interactive toys to keep them distracted and positive while I'm helping them get past whatever is stressful.

Make sure the cat has access to a comfort zone (preferably several)—meaning a safe hiding place away from noise, pets, and people.

Provide activity toys to keep your cat occupied when you can't be around.

Try to make every transition in your cat's life as gradual and easy as possible.

The Depressed Kitty

Sophia was a big, beautiful, mixed-breed cat. Her gray-and-white coat was lush, shiny, and kept meticulously clean by this very fastidious feline. She was a cat who loved to be in the center of things and was always in the lap of one of her owners, Patricia or Marc. Sophia was doted on, played with, and truly loved. Because she had been adopted as a kitten, this was the only life Sophia knew and there was no reason for anyone to think it would change anytime soon, but it did. When Sophia was seven, Marc had a heart attack at work. He was rushed to the hospital and died a few hours later.

Patricia and Marc had been married for twenty years. Patricia came home from the hospital that night, obviously still in shock. Over the next few days she began the long, painful process of grieving for her beloved husband. Friends and family remained by her side, offering help. She was watched over and cared for.

Sophia, who didn't understand any part of what was happening, began a slow descent into depression. From her point of view, one of her owners had suddenly vanished and her other owner was acting totally out of character. Sophia would attempt to climb into Patricia's lap, but one of the visiting family members would shoo her off. There were lots of strangers in the house, but no one paid any attention to Sophia. In an effort to help Patricia, a neighbor was coming over to feed the cat twice a day. Sophia's attempts at contact were ignored. Everything in her world was different but she didn't know *why*. Eventually she began to withdraw. She kept to herself, coming out from under the bed only to eat and use the litter box. She became neglectful of her personal hygiene. Her coat started looking messy and dirty. She began using the litter box sporadically, choosing instead to eliminate in the corners of closets. Food lost its appeal. Sleep became the focus of Sophia's life. As months went by, Sophia's deteriorating appearance and behavior concerned Patricia, so she called the vet. A consultation with me was recommended. When I arrived at the house, the cat I saw was a depressed, thin, dirty cat who in no way resembled the sociable beauty she had been. Cats get depressed over many of the same things we do: death, divorce, illness, loneliness, you name it. How do you recognize depression? Look for changes in your cat's normal routine, especially if there's been a crisis in the household. Note any change in: personality, activity level, appetite, grooming habits, litter box habits, sleep patterns, overall appearance.

After you've spoken to your vet, begin to bring the spark back in your cat's life. Use lots of interactive playtime. If the cat is home alone for long periods, have a friend (or a hired pet sitter) come over for daily play sessions. Provide stimulation by setting a cat tree near a window. Open the drapes and let the sun into the house. Hand-feed your cat to kick-start his appetite and also to re-connect with him. Help your cat with grooming by brushing him daily. The massage of the brush will feel great. Don't forget to break out the catnip occasionally, too!

If your cat's depression is because you have changed your lifestyle and you're gone for long periods (perhaps out of town), consider getting him a companion cat.

Make life fun again!!!

Noisy Nocturnal Adventures

You're in bed, you're just about to drift off to sleep when suddenly there's a *crash* in the other room. You sit bolt upright in bed, convinced you also heard the sound of a horse galloping down the hall. What in the world is going on? You get out of bed, switch on the light, and walk out into the hallway. Standing there, looking as innocent as can be, is your cat. On the floor next to him are the dozen roses you received from your husband that day. Also on the floor is the crystal vase that once held the roses. Of course, now it's in several pieces in a puddle of water. Your cat blinks his eyes, flicks the tip of his tail, and goes off down the hall. What sounded like a horse to you was merely your eight-pound cat revving up for a night of fun.

Cats are nocturnal creatures. While some of us are lucky enough to have cats who graciously agree to adjust to our daytime schedules, others of us aren't so fortunate. In order to ensure yourself sleep you'll need to add a few things to your pre-bedtime preparations.

If you feed your cat on a schedule, divide his meals into three portions, feeding him two at his regular times. Before you go to bed, and I mean *just* before, conduct a fifteen-minute interactive play session with him and then feed him his third meal. The exercise will release his built-up energy, and then the meal will most likely lead him to a nap afterward. Hold it, don't get into that bed yet—there's still a little more work to do. Put out an activity toy for him to discover later in the evening. So the noise doesn't wake you up, put it in a distant area of the house. It is also important to rotate toys so he doesn't become bored.

If you can, leave the curtains open in a window. Put a cat tree there so your cat can look out at the nightly activity. I keep the shutters open in the guest room because my backyard is very private. My cats love to sit on the bed and keep track of the insects and other little creatures conducting their nightly business.

Paw Prints on the Counter

The house is quiet. No one seems to be doing anything interesting so the cat walks into the kitchen and looks around. Nothing much happening on ground level, so in one graceful leap, he lands on the counter. Suddenly, out of nowhere comes his owner, yelling, charging the cat, aiming a squirt bottle in his direction, and then blasting water in his face. Panic stricken, the soaking wet cat scrambles off the counter, runs through the house, and dives under the bed. There, the terrified cat stays for the next hour. His owner replaces the squirt bottle on the shelf and goes back to watching TV in the den. What the owner is thinking: *I'll train that cat yet!* What the cat is thinking: *My owner's a lunatic!!!!!* The bottom line: This training method stinks.

The best way to keep your cat off the counter, table, or whatever furniture you decide should be forbidden is to go back to two of the three approaches I mentioned in the beginning of this chapter: *remote control* and *redirection.* Don't forget to also be consistent about which areas are to be off-limits to kitty. Don't confuse him by allowing him to be on the table or counter as long as you're not eating, but forbid him when there's food. He won't understand the difference, and it's not fair to expect him to.

I prefer to use low-stress, quiet devices for remote control deterrents. My method is to get several inexpensive plastic placemats from the discount store and place several strips of either double-faced masking tape or Sticky Paws (available in pet supply stores or through mail order) over them. Cover the counter with the placemats. The taped placemats will make the surface unattractive and the first time your cat jumps on the counter he'll immediately jump down. Keep the placemats on the counter or any surface you don't want the cat on. Remove them only when you need access to the surface, then immediately replace them when you're through. Eventually, your cat will decide that the counter isn't such a great place after all. Don't be too quick to remove the placemats permanently. A few more days of inconvenience are worth it to end up with a well-trained cat. When you do begin removing the mats, do it one at a time over the course of several days.

Another way to keep the cat off the counter is to put a few pennies inside empty soda cans (tape over the opening), then line the cans up along the edge of the counter. When he jumps up, he'll knock them over and be startled. I prefer the placemat method over the cans for two reasons: Once the cans are knocked over and hit the floor, the counter becomes very attractive again, whereas the placemats remain there. The other reason I don't like the cans is that if you have more than one pet, the noise scares not only the guilty cat but the innocent pet as well. What if one cat is innocently using his scratching post or litter box when he suddenly hears a clatter of cans? You want to direct the training at the cat who needs it. I also dislike the training method of using balloons for the same reason. The sound of a popping balloon scares *me*, I can imagine how frightening it is for a little cat.

Now let's suppose you're in the kitchen working on dinner so the placemats are off the counter. You notice your cat getting ready to jump up. What do you do? This is where a quick squirt of plain water from a squirt bottle comes in. Use a small plant mister with the nozzle adjusted to produce a stream instead of a mist. That way, you can direct the water right at the cat and not all over the counter. A stream is more effective anyway, because a cat with a thick coat may not even feel mist. You have to be fast, so keep your bottle loaded and on the counter. The secret to making this a modified version of remote control training is to be sure the cat doesn't see that the squirt came from you. Be as sneaky as you can. If you can't be out of sight, try to be as inconspicuous as possible. Just a quick squirt directed at the cat's fanny should do it. If you try to squirt him in the face, there's a good chance he'll see you. Also, it's not a good idea to get water in a cat's nose or eyes.

A squirt bottle isn't a good idea if there is fine furniture around or in any area that shouldn't get wet. There you can use a compressed air canister. It's *very* important that you only spray at the cat's fanny and never at his face or near his ears.

If you find your cat on a surface that doesn't have the placemats on it and your squirt bottle or air canister aren't around, just pick him up, say "no" (don't yell or scream, just a firm "no"), and place him on the floor. Don't knock him off the furniture or drop him on the floor. On the other hand, don't pick him up, kiss him, cuddle him, and then place him on the floor. Use your good judgment—I know you have that because you decided to become a cat owner in the first place.

Now comes the *redirection* part of the training. Cats like elevated places, so provide an alternative such as a cat tree. My cats aren't allowed on the counters but there's a cat tree for them in the kitchen by the window. They get to be up high and I don't have to explain to my guests why there's cat hair in the cheese dip.

Biting and Scratching During Play

I can usually identify the owner of a new kitten just by looking at his or her hands. Those ten fingers make such convenient and enticing toys when you're trying to get a kitten's attention. However, the message the kitten receives is that biting skin is acceptable. You won't like that very much as your cute little kitten grows.

From the very beginning, use the interactive toys for playtime so there's never any confusion. As with all the other aspects of training, consistency is important. If one family member lets the kitten bite, then he'll never be trained.

What to do if your kitten accidentally bites you during play: If his teeth are still in contact with your hand, don't pull away. This is important because if you do pull away from him, he'll instinctively bite down harder. He's responding to the movement of prey. Just freeze. At the same time, make a distracting noise with your other hand, such as hitting the table, slapping the floor, etc. He'll be startled and will let go, without associating the scary noise with you. If he doesn't let go of your fingers, *gently* push *toward* him which will automatically release you from his grasp. It will also confuse him momentarily. Prey never willingly heads toward the predator, so he'll relax his mouth, loosening his grip. After you've gotten out of his grasp, get an interactive toy so he can redirect his playful biting toward an appropriate target.

The same approach should be used if the kitten accidentally scratches you in play.

Never punish, hit, or scold your kitten for play biting. The best way for him to learn is to redirect the behavior toward a toy. Don't ever break the "no biting" rule no matter what. If you're in bed wiggling your fingers under the sheet to entice your kitten and he bites you, you'll have set the training process back several steps.

Charging the Door

Whether or not your cat is allowed outdoors, you certainly don't want him charging past you as you're opening the door.

You should never greet or pet your cat at the front door (or whatever door you enter and exit from). If you call to your kitty the moment you walk in the door, he may begin to wait there as the time of your arrival grows closer. The sound of your key in the lock could be his cue and give him time to slip through as you open the door. Instead of greeting your cat right at the door, walk over to a spot a few feet inside the entrance and make that the official greeting area. Ignore him until you get to that spot. If you do this repeatedly, he'll begin to wait for you closer to that inside spot than at the door.

To prevent your cat from running out the door when you're trying to *leave* the house, say your good-bye to him in a specific spot (such as at his cat tree). You could place a treat-filled activity toy there as you are going so he'll have something to occupy himself with. If your cat isn't food-motivated, as you're going out, toss a toy away from the door. When I was training Albie, I'd roll a Ping-Pong ball into the kitchen. He found the sound irresistible and would have to investigate. I lived in an apartment in New York at the time and I could still hear him batting the ball around the kitchen as I waited for the elevator at the far end of the corridor. My neighbors never complained, but I'll bet they weren't too upset when I moved away.

If all redirection methods fail and your cat keeps charging the door, have someone stand outside the door and open it just a little (not enough for your cat to squeeze through). If the cat goes to the door, the person is to try squirting him with water or using the can of compressed air (remember: NEVER in the cat's face—in this case, since the cat will be facing forward, aim for the chest or the front legs) to startle him. It's important that the cat not see the person. You want him to think that the door itself is responsible for this awful experience.

Begging Is Not an Attractive Quality in a Feline

I'm a pretty easygoing person, but I do have a few absolutely unbreakable rules in our house. No pets are to be fed from the table—ever. When I'm invited to a friend's home for dinner, I find it extremely distracting to eat while their dog stares at me, forming little puddles of drool on the floor in front of him. I also don't appreciate it when the cat jumps on the table or claws at my leg.

Feeding your cat from the table often upsets his nutritional balance, creates a finicky eater, contributes to obesity, and poses a health risk because many of the foods we eat are too rich and spicy for cats.

If your cat begins the behavior of begging, give him an activity toy or schedule his meal for when you eat yours.

If all else fails, keep your squirt bottle on the table with you but once again, remember that you have to be sneaky about it so he doesn't associate it with you.

Aggression

It's a scary subject. You don't want to think about the possibility that your sweet little kitty could turn into a snarling, biting, scratching attack cat, but to ignore warning signs could be disastrous for both you and your cat.

A cat who acts aggressively isn't being mean or defiant or taking pleasure in watching you recoil in fear. A cat acts aggressively because he feels he has no other choice. By your understanding more about what can trigger aggression and the different kinds of aggression, you can in many cases, avoid it from ever surfacing.

In the wild, aggression is a crucial part of a cat's survival. It enables him to catch prey, defend territory, mate, protect family, and keep himself alive.

With your cat, very often there will be warning signs leading up to aggression (such as low volume growling, skin twitching, tail lashing, and paw smacks with sheathed claws). Some cats give several signs, some give only a brief one, and there are some cats who give no warning whatsoever that an attack is about to come out of the blue. If you find yourself in a situation where your cat is suddenly and unexpectedly being aggressive, the best thing to do is leave him alone. Any attempt to touch, pet, comfort, or restrain him will only heighten his panic and get you injured. And since aggression is a behavior which can have serious consequences, consult your vet to make sure the problem isn't medical and also in case he or she feels you need to be referred to an animal behaviorist.

The following are some forms of aggression seen in cats:

AGGRESSION DURING PLAY

Your unsuspecting ankles are usually the victims of this. You walk by the bed, and suddenly your feet are ambushed by a set of teeth and razor-sharp claws. It's a hit-and-run attack, though, because he's gone in a flash, racing out of the room and down the hall.

This type of aggression is the result of a cat who isn't getting enough playtime, so he has to go for whatever moving targets he can find. Your feet are usually the most tempting.

To correct this behavior, use interactive toys and play with your kitty at least two or three times a day for a minimum of fifteen minutes each. You'll help him get all that energy out and also be teaching him what are acceptable objects to bite (the toys) and what aren't (your feet). Rotate his regular toys as well to prevent boredom.

Remember to never let your cat bite your fingers in play. If you allow your fingers to be toys, then he'll assume that approval applies to toes as well.

FEAR AGGRESSION

This is a cat who needs to be left alone. A cat who is terrified isn't thinking clearly and will view any attempts at comfort as a threat.

A cat displaying fear aggression will be crouched low to the ground, pupils dilated and ears flattened. He'll very likely be hissing and growling. His body is usually facing sideways, but his head and front paws often face his attacker. This position says that his body and hind feet are ready to get the heck out of Dodge but his head and front paws are ready to defend himself. Fear aggression is a conflicting emotion for a cat, because he doesn't want to be where he is but he'll fight if necessary.

Fear aggression is a behavior many veterinarians see when cats are brought into their clinics. This may be the only time an owner ever sees their cat behaving so frighteningly.

If your cat is showing this behavior, leave him alone. If you're at home, leave the room and let him calm down. If you know the source of his fear and can remove it, do so quickly and calmly. Then leave your cat alone and don't attempt to interact with him until he resumes normal activity such as eating dinner, using the litter box, soliciting attention from you. If your cat is injured and showing fear aggression, transport him safely to the vet (see chapter 18).

If your cat has a tendency to show fear aggression at the vet, be sure to transport him in a carrier. He may be calm on the way there, but he may become impossible to hold once you walk through the door. If your cat is too aggressive for you to handle while at the vet, let the doctor and staff handle him.

For a cat who shows fear aggression on a regular basis, consult your veterinarian. There are anti-anxiety drugs available, but that's not a route to take lightly. You must talk with your vet who may then refer you to a behaviorist.

PETTING-INDUCED AGGRESSION OR OVERSTIMULATION

It seems to come out of the blue. Your cat is lounging on your lap enjoying how your hand lovingly strokes his back. Then suddenly, seemingly without warning, he turns his head and sinks his teeth into you or wraps his paws around your hand with claws unsheathed. Let's look back at what happened. Your cat was relaxing on your lap and you were petting him. It seems innocent enough. Then, from your point of view, he suddenly attacked without warning. That's where the communication breakdown occurred, because he more than likely did give you advanced warning that he had had enough. The signs that an owner often misses include tail lashing or thumping, skin twitching, or a shifting of body position. Sometimes the cat looks back at you several times, trying to figure out why you're not getting the message. By the time he whips around and scratches or bites, overstimulation has reached a breaking point. Remember, cats in the wild aren't close-contact animals. Some have low thresholds for how much touch they can tolerate before pleasure turns to discomfort.

Be more aware of your cat's body language so you can tell if he's approaching overstimulation. If his tail begins to thump the ground or lashes back and forth, stop petting *immediately*. The same goes for the other warning signs as well. Let him just stay where he is and calm back down.

The best thing to do as an owner is to never even reach the warning phase again. If you know that your cat starts getting uncomfortable after five minutes of petting, stop after three minutes. By stopping before he begins to feel uncomfortable, you both will enjoy this interaction better and he won't begin to associate your hands with something unpleasant. You certainly don't want your cat believing that the only way to stop you from petting him is by inflicting injury on you.

If your cat has no tolerance for so much as one little stroke down the back, be content to just let him sit on your lap or on the couch next to you. Build trust by not attempting to pet him. In time, you can hold your hand out and scratch him under the chin or on the back of the head. These two spots tend to be the most comfortable for cats. Some cats don't like having their back stroked. Pay attention to your cat's cues. I have one cat who adores being petted on the head, under the chin and around her shoulders. She doesn't like long strokes down the back so I avoid that totally. She let me know what she preferred and I paid attention. As a result, she has never had to worry that I might break the rules.

Rubbing a cat's belly is another common mistake owners make when petting their cat. Rubbing this most vulnerable area sends him into a defensive response where he'll go on his back, exposing all four sets of claws. A cat who exposes his belly isn't showing submission. If you test this theory, you will always lose.

REDIRECTED AGGRESSION

Your cat is peacefully looking out the window when suddenly a strange cat appears in the yard. You walk over to see what the fuss is about and as soon as you get close to your cat, he lashes out and attacks you. You weren't the intended target of his aggression but in such an excited state, he vents on the nearest victim when unable to get to the primary cause.

Leave your cat alone until he has calmed down. Block your cat's access to that window for a while (even if it means taping cardboard over the bottom half of the window). Do your best to keep unfamiliar cats out of the yard.

In a multicat household, one cat can be the victim of another cat's redirected aggression. Instead of you walking over to your agitated cat, his companion cat comes by. BAM! The poor cat is struck without warning. Now the two friends are engaged in a fight. Then for the rest of the day they avoid each other, only entering the same room at mealtime and even then there's hissing and growling.

Unfortunately, redirected aggression can put the whole relationship at risk long after the intruder is gone. The innocent victim cat starts acting tentative or defensive in the presence of the cat who attacked him. That keeps the aggressive cat in an agitated state. They no longer trust each other. The best thing to do is to separate the cats as soon as possible after a redirected aggression episode. Keep them in separate rooms for the rest of the day. If they don't see each other, they stand a better chance of calming down and not associating this episode with each other. After they've been apart and calm, give treats, conduct low-intensity, stress-relieving individual play sessions with each kitty. By the following day when you reintroduce them to each other, in most cases the episode will have been forgotten.

If redirected aggression has caused an ongoing feud in your multicat household, separate your cats and start from scratch. Keep them apart for several days and slowly do a re-introduction, almost as if you were introducing two new cats (see chapter 11).

TERRITORIAL AGGRESSION
Since a cat is not a pack animal, territorial aggression is crucial in the wild. Your indoor cat can display that same behavior if he feels his territory is being threatened.

Turf wars can even occur within your home between companion cats. Indoor territorial disputes can occur over the one large area of your entire house or they can be broken down into many smaller areas within the home. For instance, cats may feud over territorial rights to the owner's bed. Choice spots by a sunny window, a comfy chair, the litter box, or food bowl can also be continually in negotiation.

If there is a territorial battle going on in your household, try to create some breathing room in the disputed areas. For instance, make sure there's more than one litter box so the cats don't have to come face-to-face with each other at such a vulnerable time. Each cat should have his own food bowl and, if one cat is bullying another during meals, feed them in separate rooms.

Use interactive playtime to help dissolve built-up tension and spray Feliway in the environment. Be observant of your cats' body language and the times of day or areas of the house that cause territorial rumbles.

When you see trouble is brewing beneath the surface, distract the aggressor. You see one cat is sleeping in a chair; the other cat is walking over to knock him out of there. Redirect the aggressive cat with an interactive toy. The predator in him will be aroused. If you divert his attention before he actually gets to the sleeping cat, you can lure him away with the toy. If your timing is right, the more times you do this, the quicker that *seek-and-attack* pattern between the two cats will fade.

When the two cats are in a room together and begin staring each other down, distract them with something positive. Throw a few treats in various directions (so that the cats don't collide as they go for the food) or use an interactive toy. By using something positive instead of reprimanding the cats, they'll begin to associate each other with more positive things.

MEALTIME AGGRESSION

In a multicat household, one cat may aggressively dominate the food bowl or run another cat out of the kitchen. If you feed on a schedule, each cat should have their own bowls. Don't use double bowls because it forces the cats to be uncomfortably close to each other. If necessary, feed them in opposite corners of the kitchen or even in separate rooms. Each cat should be able to eat without feeling threatened.

If mealtime aggression continues to be a problem, consider switching to free-choice feeding and provide more than one feeding station.

PAIN-INDUCED AGGRESSION

If you inflict pain on an animal, common sense will tell you that the animal is going to defend himself to get you to stop. It's another reason why physical punishment only worsens the situation you're trying to correct.

This aggression may also be seen if you groom your cat and cause pain (such as yanking on a mat). A cat's body is very sensitive and if you cause pain, he's going to react. For grooming tips, refer to chapter 12.

Another common cause of pain-induced aggression is when a cat has an abscess forming due to a cat fight and the owner is unaware of it. When you pet your cat and you touch that extremely painful area of his body, he may lash out at you. If a cat who normally enjoys petting and handling suddenly reacts violently to it, run—don't walk—to the vet because there's a good chance he may have an abscess or other injury.

PREDATORY AGGRESSION

This is *not* bad behavior, despite an owner's squeamishness or love of nature. He's a cat. Cats are predators. If there's prey in the vicinity, any predator worth his salt is going to hunt. The only way to prevent your cat from bringing home dead mice, chipmunks, or birds is not to let him outdoors.

AGGRESSION DUE TO
IMPROPER HANDLING OR ABUSE

This one's a no-brainer. A cat who has been abused or roughly handled has every right in the world to protect himself. The only problem is when you adopt a cat who has been abused, how do you convince him to trust you? Very slowly. He needs to feel as if he has control over his life again. Let your cat determine how close he wants to get to you. Hand-feed him and conduct interactive play sessions and when he initiates contact, let him see that you can be trusted. As much as you may want to scoop him up in your arms, cuddle him and show how much he's loved, he's not ready yet. Trust comes slowly. Once you've earned it, don't ever give him reason to regret believing you.

UNPROVOKED AGGRESSION

If your cat becomes aggressive for absolutely no reason at all that you can figure out, have him examined by the vet. There may be an underlying medical cause.

If he gets a clean bill of health, re-examine his environment to be sure you haven't missed any telltale signs. It could be redirected aggression.

WHEN YOU NEED OUTSIDE HELP

Chances are you'll never have to deal with a cat who goes over the edge with aggression for unknown reasons, but if you do, get the help of a professional. Unless you're prepared to handle the problem of an aggressive cat and know what you're doing, attempting to solve this behavior on your own can result in serious consequences.

Don't battle with your cat, don't try to bully him and—for goodness' sake—don't resign yourself to living in fear of your own pet. Start by consulting with your vet. When all medical causes have been ruled out, your vet can refer you to a behavior specialist he or she is familiar with. If your local vet isn't familiar with a behaviorist, contact the nearest veterinary university for a referral.

Almost all of the cases of aggression that I'm called in for have been triggered by something that I'm able to pinpoint. The owner may not be able to see it, but based on the environment, the circumstances, and the history I get from owners, I can very often explain the cause of the cat's aggression. If you're able to work with a behaviorist, he or she can hopefully diagnose the cause of the problem and customize the modification plan that your particular cat needs.

DRUG THERAPY FOR BEHAVIOR PROBLEMS

We are fortunate to have available today several effective drugs for use in behavior modification. Far superior to the drugs used years ago to treat behavior disorders, these medications have fewer side effects and many can be used long-term if necessary. If your impression of a medicated cat is one who sleeps all day or walks around in a daze, you haven't been keeping up with veterinary medicine.

That said, I caution you that drug therapy is not magic and won't make the problem suddenly disappear. It's to be used in combination with behavior modification and under the close supervision of your vet and your behaviorist.

SHOULD YOU EVER EUTHANIZE
AN AGGRESSIVE CAT?

As a behaviorist, I'm often the last call right before the cat makes that trip to Death Row. Many cats are put to death for behavior problems that could have been solved. Don't be in a hurry to give up on your cat. He's a member of the family and deserves every chance. So many of the owners I've worked with now have their relationship with their cats back on track—cats who were one phone call away from death.

In the many years I've been doing this, I have come across a couple of cats who did end up having to be euthanized due to severe aggression (the cause in those cases was due to untreatable medical conditions). It's not a decision to be rushed into. Your cat's life depends on your sound judgment. Make an appointment with your vet, sit down, and have an honest discussion about what options are available.

Turning an Outdoor Cat into an Indoor Cat

Whether you've moved to a busier street, your cat's getting old, the weather's getting bad, or you just don't want to risk outdoor dangers, you'll have to help your cat go through a lifestyle change. While you may be sitting there shaking your head, imagining this to be a difficult task, it's really easier than you think—if you can *think like a cat.*

The first thing to do is look around and re-evaluate the environment. Go through your house and try to view it from your cat's perspective. Since he's now going to lose access to all the fun things such as catching prey, watching insects, scratching trees, and lounging in the sun, what will he get in return? Will his indoor environment be as stimulating as the outdoors? With your help, it can be.

Outdoors, he had access to the best places to scratch, courtesy of Mother Nature. What will he have indoors? Provide him with a tall, sturdy, rough-textured post that will meet both his scratching and stretching needs (see chapter 9). If you've noticed the types of surfaces he has scratched on when outside, you can duplicate that with his indoor post. For instance, did he prefer the bark of the tree or the bare wooden railing of your backyard deck?

Give your cat an indoor version of a tree to climb by purchasing a multi-tiered cat tree. If, unlike me, you're handy, you can even make one for your cat. Depending on how much room you have and how unlimited your budget, you can create a feline jungle gym. You don't have to get fancy though, a simple two-post tree with a perch on top of each post will do. One post should be higher than the other to allow a less agile cat to climb to the top. The trees in my house have bare wood posts and rope-wrapped posts to accommodate the different scratching preferences of each cat. Put the tree by a sunny window and your cat will not only be able to watch the birds, he can curl up and take a nap.

Unlimited prey (or at least potential prey for the less than top-notch hunter) and the other temptations of a dynamic environment can make your newly indoor cat feel as if he has just been sentenced to Kitty Alcatraz. A regular schedule of interactive playtime will not only provide exercise and fun, but thwart undesirable, destructive behavior. A cat who is used to being active all day won't instantly take to daintily sitting by the window hour after hour.

If your cat was used to being let out at specific times of the day, he's not going to understand why you've suddenly stopped playing by the rules. He may stand by the door, staring at the door knob as if willing it to open. If the subtle reminders don't rouse you, he'll probably follow you around, meowing at regular intervals in an attempt to snap you back to reality. Finally, he may just give up on you totally and decide to break out of jail on his own. Digging at the carpet and scratching at the door are the most common escape plans. The very clever cat may act as if he has given up the fight, resigned to being an indoor pet, but in reality, he's planning to make a mad dash the minute someone opens the door. To keep your home from sustaining damage and you from going nuts, you'll need to incorporate *redirection* techniques to lure kitty away from the door. See section in this chapter titled "Charging the Door."

Use activity toys to keep your cat busy while you're at work or unable to engage in an interactive session. Cats who were used to the changing environment of the outdoors will appreciate coming across an unexpected treat-filled activity toy as well as an open paper bag or box to play in.

If your cat was never trained to a litter box because he'd take care of all his personal duties outdoors, keep him confined to a small area until you're sure he has mastered his litter box lessons. Use an uncovered box with unscented litter. The soft, scoopable litter will probably be better than regular clay, because its texture will more closely resemble the soil or sand he's used to.

8
Litter Box Survival Guide

Everything You Need to Know from Setup to Troubleshooting

There is no subject more misunderstood by cat owners than the litter box. When kitty faithfully uses it, all is peaceful in the house. Should kitty begin rejecting his box, though, life in the household is dramatically turned upside down. Tension runs high, punishment is often inflicted, and in many instances, the cat is given away to a shelter and/or euthanized. A once loving cat/owner relationship transforms into a stressful day-to-day battle which nobody wins.

You'll never "win" if you think of it as a battle—what it takes is understanding the litter box from his point of view and the role it plays in your cat's life. If the thought has ever entered your head that your cat wasn't using the litter box deliberately to spite you, then you haven't been looking at it through his eyes. Stop thinking like an owner. If you thought it was just a plastic box filled with litter that you stick in the corner of the laundry room, you're underestimating the power that it has over your cat's emotions.

By knowing how to set up the best box in the correct location, provide proper maintenance, and how to understand signals that your cat may be relaying regarding it, you stand a good chance of avoiding future problems.

There are no secret tricks. Owners keep trying to find ways to prevent litter box odor from permeating the house and unfortunately they fall victim to quick-fix temporary solutions. Wrong. The best and only way to reduce litter box odor is to keep it clean.

One of the things we find so appealing about cats is the fact that they do use a litter box, but many owners don't understand the origins of this basic instinct. The cat's behavior of burying his waste is based on a need far more important than his owner's convenience. *Survival* is the motivation behind the ritual of burying waste. A cat's urine is very concentrated and has a strong odor, which in the wild can be detected by predators. In the wild, cats urinate and defecate away from their nest and cover the waste so they don't attract any predators back to their young. For safety, cats don't eliminate where they eat, sleep, play, or raise young. Your indoor cat has those same instincts.

Which Litter Box?

I find it amazing how complex and elaborate some litter boxes have become. I'm sure you've seen the ads on TV and in magazines for boxes that are sifted and cleaned simply by rolling them over, or better yet, boxes that even clean themselves electronically. Manufacturers continue to knock themselves out trying to come up with a litter box so maintenance-free that an owner will hardly know it's there. The problems I have with those are: 1) If owners don't need to maintain the boxes as often, they also won't be *monitoring* their cats' litter habits as well. For example, if you aren't checking and sifting the box every day, you may be unaware that your cat has diarrhea. 2) Also, it has been my experience through the years that the more complicated the litter box setup is, the less likely the cat will use it faithfully.

A simple, basic box is all you need. As you stand in the store aisle staring at the dozens of boxes, consider your cat's age, size, and health. If you have a tiny kitten, you wouldn't want to start out with a jumbo box that might be too high-sided for him to climb into. You may need to purchase a small box initially and then switch to a larger one as your cat grows. On the other hand, if you have a rather large cat, the litter box needs to be of an adequate size for him to move around comfortably.

The basic litter box is a rectangular plastic pan. It comes in sizes from a small cage-sized box to a jumbo multicat model. I find that owners commonly make the mistake of buying too small of a box in order to have it fit in a corner somewhere. Look at the size of your cat and pick a box that would give him enough room to eliminate in a couple of areas and still have enough clean spots to stand on. As a general guideline, the length of the box should be double the length of an adult cat and the width of the box should be the cat's approximate length. If you have more than one cat and they vary greatly in size, base your measurement on the largest cat. It's a major part of your cat's life, so don't skimp on size just so it'll fit under the vanity. Keep your cat's needs in mind when litter box shopping. After looking through the displays at pet supply stores, if you still don't see one that fits your cat's needs, for instance, if he sprays urine over the sides of an ordinary box, go to the discount store and check out the plastic storage containers. They come in many sizes and you'll probably discover one that's perfect because the higher sides of the storage box may just do the trick.

Gee, Pam, why not just get a covered box? Good question.

COVERED BOXES

Covered boxes have two functions: to contain the smell, and to prevent urine and litter from being scattered into the room. In theory, that sounds very appealing and practical. The problem is—it appeals to you, not the cat. A covered box really *does* contain the smell—keeping it trapped inside so that your cat must endure that concentrated odor each time he enters. The cover on the box also reduces the amount of air circulating so the litter takes longer to dry, creating a perfect environment for odor.

A covered box can also create discomfort for a cat when he attempts to enter. A tall cat may feel cramped as he tries to find a comfortable position. A cat who barely squats for elimination will not like having to duck his head to avoid touching the ceiling of the box. If you're considering a covered box to reduce litter scatter or urine spray, you will do just as well to get a taller open box instead. The effect is the same, and your cat will be more comfortable.

LITTER

If you thought that there were many varieties of litter boxes, wait until you start shopping for litter. The choice can be overwhelming for a new owner. Heck, it's overwhelming for seasoned owners. So imagine how confusing it can be for a cat.

Every one of the many types of litters on the market claim to have the solution to a cat owner's ultimate quest: *odor control.* You will find litters made of clay and box after box of scoopable litters. You can even find reusable plastic litter as well as ones made of wheat, sawdust, newspaper pellets, and corn cobs. There are so many options out there. The choice depends on what matters most to you.

Some litters tout their virtually dust-free properties. Others highlight their super-strong clumping ability. Which should you choose? What's a cat owner to do? Here are the fundamentals. The first decision to make is whether you want scoopable or regular litter. Clay litter is the most basic. It was the first commercial litter, introduced by Edward Lowe, back when owners were just using ordinary sand. Clay litter is absorbable and economical. Scoopable litter is sandlike in texture. When it becomes wet, it clumps into a ball. This makes it easy for you to scoop out the urine ball, leaving the rest of the litter dry and odor free.

When you choose a litter, go for unscented. The scented kinds that smell so wonderful to us are often too perfumed for a cat's nose. He wants to be able to identify some of his own scent in the litter and the heavy perfume can actually drive him away. If you regularly scoop out the wastes, you'll have an odor-free box without all the extra perfume.

Basically, from a cat's point of view, litter should meet three requirements: 1) It has to be a substrate (base material) that he won't mind standing on; 2) it has to be loose enough for him to dig a hole and cover afterward; and 3) it shouldn't have an odor.

If you have just adopted or purchased a new kitten or cat, it's best to start out using whatever the previous owner or breeder used. Then, if you decide to switch kinds, you can do it gradually, so the cat won't reject it.

My philosophy on litter is to start out by sticking to what a cat would naturally seek out in the wild (with a few modifications, of course). Regular clay litter, the old standby for years and years, is an absorbent substrate. Some are very dusty and can raise quite a cloud as the cat digs and scratches. You may even hear a series of sneezes every time he's in there. Pick a litter that creates the least amount of dust. Scoopable litters have a sandlike feel that is soft and very easy for a cat to dig. Many cats seem to prefer that substrate and for some cats who have been declawed, the soft texture can be more comfortable. Scoop-, able litter is efficient for odor control because you can sift through it, scooping out clumps of urine as well as any solid waste.

There has always been somewhat of a controversy surrounding scoopable litter. Some people have had concerns over whether the litter, if ingested by a cat, turns cementlike in the intestines. Veterinarians report no cases of intestinal damage due to ingestion of litter. If you have any questions, discuss this with your vet.

You'll find several variations of scoopable litters. There are low tracking formulas, unscented, super-scented and heavy-duty formulas guaranteeing rock hard clumps that won't fall apart. If you have more than one cat sharing a box, then consider one of the stronger clumping formulas.

There are also numerous alternative litters. If you need a totally dust-free litter, you may prefer newspaper pellets. This clean, dust-free substrate has an ingredient in it that helps control odor as well. Don't use regular shredded newspaper because it's messy and can get very smelly when saturated with urine.

Each cat is individual in his preferences and needs, as is each owner, so if you have a specific situation which means the more commonly used litters don't work, look among the wide variety of alternatives.

DEODORIZERS
I don't care for deodorizing products for the litter. They tend to have a very strong fragrance which can drive a cat away from the box (not quite the effect you wanted).

HOW MUCH LITTER TO USE
An important aspect of odor control is how much litter is in the box. Doing my house calls I've found many owners go to extremes, using either way too much or not nearly enough. If you use too much scoopable litter, it's just a waste and ends up being kicked over the side of the box. Too much clay litter makes the urine spread out and soil more granules than necessary. On the other hand, not using enough litter results in a very smelly box because urine hits the plastic bottom of the box and forms puddles and there are not enough granules to absorb adequately.

A good guideline is to spread about a two-inch layer of litter in the box. This gives your cat enough for digging and covering. In multicat households, you don't need more litter in the box, you need more boxes.

Where to Put the Box

Location, location, location. It applies to real estate, it applies to opening a restaurant, and it most definitely applies to litter boxes. *Where* you put the litter box is more important than many owners realize. You can have the perfect box, filled with the best litter in the world, but if it's put in an area that the cat finds unacceptable, it may be rejected.

There is one rule that cat owners should never ever break under any circumstances: Don't put the litter box near the cat's food and water. Many owners mistakenly believe that having the box right next to the cat's food will serve as a reminder to him. Unfortunately, this plan can only backfire and you lay the groundwork for litter box rejection. Remember, cats eliminate *away* from the nest. Putting his food and box together sends him a very confusing message. He'll be forced to make a decision about whether to designate the area as a feeding area or an elimination spot. Since the food is only available in that one area, he'll have to search for another location for his litter box needs. If you have no choice but to keep his food bowl and litter box in the same room, at least put them as far apart as possible.

The most common place owners put the box is in the bathroom. This is a great spot provided you have the room. It makes cleanup easier and it's convenient for you to check regularly.

Another popular location is the laundry room. Like the bathroom, the laundry room is usually not carpeted, making for easy cleanup. The downside is that the sudden noise of the washer going into the spin cycle while the cat's in the box can cause him to become frightened of using it again.

Pick a spot in your home that isn't in the center of traffic to provide your cat with a feeling of privacy and safety. On the other hand, don't choose too remote an area or you'll forget to check it daily. I saw one owner who put the box in the "junk" room on the second floor of the house. No one routinely went in there, so the box got forgotten until the cat began urinating on the carpet in the den. The box had become so full and dirty that the cat couldn't stand to use it any longer. Wherever you locate the box, be sure you'll remember to check it twice a day.

A two-story home should have a box on each floor. If your indoor/outdoor cat doesn't use a litter box and prefers to eliminate outside, keep a litter box indoors anyway in case he chooses not to go out in bad weather or becomes ill.

In multicat households, more than one box will be needed. This is not just because one box gets dirty too quickly (although it does), but also because some cats object to sharing.

Multicat households can create litter box placement problems. If there are any territorial disputes going on or if your cats don't especially care for each other, the boxes should be placed far enough apart so that if one is being guarded, there is easy access to another.

There is another potential problem to consider when setting up a litter box for multicat households in which there is some feline animosity. A litter box wedged in a corner can make a cat feel trapped. If a cat thinks he doesn't have enough avenues of escape and fears being attacked, he could reject his box. This problem is covered more specifically later in this chapter.

Cleaning the Litter Box

You will need a slotted scoop or shovel to sift through the litter for solid waste. It will also enable you to separate the soiled urine clumps from the dry scoopable litter.

If you use non-scoopable litter, you'll also want to use a slotted shovel to remove any solid waste. A long-handled unslotted spoon is good for removing mounds of wet litter. Saturated litter left sitting in the box is what will create an odor. Don't stir the wet litter around too much or you'll just end up spreading it all over the box.

Keep the spoon and scoop in a container by the litter box for convenience. Scooping and sifting should be done at least twice a day. It only takes seconds and will make a significant difference in odor control. Scoopable litter will be worth nothing if your cat has to climb over old clumps from days ago in order to find one corner of unsoiled substrate.

Some scoopable litters, especially the heavy-duty formulas, aren't flushable, and clay litter should never be flushed down the toilet. The most convenient method I've come up with for disposal of soiled litter clumps is to keep a small plastic storage container lined with a plastic grocery bag right next to the box. I scoop first thing in the morning and deposit all of the clumps into the container, and tightly snapping the lid I keep the contents there until after I've done my evening's scooping. Then, I close up the plastic bag and dispose of it in the outside trash can. It doesn't matter what method you come up with, just make sure it's convenient enough so that no one in the family will have an excuse for letting litter box maintenance slide. And remember, always wash your hands after scooping out the litter box.

Scooping twice daily will not only keep the litter box clean but it will alert you to potential health problems. Routine scooping will help you become familiar with your cat's litter box habits. I know it doesn't sound like a thrilling job, but it can mean the difference between a happy, pain-free cat or one who has to endure a painful medical condition because it has gone undetected by his owner. You'll soon be familiar with your cat's habits: how often he goes, his daily urine output, the formation and consistency of his stool. Should any of that change, you'll be aware of it right away and be able to get prompt medical care.

In addition to daily scooping, the box itself will also need routine cleaning. If you use regular clay litter or one of the other nonscoopable varieties, you should do a thorough cleaning at least once a week. This involves disposing of the litter, then scrubbing the box and all related utensils. If you use scoopable litter, you can go longer than one week between cleanings. Don't be fooled by the ads for scoopable litter claiming that because the waste is being sifted out you'll never have to scrub the box. Not true. Urine will still come in contact with the plastic.

When you clean the box, don't use harsh cleansers that can leave a smell, I use bleach that I've diluted with water. Then I rinse the box until there's no trace of the bleach scent. I also scrub all of the utensils and their plastic container. Then everything gets thoroughly dried before the box is refilled with fresh litter.

Are Plastic Liners a Good Idea?

The idea of a plastic liner in the litter box seems wonderful. In reality though the animals who step into the box have *claws* so the liners can end up being more of a nuisance than a help. When you lift up the liner to throw it away, you may find litter escaping from the holes in the bottom of the plastic where your cat has scratched. Plastic liners can also make litter box odor worse because urine can pool in creases and folds, and urine that leaks through any tears or holes will sit on the bottom and become very smelly.

Your objective is to make the litter box as inviting and comfortable as possible for your cat, so you certainly don't want him struggling to dig or cover because his claws keep catching on the liner.

Introducing Your Cat to the Litter Box

The first step is to make sure your cat knows where the box is. Confine your kitten to a small area until he's using the box successfully and is comfortable with his new surroundings. If he doesn't get the idea, then after he has eaten, place him in the box and scratch a little in the litter with your finger. Don't force him to stay in the litter box, though.

If you're planning to use a covered box, don't put the cover on during this orientation process. You want to make the learning process as easy as possible. And, while you're waiting for your cat to get used to his new box, go back and reread the section in this chapter on covered boxes so you'll fully understand why they're not good.

If your cat doesn't appear to grasp the concept of the litter box and he urinates or defecates on the floor, collect it as best as you can and deposit it in the box. The scent of his own waste should direct him there next time.

Litter Box Rejection

It's high noon. The place is deserted. A few hair balls roll around lazily. There's an eery ghost town stillness in the air. The only sound is the

---

Litter Box Checklist

- the right size box
- proper location (not near food)
- unscented litter
- heavy-duty slotted litter scoop
- large unslotted spoon to collect wet litter (for clay litter users)
- washable container to hold litter scoops
- washable container with lid to collect soiled clumps
- plastic bags
- small broom and dust pan or small vacuum (to control litter scatter)
- bleach and appropriate container to use for diluting with water
- scrub brush or sponge designated for litter box cleaning
- enzyme cleaner (for accidents)
- air purifier to help cut down on litter dust (optional)

---

lonely echo of your footsteps as you enter the room. It all looks innocent enough but you know that somewhere in this room *that thing* awaits. Suddenly you see it in the corner, covered in dust. The cobwebs laced over it glisten in the sun. It is *the litter box* that your cat refuses to use.

"He's doing it out of spite!" "He knows he's being bad!" "He's too lazy to go to his litter box!" "My cat is so stupid, he pees on the carpet!" This is a small sample of the sorts of things I hear on my answering service. While I certainly can understand an owner's sense of frustration, none of the above quotes are at all true about cats. It's only when you stop interpreting your cat's behavior as mean, spiteful, stupid, deliberate, or lazy, that you stand a chance of correcting the problem.

Understanding what type of behavior your cat is displaying is crucial. *Indiscriminate urination* is usually done on a horizontal surface such as the floor, carpet, or in a tub. *Spraying* is usually done against a vertical surface, such as a wall, furniture, or drapes. There are a number of cats, though, who do spray horizontal surfaces, such as clothes or shoes on the floor. You must first identify whether your cat is indiscriminately urinating or spraying. A cat may also defecate outside of the litter box, which we will discuss later in this chapter.

If your cat is spraying and he hasn't been neutered, now would be a good time to make an appointment for the surgery. A male cat reaches sexual maturity at about seven months of age, and spraying can begin at that time. Neutering will eliminate the spraying behavior in almost all cases.

MARKING HIS TURF

If your cat has already been neutered and is spraying, there's a good chance he's feeling that his territory is in danger. Many things can prompt a cat to mark his turf, such as the appearance outside of another cat or the arrival of new cat into the household. If a turf war is being waged in your home, the cats should be separated and individual behavior modification begun (covered in this chapter). Then the cats can gradually be reintroduced. You can do this the same way you'd introduce cats for the first time. For specific instructions, refer to chapter 11.

The key to correcting spraying behavior is to find the *cause* of the cat's fear and either remove it or modify it.

The first step you should take if your cat stops using the litter box is to call your veterinarian. Indiscriminate urination is a common sign of a medical condition known as *lower urinary tract disease* (LUTD). It's not unusual for a cat suffering from LUTD to make frequent trips to the box but only be able to void small amounts of urine. As the condition worsens, the irritated bladder makes the cat feel the urgent need to urinate wherever he happens to be in order to relieve the discomfort. Sometimes a cat begins to associate the pain he feels upon urination with the

Potential Reasons for a Cat to Spray

- sexual maturity
- temperament of the cat
- the appearance of a strange cat in the yard
- the addition of a new pet or family member into household
- scent of unfamiliar cat on owner's clothing or shoes
- tension or aggression between companion pets
- number of cats in the home
- renovation or remodeling
- move to a new home
- unfamiliar visitors
- change in owner's schedule

Potential Reasons for Inappropriate Elimination

- medical condition
- dirty litter box
- covered or inappropriately sized litter box
- unacceptable litter substrate
- abrupt change in litter or litter box location
- unacceptable litter box location
- aversion to scent of product used to clean litter box
- anxiety/fear
- negative association with litter box
- punishment by owner
- increase in owner's absence from cat
- tension or aggression between companion pets
- inadequate number of boxes for multicat home
- geriatric-related problems

Some Signs of LUTD

- frequent trips to litter box
- voiding little or no urine
- blood in urine
- urinating outside of litter box
- crying while in litter box
- frequent licking of genital area
- little or no appetite
- appearing depressed or irritable

litter box itself. LUTD is very serious and can be fatal if crystals form, blocking the passage of urine through the urethra. Have your cat checked immediately should he stop using the litter box. For more on LUTD, refer to the medical appendix.

There are other medical conditions that could cause your cat to change his litter box habits, such as diabetes or kidney disease. Any change in your cat's litter box habits or food/water consumption should be checked by the veterinarian.

If you have a multicat household, you may have difficulty figuring out which cat is the perpetrator. If there is indiscriminate urination and LUTD could be the cause, don't waste time waiting to catch a cat in the act. If you notice any suspicious signs (see above), take the most likely suspect to the vet. If there's no clear-cut suspect, have all of the cats' urine tested.

If the initial urinalysis comes out clean on every cat, you may have to separate and isolate the cats to determine which one isn't using the litter box. Or you could ask your vet about *fluorescein* (an ophthalmic dye) which can be given orally. This harmless dye will cause the urine to brightly fluoresce so it can be detected using a special light or a urine odor detector light (discussed later in this chapter). After giving the fluorescein to one cat, you then check around the house with the light for the next twenty-four hours. If nothing shows up, give the fluorescein to the next cat a couple of days later, and so on until you discover who is responsible for the behavior.

BEGINNING AT THE SOURCE (THE LITTER BOX)
Take a long, hard, critical look at the litter box. I mean now, this very minute. How does it really look? Have you been keeping it clean? Have

you been sticking to your twice daily scooping and routine cleaning? If you haven't, then chances are the poor conditions of the box are driving your cat to find cleaner, less smelly places. Even if you've been scooping twice daily and routinely cleaning, that might not be enough for your particular cat. For his level of comfort, the box may have to be cleaned more often.

In certain weather when there's increased humidity, the litter box cleaning schedule may have to be adjusted. Also, if you keep the litter box in a bathroom frequently used for showers, that will raise the humidity level and litter will take longer to dry. So if you've been using a covered box and you keep it in the bathroom, remove the cover. Also, keep the bathroom exhaust fan running during showers to reduce humidity.

Check the amount of litter that you're putting in the box. Make sure there is at least a two-inch layer to permit sufficient digging and covering. If you use scoopable litter, you should periodically be refilling the box with clean litter to maintain the level as you remove the soiled clumps.

An abrupt change in litter can be enough to make a cat stop using his box. A cat takes it for granted that when he steps into the box, he'll feel the same texture on his paws and the scent (or lack of scent) will be the same as the last time he was there. A change in litter texture or a drastic change in scent or its intensity can be confusing. If you plan on changing litter brands, do so gradually so your cat has time to adjust. Start by adding a little of the new litter into the box containing the current brand, gradually increasing the amount of new litter while decreasing the old, over the course of five to seven days.

If you feel that your cat may have come to dislike his current brand of litter or maybe dislikes the texture (a couple clues may be that the cat stands with his front legs on the rim of the box, perches on the very edge, or scratches the area outside of the box when covering), you can do a test by placing a second litter box next to his current one. In the second box place a different litter. When I've done such experiments, I've found that if it's a choice between clay or scoopable, cats seem to prefer the soft texture of the latter.

There are a few signs you can look for to see if your cat is maybe uncomfortable with his litter. Warning signs include: putting only two feet in the box and bracing the other two feet on the lip of the box; not digging or covering at all (though not all cats cover their waste);

scratching the floor or carpet just outside of the box instead of the litter; eliminating on the floor or carpet right next to the box. If you catch any of these signs early enough you can make adjustments before it turns into actual litter box rejection.

It's not a good idea to place the litter box on carpet. Some cats mistake the soft feel of carpet for litter. If the box doesn't meet your cat's standards for cleanliness, the carpet will begin to look especially attractive to him. If all floors are carpeted, consider putting a piece of sturdy plastic or linoleum underneath the box. You can use a sheet of hard plastic available at home improvement centers.

There are some cats who, no matter how diligently you clean, won't use the litter box once it has been soiled. If you have this type of cat, put two litter boxes in the room so that he'll always have a clean one should you be unable to scoop up the waste before his return visit. You may also be one of the lucky owners of a cat who refuses to defecate in the same box he uses for urination. Go figure. This one's easy to solve though, just put a second box down for him. Don't place them too close together or else it'll just appear to him to be one big box. His Majesty will designate one of the two boxes for urination and one for his princely poops. It may seem inconvenient to have to clean two boxes, but I'd rather scrub an extra litter box than clean urine out of my carpet.

THE DISAPPEARING LITTER BOX

In an effort to find a location that will meet with the approval of all family members, sometimes the litter box gets moved around too much. This is where planning ahead proves very helpful. Think about the pros and cons of the area you have chosen before you start playing musical litter boxes. The harder you make it for your cat to find the box, the more inviting your oriental carpet will look to him when his bladder is full.

MONITORING A RECENTLY RELOCATED LITTER BOX

I was called in for a consultation because Sparkles, a four-year-old female cat, suddenly refused to use her litter box. The owners also had dogs. The history I received was that the cat had a very outgoing, friendly personality, loved being around the dogs, and up until two

166

months before, when she stopped using her litter box, had been the perfect cat.

Upon further investigation I learned that the box had recently been moved. Originally it had been situated in an unused extra room, but now was in the bathroom because the owners were planning to convert the extra room into an office. For six months, Sparkles had handled the relocation just fine. Then two months earlier she'd begun eliminating in the old location. Why the change in her behavior after six months? Eventually, I learned that during those first six spring/summer months, the dogs had been kept outside, as usual. However, they'd been sleeping indoors now for two months as it got colder.

The dogs had never been allowed in the section of the house where the extra room was located. The owners had installed a baby gate to keep them out. Sparkles however was free to roam anywhere, and had just hopped the gate to get to her box. But the dogs had access to the new litter box location in the central area of the house and they'd discovered the fun game of following Sparkles to the litter box and crowding her while she was trying to conduct her private business. Apparently, since moving indoors, the dogs had been anxiously awaiting the deposit of feces so they could snack on them. No owner wants to believe his or her dog would display this behavior but it is nevertheless, a relatively common one among canines.

I figured it out when the owners told me that they often saw the dogs hanging around the bathroom door. Because all of the pets got along, they never imagined there was a problem. When pressed, neither owner recalled scooping feces out of the box for the last two months. Each just assumed that the other had already cleaned it.

Understandably, Sparkles was upset at the intrusion upon her privacy, so she went back to eliminating in the old area which proved much safer. Perfectly logical.

The solution to the problem was for Sparkles's owners to relocate the box back to the section of the house that was off-limits to the dogs.

If you plan to relocate the litter box, think carefully beforehand about what potential problems and obstacles your cat could encounter in the new place. Then, after you've moved the box, monitor everyone's reactions and behavior to catch any early warning signals (in the case of Sparkles's; owners, noticing the dogs at the bathroom door).

IF YOUR CAT HAS BEEN DECLAWED

The first ten days after declawing surgery are painful for the cat. The wounds on some cats' paws remain sensitive long after the usual healing period. He'll need a special litter in his box while he is healing to keep the wounds clean. Your vet will probably recommend shredded newspaper or a litter made from pelletized newspaper. Pelletized newspaper litter is much more absorbent, and cats accept it better than shredded paper. An excellent brand is Yesterday's News.

Not only the pain can cause the cat to not want to deal with the litter box, the sudden shock of encountering a strange litter can bother any cat. Either circumstance can cause litter box rejection.

If you're set on having your cat declawed (refer to chapter 9 before making that decision), plan ahead and mix a little of the pelletized newspaper in with his regular litter before the surgery. Then, after the ten-day healing period, you can reintroduce his regular litter again. If you were previously using regular clay litter and it now seems to cause discomfort, switch to scoopable litter. Soft, sandlike texture will be gentler to his paws.

NEW HOUSE

The first time I moved to a new house was an overwhelming and traumatic experience for me. I can understand exactly what a cat must feel at such a time. Everything familiar was suddenly gone and I was faced with the task of establishing all sorts of new territory. Because I remembered how it had felt, I planned enough in advance to make transitions much easier for my cats than for me. If only someone had pampered me the way I pampered my cats.

If you've recently moved and your cat has stopped using his litter box, it's probably because of the unfamiliar surroundings. Remember that he's a creature of habit and was used to his comfortable, familiar territory. Initially, the best way to prevent pussycat panic is to set up a small area for him while he gets his bearings.

RENOVATION/NEW FURNITURE/CARPETS

The frightening sounds of renovation and all of the unfamiliar faces of construction workers can be perceived as a threat to a cat's territory and cause him to spray. A cat may also urinate away from the litter box if it's located too close to the noise or if he feels too frightened to venture near it.

The addition of new carpet or even a new piece of furniture can be threatening for some cats. They may feel that it doesn't belong in their territory until it has been sprayed with their scent.

It is imperative to keep a cat as far away from construction noises as possible. If there's a quiet room in your home (preferably not one with new furniture or new carpeting), set him up in there with his litter box. Play some soft music to block out the distant hammering and drilling.

When you bring in a new piece of furniture, rub it down with a towel that you've rubbed your cat with. Keep the piece covered with a sheet or blanket for a day or two if you're concerned that your cat may try to mark. Using a sheet that you've slept on can speed up the acceptance process because the cat will detect your comforting scent. Always do what you can to speed up the process of having any addition of new furniture take on the familiar scent of your home.

THE COMINGS AND GOINGS OF FAMILY

Whether it's the new couch cushions or the new spouse, change is change and cats don't care for it! Even though down the road it will be wonderful, any change in the family status can cause litter box rejection.

A common worry that owners have is how their cat will react to a new baby. The answer is, if you haven't prepared him for the change, he may begin to spray.

A new marriage may be the cause of a lapse in good litter box etiquette especially if your new family includes another cat or even a dog.

Remember to ease your cat through the very confusing changes of any addition to your family. Forethought could make the difference between a smooth, incident-free transition or a full-blown family crisis.

For specific information on cats and their relationships with family members, refer to chapter 11.

PEEPING TOMS (THE FELINE VERSION)

The peaceful sight of your cat looking out the window to watch the birds could turn ugly if he spots another cat in the yard. At best, your cat may perk his ears up and thump his tail. He may even issue a hiss or two. If you're not so lucky, he may view that cat's presence as a territorial threat and become concerned with marking his turf. If your cat is allowed outdoors and he confines his spraying to backyard trees, bushes and the fence post, you're okay. If your *indoor* cat feels threatened enough to spray, then we have a problem. You may notice streaks of urine on the walls under windows. Another common area to spray is around the front door. If your cat saw the uninvited feline on the patio or deck, then there's a good chance that the glass doors or any nearby drapes have been marked.

A cat with a spraying problem may or may not continue to use his box or he may only defecate in the box.

If the unwanted visitor makes frequent appearances, try to find out if he has an owner. If he's a stray, do your best to catch him because he probably isn't vaccinated or neutered and could pose a serious threat to other cats.

Check around the outsides of your doors and windows to be sure the feline stranger hasn't been spraying. Your indoor cat may be picking up on the scent so clean away any urine odor close to the house.

In the meantime, block off your cat's view through any windows from which he might be able to see the outdoor cat. You can use cardboard or anything else that can be securely fastened. You need only cover the bottom half of the window. I know it's going to look strange but I'd rather have cardboard over my windows than cat urine on my walls.

Follow the instructions in this chapter under "The Four-Step Retraining Program."

HOSTILE TAKEOVERS

In a multicat household, if you isolate a new cat in a separate room before integrating him into the cat community, it will help ease litter box disputes. Refer to chapter 11 for more on new cat introductions. Now, what if you've followed all of the correct introduction procedures and you still notice someone not using the litter box? This could happen even if there isn't a new cat in the house. One of your three longtime companion cats might suddenly begin eliminating outside of the box.

By now you know that in a multicat household it's essential to have enough litter boxes. The boxes must: 1) be kept clean and; 2) provide privacy; but also, 3) have escape routes. What? An *escape route* for a *litter box*? Most definitely! Look at it from your cat's point of view. He goes into the litter box, which is probably wedged into the corner of the bathroom. Perhaps it's even a covered box. Let's say the opening to the box faces the side of the tub or a closet door and doesn't look out at the entrance to the bathroom. If another cat comes into the room and approaches the litter (whether it's with trouble on his agenda or just a routine pit stop), the cat inside of the box is taken completely by surprise. He truly is trapped because there's only one way out and his enemy is blocking that route. If the encounter at the litter box is between feuding felines, the fellow trapped inside feels a greater sense of threat. Even an open box, wedged in a corner, may only allow one way out.

It is vital to be sure your cat feels he can escape from the litter box when you are trying to correct indiscriminate urination or spraying problems.

Look at the box from a cat's point of view and adjust it to avoid the possibility of him getting cornered. If the box is covered, remove the top. If it's in a corner, slide it out a little. If there's a more open area in the room, relocate the box there.

Another way to create an escape route is to afford your cat more warning time. Do this by making sure the box gives him a vantage point from which to view the room or entryway. If the litter box occupant can see another cat coming, that may give him a few more seconds' warning—enough time to get out of the line of fire. More than one litter box in different areas of the house is also a must to reduce anxiety. Kitty has an alternative in case one box is being guarded. So, while you may like the fact that the box is so well hidden and out of the way, a cat may feel the location is setting him up for an ambush.

If you have an inappropriate elimination problem in your multicat household, look at the places chosen for urination (or defecation). You may find that targeted areas offer a cat what the litter box can't: *escape*. Perhaps the cat is eliminating behind the chair in the living room. The cat has privacy and cover but the openness of the area allows him to view the room and offers several escape routes should he perceive a threat. I've found that very often, if the targeted spot is in a room with only one entrance, it'll be by the far wall so the cat can have a good view of the doorway.

Pay attention to the route a cat must take to get to the litter box. The journey can be tense and harrowing in a household where there's a turf war. If a more dominant cat stations himself in the long narrow hallway that leads to the litter box, a more submissive cat will want to avoid an encounter.

Within a hostile household you may encounter both spraying and indiscriminate urination. Spraying may be done by the new cat to establish a territorial space of his own, or it may be done by the resident top cat to defend his turf. The more submissive cat may indiscriminately urinate because he's afraid to go to the litter box. Finding out who is displaying the behavior (remember, it could be more than one cat) and just what kind of behavior it is will be crucial to solving the problem.

The Four-Step Retraining Program

Let's start with what *not* to do. Don't punish your cat in any way for eliminating or spraying outside of the litter box. Don't follow the old technique of rubbing his nose in his mess. This method has NEVER worked, is quite cruel, and will actually worsen the behavior. By rubbing his nose in his mess you only manage to communicate that the very act of urination and defecation are bad and he'll be punished every time he goes. He won't make the connection that you're displeased only with his choice of location. He'll assume that whenever he has to eliminate, he'll be punished. This only adds to the anxiety he already feels. For whatever reason, his litter box isn't a comfortable place so he'll soon find more secluded hiding spots to avoid your reprimand. He may also become afraid of you.

The next big *don't* on the list is: Don't hit your cat. Once again, he'll associate the act of elimination with being punished and he'll become afraid of you. Another common but counterproductive retraining method is to grab the cat while he's in the act of spraying and forcibly take him to the litter box. If you think that transporting your cat to the box while he's in the act of elimination or spraying will work, you're sadly mistaken. Trust me, he hasn't forgotten where his box is.

Now, what should you do? First, you want to reduce the appeal of your carpet or furniture as litter box alternatives. Begin with cleaning, odor neutralizing, and setting up deterrents. Cleaning and neutralizing soiled areas is more work than you think. Regular household cleansers may get rid of stains but they only mask the odor. The scent of urine on the carpet or along the baseboard of the wall can trigger the cat to soil that same spot repeatedly. It is vital that you *neutralize* the odor so that your cat's sensitive nose doesn't lead him back there again and again.

I have outlined below, a basic four-step program for retraining your cat back into the litter box. Even if your veterinarian determines that your cat has been urinating because he had LUTD, you may still need to follow the steps listed below. You'll certainly want to clean and neutralize the soiled areas. The cat may even have a negative association with the box from the pain he felt when he was urinating, so you may also need to use behavior modification.

STEP 1: THE CLEANUP

Start by gently blotting up the urine with paper towels. Be careful not to force the liquid deeper into the pile of carpet or the fabric of upholstered furniture. After you have blotted up as much as possible, you can press down to absorb the rest of the moisture. Keep replacing wet towels with dry ones. Next, use a *pet stain and odor neutralizer* on the spot (available at pet supply stores). Choose a stain and odor neutralizer that contains enzymes. These are what will effectively neutralize the smell. Nature's Miracle is the product I've used with my clients' cats. It's non-toxic to cats and won't stain carpet, furniture, floors, walls, and clothing. Always test a small area first, though.

If you're cleaning carpet, leave the enzymatic cleaner down long enough so it can reach all soiled areas. If the urine seeped through to the padding, the enzymatic cleanser needs to soak that far down. Follow the label instructions for how long to let the product sit, then blot with towels until you can't get up any more liquid, then you can set up a small fan to help accelerate drying time.

If you're using an enzymatic cleaner on an area of the carpet that's been sprayed repeatedly, you'll need to dilute the old urine residue before you use the enzyme product. All that built-up urine can be too much for the enzyme to neutralize effectively, so first treat the stain with plain water and blot with paper towels. Now you can treat the area with the enzyme product just as you would a fresh urine stain.

If you're not sure where your cat may have urinated or sprayed, you can use a special light. The Urine Odor Source Locator (by Nature's Miracle) is a black light that when held a few inches away from a surface, will cause urine stains to fluoresce. If you think your cat has hit several locations, the light will be a very worthwhile investment. The Nature's Miracle Urine Odor Source Locator is available in pet supply stores or directly from the manufacturer. Some pet supply stores may even rent the light. Refer to the resource guide.

To clean feces off carpet, slip a plastic sandwich bag over your hand and carefully remove the solid stool. If the stool is well formed, you should be able to lift it off the carpet easily. I don't advise using newspaper to pick it up because you run the risk of pushing it deeper into the rug. If you use a paper towel, be very light handed. Once you've removed the stool, treat the area with an enzymatic cleaner, following the label instructions.

If the stool is very liquid, you can avoid causing more of a stain if you carefully scoop it up from along the top of the carpet with a spoon or thin metal spatula. Diarrhea that is pure liquid should be blotted up with paper towels and the area cleaned as previously described for urine stains. Remember, never force the stain down deeper into the carpet.

If you come across a urine stain and don't have an enzymatic product, treat it with a solution of equal parts white vinegar and water. Never use ammonia because urine is ammonia-based and the smell could trigger your cat to revisit the cleaned spot.

STEP 2: BAIT AND SWITCH

When a cat marks with urine and in the process secretes pheromones, it means he's in an agitated, excited, anxious state. Usually, it's because he feels that his territory is in danger. Even if the cat isn't actually spraying, but is urinating outside of the box, it still could be a sign that his emotional state is anxious, stressful, fearful, agitated. Compare this with the behavior of your cat when he rubs his cheek along an object, or perhaps nuzzles you. He's also secreting pheromones, but his emotional state when he marks with these *facial pheromones* is calm, content, friendly, secure.

If you look around your house, you'll notice that your cat isn't urinating in the spots where you've seen him displaying facial rubbing. So what we're going to do is deposit facial pheromones on all of the areas that have been previously marked.

Feliway, when sprayed on the targeted areas, enables the cat to detect the familiar, calming pheromone. If you follow the directed program, which includes using Feliway and incorporating behavior modification, your cat should decrease his urine marking and you may eventually even see him rubbing his own facial pheromones on those areas.

If you are going to use Feliway, its important that you not clean the urine spots with bleach or detergents. The manufacturer says it may degrade the product's effectiveness. The Feliway label instructs that you use only clear water to clean. Clear water won't get stains out of carpets, so my advice is to use an enzymatic cleaner not on the carpet because you won't be spraying Feliway there, but rather, on the wall corners, furniture legs, or doorways. Use clear water to clean urine-marked areas above the carpet.

Before using Feliway, make sure the bottle has been at room temperature and shake well. Spray once at each urine site. The nozzle should be held four inches away from the area and eight inches up from the floor or carpet. Spray the area one to two times daily for thirty days. It usually takes about seven days before you start to see results. After the thirty days, if your cat has a setback, do a maintenance treatment every couple of days. Usually, though, once you notice your cat begin to rub his own facial pheromones over a spot, you can cease using Feliway.

Corners of prominent objects in the house and potential urine targets, including furniture corners and doorways, should also be sprayed one to two times a day for thirty days.

If there's tension between cats in the household, Feliway has a demonstrated positive effect. Sprayed on commonly shared areas, such as cat trees, furniture, and windowsills, it may help restore calm. Feliway must be used in conjunction with behavior modification.

STEP 3: SETTING UP DETERRENTS

If you are *thinking like a cat,* the objective of setting up a deterrent isn't to punish or scare him away. Your motive is to stimulate what comes naturally to him. It's almost like giving him a gentle nudge to guide him in the right direction. Remember, cats don't respond to forcefulness, but rather, to suggestions.

There are a number of them you can try. Some are more subtle than others. Depending on your cat's determination, you may not have to go beyond the basics, or you might need to use the whole works.

Because under normal circumstances a cat doesn't eliminate inside his nest, you can try to get him back to his original boundaries. Right now, he's viewing the carpet behind your sofa or the wall under your window as the perimeter of his nest. To change it back to inside the nest, try placing a small bowl of cat food at those spots (only do this if you have completely cleaned and neutralized the urine). If he's urinating in only one area, you can feed him there until he's been retrained. If he has been urinating in several locations, place a bowl at each spot with just a little dry food in each. You don't want to end up with a fat cat, so don't pile on the food. You can still feed him in his normal spot but just feed a bit less and divide the rest into the other bowls. The smell of the food in those spots (along with the scent of the facial pheromones that you've sprayed) will start triggering him to reevaluate the situation. Use this method for at least several weeks. Then, provided he hasn't had any mishaps, remove *one* of the bowls for a day. The next day, put that bowl back in the spot and take up another for a day and so on. If he hasn't urinated in the food-free spots, then take up one bowl permanently. A couple of days later, take up another. Continue this way until all bowls are removed.

If you don't want to leave food down, are unable to (because of a dog, for example), or if your cat still urinates in the forbidden place despite the presence of the food bowl, don't panic. The next deterrent to try is making those targeted areas less comfortable. If the cat doesn't like standing on some surface, he probably won't want to walk on it to get to the spot. At your local home improvement center, you can get plastic carpet runners. Get the heavy-duty kind often used in model homes that have little pointed grips on one side. The grips are meant to keep the runner from sliding on the rug, but you're going to position the runner so the gripping feet face *up*. Cut the runner to fit over the spot or place it along an entire wall. Your cat probably won't like standing on the grips. If you're placing it along a wall, be sure it is wide enough so your cat can't just back up to the edge of it and still spray the wall.

If your cat isn't a tenderfoot and marches right across the carpet runner, try laying a few strips of double-faced masking tape across the surface of the runner. Some cats find the combination of the tape and the pointed grips on the runner not worth stepping on.

You may imagine that using a water pistol is a good deterrent when the cat is about to spray. There are problems with this. It means that you actually have to catch the cat in the act, which is easier said than done. And, if you do catch him in the act and you spray him from nearby, he'll know it came from you. His conclusion? *I'd better stay away from my owner.* He'll just find more secluded spots to spray. The only way a squirt pistol will be effective is if you're out of sight when you use it so your cat can't see that it came from you. Save the water pistol to train him to keep off the dining-room table during dinner or not to jump onto the stove.

The next section will explain to you how to distract your cat by using *positive* methods.

STEP 4: BEHAVIOR MODIFICATION

We can assume that a cat who eliminates outside of the box is already stressed, so my method for behavior modification involves flooding him with positive, calming, confident feelings.

So far, you've cleaned and neutralized the targeted areas and you're now spraying Feliway on those spots. Whether you're leaving food down in those areas or using the carpet runners, the next part of the program is to help your cat replace his associations with those areas. You'll be turning those *perimeter* areas back into *nest* areas through play therapy. Following the instructions in chapter 6, conduct your play sessions near the targeted spots. Don't have the cat go too close to the carpet runners because you run the risk of his jumping on them to catch the toy and the discomfort will only cause a negative association with the game.

If your cat has had prior negative experiences in an area, go slowly and let him set the pace. Say for example, the narrow hallway leading to the litter box has been a scary place because that's where your resident feline bully would lie in wait to attack. Put the bully in another room and then begin a gentle game with your other cat. Stay within his comfort zone by letting him crouch mostly in the doorway if he prefers. Eventually, he'll venture out.

Sometimes, if a cat is urinating indiscriminately outside of the box (not urine marking), he may attempt to go right next to the box if the box is too dirty or he doesn't like the litter substrate. If he doesn't like the location of the box (in a laundry room, for example) and goes in other rooms, you may notice that the places he chooses are in rooms you seldom use. When I go on a house call and find that the cat rejects his box because of its location, usually the rooms he picks instead are the dining room, the formal living room (which no one sits in), or perhaps one of the empty guest rooms. It's as if he's viewing the rooms that the family seldom spends time in as the nest perimeter. Play sessions in those rooms will help transform them into central nest areas.

When you're attempting to retrain a cat to a litter box there is another very important aspect of behavior modification. It's the one aspect we tend to be short on when the going gets tough: *patience.* Many inappropriate elimination or spraying problems didn't happen overnight, so they won't be solved overnight either. Some of the clients I see have been living with a spraying cat for several years and then contact me, expecting me to fix the problem in forty-eight hours. Quick fixes don't work.

Contacting a Behaviorist

As you've read this chapter you've become aware of how complex, stressful, and sad litter box problems can be. If you're dealing with a behavior problem without success, there are options available for you. An appointment with a veterinary behaviorist can help accurately diagnose the problem, so a behavior modification program can be specifically structured for your individual cat.

Behaviorists generally work on a veterinarian referral basis. Many make house calls in order to see the cat in his own territory so they can accurately assess environmental factors. If you're not familiar with behavior counseling, discuss it with your vet.

When Behavior Modification Attempts Aren't Working

Confining the Cat

If your cat continues to urinate in many locations, the confinement method, based on the cat's instinctual need to eliminate away from the nest, may help retrain him. Confine him in a small area with enough room for his litter box, a small bed and his food/water (which will go on the wall opposite the litter). The space needs to be small so that he realizes that his only option is to eliminate in the box. If he chooses to eliminate outside of the box, he'll end up walking and sleeping on it—not at all an experience he wants (of course, you must clean it immediately though, should he have an accident).

You can use a small bathroom or a large cage to confine him. If you choose the bathroom, be sure it doesn't have carpeting.

Remember the objective of the confinement method is to *retrain* and not to *punish*. Don't lock him in the bathroom as if it's going to be his jail cell. Spend time with him, playing, grooming and petting. Keep it as positive as you can.

Keep him in the confined area for about three to four days even if he has been successfully using the litter box after the first day. Then you can begin to let him out for short periods under supervision. Conduct play sessions while he's out.

While he's confined, do a thorough cleaning/odor neutralizing of the house. Remove any heavily soiled furniture or carpets.

When he is using his litter box consistently, you can reintroduce him back into the household.

Behavioral Drug Therapy

There are times when behavior modification won't be enough to counteract all the problems that a cat may have. Maybe it doesn't work because of the serious nature of the problem, the length of time that the problem has been going on, or it could be that the cat is so overtaken by fear and stress he can't even begin to respond to modification techniques.

Appropriately used drugs can, in several cases, at least reduce, if not totally eliminate the behavior problem.

Until quite recently, the choice for behavioral drug therapy to stop spraying was hormone related, such as in Ovaban. The unfortunate part about Ovaban was that long-term use could be dangerous for the cat and put him at risk of developing diabetes. Nor was it a real success story for treating litter box problems. But it was all that vets had to work with for a long time.

Valium was and still is a drug that many vets prescribe for inappropriate elimination problems. Again, the side effects can be very dangerous for a cat, most notably, risk of liver failure.

There are now drugs used in feline behavior therapy that are very effective and have few side effects. Buspirone, an anti-anxiety drug prescribed for humans, has in many cases, reduced a cat's inclination to spray. Amitriptyline, an anti-depressant (another human drug), is also now used to treat feline inappropriate elimination and certain cases of aggression.

These are just two of the new drug therapies that veterinarians and behaviorists are using with modification programs. If there is an accurate diagnosis and the appropriate drug is used, it might save a cat with a behavior problem who otherwise might have been euthanized.

A few words of caution, though: don't, under any circumstances, take it upon yourself to medicate your cat with any drugs you yourself may be using. Most behavioral drugs haven't been licensed for use in veterinary medicine. Before you and your vet decide on drug therapy, you'll need to have a specific discussion about all aspects of this treatment, including how it might affect the medical health of your cat, the cost of the drug, and the type of monitoring required to ensure the cat's safety. No drug therapy should begin without a complete medical workup on the cat. Be sure to find out the expected duration of drug therapy as well as instructions for the tapering off of the drug toward the end of therapy.

Drug therapy must always be used concurrently with behavior modification or else you stand a very good chance of seeing the problem resurface after the drug has been removed.

It is *part* of the complete behavior modification program, not just an easy way out.

If you truly feel that only drug therapy can help, make an appointment with your vet and perhaps a behaviorist to discuss the options thoroughly. Be an informed owner—your cat's life depends on it.

Unusual Elimination Preferences

Cats mostly prefer a soft substrate that enables them to scratch, dig, and cover. Every now and then though, a cat comes along who prefers to eliminate on hard surfaces and turns his nose up at litter of any kind. Because urinating in tubs, sinks, or on floors is a common sign of LUTD, make sure such a cat has been checked by the vet. Then, if in fact the problem is behavioral, retrain him by confining him to a small room. Line all flat surfaces with old towels and sheets. Place an *empty*, uncovered litter box in with him. The only plain hard surface for his elimination will be *inside* the box. Over the next few days, gradually sprinkle a small amount of the soft sandlike litter in the bottom of the box. Add a little more each time until your cat is comfortable using a litter-filled box.

Another more common preference is the desire to eliminate only on rugs, towels, or clothing. If you have tried a wide variety of litters, behavior modification, etc., try confining your cat in a small room with no rugs and provide a litter box with no litter but a piece of carpet or towel in the bottom. If he begins to use the box, you will replace the carpet piece with a clean one and begin adding a small amount of soft litter. Each time you replace the carpet, make it a smaller piece. If you do this gradually enough, you should be able to re-accustom him to litter.

PLANT-LOVING CATS

Eliminating in the potted plants happens more often if the cat has spent much of his life outdoors. It can also happen if a cat discovers he prefers the soft texture of the soil to that of his clay litter. If you're using regular clay litter, add a second box with the soft sandlike litter. The texture may be more appealing to your cat.

Set up deterrents in the plant pots such as strips of Sticky Paws For Plants placed in a tic-tac-toe board pattern across the pot. You can also cover the soil in large planters with heavy rocks. The rocks need to be heavy so the cat can't push them away. Another option is to cover the soil with garden netting. This will prevent your cat from digging. All of the above-mentioned methods allow you to water your plants easily and they don't look terrible.

If your cat refuses to use anything but soil, then start with that in his litter box and gradually add a small amount of litter every couple of days. Eventually, he should make the transition. A reminder: Soil is very messy, so make sure you cover any carpet or remove any rugs that are near the box.

GERIATRIC-RELATED LITTER BOX PROBLEMS

As your cat ages, physical and/or mental deterioration may result in house-soiling behavior. Arthritis can make it difficult for him to get in and out of the box. Climbing and descending stairs might be too painful. Some cats can become disoriented as they age and have trouble remembering the location of the litter box. Diabetes, kidney disease, and other medical conditions that create increased water intake and urine output can also make it difficult for a cat to reach the box in time.

Provide several low-sided litter boxes that are easy for your cat to get to. If the lowest litter box is still too high, use plastic serving trays.

If your cat frequently becomes disoriented, confine him to an area of the house that's easily cleaned, and keep a good supply of enzymatic odor neutralizer on hand.

9

Scratching Posts, Sofas, Antique Chairs . . . Which One Will Your Cat Choose?

Yes, You Can Have a Cat and Nice Furniture, Too

During visits to cat-owning friends' homes, you've seen the tattered remains of what once were drapes. You've tried not to notice the shredded sofa that looked as if it had been the victim of a tiny chain saw. Now you have your own cute little kitten back at home. Is he capable of inflicting this much damage? Is this the end of your nice furniture? Should you have him declawed?

Before you decide to declaw, go back to those friends' homes and really take a closer look at things. Do you see scratching posts anywhere around? If so, are they short and wobbly? What methods did your friends use to try and redirect the scratching behavior to this more appropriate object? Was punishment the only way your friends thought they could train their cats? If you've read the previous chapters in this book, how successful do you think punishment would be? Based on what you've read so far, wouldn't it make sense to you that if a cat is scratching the furniture it might mean that either the scratching post wasn't meeting his requirements or worse yet, that there wasn't a post available?

You have the opportunity to become an informed owner for your little kitten and use productive training methods.

Having a cat declawed is extremely serious and permanent, so please read this entire chapter and make sure you understand why cats scratch, why they choose certain textures over others, and the training methods I've successfully used for years.

The Need to Scratch

Scratching is an innate behavior and serves many functions in a cat's life. The most obvious one is to maintain the health of his nails. A cat discards the outer nail sheath on his forefeet by raking them down along a rough surface. As he pulls his nails out from the material, the dead outer sheath comes off, exposing the new growth underneath.

Scratching also serves as a marking behavior as previously described in chapter 2.

If you've ever seen a cat when his owner arrives home, run to his post to scratch, you've witnessed how scratching behavior serves an emotional outlet as well. A cat will also use scratching to displace the frustration he may feel after being reprimanded or being unable to do something that he wants (for example, capturing the bird he sees through the window).

Scratching also enables the cat to stretch out the muscles in his shoulders and back. And he often enjoys a full stretch after a nap in a curled-up ball or after eating.

The Impact of Declawing

Many owners rush into the decision to declaw without understanding the consequences. Luckily, more vets are educating owners that declawing should be a last-resort surgery.

Declaw surgery is the equivalent of having the last joint of all of your fingers removed. After the joints of the cat's toes are amputated, a pressure bandage is put on the legs and remains in place overnight. The cat is in pain upon waking and most continue to feel pain for many days afterward. If the cat isn't given pain relievers, it's an even more difficult recovery.

The wounds need about a week to heal and during the recovery time, regular litter can't be used because it's painful to the sensitive paws and can also get stuck in the healing wounds.

A declawed cat is almost totally defenseless if he can't slash his enemy with the claws of his front paw. Therefore, a declawed cat can never be allowed outdoors. A cat without front nails would have severe difficulty even climbing a tree or fence in order to escape an attacker.

Declawing can sometimes affect a cat's sense of balance, and if surgery was improperly performed, one or more of the nails can grow back in a way that causes the cat discomfort.

There has been an ongoing controversy as to whether declawed cats are more inclined to become biters. Many experts will argue that there's no supporting evidence to prove that a declawed cat is likely to bite. I've seen such cats become biters and/or go through a personality change. Honestly, I've also seen cats who remained just as good-natured after being declawed. What is so unfortunate, though, is that these good-natured cats might have been the easiest to train to a post had the proper method been used. My main objection to declawing is based on the extreme pain and suffering that declawing causes a cat as well as that he loses his ability to scratch, vital to his physical and emotional well being. Declawing is, in my opinion, nothing more than mutilation.

If you have a kitten, wait until you've tried training him to a post before considering declawing. I know it seems as if his claws are always exposed, but in time, he'll learn more about how his body works and he'll figure out that he can keep his nails sheathed more often than he's doing now.

Getting your kitten used to regular nail trims will lessen damage to furniture and will help him to accept having his paws handled.

The Average Scratching Post

The cat owner tries to do the right thing by purchasing a scratching post at the local pet-supply store. The post is usually covered in a colorful carpet material and maybe even has a cute little toy dangling from the top. Home the owner goes with the best intentions of providing for kitty's needs. The post gets placed in the corner of the living room. The cat, ever curious when it comes to anything new in the home, goes over to check it out. Sniffing the post, the cat even gives the dangling toy a little swat with his paw. The owner smiles. Satisfied that this new addition to the home is harmless, the cat turns his back to it and trots over to the sofa. There, he proceeds to sink his nails in and scratch. The owner frowns.

Is the cat being stubborn and destructive? Willfully disobedient? Not at all. He just knows that the post won't provide enough when it comes to his natural, normal, and healthy need to scratch.

So what's wrong with the average post? Let's start with the cover material. Most posts are covered with carpet that's too soft and plush. A cat needs a rough textured material that he can sink his nails into to help discard the dead sheaths. If you have a cat who is scratching on furniture instead of the post, compare the two textures. Run your hand along the post and then along the furniture. The furniture wins.

Moving on down the list, the next problem with the average post is that it's usually not sturdy enough. Many have a small base so when a scratching cat leans his weight on it, it topples over. Some poorly constructed posts aren't connected to the base securely so they wobble. Because furniture is sturdy the cat has another incentive to use your sofa. He knows that it won't wobble.

Most posts are also too short. The act of scratching is also a way for a cat to get a full back stretch. Look at how long your cat's body becomes when he engages in a full stretch. Stretching out feels so wonderful that he's going to return to the place he knows will provide that—your furniture.

Choosing the Right Scratching Post

When you go out shopping, keep three rules in mind. A scratching post must be:

1. covered in the right material

2. sturdy and well constructed

3. tall enough for a full stretch

You can't go wrong if the cover material is sisal. A rope-covered post is another great option. Rough texture is very appealing. As you run your hand along the various posts, the rougher it feels, the better. Think of a nail file. You wouldn't want to use a dull, smooth file, right? Neither does your cat.

Some carpet-covered posts are acceptable if the material is rough enough.

If you're unable to find a sisal-covered post, you can order one by mail. There are several companies making sisal- and rope-covered posts. My favorite is the Felix post. It stands about thirty inches high, has a large, heavy base, is well constructed, and can take a lot of abuse. The Felix Company is listed in the resource guide.

MAKING YOUR OWN SCRATCHING POST

You'll need a 4-inch-by-4-inch piece of wood, thirty inches in length for the post. For the base, a 16-inch-by-16-inch square ¾-inch piece of plywood will work. Select cedar, redwood, fir, or pine for the post. Oak, which is a hardwood, will be more difficult to drill.

At the store, you'll probably find both *treated* and *untreated* wood. Don't choose the treated kind because it has an obvious odor that neither you nor your cat will like. If your local lumber company only has treated 4-inch-by-4-inch posts, then get a regular untreated 8-foot, 2-by-4-inch. Cut two 30-inch pieces and screw them together to form a 4-inch-by-4-inch-by-30-inch-long post.

If you plan on leaving the base uncovered, be sure to sand it well so you won't get splinters should you stub your toe on it while on your way to the bathroom in the middle of the night.

To fasten the post to the base, you will need five #8 2½-inch drywall screws. Mark on top of the base where the post will sit. You should now have a square marked in the center of the base. In this square, make two diagonal lines from the corners to mark the center of the square. Drill one hole in the center and one hole on each diagonal line, 1 inch from the corner. Coat the screws with soap so they'll go in more easily. Turn the base upside down and run the center screw through the bottom of the base into the positioned post. Double-check the location of the post with the marks you made on the top of the base before running the rest of the screws. When you've finished, if you still think the post isn't sturdy enough, attach a small metal angle iron on each side of the post bottom where it meets the base.

There's one common mistake that many owners make about cover material: They hunt down that carpeting they had leftover. As with what

Supplies Needed for Making a Post

- 4-inch-by-4-inch-by-30-inch piece of wood
- 16-inch-by-16-inch square of ³/₄-inch-thick plywood
- cover material for post
- cover material for base (optional)
- sandpaper (to smooth base)
- five #8 2 ¹/₂-inch drywall screws (more if using a 2″ x 4″)
- four small metal angle irons (optional)
- carpet tacks (if using carpet for cover material)
- heavy-duty construction staples (if using rope for cover material)
- drill (for drilling holes through the base)
- screwdriver (electric will be much easier)
- soap (to coat screws)
- safety glasses
- catnip (to rub on the finished post)

is on most store-bought posts, that carpeting is usually too plush and soft. However, if you want to use what you already have, attach the carpet to the post with the back side facing *out*. Rough carpet backing can be a very appealing scratching material. Fasten the carpet to the post with carpet tacks.

I've found that the easiest covering for a post is rope. When you purchase it, get more than you think you're going to need because it'll be wound very tightly around the post. You can also use rope to cover an already fluffy carpeted post that your cat has been ignoring. Secure it at the top and bottom with heavy-duty construction staples. To protect your hands, wear work gloves when winding the rope.

Some cats prefer to scratch on plain old wood. You may have noticed this if your cat scratches on the logs stacked by the fireplace. If that's the case, the easiest thing to do is make an upright log post. Nature has already supplied the ideal cover material for you. If your cat scratches on bare wood, you can strip the bark off the log or use a plain 4-inch-by-4-inch piece of wood.

Cats can have such individual and unique preferences for scratching, so you may have to use great creativity to come up with the ideal post. Don't give up!

Where to Put the Scratching Post

Don't make the mistake of trying to hide the scratching post. It may not be the greatest-looking addition to your decor, but your cat needs to know that it's there. The post, conveniently located, can be a visual reminder.

Many cats enjoy scratching and stretching after a nap or after they've eaten. Because scratching is also an emotional outlet, many cats will want to use the post when their owner comes home or as they anxiously await dinner.

If the post is for a kitten, keep it right in the middle of his room or area so he can't miss it. If your kitten has access to the entire house, invest in more than one post. You can't expect him to keep a lid on his desire to scratch while he searches from room to room for his post. Make it easy for the youngster.

Training Your Cat to Use the Scratching Post

Scratching, for a kitten, is actually just a means of climbing to higher ground. To a new cat owner, it may appear that your kitten has Velcro paws, as you watch him scale furniture, drapes, beds and the clothes hanging in the closets. Take a deep breath and be patient. This phase will pass. Even though your kitten may do nothing with the post other than climb up and over the top, very soon he'll discover scratching behavior and you'll want to be ready.

The training method is the same for a kitten or an adult cat: Make it a game. Dangle a peacock feather or other enticing toy right next to the post. As your cat goes for the toy he'll feel the irresistible texture of the post. With your own nails, gently scratch up and down the post. Often, that scratching sound can inspire him to join in.

If your cat doesn't have a clue about what to do with the post, lay it on its side and dangle the toy all around it. As he jumps on the post or paws at the toy, he'll discover the texture. He may then begin scratching the post in earnest. Once he has discovered its true purpose, you can stand the post upright again.

Never force your cat to scratch by taking his paws and putting them on the post. No matter how gently you do it, your cat won't like the experience and it'll just cause confusion. His attention will be focused on getting out of your grasp and you will have done nothing but create a negative association with the post.

Make the games around the scratching post a regularly scheduled event for a kitten.

Keep your training methods consistent so you don't confuse your kitten. Don't drag the toy under fabrics such as comforters, chair cushions, clothing, or behind drapes, etc. That could encourage him to scratch there as he claws at the toy. Don't run the toy up and along furniture. That will cause your kitten to extend his claws and climb. Never send mixed messages.

Retraining a Cat to the Post After He Has Discovered Your Furniture

It can be done. First, though, you must have the right kind of post. Make sure you've followed my instructions and purchased or constructed an appropriate one. If you already have a post in your home that has sat for years gathering dust, don't even attempt to retrain your cat to it. If he'd thought it was acceptable in the first place he would've been using it, so just get rid of the relic (or if it's tall and sturdy enough, recover it using a better material).

Next, look at the areas where he's currently scratching. If it's the sofa or chair, you'll have to make the object no longer appealing. If the scratched area of the furniture is limited to certain sections, lay strips of Sticky Paws (a double-faced transparent tape made especially for this purpose) across them. Plain masking tape can leave a residue behind. According to the manufacturer, Sticky Paws has an acrylic base so it won't leave any residue when removed from the furniture. Sticky Paws is also water-soluble.

If the cat has been working on the entire chair, cover it with a sheet, carefully tuck it in all around and tape the bottom so he can't climb up underneath it. Place strips of Sticky Paws or double-faced masking tape at several locations. Now you've turned this great scratching surface into an unacceptable one. The next step is to put the new post next to the covered furniture. That way, when he goes over for his routine scratch and realizes that his usual spot has disappeared, he'll discover something even better. You can further entice him by using a toy around the post to get his attention. Also, rub the post with catnip to ensure getting his approval.

If you catch your cat attempting to scratch the furniture during retraining, don't punish, hit, or yell at him. Scratching is a normal, natural behavior, so you can't reprimand him. Just make the furniture a little more unattractive by placing something under one corner so it becomes unsteady (inform family members before they attempt to sit down). By making the chair or sofa unstable, it'll no longer be a secure scratching surface.

Some people have used deterrents such as taping balloons to the furniture, but I'm strongly against that because it's too frightening. If your cat is timid or nervous, bursting balloons could make him even jumpier. Your cat may become too scared to even use the post. Other animals in multipet households can be frightened by the popping balloon sound as well.

Keep the furniture covered until your cat has been using the post routinely and no longer attempts to get at the furniture. Then gradually move the post over to where you want it permanently located. I recommend that you keep it relatively close to the same area though, to remind him. When you feel that he's retrained and goes right for the post without so much as looking at the furniture, go ahead and remove the sheet or tape.

If your cat is scratching by the front door or around entrances to rooms, he may be doing more marking behavior than nail maintenance. Put a scratching post near the doorway and cover the scratched area with double-sided tape. In narrow hallways or anywhere else it would be impossible to put a post, use sisal covered pads made especially to hang on doorknobs. You could also make a flat scratching pad with carpet backing and attach it to the wall.

If your cat is motivated by food rewards, give him a treat when he makes any kind of contact with the post.

If you have more than one cat, you need more than one scratching post in case one cat decides to claim it for his own use exclusively.

Once you have your post(s) in place you can monitor how successful it is by looking at the base. If your cat is using it, you should begin to see small crescent-shaped nail sheaths there.

Once a week during retraining, rub a little catnip on the post as a little hint. When retraining is complete, use the catnip on the post periodically as a treat.

WHEN DO YOU SURRENDER?

It's one of the most common things I hear from owners. In desperation, they decide to give in and let the cat destroy a chair because they plan on buying a new one eventually. The problem with that logic is that the cat won't understand why he isn't allowed to scratch the new piece when he was allowed to scratch the old. Don't send mixed messages to your kitty. Invest in a great scratching post.

Horizontal Scratching

Not every cat reaches up and scratches vertically. There are some who prefer stretching out and scratching flat surfaces. You may notice your cat scratching on the carpet, welcome mat, outdoor deck flooring, or along the tops of furniture. There are also many cats who enjoy both horizontal and vertical scratching. If you notice that all of the scratched surfaces are horizontal, that may be why attempts at training your cat to a vertical post have been unsuccessful.

There are many commercial scratching *pads* available for horizontal scratchers. The Felix Company makes a pad covered in the same sisal material used for their great posts. Many inexpensive pads made of corrugated cardboard are available. These are terrific and come in narrow and wide widths so they can fit anywhere. There is even a corrugated cardboard scratching pad built on an incline for the cat who is both a horizontal and vertical scratcher. The Cosmic Cat Alpine Scratcher is a wide pad built on an incline. Kittens especially seem to enjoy the corrugated cardboard pads. These pads are convenient in case you have to travel with your cat.

The Application of Plastic Nail Caps

A brand of little plastic caps called Soft Paws can be placed over your cat's nails. A permanent glue is squeezed into the cap and then it's fitted over the nail. The caps last from one to two months. Your cat's nails grow, so any caps that don't fall off or aren't chewed off will have to be removed.

The cat will still attempt to scratch with these nail caps in place but obviously won't be able to penetrate anything.

For owners who are totally unable to train their cats to a post but also don't want to declaw, these nails caps are an option.

I'm not a big fan of this product (but I would prefer you use these instead of declawing) because once the caps are in place, the cat is unable to retract his nails fully. I'm not sure how comfortable that would be over the long term. Also, the caps prevent the cat from enjoying natural scratching behavior.

The first time the caps are applied, it should be done by your veterinarian in case your cat has any reaction to the glue.

Nail kits are available for at-home application and come in various sizes. Don't attempt to do this at home if your cat is aggressive. Even if he isn't, you'll need an assistant to hold the cat while you apply the caps.

I've found that many cats manage to chew at least one or two of the caps off shortly after being applied. So you can't just put the caps on and forget them. Check periodically to make sure they're all still in place because two or three exposed nails will still cause damage to your furniture.

If you're interested in Soft Paws, talk with your veterinarian.

Indoor Trees

Every home should have at least one. Not only do they provide a tall, sturdy scratching surface, but they enable a cat to climb and perch on his very own furniture. There are a wide variety of trees available. You can get multitiered ones so that two or three cats can share, and they come in many different configurations and heights.

The support posts on the trees can be covered in rope, bark, sisal, or left as bare wood. Multitiered trees with two or three posts can have several coverings. It's pure heaven for a cat!

Should You Replace That Well-Used, Worn-Out Old Post?

Your cat has been faithfully using his scratching post for years. So much so that it's now just shredded rope hanging from a mangled post. You lovingly rewrap the post with a new rope, or you throw the whole thing away and surprise your kitty with a brand-new one. Guess what? There's a good chance he's not going to like it. He'd gotten that post the way he wanted it, with all of its visual and olfactory marks. It was truly his! Then suddenly, to his horror, his post is gone . . . vanished.

Don't get rid of a post that your cat is strongly attached to. Rather, get an additional post and place it nearby so he'll have a great new scratching option. Remember, scratching isn't just for maintaining the health of the nails, but also for marking and emotional expression. If he truly abandons the worn-out post for the new one, then you can dispose of the old one.

In our house, we have two large scratching posts and three cat trees. All five get well used so I know my cats are happy with them. The most popular post is ten years old.

10

The Kitty Chef

Finicky Eaters Aren't Born—They're Created

As a new cat owner, you're no doubt, very concerned with providing the best possible nutrition for your growing youngster. *What* you put the food in and *where* you place it can have a surprising impact on whether your cat runs in delight to the bowl at mealtime or sits and stares at it (and you) in disgust. It's about presentation.

There are several options when choosing your kitty's food and water bowls. Before you go out and spend big bucks for a jewel-encrusted, personalized dish or dig through the attic for that old water bowl you've saved from the German Shepherd you had eight years ago, evaluate your cat's needs.

A bowl is a bowl, you say? This is true, but what you're looking for is the *best* bowl for *your* cat. Bowls are generally made of plastic, glass, porcelain, or stainless steel. Here are some things to consider when making your choice:

Plastic. Probably more bowls are made of plastic than anything else. It's inexpensive, lightweight and unbreakable. I don't like them, though. Some cats can develop allergies from eating out of plastic bowls. The allergy will show up as hair loss or acne on the chin. Some cats can even develop quite serious lesions. No matter how hard you clean it, the dish still retains odors. Plastic bowls are also easily scratched which can lead to food residue and bacteria collecting in the scratches. A scratched plastic surface can also be abrasive to a cat's sensitive tongue. A scratched bowl has to be replaced, so even though you may initially feel as if plastic is inexpensive, the repeated cost of replacement bowls make them not such a bargain.

Finally, I dislike plastic bowls because they *are* so lightweight. My cats don't enjoy having to follow their bowl all around the kitchen as it slides along the floor. While you may think it's kind of cute and funny, in hostile multicat households, *distance* during meals is critical. A food bowl sliding in the enemy's direction can lead to big trouble.

Glass and Ceramic. A good choice because they're heavier than plastic, so they won't go on trips around the kitchen. They're breakable, though, so you have to take care when washing to avoid chips or cracks which can injure a cat's mouth and tongue. Additionally, some ceramic bowls have imperfections which create a rough texture. This can be irritating to the tongue. When choosing ceramic, look for manufacturers who state that their products are "lead-free." Some ceramic bowls made outside of the U.S. contain lead in their glaze.

Stainless Steel. Virtually indestructible. This is a great choice. Because they can be lightweight though, you may want to look for the bowls that have nonskid rims. To maintain cleanliness, if the rubber nonskid rim is removable, don't forget to wash underneath where bacteria can hide.

SIZE AND SHAPE

Choose the size appropriate for your cat. With a tiny kitten, if you give him a large bowl, guess what's going to happen? He'll end up stepping in his food. You can save the larger bowl for when he has grown a bit more.

Deep, narrow food bowls that severely crowd the cat's whiskers aren't a good idea. With longhaired cats, deep bowls will cause the fur around his face to become soiled. This type of bowl is also not recommended for short-nosed breeds such as Persians or Himalayans. They need a wide, shallow dish.

DOUBLE BOWLS

If you have two cats and you purchase a double bowl, you may be creating a potential behavior problem. Some cats require a greater space around them as they dine (remember that in the wild a cat often takes his prey somewhere private and safe to eat). Making the cats eat so close to each other may encourage the more dominant one to bully the other away from the food. The more submissive cat may be afraid to approach the bowl until the first cat has finished eating (and by then, all of the food may be gone). Give them at least a few feet between bowls.

Some people use a double bowl to hold food on one side and water on the other. There are a couple of reasons why I'd recommend that you not do that. Some cats don't like their food that close to the water. The result may be a cat with a finicky appetite or a cat who gets his water from other sources (such as the toilet bowl). The other reason why I dislike food and water in one double bowl is that pieces of food usually end up falling into the water, making it less appealing. If you leave the food/water bowl down for free-choice feeding all the time, then the water can become contaminated.

AUTOMATIC FEEDERS AND WATER DISPENSERS

I think automatic dispensers are okay if you're leaving your cat alone for a night or two. On a regular basis, though, I feel they're wasteful. Water that sits out for a prolonged period loses oxygen and will taste stale. Some cats will not drink as much as they should once it loses its taste. The same thing happens with the food—as it becomes stale, the cat may be less inclined to eat.

In multicat households, if one or more cats drink lots of water (perhaps due to a medical problem) and you aren't around to refill the bowl, then an automatic dispenser is a good idea. Just be sure you frequently clean it and replace with fresh water.

WASHING THE BOWLS

No matter what type of bowls you decide on, keeping them clean on a daily basis is essential. Wash with dishwashing liquid by hand or in the dishwasher, following manufacturer's directions. If washing by hand, be certain to rinse off all traces of soap. Any residue can be irritating to the cat's mouth and tongue. When you're sure you've rinsed the bowl enough—rinse again.

FOOD AND WATER PLACEMENT

I've said it before, I'll say it again: The one place in the house you should *never* put the food is near the litter box. I can hear the footsteps now as some of you are running to the litter box to see just how close . . . uh-oh, there it is—the food bowl and the litter box side by side. OH, NO! Why is this so bad? To understand, let's go back to the cat's survival instinct. In the wild, a cat eliminates away from the nest to avoid attracting predators. By having the food so close to the litter, the cat receives conflicting messages. *Is this my nest or the perimeter?* The behavior problem that develops is that the cat chooses to eat the food at that location (since it's the only place the food can be found) and then goes somewhere else to eliminate. I promise you, his choice of location for elimination won't be one you'll like very much.

Other bad choices for food placement are any areas that are noisy, scary or unpredictable. If you have a timid, jumpy cat, and you put the food in the laundry room, guess what's going to happen when the washer goes from *rinse* to *spin*? Your cat's going to bolt out of there. If you have a dog and the cat's food is very appealing to him, then placing the bowls on the floor means the cat may get pushed from his own food.

The most obvious place for the food and water is in the kitchen, but based on your particular circumstances, that may not be possible. If your cat is timid and the activity in the kitchen is overwhelming, then put his food in a quieter area of the house. Owners can get very creative to meet their cats' needs. Just remember, meals should be a time when the cat can feel safe so he can enjoy his dinner.

Once you've settled on the best spot for the food, don't switch locations if you can help it. Being such creatures of habit, cats don't like it when they go to their usual feeding spot only to discover it has disappeared.

Elderly cats may require adjustments in their usual feeding routine or location. If you've always kept your cat's food in an elevated spot, be sure he's still able to make that leap up and down. You may have to lower his food to the floor or create a way for him to easily climb to the spot.

PET PLACEMATS

For seriously messy eaters or cats who love to spill their water bowls, you can find placements with raised edges that contain the water and prevent damage to your floor or carpet. These placemats are available at pet supply stores.

The Confusing World of Pet Food

If you've been in a supermarket within the last decade, you've probably noticed how much shelf space is devoted to pet food. The variety is mind-boggling. Then there are also the brands sold exclusively to pet supply stores, via mail order, and the foods available from your veterinarian.

The pet-food industry is a big, big business. Pet-food advertising can be very misleading and targeted toward *our* impression of food. Some companies create food that looks as if we ourselves could eat it—slices of beef, smooth gravy, peas, tiny carrots, etc. Do you think that those things really matter to a cat? If your kitty took over the duties of chef at your house, you'd be sitting down to a plate of one small mouse with a side dish of butterflies and grasshoppers. Tomorrow's menu would probably include Bird à la Felix, seasoned to perfection with a hint of catnip. Hungry yet? Me neither, but cats would be lined up for miles for a meal such as this.

This chapter will help guide you toward understanding what your cat's nutritional requirements are and how to supply them. I don't want you paying more than you should for gimmicky food just because it's well advertised, but I also don't want you loading up the trunk of your car with forty pounds of some economy brand that won't help your kitty grow and thrive. Sound nutrition will give your cat: optimal health, a glorious coat, and increased energy. He'll have higher resistance to disease and fewer behavioral problems, and is more likely to live to a ripe old age.

UNDERSTANDING THE BASICS

Protein

Cats need protein for growth, energy, and to allow the body's tissues to function. Cats require a higher amount of protein in their diet than dogs. A kitten requires even more protein than that of an adult cat.

Protein is made up of *amino acids.* There are two kinds: *essential* and *nonessential.* The nonessential amino acids can be synthesized by the body. Of the approximately twenty-two amino acids, eleven are referred to as *essential* because they can't be synthesized by the cat and *must* come from food sources.

One of the amino acids, *taurine,* is of particular importance to the cat. Not too long ago, cat foods lacked sufficient amounts of this, and health problems arose from the taurine deficiency. Blindness and heart disease are two extremely serious conditions that can result from an inadequate supply of taurine in the diet. Luckily, pet-food manufacturers responded to the need by supplementing with more taurine. Canned food must be supplemented with more than dry due to changes that occur during the canning process. Since taurine supplementation, deficiencies are seen less frequently. Cats who are fed dog food are still at risk. Because dogs don't have the same need for taurine supplementation, a cat fed a diet meant for a dog will become deficient.

Why Cats Can't Be Vegetarians

Cats are carnivores, period. They must get their vitamin A, along with other *essential* nutrients from meat sources. Unlike us, cats' bodies are unable to convert beta carotene into usable vitamin A.

You may be on an exclusively vegetarian diet and might even be strongly against the consumption of meat under any conditions. With all due respect to your beliefs, your cat must have meat or his health will rapidly decline.

Fats

The very word *fat* strikes fear in most of us these days. We spend so much effort trying to eliminate it from our diet. Cats, on the other hand, have a higher need for fat than humans. Here's another case, as with their need for meat, where we have to understand the differences between our nutritional requirements and our cats'.

Fat is a concentrated source of energy, and animal-source fats provide the body with essential fatty acids. Fatty acids group together to form fat. Fat soluble vitamins (A, D, E, and K) require fat for proper absorption and delivery throughout the body.

Even though cats require more dietary fat than we do, not any fat will do. *Polyunsaturated* fat (from vegetable oil) can't be converted by the cat, so the essential fatty acid, *arachidonic acid,* must be obtained from animal sources.

Fat also adds to the food's palatability. That much we *do* have in common with cats—we both like the way fat makes our food taste better.

Carbohydrates

Carbohydrates are comprised of sugars, starches, and cellulose. Besides being a source of energy and fiber, carbohydrates assist in the digestion of fats. The cellulose in carbohydrates is not digested and acts as fiber, which helps to promote normal fecal elimination by absorbing water in the intestine.

Vitamins

Vitamins are either *water soluble* (vitamin B complex, niacin, folic acid, pantothenic acid, biotin, choline, vitamin C) or *fat soluble* (A, D, E, K).

As long as you're feeding your cat a high-quality, well-balanced food that's appropriate for his age, there's no need to supplement with additional vitamins. To do so without the advice of your vet could cause possible toxicity. Unused water soluble vitamins are excreted in the urine, but the fat soluble vitamins build up in the body to dangerous levels. Some cats, though, due to age or illness require additional vitamins— your vet will determine if that's necessary.

As I mentioned previously, cats are unable to convert beta carotene into a useable form of vitamin A, so they must obtain it from meat sources—so save the carrot sticks for your own lunch.

Mineral oil or petroleum jelly–based hair ball prevention products can interfere with proper absorption of fat-soluble vitamins. If you have a cat who suffers from frequent hair balls, be careful not to overuse the prevention product. This also applies to the excessive use of mineral oil or petroleum jelly. For more on hair ball prevention, refer to chapter 12.

Minerals

As with vitamins, your cat requires minerals in the proper amount to maintain health. The minerals *calcium* and *phosphorus* must be maintained at a certain ratio. If the balance shifts significantly, the cat can experience debilitating medical complications. Cats who are fed an all-meat diet, which is deficient in calcium, can develop bone disease. A diet too high in calcium can interfere with normal thyroid function.

The best way to be certain your cat is getting all of the minerals he needs in the proper amounts is to feed him a high-quality, well-balanced food that's appropriate for his stage of life.

Water—the Forgotten Nutrient

Every process of life depends on water. A cat can go without food longer than he can exist without water. His body is made up of almost 70 percent water. So when thinking about how to supply your cat with the best nutrition, don't forget that overlooked essential nutrient: *water*.

Your cat needs to have access to clean, fresh water at all times. Your responsibility doesn't end with just filling up the water bowl every time it's empty, though. Your responsibility includes monitoring how *much* or how *little* your cat drinks. Note any changes in water consumption, as it could indicate a medical problem (such as diabetes or kidney disease).

The water in your cat's bowl should be changed daily and the bowl itself washed to avoid contaminating any fresh water you refill. Don't get a huge bowl thinking that you'll only have to refill it once a week. Water gets stale, and cats can taste that.

If you notice food particles or dirt in the water, clean the bowl, and refill with fresh water. Make the water your cat drinks as appealing as possible.

Some cats are particular about the shape and size of their bowl. Your cat may prefer a more shallow bowl rather than a deep one. If that's the case, be aware of the more frequent need to refill.

If you share your life with not only a cat but a dog (especially a big one), the cat may not want to share one large community water bowl. To a tiny cat, your big dog's water bowl may look more like a swimming pool. If that's the case, place another, smaller bowl in an elevated spot for kitty's exclusive use.

A number of cats prefer to combine two activities at once: playtime and water drinking. They enjoy, and sometimes insist on, drinking the dripping water from faucets. While you may initially view this as cute, take my word for it, the cuteness of it wears thin in no time. You'll soon find yourself being trained by your cat to either turn on the faucets whenever he sits and cries near one, or worse yet, you'll give up and just leave the faucets dripping. Neither option is a good one. If you have a kitten, don't even put the idea in his fuzzy little head that a dripping faucet is a great game. If your cat has already developed a faucet fixation, there are products available that will meet his running water requirements and keep him away from your sink. The one that I think works best is the Drinkwell Fountain, which continually recirculates water by way of an aquarium pump and filter. Available through mail order catalogs or directly from the manufacturer (see resource guide). Keep in mind, though, that despite the plus side of the water recirculation devices, they do need to be kept clean, which becomes more involved than just washing a plain water bowl. Unless your cat already has a faucet fixation, don't get him started—it just creates more work for you.

To keep your cat from drinking the toilet water, always keep the lid down. The detergents and chemicals used to clean toilets can be deadly to pets.

If your cat goes outside, make sure he has access to clean fresh water out there. This is especially important in hot weather.

Is There Really *Ash* in Your Cat's Food?

Ash refers to what's left of a food's mineral components after a sample is burned.

Ash used to be blamed as the culprit behind cats developing urinary crystals and stones, but it's actually high levels of magnesium that contribute to urinary stones. So, just because a manufacturer advertises *low ash* on the label doesn't necessarily mean it's *low magnesium*.

Your Cat Isn't a Dog, so Don't Feed Him Dog Food

Sounds pretty basic, right? Yet, many owners are under the misconception that dog and cat foods are interchangeable. How many times have you seen the cat with his nose in Fido's food or the dog pushing the kitty out of the way to steal a few of his tasty morsels? This practice, unfortunately, can cause serious health complications for both pets.

If your cat eats dog food, he is at serious risk of developing health problems. On the other hand, a dog who is allowed to eat cat food will be consuming far more protein than he requires, which can lead to serious medical conditions. Additionally, the higher fat content in cat food will lead to obesity in your dog. I know it's difficult to play referee at mealtime to make sure everyone keeps their nose in their own bowl, but the consequences of not monitoring it are far too great. Unfortunately for dogs, the fat content in cat food tends to make it taste more appealing, so once Fido gets a taste of Fluffy's dinner, he'll become even more determined to switch the bowls when you're not looking.

Which Foods Are Right for Your Cat

There are a frightening number of choices out there. Every company, from the small mom and pop ones to the large well-known companies, claim to meet your cat's nutritional needs. How do you decide? It's enough to give an owner a headache.

My advice—based on years of having researched pet food, consulting with vets, cat owners, and the often very opinionated cats themselves—is to follow these basic rules:

- Learn to read labels. Although you won't be able to identify every last ingredient, you'll at least be better able to make comparisons between brands. We'll talk about this in detail later in this chapter.

- Stick with the foods manufactured by major companies. These manufacturers have invested a great deal of money and research into providing quality food that meets a cat's nutritional needs. Taking a chance on alternative, store-brand, discount, or unfamiliar manufacturers is risky because of the lack of research, quality control, consistency, and years of experience. The "innovative" new food you purchase today may not be around tomorrow. Some of the innovative new foods may well prove to be great, but don't experiment on your cat—wait until the companies have proven themselves. For my money, I depend on the manufacturers that I know have dedicated years to maintaining the quality of their products and improving the field of feline nutrition.

- Feed your cat the diet that is correct for his stage of life. Growing kittens need a *growth formula* food. Less active cats who tend to put on weight should be on a *lighter formula.* Pregnant or lactating cats are generally put on a *growth formula* due to the increased nutritional demands placed on them. Be aware of what dietary adjustments may be needed as your cat goes through life. Consult your veterinarian if you're uncertain about whether your older cat should be switched to a *senior* or *light* formula.

- Don't feed one food exclusively. Feed a variety of foods so you don't end up with a finicky eater. Vary the diet with different flavors (i.e., beef, poultry, etc.). Also, choose a couple of manufacturers and alternate. If you vary the diet from the beginning, you'll raise a cat who won't become *addicted* to one kind of food (it does happen). If your cat's stomach is sensitive to change, or you've always fed one kind of food, mix in a little of the new food each time so the changeover is gradual. This way, you'll avoid rejection of the food.

  By including more than one flavor and more than one manufacturer, you avoid going into sheer panic should a flavor be discontinued or your grocery store is out.

- Follow your veterinarian's instructions concerning prescription food. If your cat needs to be on a special food, make sure you understand *why* and *how long* it should be fed. Many times, I've found that owners don't really understand the reason why their veterinarian has prescribed a specific food, so they don't understand the *risks* of not complying with the diet. If your cat's on a diet due to kidney failure, it doesn't help if you're supplementing his meals with leftover ham and bacon. Don't leave the vet's office with those cans or that bag of food until you understand your instructions completely.

The Three Types of Cat Food

CANNED

The great thing about canned food is that it has a long shelf life. Cats usually love the taste and, depending upon the manufacturer, the flavor combinations are almost endless.

Canned food is lower in carbohydrates than dry food and much higher in water content. On the average, canned food contains about 70 percent water.

Canned food is more expensive than dry food. If you have several cats, you can buy the large cans as long as everyone agrees on the same flavor. If you have a single cat and you try being a savvy shopper by buying the large size can, I can predict with a fair amount of certainty that he'll decide he no longer cares for that flavor when there's still three-quarters of a can sitting in the refrigerator. Buying the small, single-serving cans will most likely be the most appealing to your cat, but it's also much more expensive.

If you decide to feed free choice (leaving food available at all times), then canned food isn't a good idea. It'll dry up and turn extremely unappetizing in about twenty minutes. I'm sure the last thing you want to do when you come home from work at night is to try scraping rock-hard cat food out of the bowl.

Because it's easy to chew and has an appealing aroma, canned food is often the best choice for ill or convalescing cats. Elderly cats who have difficulty chewing hard food do better with canned as well.

Allow leftover canned food that has been refrigerated to come to room temperature before serving it to your kitty. Not only would the chilled food perhaps upset his stomach, but a lump of cold day-old food stands a good chance of feline rejection. And always keep it tightly covered. Most manufacturers supply fitted plastic lids. Once opened, a can of food should be used within a couple of days.

Some owners feel that they're not serving their cats the very best unless they buy those teeny weeny cans of so-called *gourmet* food. Those foods are highly palatable for sure, but don't assume they're more nutritious. Their whole appeal is *taste*. When it comes to providing sound nutrition for my cat, I prefer to stick to the manufacturers whose main objective is balanced nutrition. What about as an occasional treat? I don't think it's necessary. The strong taste of the food might make your cat's normal diet pale in comparison in taste bud trials. My best use for the gourmet food is to entice stray cats to get close enough for me to catch them, and to jump-start the appetites of cats who have completely stopped eating.

I include several canned food meals (not the gourmet type) during the week for my cats, with the large portion of their diet consisting of dry food.

DRY

Dry food is higher in carbohydrates than canned food. The moisture content of dry is somewhere around 10 percent.

Dry food offers much more versatility. If you choose to feed free-choice, you can fill the bowl in the morning and it'll still be appetizing by evening. Dry food also offers the convenience of allowing you to leave your cat overnight and still make sure he has sufficient food.

Another advantage of dry food is that it helps reduce the buildup of tartar on the teeth.

Less expensive than canned, dry food comes in various sized bags and boxes. Once opened, if stored in an airtight container, a bag will stay fresh for several months.

One thing I especially like about dry food is that it forces Beatrice to eat a little slower. Whenever I feed her canned food, the bowl is emptied before I can even place it on the floor. With dry food, Beatrice actually *chews* her food before swallowing.

SEMI-MOIST

Sort of a cross between canned and dry. This food is shaped like dry food but has a soft consistency. Semi-moist food is higher in sugar than other foods. I think these foods were created to appeal to *us* more than to cats. The kibble comes in cute little shapes, is often multicolored (although I have yet to meet a cat who chooses his food based on color), and has less of an odor than canned food. Again, the manufacturers are appealing to the owner.

As far as price goes, semi-moist food is more expensive than dry food.

If you have a cat who for some reason doesn't like canned food and is unable to eat dry, at least you have another option. Realistically, though, I don't see the value in making semi-moist food a regular part of a cat's diet.

Read Those Labels

The American Association of Feed Control Officials (AAFCO) was started to develop and maintain consistent standards in the pet food industry. An advisory board of feed control officials from all of the states establish guidelines regarding the nutritional claims from pet food manufacturers. AAFCO defines the product labeling guidelines based on their testing requirements.

Although AAFCO has no power to enforce these guidelines, its rules are accepted by the FDA, and the better pet food companies comply with them. Those companies will state on their labels whether the food has met or surpassed AAFCO standards and by which method. There are two ways a manufacturer can substantiate their claims. They can conduct feeding trials based on AAFCO protocols or they can do it based on nutrient analysis (also based on AAFCO protocols). Feeding trials are preferable because you know that live cats actually were fed the food and it met the nutritional claims stated by the manufacturer.

When shopping for cat food, always look for the AAFCO feeding trial statement on the label.

If you want to learn more specifically about AAFCO guidelines you can contact them directly. The address is listed in the resource guide.

PRODUCT NAME

AAFCO rules dictate how an ingredient can be used in the product's name. For example, in order for the food to be named as "ABC Chicken Cat Food," chicken must constitute at least 95 percent of the total weight of all ingredients (minus water used for processing). If chicken doesn't meet 95 percent, it can still be in the name, according to AAFCO, if it constitutes at least 25 percent but it must then be referred to as *dinner, grill,* or other descriptive term. So the name of the product might then be "ABC Cat Food Chicken Dinner." If there's more than one ingredient in the name, they must appear in order of weight. Also, if a combination of ingredients are used in the name, each ingredient must constitute a minimum of 3 percent of the product weight (less water used for processing). So, now the name is "ABC Cat Food Chicken & Shrimp Dinner." You know that the chicken and shrimp combination make up at least 25 percent of the total weight, there's more chicken than shrimp, but the shrimp constitutes at least 3 percent of the product weight, less water for processing.

INGREDIENT LIST

Ingredients are listed in order of their proportions. The first few ingredients that head the list are the main protein sources. In canned food, of course, water is the first ingredient listed.

As you look at the ingredient list you may see the term *by-product.* AAFCO guidelines exclude certain ingredients for use as by-products. They include feathers, feet, teeth, head, hair, hooves, horns, contents of stomach, or intestines. Some owners worry when they see *by-product* listed on the label but actually, organ meat is technically a by-product and it's an excellent protein source. Remember, when a cat eats a mouse, he eats those *by-products* of the prey.

Vitamin and mineral supplements as well as preservatives are also listed.

NUTRITIONAL ADEQUACY CLAIM

This tells you for what stage of life the food is intended.

The manufacturer must show how the *complete and balanced* statement made on the label can be guaranteed. This is where it's explained that the claim is based on feeding trials or nutrient analysis using AAFCO protocols. Remember, feeding trials are better than nutrient analysis.

FEEDING INSTRUCTIONS

Amount to feed per pounds of body weight is the usual instruction. Remember, these are *general* guidelines.

GUARANTEED ANALYSIS

This is shown as either guaranteed minimum or maximum quantities. For example, minimum guarantee means there's a limit to how little of that ingredient is in the food but no upper limit to the amount.

MANUFACTURER'S NAME AND ADDRESS

The label must include this information to identify the company responsible for the product. Some manufacturers include a toll-free number as well, for consumer questions or comments. If you have a question concerning the product, any of its ingredients or have a comment or complaint, don't hesitate to contact them. Manufacturers want to please you, so they're very willing to provide customer service.

Premium, Regular, All-Natural, and Generic Cat Food

PREMIUM

Premium foods, sold in pet supply stores and sometimes through your veterinarian, are the most expensive. In general, these products have higher amounts of protein and fat that are of consistent quality. Premium foods are more *nutrient dense,* meaning the cat won't have to eat as much as he would of regular or generic food to receive the same amount of nutrients. Several formulas are available in canned and dry for various life stages, and most cats find the taste very palatable.

Premium foods make their nutritional claims based on AAFCO feeding trial protocols.

REGULAR/STANDARD

Regular or standard cat foods are the kinds you find in pet supply stores and supermarkets. Manufactured by the major pet food companies that you're used to seeing in numerous advertisements, these foods come in several formulas for the various life stages and seemingly endless flavors. With canned foods, many manufacturers offer choices between consistencies and textures such as sliced entrees, gravies, stews, and bite-sized chunks.

Less expensive than premium foods, regular/standard cat food still provides the nutrients needed for your cat to live a long, healthy life. Regular cat food may be less nutrient-dense, so your cat may need to eat more than he would of the premium brands.

When feeding regular cat food, vary flavors and brands to keep from developing a finicky eater.

Within the aisles of regular cat food at the supermarket, you'll find the so-called gourmet brands. As I mentioned before, they're highly palatable but not necessarily well balanced. Don't make them a regular part of your cat's diet.

Read and compare labels. Look for the AAFCO substantiation statement.

ALL-NATURAL

Sold in natural food stores, some pet supply stores, as well as through mail older, these products are made without any non-natural ingredients and use natural fat preservatives.

All-natural products may seem very appealing, but be sure of what you're really getting. Just because it's natural doesn't mean it meets your cat's nutritional requirements. Read the label and compare it to the premium foods. Also, check the label for how the nutritional guarantee is substantiated: AAFCO feeding trials or just nutrient analysis.

GENERIC

Available in supermarkets, warehouse clubs and discount stores. I would be *very* cautious when evaluating generic food. Nutrient quality and consistency can vary greatly. Remember, the quality of your cat's nutrition plays a vital role in whether he lives a long, healthy life.

Very often, the generic foods are misleading because you're initially paying less for the food, but you may notice that you're having to clean more waste out of the litter box. That means less of the food going into the cat is being used and much of it is ending up as waste. So you *paid* less but also *got* less. Not such a bargain.

Even though on label comparisons the numbers may look the same as the regular or premium foods, remember the *quality* may not be the same. I've even found vast differences in consistency from can to can within the same brand of generic food. That doesn't make me feel very confident about feeding that to my cats.

Storing Cat Food (Out of Kitty's Reach)

A cat on a diet can be one determined kitty, so make sure you've stored unused portions of food safely away.

Dry food should be placed in airtight containers. I prefer the plastic containers with snap-on lids. I also keep a little measuring cup in there so it's convenient for anyone in charge of feeding duty. They can easily dispense the proper amount.

Once you open a bag of dry food, don't just fold over the top and shove the bag in the cabinet—that's a sure way of: 1) accelerating spoilage, 2) tempting your cat (or dog) into thievery, and 3) attracting ants and rodents.

Canned food, once opened, can be stored in the refrigerator. I prefer to remove it from the can and put it in an airtight container. If you store food in the can, get one of those snap-on lids. Don't just cover the can top with plastic wrap because the contents will spoil faster and the aroma of the food will be detectable every time you open the refrigerator.

How Much to Feed

"How much should my cat be eating?"

Owners often ask me this, but more often than not, the ones who never ask are the ones who should. They're the owners who have been stuffing their kitty like the Thanksgiving turkey. I'll look at that mass of fur waddling into the room and am shocked that the cat's owner considers this normal. When I ask them about it, very often their reply is that they're just following the instructions on the bag of food. Just because the label says to feed one cup or a half cup, doesn't mean *your* cat needs that exact amount. Individual adjustments often have to be made. Based on the specific factors concerning my own cats, if I followed the manufacturer's exact feeding recommendations, I'd have a house full of overweight kitties.

When trying to decide how much food your cat needs, there are several things to take into consideration:

- the cat's age

- the cat's health

- size of the cat or specific breed considerations

- activity level

- type of food being fed

- whether the cat is pregnant or nursing

The instructions on the bag or can are *general guidelines*. Your individual cat may need more or less based on the above factors. For example, an active outdoor cat will most likely require more food than a sedentary indoor one (don't count on the mice and birds the cat may catch as his source of nutrition). Your veterinarian will be able to advise you on whether the quantity needs to be adjusted. By looking at and examining your cat, you should also be able to tell if you're on track. You should know what your cat's ideal weight range should be and periodically weigh him. To do this at home, weigh yourself first, then weigh yourself while holding your cat. Subtract the difference to get your cat's weight. If you have any questions concerning how much to feed, the best person to ask is your veterinarian. If you still believe that old myth that a cat will never overeat, you apparently haven't looked around lately—there are a lot of fat cats out there.

Dinner Is Served

FREE-CHOICE FEEDING

The most popular method of feeding a cat is called *free-choice* or *free feeding*. You just leave dry food in the bowl at all times so kitty can nibble whenever he's hungry. This works well if you're gone for long hours or overnight. I don't think it works well with canned food though because the food dries out too quickly and becomes unappealing.

In multicat households where there is hostility among cats, setting up more than one feeding station can help reduce tension in case the food bowl is guarded by a dominant cat.

Free-choice feeding works well in households where each cat tends to have appetites that peak at different times of the day.

Recent studies have now discovered that free-choice feeding may actually *help* prevent occurrences of Lower Urinary Tract Disease. Several small meals during the day reduces the alkaline swing so the urine pH doesn't rise as much. The combination of feeding a low-magnesium food on a free-choice basis may be beneficial, especially if your cat is prone to LUTD. If you have any questions, consult your veterinarian.

SCHEDULED FEEDING

This method works best for canned food eaters and also multicat households where one cat is on a special diet.

If you're trying to get a hesitant cat to bond with you or gain the trust of a troubled cat, scheduled meals allow you to be associated as the *provider* of the food, which can accelerate the acceptance process.

With scheduled meals, unless you're feeding kittens or your vet has put your cat on a specific timetable, you'll need to provide two or three meals a day. Once-a-day feedings aren't recommended, because the cat gets too hungry and will have a tendency to gulp his food.

Don't feed your kitten or cat the very second you walk in the door from work at night or else you'll raise a cat who will become stressed every time you're late coming home from work. This rule applies to A.M. feedings as well. Don't feed him the second you wake up—unless, of course, you *want* a cat who sits on your chest at 5:00 A.M., demanding his breakfast.

Home-cooked Meals for Kitty

Even if you didn't mind the time-consuming job of cooking for your cat and would lovingly chop every vegetable and each piece of meat into bite-sized chunks, from a nutritional standpoint you'll probably do more harm than good.

High-quality commercial cat foods are so nutritionally balanced that there's really no reason to risk the chance of not providing all of the nutrients needed in the proper amounts.

Do's and Don'ts of Cat Treats

For training purposes, cats generally respond to treats rather than praise. If you've ever watched professional cat trainers, they often use canned cat food on a long spoon to guide their cats through various tricks.

I use treats to reward my cats for positive behavior especially when they could have easily opted for negative behavior. I also use treats to distract a cat away from a negative situation. For example, Olive was looking out of the window one day and a cat was in the yard. Now this particular cat just happens to rub Olive the wrong way. Since Olive's first love is food, I tossed a treat in her direction. Well, that got her attention immediately. After she finished the treat in record time, her attention shifted from the feline intruder outside, to me, the treat-giver.

Even though treats can help with behavior, remember that they *are treats* and *not meals*. Your cat doesn't need a mouthful of them to feel rewarded although he'll probably try to convince you otherwise. Depending upon the size of the treat, I might even break it in half. Your cat won't realize that he only received a half or a quarter of the treat. What registers in his head is "Treat, I got a treat!"

Don't get in the habit of giving treats to your cat like clockwork. He'll soon figure out that he doesn't have to *do* anything for them, which means you've lost a powerful behavior modification tool. He may even sit by the drawer or cabinet where the treats are stored and begin demanding them.

Foods to Stay Away From

MILK

Once weaned, a cat no longer produces a sufficient amount of the enzyme *lactase,* which is necessary to digest the *lactose* in milk. Cats ironically—given the myth—are lactose intolerant. Feeding milk to your cat could result in diarrhea. If you want to give your cat a little milk as an occasional treat, watch carefully for any digestive problems.

The milk fed to kittens is different from the cow's milk we drink. The milk from the queen (mother cat) is higher in protein and arachidonic acid (which kittens need). If you're hand-raising a kitten, consult with your vet concerning the appropriate kitten replacement formula to feed.

TUNA

Cats love it. But the tuna meant for humans is, unfortunately, not a good food for your cat. It's high in polyunsaturated fats, which cats don't metabolize well. A steady diet of tuna depletes their bodies of vitamin E and can lead to a very painful condition called *Steatitis*. Tuna-flavored cat foods are supplemented with extra vitamin E to prevent this, but straight tuna is not.

Cats can quickly become addicted to the strong taste of tuna. No matter what food you place before him, your cat will only want his tuna. To get him off of it, you have to gradually mix in other food. It's not easy trying to reform a tuna junkie, so try not to create one.

RAW EGGS

Raw egg whites contain an enzyme called *avidin*, which destroys biotin in the body.

CHOCOLATE

It's extremely toxic to a cat. A mere few ounces will kill him.

TABLESCRAPS

Feeding tablescraps to your cat can seriously upset his nutritional balance. The good-quality cat food that you feed him is well balanced with the precise amount of protein, fat, and the correct ratio of vitamins and minerals. Adding your leftover turkey, unfinished hamburger, or piece of bacon causes that scale to tip. While your cast-iron stomach may look forward to those spicy dishes and rich desserts, they're certainly not good for a cat. By allowing your kitty to nibble on your burrito or sample your spaghetti sauce, you risk causing him intestinal upset and perhaps a nasty case of diarrhea.

From a behavior standpoint, I'm so against feeding a cat from the table that when I'm a guest at someone's home, I just about have to bite my tongue in half to keep from reprimanding the host as I watch them tossing little goodies to their pets.

Feeding from the table encourages begging, which is only cute when you're in the mood for it—otherwise, the novelty of your cat clawing repeatedly at your leg while you're trying to eat, wears off very rapidly. The begging behavior can escalate into jumping on the table (your company will not find this amusing, especially the ones who aren't cat lovers). When the cat is allowed to eat tablescraps, it also becomes more difficult to keep him off the kitchen counters when food is present. You may also find yourself with a garbage-can raider. Basically, everything becomes fair game at that point as he decides there's no reason to wait for you to hand him the food, he can just serve himself.

Not feeding tablescraps can be a more difficult rule to enforce in a family with children. If they're old enough to understand, explain the dangers of sharing people food with the pet cat. If they're not old enough, then you'll have to make use of those eyes in the back of your head—standard equipment in parents.

If you absolutely can't resist the urge to treat your cat to the occasional tiny piece of cooked chicken or piece of cheese (I use these for the purpose of training), do it *away* from the table so the cat doesn't make the connection that whenever the family sits down to dinner, there'll be something in it for him. Also, never give your cat the food when he begs—otherwise you've just shown him the way to train *you*. Veterinary nutritionists advise that tablescraps comprise no more than 10 percent of the cat's normal daily diet. As a behaviorist, I say it should be even less than that or you run the risk of creating a finicky eater.

Finicky Eaters

We actually cause this problem ourselves. When our cat shows a preference for a particular food, we buy a truckload of it. If that flavor or brand becomes unavailable, after years of eating the same food, the cat refuses to even taste anything else. Finicky eaters are also created when we repeatedly spruce up the cat food with tablescraps or strong-tasting foods. Then, at the next meal when the dish placed before him contains plain, ordinary cat food, he feels cheated. Knowing that by holding out, turning away from the food in disgust or pawing the ground in a mock attempt at covering this boring meal, the cat will get something much tastier. While apologizing profusely, we rummage through the refrigerator for something special, or we race to the store for something, *anything* that will meet Fluffy's approval. And thus is born the *finicky* eater.

To avoid raising a finicky eater and spending your days opening countless cans or bags of food for your cat's inspection, feed a variety of flavors from a couple of manufacturers. Feed both dry and canned food so your cat becomes comfortable with different tastes, smells, and textures.

Taste is not the only consideration in your cat's decision to accept or reject a food. *Smell, texture, size,* and even the *shape* of the food are important issues to him. In terms of dry food, some cats prefer the way a triangular shape feels in their mouth, while others will accept only round pieces of kibble. Don't laugh, it's true. What's more, pet food manufacturers have spent lots of money evaluating which shapes, sizes, and textures are preferred by cats. To avoid having a cat with a shape or texture preference, the two brands of dry food I feed have different shapes and textures and are slightly different in size. My cats have been exposed to that since kittenhood, so they're much more accepting of variations.

Tipping the Scales

I don't know about you, but whenever I watch one of those nature shows on television I never see any fat lions or other overweight cats. Looking around me, I also don't see fat strays or feral cats. But in homes all over America, I see fat house cats. Some are so fat that any slight movement requires great effort. We're killing our cats with kindness. The over-abundance of food that we endlessly offer our kitties is shortening their lives. We need to take a lesson from the wild cats. Let's examine the situation.

Cats in the wild have to *work* for their food. A stray cat, if he's lucky, may catch a number of prey in one day but I can assure you that they don't march up to him and offer themselves up as a meal. He has to *hunt* before he can *feast*. Then there are our beloved, doted on, spoiled cats. All they have to do for a meal is basically *show up*. They don't have to hunt—they can skip that part and go right to the feast. What's even worse is that it usually is truly a *feast*. We simply feed our cats too much. Unless your cat has found a way to sneak into the cabinet and open the container of food himself (and some cats are probably smart enough to do that very thing), then *you* must take responsibility for his condition.

As owners, we've taken away a vital part of our cats' lives—*activity*. It all boils down to: too many incoming calories + not enough calories burned off = a fat cat.

Another common mistake owners make is not adjusting the amount of food needed as the cat matures or goes from a revved-up kitten to a more sedentary adult. Overfeeding commonly occurs with cats once they've been neutered or spayed. Many owners blame the neuter or spay procedure on the cat's weight gain but in reality, the cat simply doesn't require as many calories due to reduced metabolic needs.

Many owners follow feeding instructions on the pet food label without making adjustments for their particular cat's physical shape. This contributes to weight problems, because the owner continues to feed the suggested amount despite the fact that the cat is getting fat.

An obese cat is more susceptible to heart disease, diabetes, and arthritis. As your cat gets older, if he does develop arthritis, the extra weight on those joints will cause even more pain. Obese cats undergoing surgery are more at risk from anesthesia as well.

Feeding tablescraps and offering too many treats contribute greatly to obesity. You may not realize how many calories your cat is consuming because it's happening gradually over the course of the day—you share a piece of bacon with him at breakfast, a few cat treats later that morning, refill his empty food bowl, treat him to the remains of your sandwich at lunch, a cookie that was dropped on the floor by your son, some samples from dinner, refill his empty food bowl, and then maybe several licks of the melted ice cream you left from dessert. Then you wonder why he's not losing weight, even though you've put him on a reduced-calorie cat food.

HOW TO DETERMINE IF YOUR CAT IS OVERWEIGHT

The first place to start is at your veterinarian's office. A physical exam will be done, possibly along with additional diagnostic testing.

Certain purebred cats have very different body types. A Persian's ideal cobby body is very different from the ideal slender Siamese body type. If you have a purebred and you aren't sure what his ideal body weight should be, consult your veterinarian.

Stand over your cat and look down at him. How do his sides look? Can you make out any kind of waistline above his hips? A cat of ideal weight has a little fat over his ribs (remember, I said a *little*) and a detectable slight indentation just behind the ribs, above the hips. If he looks more like a furry football than a cat, he's overweight.

Put one hand on either side of him. By firmly stroking his sides, you should be able to feel his ribs (if you can actually see his ribs, then he's underweight). If you can't feel his ribs without applying very firm pressure, then he's overweight.

If you're unable to feel his ribs, his chest feels soft and padded with fat, or you can feel fat pads along the backbone, then he's not just overweight, he's *obese*.

Look at your cat in profile. Does his underside hang down in a pouch of fat? If so, he's overweight.

Lift up your cat's tail and check his anal area. Does it look clean and well groomed or dirty and neglected? Some cats become so obese that they no longer can reach back there to do normal grooming.

Does your cat snore? Sometimes obese cats wheeze and snore in their sleep due to the increased fat putting more pressure against their lungs.

PUTTING KITTY ON A DIET

Your veterinarian will be able to give you an idea of what your cat's ideal weight should be and how to *safely* reach it. The reason I emphasize the world *safely* is, because if you attempt to put your cat on a crash diet or restrict his calories too severely, it can result in serious health complications. That's why you'll want to do this under the veterinarian's supervision. The cat's liver can't handle severe calorie restrictions, and *hepatic lipidosis* could result. When a cat misses too many meals, fat gets deposited in the liver, which results in liver failure.

Your vet will determine how much to feed your cat and what type of food is best to use. Depending on how overweight he is and how much food he has been getting, you may be instructed to simply cut down the portions of his regular food. Reducing the diet by no more than a quarter is medically safe and less upsetting for kitty. In other cases, a changeover to a reduced-calorie food may be necessary. If your cat is obese, he'll be put on a prescription food. Whatever option your vet decides is necessary will be successful only if *you* comply. That means no sneaking treats to your cat because you feel guilty. You have to be strong. Being the owner of a cat on a diet isn't fun. In fact, it'll be one of the hardest things you'll ever do. Be warned, your cat is going to pull out all of the stops. He's going to sit on your lap and stare into your eyes with the most pitiful look. He'll lay by his empty food bowl as if in mourning over those long lost meals. He'll cry, meow, and maybe even be demanding. He'll follow you from room to room, convinced that surely you've lost your mind and forgotten the way to the kitchen.

Another trap that you'll have to avoid is attempting to make your cat's diet food more appealing. Sometimes when the vet prescribes a reduced-calorie food and the cat doesn't care much for it, the owner tries to entice him by adding little goodies into the food. Don't sabotage his diet in the name of love.

DON'T FORGET EXERCISE DURING DIETING

It's true for humans and it's true for cats. Exercise and activity are crucial to a successful weight-loss program. Now, if the vision of putting your cat on a treadmill or signing him up for kitty aerobics is worrying you, relax. The best exercise for your cat is based on what he loves to do—*hunt*. Of course in the case of some cats, it's based on what he *used* to love to do before he got so fat. Use your cat's natural instinct as a predator and engage in daily interactive playtime. For more specifics, refer to chapter 6.

ACTIVITY TOYS

Try putting pieces of kibble in *activity* toys and leaving them around the house (take a few pieces from his regular amount so you're not increasing his intake). The cat will have to work for the food, which will keep him occupied, and then he'll enjoy the reward of the food. Refer to chapter 6 for specific instructions on how activity toys work.

FEED SMALLER MEALS MORE OFTEN

Free-choice feeding method may not work if you have an overweight cat who doesn't know how to limit himself to several small meals during the day. He may eat everything in his bowl the minute you put it down and then go hungry the rest of the day. This isn't a good plan. Instead, control his diet by feeding him several small meals on a scheduled basis throughout the day. Don't give him an increased amount of food, just divide his prescribed portion. He won't go as hungry and you'll get him out of the habit of gorging himself.

One of my cats would eat more food than she really needs in one sitting, allowing herself to become stuffed. By dividing her correct portion of food into several small meals during the day, she's convinced that she has conned me into giving her *extra* food.

Food Allergies

Food allergy reactions may show up in several forms, including diarrhea, vomiting, or other digestive problems. Food allergies may also appear as an itchy skin rash anyplace on the body. Food allergies can cause behavioral changes as well, such as anxiety, restlessness, or aggression.

What's so ironic about a food allergy is that it may be caused by a specific food that your cat has been eating for years.

If your vet suspects a food allergy, he or she may prescribe a *hypoallergenic* diet. This diet contains food sources not normally found in cat food (such as lamb) and doesn't contain the usual (such as beef or chicken). If the rash clears up, the normal diet may be reinstated to confirm diagnosis. If the rash returns, it's a pretty sure bet that it's one or more of the ingredients in the cat's food. Determining which ingredient is the specific cause can be difficult and costly, involving skin sensitivity testing. Very often, the cat is maintained on the hypoallergenic diet.

Changing Over to a Better Nutritional Program

If you've been reading this chapter and realize that you've been compromising your cat's nutrition by feeding bargain brand foods or ones that are inappropriate for his stage of life, don't make an abrupt change. The transition needs to be gradual for two reasons: 1) to avoid digestive upset, and 2) to avoid rejection. If you've been feeding a low-quality food and are now going to switch to a high-quality one, you have to allow the cat's body time to adjust. Make the changeover gradually by adding a little of the new food in with the old diet. Gradually increase the amount of new food while decreasing the old food over the course of seven to ten days. If your cat begins to reject the new food, go even slower. Some cats may take three weeks for the changeover—but be patient, it'll all be worth it when you see the difference in your cat's health, physical appearance, and disposition.

Feeding Kittens

Good-quality protein and nutrients will play a vital role in your kitten's development since his body is going to encounter major transformations. He will double in size several times in a short period of time (just mere months).

After weaning, kittens should be eating four meals a day until they're four or five months old. At that time you can reduce it to three meals (although keeping them at four meals is just fine). At six months, you can reduce the meals to two or three times a day if you are planning on scheduled meals. If you're doing free-choice feeding, then just provide access to growth-formula food at all times until the kittens reach one year of age. At that time you'll switch to an adult formula. If you are free-choice feeding, make sure all kittens are eating successfully without any problems and are gaining the appropriate amount of weight. Replace food often and wash the bowl to keep food fresh and appealing. You may even want to set up more than one feeding and water station if you have several kittens.

Feeding a Geriatric Cat

See chapter 16.

11

Relationships: Other Cats, Dogs, Kids, and Your Grumpy Aunt Esther

Does Your Cat Hate Your Spouse? Will He be Jealous of the New Baby? Should You Get a Second Cat? How About a Dog?

Although cats have been labeled asocial, the truth is they *do* enjoy companionship. To most dog owners, the idea of introducing a second dog into the household brings to mind images of the two pets playfully romping as they get to know each other. For cat owners, though, any initial images of playful romping when introducing a second cat into the home are quickly squashed by the reality of hissing, growling, and the feline version of the nuclear war. Does that mean you shouldn't risk bringing in a second cat? Absolutely not. Many single cats benefit from the addition of a companion although they may raise quite a considerable fuss initially. As an owner, being prepared beforehand, and knowing how to do the introduction in the least stressful way, will do wonders for getting the two cats to give each other a chance. By understanding their need for territorial security and individual comfort zones, you can definitely make this process go more smoothly.

Will every cat like it? No way. There are some cats who are so territorial that they could never accept any competition. Unfortunately, though, when many owners see their resident cat's initial hostile reaction to a new cat in the house, they interpret it to mean that the cat could never share her home with another and they give up. On the flip side, there are some cats who are forced to share territory in the name of companionship, where they spend day after day terrorizing each other. Call it bad chemistry, mismatched personalities—they just get under each other's skin day after day after day. Some owners don't pay enough attention to the personality and temperament of their cat and then they bring in a second cat who creates competition instead of companionship.

What kind of a cat would benefit from a feline companion? If your cat is lonely, spending long hours by herself due to your work schedule, another cat would be a wonderful friend. If you travel often and leave your cat at home in the care of a pet-sitter, having two would provide comfort for one another in your absence. A very active cat who never seems to wind down would most likely enjoy being able to run around with a friend. The addition of another cat into the household may put the spark back into the life of a sedentary or overweight cat. There are many reasons to provide your kitty with a companion.

When *shouldn't* you consider a second cat? Never try to introduce a new cat when your current cat is in the middle of a crisis. For example, if your cat just lost her longtime companion, don't try to take her mind off things with the sudden appearance of a kitten. While she has just begun grieving isn't the time to confuse her with such an overwhelming experience. I advise cat owners to avoid compounding one already stressful situation with another. Make sure your cat is in the right frame of mind to handle the process of a new cat introduction.

If your cat is ill, the addition of another cat could compromise her recovery due to the added stress.

In general, know your cat's temperament. Some cats just won't tolerate any other cats. Look at things from her side and use that insight to do what's best for her when it comes to choosing her buddies.

Bringing a Second Cat into the Home

How well you handle this introduction can make or break the relationship the two cats have. Yes, it all rests on your shoulders. Talk about pressure! So, let's get it all planned out in advance so everything goes smoothly (well, relatively speaking, that is).

The first thing I want you to keep in mind is that you're going to be introducing one animal into another animal's established territory. Plopping the new cat down in the middle of the living room is guaranteed to create hostility, panic, terror, aggression, and maybe even injury. So, let's just cross that method off the list, shall we? How should you do a new cat introduction? *One sense at a time.* This element is so important that I want you to write it on a piece of paper and tape it on your bathroom mirror if you have to in order to remember. Introducing two cats one sense at a time allows them to process each step, avoid overreacting, and gives you the opportunity to adjust the speed of each phase. Head off a feline circuit overload. One sense at a time is far less threatening for both cats. Not only do you have to concern yourself with how *your* cat is feeling, but also the new cat as well. Remember, he'll be in an unfamiliar territory.

Remember to have any new cat checked by the vet. Never bring an unvaccinated cat into your household with existing cats. Have the cat checked for parasites as well. You certainly won't want to bring home uninvited guests such as fleas or ear mites.

Before you bring the newcomer in, set up a sanctuary room for him. In it should be several hiding places (they can be boxes lined with towels), a litter box, some toys, and a bowl of water. Whether food is left out depends on if you plan on feeding free-choice or on a schedule. Keep the door to the sanctuary room closed.

Bring your new cat into the house in a carrier. Just casually bring him right into his room. Set the carrier in the corner of the room, open the door, place a treat on the floor just outside the carrier, then leave. The new cat may or may not choose to leave the safety of her carrier. After you leave the room, he'll be able to do an initial investigation and choose his own hiding place.

Your immediate concern needs to be your resident cat, who may be completely unaware of what has just taken place in her home or may be right outside the door with a look of distrust and disgust. Act casual as you shut the door and walk past your cat. If you have another treat, you can drop it behind you. (As you can tell, I'm a big fan of sensible bribery.)

At this point you can conduct an interactive play session with your resident cat, feed her, or leave an activity toy out for distraction. Don't be surprised, though, if she shows little interest in anything but what's beyond that closed door. She may sniff around the door, camp out in front of it, even hiss and growl. Don't be alarmed—those are all normal reactions. The good thing about having the newcomer out of sight is that only a portion of your cat's turf is violated.

Pay lots of attention to your cat but in a casual, nonclingy way. Don't try to comfort her by holding. Keep the tone of your voice and your body language very normal—at ease and soothing.

Let your cat get used to the idea of the fact that somebody's behind the door. Depending on your individual cat, that could take days or several weeks.

When you go in to feed or visit the new cat, try to do it on the sly so your resident cat doesn't sit outside the door feeling upset. Visit with the newcomer when your other cat is eating, sleeping, or in another room.

Helping the new cat to bond with you and come out from hiding places may take time, depending upon whether he's a kitten or an adult and what kind of socialization he had. Use treats, food, and interactive playtime to win him over. With a kitten, it won't take much convincing—he'll be eager to be with you—but an adult may be a little more skeptical. Refer to chapter 6 for tips on how to begin the bonding process and build trust.

The next step toward introduction of the two cats will involve *scent*. For this you'll need a pair of socks. Put one sock on your hand and rub the new cat down to get his scent all over it. Rub around his face, being sure to go along the sides of the mouth. When you feel you've done a good rub-down (the cat will most likely enjoy it), leave the scent-filled sock in your resident cat's territory. Use the other sock to rub down your cat and then leave that one in the newcomer's room. This enables the cats to begin getting familiar with each other's scents in a controlled, nonthreatening way. You can do this several times, using a few socks.

After your resident cat has investigated the sock, reward him with a treat or conduct an interactive play session so that the experience ends on a positive note.

When the scented sock exchange has been going well, you can then move on to a room exchange. Let your cat investigate the newcomer's room and let the newcomer out to investigate the rest of the house. This lets them do a more thorough scent investigation, including checking out each other's litter box. About an hour of this is probably a long enough time. Continue to do the room exchange a couple of times a day for about a week.

Now, if everything is going well and your resident cat hasn't declared World War III, you can open the door to the sanctuary room halfway. Be casual about it but also be ready with tools for distraction. If the cats are food-motivated, have treats or pieces of special food such as shredded cooked chicken, to toss on the floor in case they get too negatively focused on each other. Having treats also helps the cats connect positive things with each other.

If your resident cat or the newcomer seem dangerously aggressive or the step from the room exchange to the open door is too drastic, you can put three baby gates up to cover the open doorway. Use the hinged kind so you can go in and out relatively easily. That way, the cats can see each other but no one will get hurt.

Once the cats begin sharing space in the house, keep the sanctuary room set up for a while so the newcomer has a safe place of his own during initial tense encounters.

Keep two litter boxes set up in different locations, not next to each other. This way, if your resident cat is feeling territorial, the newcomer will have another place to go.

Take a close look at your home and be certain that each cat will have enough space to call their own. For instance, is there only one window perch? One food bowl? Don't put the cats in the position of having to share.

Enemies under One Roof: Easing the Tension in a Multicat Household

Now that the cats are out and about the house, there are bound to be some tense moments and unfriendly encounters as they renegotiate territory and establish personal space.

Whether they're two cats just beginning the tentative process of getting to know each other or longtime companions barely tolerating one another year after year, there are things you can do to ease the hostility.

The first rule is to make sure there's enough of everything for everybody. No one should have to share a litter box, food bowl, scratching post, bed, or toy if they don't want to. Ideally, there should be an equal number of litter boxes to cats (or close to it) and several safe sleeping retreats available.

If you don't have a cat tree, I strongly recommend that you invest in one. By adding *levels* you increase territory. A multi-tiered tree can allow two or more cats to occupy the same area without anyone feeling that their personal space has been encroached upon.

Besides making sure each cat has their own comfort zones, safe retreats and undisturbed access to the food and litter box, two powerful tools you'll need to use are *bribery* and *redirection*. You know I've talked about them in other chapters, and that's because they work when it comes to cats.

If you're trying to get two cats to like each other, making them see that in the presence of their "enemy" they get more treats, more playtime, etc., they'll eventually begin to develop a more positive association with each other.

The fine art of bribery involves either the use of treats, special food such as shredded cooked chicken, or dry kibble. When the two cats are in the presence of each other, toss a treat to each one. If you're introducing a new cat and he's still behind the baby gates due to the extremely hostile reaction of your resident cat, feeding each one some irresistible food will help. You may have to start by feeding them at quite a distance from each other and then gradually work closer. Never get to within *swatting* distance though. I prefer using shredded chicken as my bribery tool because it's something my cats never get, so it certainly is a real treat. The smell of it is so distracting that my food-motivated cats can't bypass it no matter how ticked off they are at each other.

Redirection tactics involve interactive toys. Keep one with you, such as the Cat Dancer, which is easy to curl up and hide. The scenario: you're sitting on the couch watching TV. One cat is peacefully sleeping in his cat tree when suddenly, out of the corner of your eye you spot your other kitty walking into the room. She has the look of a gunslinger at high noon. She's staring at the sleeping cat and you just know she's about to launch an attack. Quietly and very quickly pull out your interactive toy and distract the aggressive cat. Being a predator, she'll very likely prefer to go after the toy. She then will get her aggression out in a positive way and forget what her original intent was. The more cat-to-cat attacks you can prevent through redirection, the more likely they'll begin to tolerate each other. Tolerance may then progress toward actually liking each other. In a hostile household, keep interactive toys in each room so you'll always have one handy.

When you use redirection, try to get in there *before* an actual attack.

Even if you only suspect that something is about to happen, use diversion. Since you're using a positive method, even if you're wrong, what's the worst that happens? Your cat gets an unexpected play session.

If both cats are staring each other down from across the room but a fight hasn't taken place yet, use either diversion or bribery in a big way. Grab a toy or toss several treats across the floor. By diverting their attention with something fun or tasty, you'll help them to avoid a continual buildup of hostility. Here's a little scenario from your own childhood which may help to put it in perspective: You and your new friend (whom you aren't sure you like yet) are playing in the yard when you begin fighting over a toy or the rules of a game. Your mother comes out and orders your friend to go home and you to go to your room. You march into your room where you sit on the bed and proceed to stew in anger at how your friend got you in trouble. Boy, are you mad at that friend. So even though your mom put a stop to the fighting, you're left with a negative feeling toward your friend. Let's go back to the beginning of that scenario where you and your new friend are beginning to fight, only this time your mother comes out and announces that she just made a batch of cookies, or maybe she's standing there with two ice cream cones in her hands. You and your friend put the game (and your fight) on hold as your attention is redirected to something fun. By using a positive approach, your mom stopped the escalating tension and no damage was done to the blossoming relationship.

Anytime you see or sense mounting tension, use positive redirection whenever you can to change the mind-set of the cats. If the fight has already broken out, the chances of either cat responding to or even noticing a treat or toy is very slim. In that case, make a noise such as clanging a pot or clapping two pot lids together. Whatever you have, use it to make a noise to startle the cats. Don't attempt to physically break up the fight because you'll most likely get injured. If the noise doesn't stop the fight, use a squirt of water.

Once you've startled the cats, they'll very likely head off in opposite directions. Don't try to cuddle or pet anyone, because they'll still be in a highly aroused state. Make sure they stay separated for a while so they can calm back down. Divert each one's attention back to something positive by casually tossing a treat or activity toy or by using an interactive toy. Be *very* nonchalant and don't toss the treat or toy in the direction of the cat. She should feel safe and even hidden if she prefers. You'll just happen to be doing something irresistible or at least interesting in the same room. A toy such as Quickdraw McPaw is great for this type of situation because the in-and-out appearance and disappearance of the feather will be hard for the cat to ignore.

Introducing a Dog to Your Cat

Despite what you may have believed in the past, cats and dogs can get along. A natural pack animal, a dog will, in most cases, adjust easily to life with a cat. Some cats who are unable to tolerate the addition of another cat into their territory may more easily accept the introduction of a dog. The upside of bringing a cat and dog together is that their views on territorial rules usually don't compete with each other the way a cat-to-cat introduction can. The downside of bringing a cat and dog together is that they speak two different languages and you need to help them find a common ground.

PRE-DOG CONSIDERATIONS

Before you introduce a dog to your cat, take enough time to think about the commitment involved. Day-to-day dog owner responsibilities are different than that of a cat owner. Unless you're taking in a dog as part of a family package, i.e., blending families as in the case of marriage, consider what type of dog would be best for your cat's personality. A timid cat wouldn't appreciate a hyper, tenacious dog. If you adopt a puppy, you have the advantage of training him to be cat-compatible. Puppies are very energetic and require time and training, though, so be certain you can supply the amount of attention needed to raise a well-behaved dog.

If it's an adult dog you're taking in, you may have the opportunity of choosing one whom you know is cat-friendly. If you aren't familiar with the dog's background, use extreme caution and always supervise the pets until you know that they can be trusted together.

Some cat owners are faced with the difficult situation of having a dog introduced into their lives who has had a history of not being cat-friendly. If that's the case, you must consult a behaviorist or dog trainer to evaluate the situation. Some dogs, even after working with a trainer, can never be trusted with a cat. I've seen dogs who have been trained to control their behavior toward the cat in the presence of the owner, only to attack when the owner wasn't home.

Even though the dog is a sociable creature, be aware of the fact that excitement and playful intentions can get out of control in certain situations. A dog who has a history of rough play or is too stimulated can not only frighten a cat but poses a very serious danger to her. If more than one dog will be coming into the cat's life, their *pack mentality* can cause one dog's excitement to feed the others, creating a highly charged pack who can gang up on a cat. You must be aware of any potential for danger.

PREPARATIONS

Before the actual introduction, your cat would greatly appreciate a little heads-up as to the major upheaval her life is about to encounter. Start by taking your portable cassette recorder to the neighbor's house (the one with the noisiest dog) and ask them to record their dog barking. Inform them that this isn't so you can use the tape as evidence that their dog is a neighborhood nuisance, but because you want to get your cat used to the sound. When you get the tape, begin by playing it at a very low volume, gradually increasing it over time. Engage in absolutely state-of-the-art interactive play sessions while the tape is on to help your kitty become used to the sound in a positive way.

With a dog coming into your home, some environmental changes may need to be made in order to safeguard your cat's territory. Doing so gradually, before the pup's arrival will enable your cat to make a comfortable, easy adjustment. For example, if your cat's food bowl is normally left out on the floor for her to nibble free-choice, you'll have to change to an elevated feeding station. By creating an elevated station or feeding in a room that will be off-limits to the dog, mealtime won't be stressful.

Think carefully about the litter box. The last thing a kitty needs is to be suddenly ambushed by a playful dog while trying to attend to business in the litter box. Preventing the dog from having access to the box will also keep him from eating cat poop, viewed as a delicacy by many dogs. Because the cat's diet is higher in fat, dogs tend to find those little litter box nuggets very tasty. Using a covered litter box may not stop a determined dog so the best setup is to keep the box in an off-limits area. If the dog is small, you can put the box in the guest bathroom tub. You can also use a baby gate to keep the uninvited canine out of the room. Many owners have installed a pet door to the cat's area (one that the dog can't fit through).

If you'll be changing the location of the litter box, move it gradually until it's in the final spot, well in advance of the dog's arrival. Don't make abrupt changes, because your cat won't tolerate that well. Move the box an inch at a time each day if necessary so your cat doesn't have to deal with the "now you see it, now you don't" disappearing box.

Providing your cat with a safe retreat is very important when there'll be a dog in the house. A cat tree can be a haven for a kitty being chased around by the new pup. The bigger the dog, the taller the tree should be, so if it's in your budget, let your cat have a place she can climb to for an undisturbed nap.

Also needed before the introduction is to make sure everyone is healthy and free of parasites. You certainly don't want your indoor cat infested with fleas from the new dog. Take care of any problems before the introduction. For more on fleas, refer to chapter 13.

If you and your cat will be moving into the dog's environment, a sanctuary room will need to be set-up for the cat so she'll have time to adjust to the new surroundings. Introducing her to a new home and a dog all at once is frightening. Once she has adjusted to her new surroundings in the sanctuary room, let her out to explore the new house and become familiar with everything before you attempt the dog's introduction. If it's possible to bring the dog over to the cat's home for a gradual introduction before you move, that may help her to accept him more easily. She'll be in her familiar territory and will know where she can go to feel safe.

Don't attempt to introduce an untrained dog to your cat. If you don't have verbal control over the dog, enroll in a training course or work with a private trainer.

THE INTRODUCTION

Allow the dog to work off energy before attempting an introduction, by taking him out to play. Then feed everyone, because pets with full tummies are usually not as energetic. If possible, having someone assist with the introduction will make things much easier on you.

Start by having the dog on a leash. If you're in the dog's territory, have the cat in a carrier so she doesn't panic. If the introduction is to take place in the cat's territory she can either be in a carrier or loose (with several available boxes or other hiding places), depending on how nervous a cat she is. If she tends to be curious and will sit in the room to watch the goings-on, then she can be loose. If you think she'll just bolt for the farthest corner of the house, have her in a carrier. Don't, under any circumstances, let anyone attempt to hold her in his or her arms. Not only will she feel confined, the person holding her stands a very good chance of becoming injured.

The first sight the animals have of each other needs to be at a safe distance. Let them size each other up from across the room. Don't allow the dog to approach the cat yet. Keep the dog calm by using voice commands and praise. Don't get the dog excited with high pitches, short verbal commands, or baby talk. Use a soothing tone of voice, stretching out your words ("gooood doooog") and dip your voice down at the end. The dog will take his cues from you, so if you're excited, the dog's going to get excited and that will only panic the cat.

The dog should be petted gently on the chest, using long strokes. Don't do short petting or slapping. Avoid petting him on the top of the head or back, as this can cause excitement. Chest stroking can have a calming effect.

Once the two pets have seen each other for a while, take the cat or dog (depending on whose territory it is) to their sanctuary room. Continue this gradual introduction several times a day as the two get used to each other. If they appear comfortable, you can let them get closer. With the dog on the leash, allow him to walk a little closer to the cat. If he attempts to run or pulls against the leash, give a slight correction with a quick tug of the leash and a verbal command. He needs to learn that his approach to the cat must be slow and that as long as he moves that way, he'll have slack on the leash, but should he attempt to bolt or pull, he'll be corrected. Reward the dog every time he reacts correctly.

Cats have a larger "personal zone" than dogs, so the pup will have to learn to respect that. If he goes rocketing up to the cat, he'll more than likely encounter a series of paw smacks and hisses. The cat needs to set the pace for how much personal space she is willing to share.

Don't let the dog off the leash until you're sure both pets are comfortable with each other. Don't rush this step, because a mistake could have serious results.

If the dog is not very tall, you may want to set up a baby gate across the cat's room so she can hop in and out of her sanctuary as needed to have some time away from the dog. Even with a large dog, you can train him not to jump the baby gates, which may give your cat a sense of security knowing that one room in the house is exclusively hers.

As the two pets begin to settle in and get comfortable with each other, continue to watch for any potential trouble. Observe the dog during meals to watch for any hint of food aggression. Also, since play methods differ (cats stalk and dogs chase), make sure there's no miscommunication happening.

Overcoming Fear of Strangers

The doorbell rings and your cat vanishes right before your eyes. To help her overcome this common fear, refer to chapter 7.

Why Your Cat Insists on Sitting in the Lap of the One Guest Who *Hates* Cats!

It never fails. You invite four or five friends over, and your kitty ignores all the cat lovers and focuses her attention on the guest who doesn't just *dislike* cats, but absolutely *detests* them. If you look at it from the cat's point of view, though, it makes perfect sense. Being a territorial animal, the cat is suddenly faced with a bunch of invaders in her domain. She needs to check them out and make sure they're okay but the cat *lovers* usually walk right over to her, reach out to pet or—even worse—try to hold her. The cat hasn't had time to evaluate the strangers and certainly doesn't want to be trapped by them. The only one who makes no overture to her is the cat *hater*. That person sits on the couch and completely ignores your kitty. That behavior allows the cat freedom to conduct her investigation. She's able to get close, sniff the guest's shoes, maybe even jump up on the couch and conduct a closer inspection. The cat's able to do all of this without so much as a hand reaching over to her. So it's not a big mystery—it's just a cat using common sense.

What to Do When Your Cat Hates Your New Spouse

I find this subject so interesting. Over the years, I've come across quite a few owners who would just as soon get rid of the spouse if they didn't meet with the cat's approval. When I was single, Albie was my "date barometer." I found that if Albie didn't care for my date, he'd sit on the coffee table, directly in front of the guy and stare him down. If my date attempted to pet him, Albie would bob and weave just enough to stay out of range. I soon found out that the men that Albie sat and stared at usually did turn out to be jerks. I learned to trust Albie's assessment and breathed a sigh of relief when he didn't engage in a staring contest with my future husband, Scott.

From a cat's point of view, the unexpected addition of a new person to the *nest* can be very alarming. If the new spouse is moving into your home, the cat is faced with not only the intrusion of a new person, but their strange belongings as well. The cat, a territorial creature of habit, watches as her environment is turned upside down. Furniture usually gets rearranged, schedules get disrupted, and worst of all, her usual sleeping spot on the bed may become off-limits to her. Add to that, the lack of attention she may receive due to the hectic activity surrounding the wedding and honeymoon. Poor kitty can easily get lost in the shuffle.

If you and your kitty move from your home into your spouse's home, or even to a new home, imagine how much of an adjustment that becomes. It's a stressful time for you, but *you* entered into this willingly, whereas your cat had no choice. So here she is, in a new home, with a stranger (and maybe other pets or even children), and the only thing familiar to her is *you*. The techniques in chapter 14 will help her adjust to this new environment.

When you talk about a cat hating your spouse or appearing jealous, it's really that she's anxious, confused, and fearful. She's having to make many overwhelming adjustments in a short amount of time.

If your cat seems uncomfortable or even aggressive toward your new spouse, you need to slow down and give her the opportunity to adjust at a more comfortable pace. She needs as much of her familiar routine as possible during the transition. Banishing her from her usual spot on the bed will only heighten her confusion and anxiety. She needs to be an included family member—not an excluded pet. So as you all make the transition, continue to look at the situation from the cat's point of view.

One thing that can cause a cat anxiety with a new spouse has to do with the sound of his or her footsteps and the types of movements s/he makes. A cat who has only been exposed to a female owner may need time to adjust to the heavier sounds of a man's footsteps as well as his deeper voice or broader movements. It will help if you can ask your spouse to be aware of trying to walk and talk a bit softer for the first few weeks. The same adjustment applies to the cat of a male owner who must now adjust to quicker movements and higher pitched sounds. The new female in the house will need to try to avoid sounding too high-pitched or moving too fast.

One of the best ways to help a cat to bond with her owner's new spouse is through playtime. Using an interactive toy, the spouse can help the cat develop a positive association. Teach your spouse how to use the toys and let him or her conduct play sessions. It's important that your spouse remain still and nonthreatening throughout the game. If your cat refuses to play, *you* can start the interactive session and eventually hand the toy to your spouse. Watch to make sure that your spouse conducts playtime in the way your cat is used to—with lots of successes and captures. Even if your spouse isn't a cat lover, I've found that much of that feeling comes from not being around cats, which prevents getting to know them. Through play sessions, both your cat and your spouse will begin to relax around each other. Your spouse will also start to view your cat in a different light while watching how graceful, fast, and comical she can be during play.

Your spouse should also take over feeding duties. Even if you normally leave food down free-choice, your spouse should be the one to do it, leaving the scent of their hands on the food bowl. Treats should also come from the spouse.

Let the cat set the pace of things and offer her plenty of opportunities to investigate your spouse without the fear of being picked up, pushed away, or held. Your spouse may be dying to hold or pet your cat in a show of friendship, but the cat may not be ready for that. Eventually, through positive association surrounding playtime, meals, and treats, your cat will very likely see those same wonderful qualities in your spouse that you do.

Preparing Your Cat for the Arrival of a Baby

When the wife finds out that she's expecting a baby, all too often, she starts to panic about what to do with the cat. Well-meaning friends and neighbors warn her about how dangerous cats are. Many cats, once loved family members, soon find themselves living in a cage at the shelter, never to see their owner again. Some cats, while not relinquished to a shelter, may become banished to the outdoors—something horribly traumatic and potentially deadly for a once indoor-only cat.

By now, I'm sure you don't believe that cats suck the breath from babies. Perhaps what we now know as SIDS was once blamed on innocent cats for lack of any other explanation. The one concern a pregnant woman should have, though, has to do with toxoplasmosis. With proper litter box maintenance and a little education on your part, you can avoid this danger. IT IN NO WAY MEANS YOU MUST GET RID OF YOUR CAT! Refer to the medical appendix, which will explain what toxoplasmosis is and how to avoid it.

Some cats handle the arrival of a new baby without so much as a whisker getting out of place. Some others, though, appear to view it as the ultimate invasion of a hairless, strange-smelling, noise-making alien. Realize that it's *anxiety* and not *jealousy* that may cause your cat to hiss or act less than friendly. Don't punish your cat or banish her to the garage for being apprehensive. Instead, use patience, love, and positive reinforcement to help her through this so you can all be one happy family.

Unless, due to some unforeseen circumstances, you suddenly have a child in your home, you have plenty of time during pregnancy to prepare your cat for the arrival. Even if you are adopting a child, you'll most likely have adequate preparation time. By taking the time to ease your kitty through the transition, you'll have a calm cat well-equipped for the changes the new baby will create in the family.

If you're planning to create a nursery, complete with new paint, wallpaper, carpet, or all new furniture, do it gradually. Start early and do a little bit at a time to give your cat a chance to adequately adjust. Remember, a cat is a creature of habit, so if one room in the house is suddenly transformed in a whirlwind of activity, she's going to be a little concerned. Do one thing at a time and allow your cat the opportunity to investigate. If you're remodeling, take breaks to play with the cat if she seems stressed by the goings-on. If workers are in the house, take time after they've finished before you go on to the next phase. Let your cat get comfortable with the changes in the room. Conduct play sessions in there so she continues to have positive feelings about every part of her territory.

Buy the crib well in advance of the baby's arrival so you have enough time to train your cat to stay out of it. My favorite method is to fill the crib with lots of shake cans. A shake can is an empty soda can with a few pennies inside and the opening taped closed. Fill the crib with the cans so that she won't be able to find a quiet, comfortable spot to nap in there. Keep the shake cans there until the baby's arrival. If the cat attempts to climb in the crib once the baby comes, you can buy netting at the baby furniture store to place over the crib.

The sounds a baby makes can be very disconcerting to a cat (and to

Don't lavish an overabundance of attention on your cat before the baby arrives, because chances are you won't be able to maintain that schedule when the baby is home. If your cat gets used to this seemingly endless amount of affection for nine months and then becomes all but forgotten after the delivery, you'll cause her even more anxiety. Maintain a normal schedule before the baby's arrival.

parents as well). Remember the technique used to help the cat adjust to a dog? Begin getting your kitty used to the noise by playing a tape of baby cries. Ask a friend to make a tape of their baby crying. I once sat in a pediatrician's waiting room with my trusty cassette recorder in order to make a tape of baby cries for a client of mine. I was able to successfully tape many samples of crying babies and only required two aspirins to get rid of my pounding headache.

Play the tape at a low volume while the cat eats and during your play sessions. Gradually increase the volume until it reaches the real-life baby cry level. Place the tape in the nursery so the cat becomes comfortable with where the sound comes from.

If you have any music boxes, musical mobiles, or any other sound-making baby toys, play them while the cat engages in a game or eating so that by the time the baby arrives, all of these noises are old news to kitty.

If you have a friend with a baby, invite them for a visit so you can gradually get your cat used to the sight and smell of a baby. You don't want a toddler going all over the house, so try to pick a friend with a baby who can just sit quietly in a baby seat or the mother's lap. Conduct a play session with the cat at whatever distance she feels most comfortable.

Scent is very important to cats, so before the baby arrives, the mother-to-be should start wearing baby powder, lotion, or whatever other products that will be used on the newborn. This will help the cat associate those scents with her owner so they'll be familiar when she smells them on the baby.

If possible, when the mother gives birth, the father or someone in the family should bring home a blanket or towel that contains the baby's scent. Then, when the baby is brought home, allow the cat to sniff the baby's things. Try to be calm and relaxed as you greet your cat. Play with and pay attention to the cat. It's an exciting time for the family but an anxious time for the cat and she needs to be reassured.

Keep the cat's schedule as normal as possible. Don't skip her play sessions even if it means that one family member plays with her while the mother tends to the baby. Allow the cat to be a part of things. If the mother is nursing the baby, there's no reason why the cat can't be in her lap or sleeping by her side.

One thing to be aware of is that the increase in visitors to your home to see the baby can be stressful to the cat. Use Feliway as needed, conduct play sessions, and don't have too many guests over if your cat appears to be getting anxious.

If you find that your cat is too fascinated with the baby and you'd prefer that she stay out of the nursery completely, you may want to install a screen door at the room's entrance.

Small Children

One of the scariest sights your cat may encounter is your toddler coming down the hallway in her direction, with fingers ready to grab a fistful of hair. Ouch! Always supervise small children around the cat. It's so easy for a tail to be grabbed or an ear pulled. A cat who feels trapped by a toddler may react by scratching or biting.

Teach children that the cat is a member of the family who should be treated with gentleness and respect. The cat is not a toy to be teased, dressed up, or restrained. Show your children how to pet with an open hand. Instruct them to pet with one hand only to avoid the cat feeling confined. As soon as the children are old enough, teach them how to interpret the cat's body language and means of communication so they'll begin to learn when the cat prefers to be left alone.

The litter box, feeding station, and where the cat sleeps are three places that should be off-limits to children. You may want to install a baby gate across the doorway to the room where the litter box is kept.

If your children want to play with the cat, provide them with safe interactive toys, such as Quickdraw McPaw. Instruct them on its proper use and make sure they don't put it in the cat's face. A fishing pole–type toy can be used if the children are old enough to use it correctly. With children, you have to watch that they don't accidentally poke the cat with the pole or tease her by keeping the toy out of reach. Explain to your children how it makes the cat feel good to have successful captures, just as they themselves feel happier when they win at a game.

I often see the family cat being hauled around by a child with only a small portion of the body supported. She ends up hanging from the child's arms as she's barely supported under the armpits with her front paws almost straight up in the air. Teach your children how to properly lift and carry the cat. If they aren't big enough to support the cat's full weight, they shouldn't carry her at all.

You're Responsible for the Cat's Welfare

When children are old enough, it's certainly a good idea to have them help with the responsibilities of caring for the cat. They can fill the food and water bowl, you can show them how to brush the cat, or they can scoop the litter, but a child can't possibly handle the total responsibility of the cat. You must monitor to make sure the cat is getting everything she needs. A child won't notice if the cat hasn't been urinating in the box or isn't eating. A child also may not notice if the cat has diarrhea or is constipated. Neglecting the cat because she belongs to your child will not teach anyone any lessons—it'll only cause the cat to suffer.

Unfortunately, in some families, animal abuse by children occurs. Do not tolerate any mishandling of the cat and be alert for signs that any "accidents" may have been intentional. If you suspect abuse, move the cat to a safe environment immediately and seek professional help for your child.

Provide your cat with a sanctuary room when unfamiliar children come over and want to "play" with her. Even if children don't mean any harm, they're often unable to read a cat's warning signs. As a responsible owner, use your good judgment and always provide for your cat's safety.

12

Glamour Puss

How to Make Grooming a Pleasurable Experience (Really, It Can be Done)

If a cat isn't sound asleep, there's a pretty good chance that he's grooming himself. Hardly an activity goes by in a cat's life that won't end with either a grooming touch-up or full-scale coat maintenance. Cats are master groomers.

Grooming serves many important functions in a cat's life. Although the people who dislike cats will tell you that they groom solely for the purpose of being able to throw up a hair ball on your bed, that's far from true.

As the cat runs his raspy tongue over his coat, he's able to pull out the dead hair. His tongue also cleans dust, dirt, and particles from the coat. He does his best to remove parasites such as fleas, by biting and licking. Spreading his toes, he cleans between them, under and around each nail. When he's satisfied that he's done an adequate bathing job, his tongue smoothes out each hair to provide maximum insulation from cold or heat. Licking helps evenly distribute the natural oils in his coat, which affords him some waterproofing and imparts a glorious sheen.

For an animal who uses scent as a major form of communication, grooming distributes his scent over his coat. After being petted, you'll often notice your cat groom himself right at the spot you touched him. He's reinforcing his own scent on his coat and also enjoying yours as well. On the other hand, after a negative encounter (such as being handled by the vet), the cat will go through an elaborate grooming ritual once he gets home. He'll want to wash away the bad scent and redistribute his own comforting scent.

After a hunt, the cat will end his meal by grooming to rid his coat of the prey's scent. This helps him to not alert other prey or predators of his presence.

Social grooming among companion cats is another way in which they bond by mixing their scents.

Grooming is also used as a displacement behavior. When a cat wants to do something and is prevented from it, he often will groom himself to relieve his anxiety. You may notice this when your cat watches the birds outside. He can't get to them and needs to do something with his energy. I see it with Olive when she walks into the kitchen. When there's food on the counter, she'd like nothing better than to jump and sample it all but she knows that's forbidden. To relieve her frustration, she'll jump onto her cat tree and do a quick face washing.

Why You Need to Groom Your Cat

Even though they are so meticulous about their personal hygiene, your cat still needs your help in maintaining his glorious coat. The coats of longhaired cats are glorious to look at but the unfortunate side of breeding to enhance the coat makes them unable to be maintained by the cat alone. Even your shorthaired cat will benefit from being brushed, though you don't have to brush as often as you would a longhaired cat. The more meticulous you are about grooming your cat, the more beautiful and healthy his coat and skin will be.

Cats have two major shedding seasons each year, one in preparation for winter and one for summer. Indoor cats exposed to artificial light and consistent year-round temperatures shed year-round but at a more moderate rate. Grooming your cat helps tremendously. If you brush your cat, not only will it cut down on the amount of hair that ends up on the couch, chairs, and bed, it will reduce the amount of hair that your cat will ingest during self-grooming. And this in turn will lessen the likelihood of hair balls, which can be a serious problem for cats who ingest too much hair. They're also a problem for owners who walk around in bare feet because cats always manage to vomit hair balls where you're sure to step on them (see section on "hair balls" in this chapter). Regular brushing, along with other routine feline maintenance, may also help those in your family with allergies.

Most cats enjoy the gentle massage and attention they get while they are being brushed. For my cats, this is our time for bonding. When Albie was a kitten, I gently began getting him used to being groomed, so he has always viewed it as a pleasurable experience. Olive, though, whom I rescued when she was about a year old, needed three weeks before I could even introduce the idea of a brush. By being gentle, patient, and making brushing an extension of petting (and even that took quite a while for her to accept), she began to actually enjoy it. Nowadays she relaxes so much while being brushed that she falls asleep. We've certainly come a long way from the cat who thought being touched by a human was to be avoided at all costs.

Grooming your cat on a regular basis also allows you the opportunity to do a health check. When I groom, my hands go over every inch of the cat's body and I can catch any lump, bump, sore, or rash early. I can feel if there's been any weight loss or gain. I check for fleas and when I clean their ears, I also look for any signs of infection or ear mites. When I brush the cat's teeth I look for any signs of gum swelling or tenderness. Owners who don't groom may not notice that small lump or wound on their cat until it has advanced. Grooming lets owners of cats allowed outdoors check for ticks that can hide in places where you wouldn't detect them otherwise—such as between the toes, in the ear folds, or under the tail.

Finally, if you don't get your cat comfortable with being groomed, you'll probably have trouble medicating him should it ever become necessary. Trying to put ear drops in a cat who isn't used to having his ears touched often results in more medicine getting on your clothes or the walls than in his ears.

The Tools You'll Need

Having everything in one convenient case will make it easier for you than if you have to leave your cat to go find the last place you left the nail trimmers or the comb. The tools you'll need will depend on the type of coat your cat has. The instructions provided are meant as general grooming guidelines for keeping your cat's coat clean, healthy, and free of mats. If you're grooming for show competitions or have a cat with specific care requirements, work with a top-notch professional groomer or get instructions from the breeder who'll be knowledgeable on show requirements.

LONGHAIRED CATS

A pin brush, which resembles a pin cushion with a handle, works best. The bristles are straight and get through the dense, fine coat. You'll also need wide, medium, and fine-toothed combs. For when your cat gets tangles you can't brush or comb out, you can buy a special detangling spray made for cat hair or you can sprinkle cornstarch into the coat. The spray is less messy. Some longhaired breeds tend to stain under their eyes. To remove this, use a tear stain remover that's safe for cats. I also finish off the session by polishing the coat with a soft bristle brush.

SHORTHAIRED CATS

A *slicker* brush, the small, gentle one, with thin wire bristles bent at the tips works well on short coats. If your cat has very short, dense hair, you can use a soft bristle brush instead of the slicker brush. To loosen dead hair and give your cat an enjoyable massage, you'll start off with a rubber currycomb or you can use the Zoom Groom, a rubber brush with longer nubs. If your cat objects to being brushed, you can start with a grooming glove to get him used to the procedure. The glove has little rubber nubs that trap the hair as you pet your cat. It's not as effective as the currycomb but if that's all the cat will let you do for now, it's better than nothing. A fine-toothed comb, also known as a flea comb, will enable you to run through the hair and trap not only fleas, but their excrement (dried blood) and their eggs. It really keeps the coat clean. And, nothing finishes the grooming process on a shorthaired cat like a piece of chamois or velvet rubbed in the direction of the hair growth.

KITTENS

No matter whether he's longhaired or shorthaired, start familiarizing him with being groomed by using the gentle slicker brush or a baby brush.

SPECIAL COATS

If you have a wire-haired or crimped-haired cat, you'll need the same tools that you'd use for a shorthaired cat. If your cat's hair is very sparse, use a soft baby brush instead. You'll also need a flea comb. For a Sphinx cat, a rubber currycomb works to massage and remove the fine down that covers the skin. The skin on the Sphinx can get oily, which attracts dirt in the folds. You may also want to keep baby wipes on hand for touch-ups in between bathing.

TOOLS OF THE TRADE NEEDED FOR ALL CATS

A rubber bath mat, which you'll put on the table, prevents your cat from slipping. You'll also use it if you bathe your kitty.

You will need nail trimmers even if your cat has been declawed (in case the nails on the hind feet need a trim). Buy trimmers designed for cat's nails. Dog trimmers are too big and with them you risk injuring your cat. Regular human fingernail trimmers aren't really designed for the shape of a cat's nail, and if you use them, the end result could be ragged. However, if you're more comfortable using those and they work well for you, then stick with them. You'll also need some styptic power on hand just in case you cut too much and cause the nail to bleed.

Keep a supply of cotton balls to protect your cat's ears while you are bathing him. They can also be used for ear and undereye cleaning. Gauze pads are handy for wrapping around your finger to brush the cat's teeth in case you aren't comfortable using a toothbrush. Gauze pads can also be used for ear cleaning. Also, a cat-safe ear cleanser should be part of your grooming supplies.

Keep a supply of cotton swabs on hand to apply the styptic powder. I don't recommend using cotton swabs for ear cleaning though because you could easily puncture the cat's delicate eardrum.

To clean teeth, you can either use the gauze, a pet toothbrush, finger toothbrush, or even a baby toothbrush. You'll also need a toothpaste designed especially for pets. Don't use toothpaste for humans because it'll burn the throat, esophagus, and stomach.

Getting Started

When you first get your cat is the time to begin getting him used to being groomed. Start by getting him comfortable with being touched.

Start by introducing grooming tools slowly. Sit with your cat and pet him, than take a brush and lightly stroke behind his head (that's usually a cat's favorite spot to be petted or brushed). If you have a rubber currycomb, that'll probably feel the best. After one stroke, go back to petting with your hand. Make brushing just an extension of petting. Once he makes that connection and it's enjoyable, grooming will be a pleasure for both of you.

Before you actually begin grooming, there are a few rules that I'm sure your cat will want you to know about. The first one is *don't hurt your cat.* One reason so many cats hate to be groomed is that it truly becomes a torture session. Don't pull, yank, or be rough in any way. A cat's body is *very* sensitive. His skin can easily tear. Also, because the skin is thin, raking a comb or brush over the spine or various other bony parts will be very painful. The moment you hurt your cat, he'll tense up and begin to dislike being groomed. My cats don't struggle to get away when they're being groomed because they trust me—I make sure that I never hurt them. Before you use any brush or comb, run it along the inside of your forearm to get a feel for how lightly you should brush.

Another reason cats hate grooming is that often it goes on for an intolerably long time. The owners of longhaired cats who brush only when they remember or when they feel a mat, end up subjecting the cat to thirty minutes or more. Owners who brush daily can get the whole thing done in under three minutes. If you have a longhaired cat, you must brush him daily. That's the only way to prevent tangles and mats. Even if you have a longhaired cat whose hair doesn't mat, daily brushing keeps the coat in good shape and reduces shedding and the risk of hair balls. Daily brushing for short periods also keeps it a familiar, comfortable routine in the cat's life.

Brushing shorthaired cats once or twice a week is enough to keep the coat looking nice. If your cat has a problem with hair balls, you may want to brush more often.

You won't have to do ear cleaning and nail trimming every time. Nails usually need a trim about once a month. Your cat's ears may be very clean and only need to be wiped out every few weeks. Some cats need it weekly. The point is, by checking the ears every time, you can catch problems early.

Teeth should be brushed daily. It's a quick process (described later in this chapter) and once you get the hang of it, you can do it in ten seconds. But, now that I've said that it should be done daily, I'll tell you that most owners don't follow that rule. Unfortunately, many owners don't brush their cats' teeth at all. That's a big mistake because if you do preventive maintenance, your cat may not have to go under anesthesia to have his teeth professionally cleaned by the vet as often. You can also, in many cases, prevent gingivitis and periodontal disease. Your cat's breath will also stay very sweet. Brushing daily would be best but do it at least three times a week. I try to do it daily to all of my cats, but some weeks I only manage three or four sessions. Still, my cats have seldom had to have their teeth professionally cleaned, so I know that at least a few times a week still helps.

WHERE TO GROOM

If you groom on a table or elevated surface, it will certainly be much kinder for your back. Place a rubber bath mat or at least a towel down on the table or counter so he will have something to grip. He'll feel much more secure than if he's sliding all over the place and scrambling to keep his footing. The table or counter has to be a surface that your cat is normally allowed on, so you don't send a mixed message. If you have a longhaired cat, it's worth checking into purchasing a grooming table.

If you're more comfortable with the cat in your lap, just place a thick towel across your legs to catch the hairs and prevent injury to you should he dig his nails in. I find that cats get more impatient being groomed on the owner's lap because they get hot. It's also more difficult to reach all areas of the coat when the cat's curled up on your lap.

Brushing Techniques

SHORTHAIRED CATS

Start by using the rubber currycomb in a circular motion to loosen the dander and dead hairs. Your cat will most likely enjoy this. Then take the slicker brush and gently do long strokes from the back of the head, down the body, on either side of the spine. Don't rake the brush over the bumpy spine. On the parts of the body where you need to do shorter strokes, be very gentle each time you lower and lift the brush. Brush against and then with the direction of the hair growth. Be extra gentle when you brush against the hair because some cats are sensitive to the way that feels.

Doing the cat's chest and tummy can be very tricky. One way is to raise your cat up so that he's standing on his hind legs. I do it by having my cat face away from me while I lean over him a bit so he has the extra support of feeling me close to his back. I hold him up by gently supporting him under the front legs. If your cat prefers to sit, gently lift one leg at a time to reach the armpit and underneath areas. Don't twist your cat's leg, just hold it high enough to reach the area beneath.

During flea season, take the fine-tooth comb and pull it through the coat to trap fleas and their debris (comb in the direction of the hair). Then, when you've finished brushing, polish the coat by rubbing the cat down with a chamois or piece of velvet to bring out the coat's sheen. Go in the direction that the hair grows.

If your cat has a very short coat that lies close to the skin, go from the rubber currycomb to a soft bristle brush. Don't use the slicker brush. Finish with the chamois. The fine-tooth comb will still be needed to search for fleas.

LONGHAIRED CATS

Start with the wide-tooth comb. Start at the tail base and do one section of the coat at a time. Lift a section to comb the area underneath. This is the best way to get all the way through a dense coat and check for hidden mats. Work your way up to the cat's head. Pay close attention to trouble spots such as armpits, behind the ears and the groin area, because mats here can be easy to miss. Be very gentle because you may come across a tangle. If you come across a tangle or mat, gently work it apart with your fingers. Don't pull on the cat's skin. If you have trouble separating a mat, use the detangling spray or sprinkle cornstarch into the hair and keep combing it out. Don't forget to comb the neck ruff, chest, and tummy. Hold the cat up as described in the section on shorthaired cats. Some owners find it easier to groom the underside when the cat is stretched out on his side. You and your cat will learn what works best for each other as you go. When you have finished with the wide-tooth comb, use your medium-tooth comb, again moving slowly and gently. This comb will help test for mats that you may have missed.

As you groom you may notice your cat's tail in motion. This could indicate that he's losing patience with the whole procedure. Work quickly and gently. Oh, and speaking of tails in motion, when you attempt to brush his, again, be gentle and quick. Cats don't appreciate having their tails restrained.

When you can comb through the coat freely, you can then use the pin brush. Lift sections of hair as you go. Brush against the hair and then back in the direction of the hair growth.

HAIRLESS CATS

If your Sphinx has oily skin, you'll probably need to bathe him every seven to ten days. This cat needs to be kept warm, though, so make sure the bathroom is a comfortable temperature. Wrap the cat in warm towels and keep replacing the wet one with warm, dry ones. The towels can be warmed in the dryer beforehand.

If oil buildup is a problem between baths, use baby wipes to clean in the folds of the skin.

If your Sphinx develops clogged pores from an overproduction of oil, you can ask your vet to recommend a safe astringent to use on those areas.

Nail Trimming

You may want to do this first when you groom. It'll certainly lessen any damage done to your skin or clothes should your cat scratch.

If you have a kitten, he may feel more secure if you hold him against you. Using your arm to support him puts you in a perfect position to hold the paw and extend the nails with the hand of the supporting arm. Your other hand can work the trimmers.

Put your thumb on the top of the paw and your fingers underneath for support, then gently press and the nails will extend. Clip only the very tip of the nail which is the non-living cuticle. If your cat has light nails, by looking closely you can see where the pink area starts. This is the vein and accidentally cutting it will cause pain and bleeding. If your cat has dark nails it'll be impossible to see the vein so only trim the tip of the nail. Don't go beyond the start of the curve. If you're at all unsure of how to do it, ask your veterinarian for a demonstration. Don't forget to trim the dewclaws on the front paws. They look like little thumbs.

If you do accidentally cause the nail to bleed, apply the styptic powder to the end of the nail. If you don't have styptic powder, gently dab the toe with a bar of soft soap. Remember, trim less than you think you should. If you continue to cut the *quick* of the nail, your cat will resist having his nails trimmed due to the pain you cause him each time.

If your cat struggles during nail trimming, don't try to get all of the nails done at one time. It's not worth wearing out his patience and you possibly getting scratched by the very nail you just worked so hard to trim.

Polydactyls are cats with extra toes. If you have one of these cats, don't forget to trim the nails on those extra tootsies.

CatwiseClue

If things aren't going well and your cat is getting upset, take a break and resume later. Trying to finish the job with an agitated cat will only make him hate future grooming.

Brushing Your Cat's Teeth

To brush your cat's teeth, you can use a finger toothbrush (available at pet supply stores or from your vet), a pet toothbrush, or even a baby toothbrush. You can even wrap a piece of gauze around your finger if you're not comfortable using the toothbrush. Use whatever tool enables you to wipe or brush the outside of the cat's teeth easily. As for toothpaste, use one specifically made for pets. They come in flavors such as malt or poultry. Never use toothpaste meant for humans, as it'll burn all the way down to the stomach.

If you're just unable to brush your cat's teeth no matter how you've tried, there are plaque-reducing liquids available that can be squirted in the mouth; they won't taste as appealing, but it's certainly better than nothing. If you have trouble with brushing, ask your vet for one of the liquid products. In order for them to be effective, be sure and follow the label directions carefully. For instance, you shouldn't feed your cat for at least one half hour after using the dental rinse.

Also, if you can't brush the cat's teeth or he won't even let you apply the dental rinse, talk to your vet about feeding one of the tartar-reducing dry foods. Canned food sticks to the teeth, creating a perfect setup for plaque (which turns to rock hard tartar). Dry food scrapes the tooth surface as the cat chews which cleans away some of the bacterial growth that leads to plaque formation. If you give your cat treats, offer him the tartar-reducing kind instead of regular ones. One brand that my cats like is C.E.T. Forte Chews. Special dry food and treats aren't a replacement for teeth brushing, but every little bit helps.

Ear Cleaning

Look inside your cat's ears before you start to clean them to check for signs of infection, sores, or ear mites. If a blackish-brown crumbly material is visible in the ears, that's a sign of ear mites. Your cat will need to go to the vet and will require ear medication (for more on ear mites, see the medical appendix).

If the ears look inflamed, are sensitive to the touch, or have an odor, the cat needs to be examined by the vet. Don't clean the ears in that case, just get him checked out. If you attempt to clean inflamed or sore ears, you'll make them more irritated.

If the cat's ears are healthy but have dirt or wax in them, pour a little ear cleanser on a cotton ball and wipe the inside of the ear. Don't use a cotton swab, because you could injure the delicate eardrum.

Fleas and Other Itchy Things

Scratch . . . scratch . . . scratch. You hear it in the night when you're trying to sleep. During the day you notice your cat is about to pounce on a toy when suddenly he stops, sits down, and scratches frantically at his neck. It could be something as simple as being uncomfortable with his collar, or it could be any number of skin problems that can plague a cat at any age. Allergies, fungal disease, and parasites can drive a cat crazy. One of the most common causes of skin scratching is the pesky little flea. If your cat has an allergy to fleas, it just takes one to cause him (and you) sleepless nights.

If your cat appears to have skin problems such as a rash, inflammation, oily or dry skin, bumps, or anything else that looks or feels suspicious, get it checked by the vet. In addition to any oral or topical prescription, a special medicated shampoo may be needed.

With fleas and ticks, because cats are such dedicated groomers, you may never actually see the parasite but you may be able to see the excrement they leave behind on the cat's skin.

With the availability of the new generation of flea control products, such as Advantage, Frontline, and Program, your cat really doesn't have to suffer the discomfort of flea infestation. To learn more about total flea and tick control for your cat and his environment, refer to chapter 13.

Oh, Those Overactive Oil Glands!

Stud tail is an overproduction of oil that usually appears as a greasy spot on the end of the tail of males (mostly unneutered). You can control the greasiness by cleansing the tip of the tail with an oil-cutting shampoo. If the condition worsens, creating hair loss or inflammation, see your vet.

Feline acne, the result of those oil glands working overtime on the chin, shows up as dark, crusty blackheads. It can also cause more serious pustules. To clean mild acne, use a gauze pad or washcloth and warm water. If it continues to be a problem, your vet will recommend more specific treatment.

Refer to the medical appendix for more on stud tail and feline acne.

Hair Balls

Due to the backward-facing barbs on the cat's tongue, the hair he grooms must be swallowed. Some of this swallowed hair passes through the digestive system without a problem. If he swallows too much hair, the cat may vomit up a tubular-shaped glob of wet hair known to those of us who end up stepping on them, as *hair balls*. Not all hair balls get vomited up or passed out with the stool though. Some swallowed hair ends up trapped in the intestines, causing a blockage. If you notice your cat passing rock hard feces or no feces at all, it could be due to a partial or complete hair ball blockage. Call your vet immediately.

Some cats never have a problem with hair balls. They're more of a problem for longhaired cats just because of the length of the hair that gets swallowed. Shorthaired cats do get their share of them, though, especially the cats who aren't groomed regularly. In multicat households, shorthaired cats who groom their longhaired companions can end up with unexpected hair ball trouble.

Solution? Brushing!

For cats who have a problem with hair balls despite your diligence, there are hair ball prevention products available. Basically a laxative, the paste products come in a tube and are usually malt-flavored. They're mineral oil–based so they aren't absorbed by the body and just work as a lubricant. They shouldn't be used more than twice a week though because mineral oil inhibits the body's absorption of fat-soluble vitamins. Squeeze out a one-inch strip onto your finger and offer it to your cat. Many cats like the taste and will lick the paste off your finger. If your cat doesn't, you can open his mouth and slide your finger along the edge of his upper teeth to deposit the paste onto the roof of his mouth. Some owners of reluctant cats try rubbing the laxative onto the paw, knowing that the cat will ingest the paste when he grooms himself. I've seen more hair ball laxative splashed across walls because the cats decided to shake the stuff off rather than use their tongues. It can also be very messy on the fur, so if you feel you must resort to this method, place only a small amount on your cat's paw until you're sure he'll lick it off. If a dose of hair ball laxative once or twice a week isn't sufficient, talk to your vet about increasing the amount of fiber in your cat's diet.

Bathing Your Cat

I must be kidding, right? Perhaps the very idea of it brings on hysterical laughter. You're sitting there, shaking your head thinking, *no way, not me, I'm not bathing my cat!* Do you imagine a soaking wet cat covered in suds, racing through the house shrieking, with you in hot pursuit?

You most likely will never need to bathe your cat. (Is it my imagination, or did I just hear you breathe a sigh of relief?) Some longhaired cats require frequent baths because their coats get oily, and shorthaired cats may need an occasional bath depending on their coat condition or what they may have gotten into. It can be a relatively easy procedure, or it can be an exhausting battle where you end up wetter than the cat as he shreds the shower curtain before escaping from your grasp and racing out of the bathroom. Doing it the easy way is better for you, your cat, your bathroom, your home furnishings, and your relationship with your spouse.

Start by having everything you'll need all in one place. After the cat is wet isn't the time to remember that you forgot the shampoo. Choose a shampoo made for cats. Base your choice on your cat's individual needs; there are specific shampoos designed to enhance whiteness, reduce oil, etc. Don't use dish detergent because it's too drying. Even if you never need to bathe your cat, keep a shampoo on hand just in case. Longhaired cats will need a creme rinse as well to help detangle them. You'll also need a shower attachment or portable sprayer that slips over the faucet, a baby washcloth, and plenty of towels to bathe your cat. If your hair dryer runs at industrial power and volume, purchase a quiet one with low settings.

Reminder list:

shampoo meant for cats

creme rinse (for longhaired cats)

several absorbent towels

cotton balls

brush

rubber bath mat

shower attachment

baby washcloth

hair dryer

Before one drop of water ever hits the cat's coat, you must brush him to get all the tangles and mats out. If you bathe the cat with mats in his coat, they'll tighten so much you'll have to cut them out. Take the time before the bath to do a good brushing.

You can bathe your cat in the sink, using the hose attachment or in the tub, using the shower attachment. If you don't have a shower attachment, you can get a portable hose attachment that slides over the faucet. Bathing your cat in the kitchen sink or laundry tub is easier on your back but you may feel as if you have more control by being able to close the bathroom door. It's also easier to keep the smaller bathroom warmer. I make such a mess when I bathe my cats that I have no choice but to do it in the bathroom or else there'd be puddles everywhere.

Lay the rubber bath mat in the bottom of the sink or tub. This gives your cat something to dig into which will make him feel more secure. Some groomers lay a small window screen in the tub or along the side of the sink for the cat to claw. You can also place a towel along the bottom of the tub if you don't have a bath mat handy. Use whatever makes your cat feel most secure and allows you to get the job done without too much stress.

Before bringing the cat in, I run the water to warm up the tub and the room. Open your shampoo bottle so you won't have to fumble with it later. Gently place a cotton ball in each of the cat's ears. For a small cat use half a ball in each ear. I keep a couple of extra ones nearby also, in case my cat manages to shake one loose.

When you place the cat in the tub, be certain to keep a secure hold on him. Don't restrain him more than necessary but if you loosen your grip, I promise you, the cat will be out of there in a flash.

Wet the coat completely by using the hose attachment. Don't dunk your cat under the water. The water should be comfortably warm. Check it against your inner forearm to be sure it's not too hot or too cold. Never pour water over the cat's head. If you have to clean or wet the hair on the head, wipe with the baby washcloth. You want to avoid getting any water in the cat's ears, eyes, nose or mouth.

Soap the cat all around the neck first. If you do the back first and there are any fleas on the cat, they'll race up to his head and crawl into his ears, eyes, nose and mouth. Shampooing around the neck will prevent this. If there are fleas around his face, use the baby washcloth to wipe the area—don't douse him with water. Suds the body and legs. Don't forget to do under the tail and completely down the legs. Don't vigorously scrub the coat, especially with longhaired cats or you'll create knots and tangles.

Using the wet baby washcloth that has been squeezed (you can do it with one hand), wipe all around the face. For cats with tear stains, pay close attention to the undereye area.

Rinse the coat thoroughly. Holding the sprayer right against the skin will lift the hair to remove traces of soap underneath. If the cat is very dirty, you can do a second sudsing.

Rinse, rinse, rinse. Any shampoo residue left on the cat's skin after he dries will cause itching or irritation.

When you've finished rinsing, gently press the coat with your hands to remove the bulk of the water. Then remove the cotton balls from the cat's ears.

Wrap your cat in a towel and pat him dry to absorb the water. Don't rub the cat down. With longhaired cats, rubbing will create knots. Cats aren't too fond of vigorous rubdowns, anyway.

Keep patting and replace the wet towel with a dry one and keep doing that until you've absorbed most of the water. If you're going to use the hair dryer, it must be set on *low* and keep the dryer in motion. Don't hold it in one place on the cat's body, because it can easily burn him. Never aim the air flow at the cat's face. And don't feel as if you have to dry every last hair, especially if your cat's patience is wearing out. He'll finish drying on his own.

Use a soft-bristle brush as you dry to fluff and lift the hair. With a longhaired cat, be careful when drying so you don't create tangles.

If your cat doesn't tolerate the hair dryer, keep him in a warm room until he's dry. Watch him to make sure he doesn't get chilled. Turn up the heat if necessary until he's dry.

Reward your cat when you've finished and then while he goes off to groom himself in order to get his coat back to the way *he* likes it, you can go clean the hair out of the drain.

Waterless Baths

If your cat won't tolerate a bath or is not well enough, you can use a waterless bath. There are several products available. Powders have been around a long time. There are also foam products, which I think work better. While these products certainly aren't as effective as a bath, they can come in handy when a bath isn't possible.

Ugh! My Cat Has Been Skunked!

My best suggestion is to put him in a cardboard carrier so he doesn't run all over the house. You can toss the carrier in the trash afterward.

You can either bathe your cat yourself or call your veterinary hospital. They often have someone on staff who will do the bath for you.

If you're bathing your cat at home, wear old clothes that you won't mind throwing away because the smell won't come out of them. You'll need old towels as well. Bathe the cat first in his regular shampoo, then in tomato juice or a de-skunk solution (available at pet supply stores or from your vet). Follow that with another sudsing in his regular shampoo. If you're unable to use a hair dryer on him, keep him in a carrier until his coat is dry so he doesn't stink up the whole house. By the way, you're probably going to need a bath yourself.

When You Need Professional Help

No, I'm not referring to a psychiatrist, although after attempting to bathe an uncooperative cat you may feel as if you need one. The type of professional I'm talking about is a *groomer*.

If you have a longhaired cat and are unable to keep the coat mat-free, you'll need the services of a professional groomer. If the cat is very matted, he may have to be clipped.

Some owners schedule regular grooming sessions with a professional groomer to do bathing.

Ask your vet and other cat owners for a recommendation on which groomers are best. Before leaving your cat with a groomer, check them out carefully. Make sure your cat won't be caged near other cats or dogs. What do they use to clean their tables and equipment? Does the groomer require cats to be up-to-date on vaccinations? If not, that puts all the cats at risk. Do you see pet hair everywhere? If the groomer doesn't appear to enjoy his or her work or seems impatient around cats, grab your kitty and get the heck out of there. Cats require a gentle touch, so go in search of a groomer who practices that.

13 The Pest Patrol

Taking the Bite Out of Fleas and Ticks

Fleas are the most common parasite found on cats and these little creatures can cause big trouble. Adult fleas are fast and high jumpers, making it very difficult to trap one in your fingers. Cats, because they're such lightning-fast groomers, often lick away evidence of fleas before an owner even knows that there's an infestation.

Fleas are more of a problem in the summer months. A warm, moist environment is crucial to complete the life cycle.

Fleas live by feeding on the blood of the host. They spend their entire life on the cat, in a constant cycle of eating, eliminating, and reproducing. Females lay their eggs on the cat, the eggs soon fall off the animal and settle in the carpet, bedding, ground, or furniture to complete their incubation. In ten days, the eggs hatch into larvae, where they settle deep into the carpet pile or under your furniture. There, they feed on debris, mainly adult flea feces.

After about a week, the larvae spin a cocoon and enter the pupal stage. It is from these cocoons that adult fleas emerge. Depending on the environment, the adult can stay in the cocoon until conditions are favorable to emerge (even if it takes months). As soon as the adults emerge, they begin their search for a host.

Some cats have a sensitivity to the antigens in flea saliva, and develop an allergic reaction. Red, irritated skin, scabs, and bald patches (usually on the rump, near the base of the tail) are a few telltale signs of *flea allergy dermatitis*. For a cat with a flea allergy, it only takes one to start the reaction.

Fleas are the intermediate host for tapeworms, so as the cat attempts to rid herself of the fleas, she may swallow one containing tapeworms.

Heavy flea infestation can cause anemia in some cats because of the significant blood loss. Kittens, cats weakened by illness, and older cats are especially susceptible.

How to check for fleas: Separate the hairs of your cat's coat and look for signs of the small, brownish-black fleas. Because they move so fast, you may not actually see a flea itself, but you may see their feces. Flea excrement, which is digested blood, looks like specks of pepper. You may even see some white specks, which are flea eggs. Check your cat around the rump, tail, neck, and groin area.

Treatment: To effectively treat for fleas, you have to do all of the pets in your house. A mistake that some owners frequently make is to only treat the pet who goes outdoors, not realizing that the fleas will just as easily infest any indoor cats.

The secret to successful treatment is to start early, *before* the fleas have a chance to get on your cat or in your house. Fortunately, we now have truly effective flea control products. They won't work, though, if you don't use them correctly.

When beginning a flea treatment program, I urge you to first go to your vet to discuss all of the available options and what would be best for your individual cat. He or she will make suggestions based upon your cat's age, health, the severity of the infestation, your financial concerns, and his or her experience with particular products. Don't just run to your local grocery, pet, or discount store and buy products you aren't familiar with. Toxicity levels of products vary, and you may end up doing more harm than good. If you have a kitten, you must be especially careful with what products you choose. Remember, anything you put *on* your cat will also end up *in* your cat due to self-grooming. There are also products on the market that do absolutely nothing and are a waste of money. Your veterinarian can help you to plan an effective and safe flea treatment program.

Another aspect of successful flea control is treatment *duration*. Depending upon the type of climate you live in, you may need to practice flea control year round. In areas where winters are warmer, fleas thrive all year. Even in areas that experience cold winters, if you haven't eradicated the flea infestation inside of your house, they'll set up camp in your nice warm home no matter how low the outdoor temperature drops.

Three Great Flea-Control Products for the Cat That Really Work (available from your vet)

PROGRAM (ACTIVE INGREDIENT IS LUFENERON)

This product is taken orally once a month. There is also an injectable version that is given by your vet every six months. When an adult flea bites the cat and ingests the blood containing Program, eggs that the flea lays will not be able to hatch. It's a flea birth control method that's easy to administer. The oral version comes in a liquid or a flavored tablet. The liquid can be mixed with food. Because this is an internal product, it's effectiveness isn't reduced by grooming or bathing, which means your cat stays protected.

Program doesn't kill adult fleas, and though it will greatly reduce the population, your cat may still get bitten. This is something to be considered if your cat has a flea allergy.

If you decide on Program, all the pets in the house should be on it as well, not just the ones who go outdoors. Otherwise, adult fleas who bite the unprotected pet will lay eggs that can hatch.

FRONTLINE TOP SPOT (ACTIVE INGREDIENT IS FIBRONIL)

A topical product that is applied once a month to cats and kittens over twelve weeks of age. You snap open the small plastic pipette applicator, part the cat's hair between the shoulder blades and squeeze the entire contents onto the skin. The placement of the product on the back of the neck is to prevent the cat from reaching around and licking it all off. The product spreads over the cat's entire body. Initially, the spot on the back of her neck will look oily but by the following day you won't be able to detect any trace. Frontline works by adhering to the sebum and hair follicles. The product is waterproof and remains effective even if the cat is bathed or out in the rain.

Frontline kills adult fleas and ticks. What I like about this product is that the application is easy and causes no stress to the cat, as opposed to sprays, foams, and powders.

ADVANTAGE (ACTIVE INGREDIENT IS IMIDACLOPRID)

A once a month application is placed on the skin in one spot. As with Frontline, applying the contents of the tube to the back of the neck ensures that your cat won't be able to lick it off.

Within twelve to twenty-four hours, Advantage will have killed all the fleas on the cat's entire body.

Advantage doesn't lose its effectiveness if the cat gets wet.

I've been using these products on my dog and cats since they first came out, and we haven't had a flea since. I make sure I begin using them in advance of flea season and continue into the colder months. I also make sure to mark the day of application on the calendar so that we stay on schedule. That's all it takes, and my pets are probably very grateful that they no longer have to endure the sprays, powders, foams, and other regimens of the past.

Since cats generally hate being sprayed or powdered, the previously mentioned products greatly reduce the stress involved with application. You'll be done before the cat even realizes you've applied something to her. Another thing I really like about Advantage and Frontline is that they don't leave an odor on the coat or give it a greasy look.

By using Advantage or Frontline, you may very well eliminate the need to have to treat the environment. That's how effective these products are.

OTHER BRANDS

New topical flea control products are becoming available at a rapid rate. Before you choose a product from your local store or mail order catalog, ask your vet's advice.

How Effective Are Other Flea Control Products?

In my opinion, all other products pale in comparison to Advantage and Frontline in terms of effectiveness, ease of application, and safety to the cat. Why go through the battle of trying to spray the cat or fog the house? Just in case you're not familiar with what else is out there or you're not convinced yet, here are those old, traditional flea control methods:

FLEA SPRAYS

In general, cats hate them. It usually turns into a wrestling match to apply it and just as soon as you've finished, the cat proceeds to lick it off.

While sprays do work, the experience is often a stressful one for both cat and owner. In a multicat household, while you're spraying the first cat, the others head for the farthest corners of the home. Pump sprays tend to be less frightening than pressurized sprays but it still ends up being a wrestling match.

Flea sprays often leave a strong insecticidal odor that remains even after they've dried. They can also leave the fur looking clumped and greasy. Another thing I hate about them is that you have to repeatedly apply them, which often adds to your cat's stress.

Some cats groom themselves extensively after being sprayed and then salivate excessively and even foam at the mouth. Sprays containing alcohol can be especially irritating to the skin if the cat has sores from a flea allergy or any other skin condition. Choose a water-based spray to reduce skin irritation.

Flea sprays will kill the fleas currently on the cat, but for total flea control, you're better off with Advantage or Frontline. The fleas on the cat will be dead within twenty-four hours.

If you simply must use a spray, be sure the label states that it's safe for kittens and cats. Don't use any sprays that contain organophosphates. Do the cat's face first to prevent the fleas from running into her eyes, nose, and mouth, because as soon as you spray, they're going to dive for cover. Don't direct the nozzle at your cat's face, spray your hands and then rub around her head or spray a paper towel. Be certain to reach all areas on the body such as the stomach, under the chin and down the legs and tail. Fleas will run to wherever you've forgotten to spray.

After spraying, rub the cat's coat to ensure that the spray reaches all sections and gets down to the skin.

When spraying for the first time, keep an eye on your cat afterward in case she has a reaction to the insecticide.

FLEA MOUSSE OR FOAM

More easily tolerated by cats than sprays or powders. The sound of the pressurized nozzle can be startling so you may want to squirt it in your hand while in another room, out of earshot. Follow label directions carefully because a little foam goes a long way.

POWDERS

Thumbs down! They're so messy and you can end up with a sneezing cat as the powder continues to invade her nostrils. The powder must be worked thoroughly through the coat, with repeat applications done two or three times a week. As with sprays and foams, cats generally aren't too wild about having this done to them.

Powders have a tendency to dry out the coat.

FLEA SHAMPOOS

Shampooing will kill the fleas currently on your cat but won't have any residual effect. Be sure you use a shampoo that's safe for kittens and cats. The bad part about flea shampoos is that as soon as you're finished, more fleas will jump on the cat again. Bathing a flea-infested cat is a good idea to clean her of all the flea debris. You don't need a flea shampoo, though—you can use any shampoo meant for cats. After bathing, when the cat is dry, apply Advantage or Frontline. For bathing instructions, see chapter 12.

FLEA COMBS

You need one. An excellent (and nontoxic) way to remove fleas, their excrement, and eggs from the coat. As you comb, the fleas become trapped in the tiny, narrowly spaced teeth. Either spray the comb with flea spray or dip it in water that has a thin coating of flea spray on the surface. As with shampooing, once you've finished combing, more fleas will hop right on your cat, though, so flea combing should be part of an overall control plan.

If you can't bathe your cat, flea combing is an excellent way to clean the coat of flea excrement and eggs.

FLEA COLLARS

A big waste of money. I've seen many cats wearing flea collars who still were loaded with fleas.

If you still don't trust me and decide on a flea collar anyway, make sure it's intended for use on cats and is a *breakaway* collar. Keep an eye on the skin around your cat's neck in case she should have a reaction to the insecticide in the collar. Remove the collar should it get wet.

HERBAL PRODUCTS

If you're against using insecticides on your cat, there are many herbal shampoos, collars, and sprays available. Just because a product says *all natural* doesn't mean it's safe, though. Your cat still can have a reaction to the herbs used in these products. Read labels carefully and use caution when applying the preparation. Like most owners, I've tried many herbal products in an effort to eliminate the use of chemicals but I haven't found anything that works well.

ULTRASONIC REPELLENTS

Somebody's making a lot of money selling these useless things to desperate owners. Whether on a collar or an in-home device, I have yet to see one that works. Additionally, since a cat's hearing is so sensitive, I'm not convinced that she won't be aware of the sound.

Treating the Indoor Environment

PLUG IN THAT VACUUM

Don't overlook the house when planning your attack on fleas. Unless you have a serious infestation, using Advantage or Frontline may be all you need to do. With Program, you'll probably still need some environmental flea control.

I hate to vacuum and usually look for any excuse to get out of the task, but it's a good step in environmental flea control. The more eggs and pupae you can suck up out of the carpet, under the furniture and off the chair cushions, the better. Frequent vacuuming will help reduce the flea numbers. Be merciless and suck up those little creatures, then afterward, squirt a good amount of flea spray into the vacuum bag and toss it in the *outdoor* trash can. If you vacuum and neglect to toss the bag, all those sucked up eggs will hatch inside the vacuum cleaner.

When vacuuming, do a thorough job *under* the furniture (I sound like your mother, right?) and also lift up any cushions, because fleas and their pupae can hide deep down in chairs and sofas. Don't forget pet bedding, cat trees, and windowsills. Vacuum as if your mother-in-law is coming for a visit, wearing her white gloves.

Foggers

Foggers are effective if you have a wide open area but they're limited when it comes to all the nooks and crannies that most houses have. If you use a fogger, you have to leave closet doors open, lift up the cushions from chairs, bed skirts and anything else that fleas could hide behind. For complete coverage, first use a premise spray beneath furniture, around baseboards, or anywhere you feel the fogger may not reach.

All pets must be removed from the house during the use of foggers. Carefully read all label directions concerning safety and correct application. Choose a fogger that not only kills adult fleas but has an insect growth regulator (IGR) as well. This prevents the immature fleas from developing.

Timing of fogger reapplication is important for success. After the initial fogging, a second one should be done in two weeks, due to the virtual indestructibility of the flea's cocoon stage. Discuss the correct use of foggers with your vet so you can plan an effective attack.

Professional In-Home Services

Using either a powder or liquid, the carpets, furniture, and floors are treated. The products are odorless and nontoxic to pets and humans.

The companies claim that their treatments are effective against fleas for up to a year. Discuss this option with your vet if the flea infestation in your home is extensive.

OUTDOOR ENVIRONMENT

Outdoor treatment should be done at the same time as the indoor, and more than one application will be needed during flea season.

Mow, rake, and remove all debris before spraying or dusting (your neighbors will love you). Follow the label instructions and don't allow pets back outside until the insecticide has dried.

Try, if possible, to limit your outdoor pets' access to popular flea hideouts such as crawl spaces under the house, deck, or porch.

DON'T FORGET YOUR VEHICLES

Owners take their cat to the groomer for a flea bath and while she's gone, they fog the house and spray the yard. This well-intentioned plan is great, except they forget about the fleas that may be nestled inside of the car. Use a small size fogger or a premise spray and treat whatever vehicles you use to transport your pets. Don't overlook anything when fighting fleas. Those tenacious little pests will even jump into bed with you.

Ticks

Because of the cat's frequent grooming, you may not find a tick on her. If you do see one, it's usually on the head, neck, or in the ears because of the cat's inability to access those areas. Ticks can even be found between the toes.

Ticks attach themselves to the skin and then burrow their head underneath. Before feeding, when they aren't attached to the skin, they resemble tiny spiders. When attached, though, a tick often resembles a wart on the skin. As it feeds on blood, the tick's body becomes bloated. That's usually the time that an owner first sees or feels the parasite on the cat.

To remove a tick, cover it with a drop of alcohol or mineral oil. Wait a few seconds for the tick to release its hold and then grasp it gently with tweezers. Position the tweezers close to the *head* of the tick to be certain that it doesn't remain embedded in the skin. There are also products available in pet supply stores for tick removal. They look like plastic spoons with a notch cut out in the center.

After removing the tick, drop it into a small cup containing alcohol to ensure that it dies and then give the little creep a proper send-off by flushing him down the toilet.

Never use a hot match to remove a tick because the chance of injuring your cat is too great.

If you have trouble removing a tick or feel that the head is still embedded, see your veterinarian.

Some ticks carry disease, so don't attempt to remove them with your bare hands. Always use tweezers or a tick-removal tool. Deer ticks can carry *lyme disease,* a blood-borne disease which is known to be transmitted to humans and dogs. It has yet to be confirmed whether cats are actually susceptible to this illness. The wide ranging signs of lyme disease in people and dogs can be devastating. The most common symptom is joint pain. Treatment involves antibiotic therapy. There is a canine and human vaccine available.

14
Fasten Your Seat Belt

Traveling Without Trauma

"T ravel" is a four-letter word in the feline dictionary. If cats ruled the world, vacations would consist of: a week of unlimited countertop access, first dibs on the bird feeder, an endless supply of mice, seven days of not having your teeth brushed or ears cleaned, and of course, eighteen hours a day of beauty sleep. Nowhere in this vacation plan would *travel* ever be considered. Most cats prefer staying home. They'd also prefer it if *you* stayed home as well. We love adventure—cats love routine. We love exotic new locations—cats love their own familiar location.

If you have a kitten, you can spare yourself much trauma by getting her comfortable with travel at an early age. That's not to say that as an adult she still won't play hide-and-seek when she sees your suitcase come out of the closet, but it'll be a heck of a lot easier than if you only venture out with the cat once a year for that dreaded trip to the vet when it's time for her annual vaccinations.

With an adult cat, it's still not too late to make the travel experience less frightening. She may never learn to appreciate the adventure of travel but you can hopefully greatly reduce the anxiety and avoid long-term negative effects.

Like it or not, travel is necessary for cats—whether it's the trip to the vet, a move to a new house, or even an appointment with the groomer.

Why Every Cat Needs a Carrier

No matter how well trained and comfortable with travel your cat becomes, she needs a carrier. Transporting a cat in a carrier is the only way to ensure her safety. Whether you're traveling by car, plane, or just taking her across the street for a visit with the neighbor, she must be in a carrier. It provides her with a feeling of security, by allowing her to feel she's in a hiding place. If she becomes frightened, aggressive, or uncontrollable, having her in a carrier means she won't escape. Imagine trying to hold a growling, struggling cat in your arms. Attempting car travel with a loose cat running around the vehicle is extremely dangerous and can cause an accident.

Think of the carrier as one of the most important safety items for your cat. Even if you never plan on going anywhere, your vet makes house calls, and you hate vacations, you still need to own one.

Having a carrier enables you to safely get your cat out of the house in the event of an emergency. Should I have to quickly evacuate my home in a fire, I would never be able to handle my four cats unless they were in their carriers. I keep them set up and ready to go, so I'll always be prepared.

Choosing a Carrier

A carrier should give your cat a sense of security, provide safety, be easy to clean, and enable you to get your kitty in and out without anyone getting injured.

WIRE
This is about the most frightening way for a cat to travel. She's trapped in a cage, yet feels totally exposed. By the time you reach your destination and attempt to remove her from the carrier, she'll very likely be quite upset. *Upset* cats are not easy to handle.

SOFT-SIDED

They resemble the kind of soft-sided luggage you'd use for yourself. In fact, I actually used a soft-sided carrier as a suitcase for myself on one overnight trip out of town when my own luggage remained missing-in-action from a previous flight.

Soft-sided carriers are lightweight and most are approved for airline travel (if you're taking the cat in the flight cabin with you). The bad part about these carriers, though, is that during travel, if something falls on them, there's no protection. They're also more difficult to clean if your pet has an accident.

If you choose a soft-sided carrier, look for one that's sturdy, has a firm floor, and is well constructed so the sides won't end up caving in on the cat. Sherpa makes a good quality soft-sided carrier.

WICKER

It may look cute but it's a horrible choice. Just try cleaning urine or feces out of a wicker carrier.

PLASTIC

The best choice. They're sturdy, safe, easy to clean, and come in many different sizes. Most come with a grill front entry door made of metal or plastic. Some carriers have top entry doors as well. Many are airline-approved and the smaller carriers are usually approved for in-cabin travel.

Virtually indestructible, the plastic carrier will probably last for the life of your pet. Doskocil makes a sturdy, dual-entry carrier that has both a front and top entry grill door (which can make it easier to get an agitated cat out). Since your cat will feel more secure by being hidden, if you choose a top entry carrier with a grill or transparent door, cover the top with a piece of fabric. Cut a hole in the middle of the fabric for the handle to go through.

Even though you want your cat to be comfortable during travel, don't buy a carrier that's too large. She is unlikely to need to move around much in there, in fact, cats feel more secure when they can feel the sides of the carrier around them. A large carrier is awkward for you to handle and the cat will end up being jostled from one side to the other.

CARDBOARD

They're very inexpensive and sometimes even free. If you adopt a shelter cat, you'll probably be given one to take her home in. A cardboard carrier is okay when you have a kitten but it's not durable enough for an adult cat. A determined cat can claw or chew her way out of a cardboard carrier in the blink of an eye. Even though the cardboard is coated on the inside of the carrier, once a cat urinates or vomits, the box is pretty much useless. It scares me when I see an owner trying to contain a large, very unhappy cat in what's left of a cardboard carrier that's falling apart. While at the animal hospital I've seen the bottoms of carriers give way and the cats go crashing to the floor—or worse—the *parking lot*.

There are a couple of things I *do* like about cardboard carriers, though. Because they can be disassembled and stored completely flat, they make great extra emergency carriers. If you have ten cats and can't afford ten carriers or don't have the room, keep a few plastic ones and the rest cardboard. That way, if you had to remove all of your cats from the house, everyone would have a carrier.

Getting Your Cat Used to the Carrier

Not training a cat to a carrier will result in the exercise of retrieving your hissing, growling cat from under the bed, attempting to fold four outstretched, scrambling limbs into the carrier while trying to avoid the eighteen unsheathed claws moving at lightning speed in your direction. Loosen your grip for just a fraction of a second and the cat crawls up over your head, leaps to the floor, and dashes back under the bed. Bleeding, covered in cat hair, wearing clothes that now sport countless pulls and holes, you tiptoe back to the bedroom to begin the adventure all over again. Your other option is to train your cat so that you can easily place her in the carrier without it being a fate worse than death.

Begin the training process by placing the carrier in a corner of the room. If the door can be removed, take it off for now or at least secure it so it stays in the open position. Line the bottom of the carrier with a towel. If your cat is extremely suspicious of this set-up, just go about your normal business and leave the carrier set up for a couple of days without proceeding to the next step. Eventually, she'll get used to the presence of the carrier (even though she may not venture anywhere near it). Conduct an interactive play session in the area around the carrier but don't bring the toy too close to it.

Now place a few treats in front of the carrier but at a safe enough distance away from it so your cat feels comfortable. When she has accepted those treats, place the next round a little closer. Put a treat on each side of the carrier and a couple in front. Don't be in a rush to put them too close to the carrier. By going slowly, your cat won't become suspicious or feel threatened.

The next day, place a couple treats directly in front of the carrier. Then the next day, place them on the edge of the carrier. Each time, move the treats a little bit farther into the carrier. For now, make the carrier the only place your cat receives treats.

Now that your cat freely goes in and out of the carrier and realizes that it's no big deal, you can put the door back on. Then, when she goes in to eat a treat, close the door, count to five and then open it up. Have a toy ready to engage in an interactive play session as soon as your cat emerges from the carrier. Do this a few times so she gets used to the closed door.

Next, toss a treat in the carrier and when the cat goes in, close the door, pick up the carrier, walk a few steps and then place it back down. Open the door, let your cat come out and engage in either a play session, offer a treat, or feed her dinner.

Practice the above step every day, each time walking a little farther. Keep the experience positive, talk soothingly to your cat, and hold the carrier as still as you can. Once your cat no longer views the carrier with dread, you can occasionally put her in there yourself. Gently pick her up and guide her in. Once she's in, close the door, take a few steps with the carrier and then place it back down. Don't shove your cat inside. Again, keep the experience positive and reward her each time.

You can also teach your cat to go into the carrier through a verbal command as you would with a dog. Just say the word "kennel" every time you toss the treat in the carrier. You can hold the treat in front of your cat's nose and lead her toward the carrier, repeating the word "kennel." Make your voice upbeat and positive. Give her the treat when she steps inside the carrier.

Begin getting her used to the actual traveling part of being in a carrier by taking her in the car for short rides. Start by just going around the block and home again. Reward, reward, reward as soon as you get home. Increase the distance you travel gradually.

To prevent your cat from only associating her carrier with the awful experience of going to the vet, take her for brief rides so she can see that something bad doesn't have to happen every time she goes there. With a kitten, bring her to the vet regularly as she grows just to be petted and greeted by the staff. This helps her to become less afraid of the hospital smells and sounds.

Before you even start training her, leave the carrier out with a towel inside for her to use as a little hideaway. In fact, leaving it out all of the time will avoid the dreaded panic that ensues the second it's brought out of the closet right before you attempt to put your cat inside of it.

How to Get the Most Uncooperative Cat in a Carrier

You haven't carrier-trained your cat and need to get her in one NOW. She's fighting you tooth and nail. Here's the quickest and least traumatic method:

Spray one squirt of *Feliway* in the carrier one-half hour before loading your cat. Stand the front-entry plastic carrier on its end so the opening is now on top. Scruff your cat with one hand and hold her hind legs with the other (scruffing refers to holding a cat by the loose skin on the back of the neck—similar to the way a mother cat carries a kitten). Quickly and carefully lower her into the carrier, hind end first. As soon as she's in, quickly let go of the scruff and close the door (be careful not to slam it on her paws or ears). Latch the door quickly, before your cat has an opportunity to lunge at it. Slowly upright the carrier back to its normal position. Whew, mission accomplished—cat in carrier and no injury to human.

Should Your Cat Travel?

Even if you've carrier-trained your cat, it doesn't mean she should travel everywhere with you. Take into consideration her temperament, health, type of travel you'll be doing, and the time of year. Cats who are easily stressed will be much better off staying at home while the family vacations at Disneyworld. Take into consideration whether your destination would actually be good for your cat. Just because you like to go to the beach every weekend doesn't mean your cat wants to also. Dragging kitty to cat-hating Aunt Esther's house for a holiday with the entire family would most likely be extremely stressful (for Aunt Esther as well as the cat).

If you're traveling by plane, I'd leave the cat at home unless she can ride in the flight cabin with you (see "Air Travel" later in this chapter).

The experience of riding in the cargo hold can be terrifying and even life-threatening.

Persians, Himalayans, Exotic Shorthairs, and other short-nosed breeds shouldn't travel in hot weather unless you'll be in an air-conditioned environment.

If you're in doubt as to whether your cat is up for the trip, consult your veterinarian. If staying home isn't an option and you're worried about how your cat will handle the trip, discuss with the vet the possibility of a mild sedative for your cat. Don't use it unless you absolutely have to, though. If you've never sedated your cat before, it's not a good idea to make the first time when you're going to be on a plane or on a long road trip.

Traveling by Car

When traveling by car, if you're going to be staying in motels or hotels, find out ahead of time which ones accept pets. To prevent the house-keeping staff from opening the door to your room and having the cat escape while you're out, make sure the front desk knows that there's a pet in the room. They can arrange for housekeeping to be done while you're there in the room. In addition, put the DO NOT DISTURB sign on the door and to be on the safe side, close the cat in the bathroom with a big note on the door, just in case.

CARRIER

Your cat will need to be in her carrier throughout the trip. For long trips you may want to get a large size (a dog crate) so you can place a small litter box in the corner. If you can't fit a small litter box in her crate, whenever you stop to stretch your legs, let your cat have access to a litter box but be *sure* the car doors and windows are closed.

HARNESS, ID, LEASH

Even if you never plan on taking your cat outside to walk on a leash, you should leash and harness train her for added safety when traveling. Keep the harness on your cat during the trip and make sure she has an ID tag attached. When you take her out of the carrier, put the leash on her. When you get to your hotel or other destination, remove the harness and put her collar on (with ID) whenever you aren't traveling. Make sure she's always wearing an ID tag that has both your home phone number and your vacation number.

LITTER BOX AND LITTER

You can buy a package of disposable litter boxes that are made of coated cardboard. It's much easier than having to wash out a plastic box. If you do have room in the car and will be at your vacation destination for a while, bring along a regular-size litter box. It'll certainly be more comfortable for the cat. Bring your cat's usual brand of litter because you may not be able to find it at your destination location. If your litter comes packaged in a bag, you may want to transfer it to a plastic storage container with a tight-fitting lid. I've had to vacuum litter out of the car after an opened bag fell over and it's not fun. Bring along a plastic cup to fill the litter box with litter.

Don't forget the all-important litter scoop. If you're using a reduced-sized box you'll need to be very diligent about frequent scooping. Pack it in a sealable plastic bag. Bring a box of plastic trash bags so you can have somewhere to empty the dirty litter that you've scooped while in the car. If you're staying in a motel or hotel, you'll need to empty the dirty litter in the sealable trash bags because you certainly can't dump the litter right into the room's wastebasket.

Bring along a small bottle of hand sanitizer (available at supermarkets and drug stores) so you can clean your hands after scooping the litter.

Extra towels are needed in case of spills and accidents. Baby wipes come in handy in case the cat messes on herself during the trip. Buy the plain, alcohol-free, unscented ones. Pack the enzymatic cleaner too.

Pack your cat's usual food. If you feed canned food, buy the smallest sizes. If the cans aren't pop-top, remember to bring a can opener and plastic spoons. Bring a bottle of water so you can offer some to your cat periodically during the ride. To prevent any stomach upset due to a change in water, bring along a plastic jug filled with your regular water from home. When you reach your destination, fill the cat's bowl with the water from home and gradually add the new water. Don't forget to pack her bowls and, while you're at it, toss a package of treats in her suitcase as well.

Carry copies of your cat's medical records in case she should require veterinary care.

If your cat is on any prescription medication, don't forget to take it along. It's not a bad idea to bring along a scaled-down version of her first aid kit as well (see chapter 18).

Basic grooming supplies should be packed, especially if you have a longhaired cat, because you'll need to maintain her grooming schedule. Bring along a travel-size bottle filled with her pet shampoo in case she messes herself so much that you'll have to bathe her once you reach your destination.

Oh my gosh, don't forget to pack at least one interactive toy or it certainly won't be a vacation for your cat. She'll appreciate the diversion when you reach your destination. I also pack a little catnip and a couple of activity toys whenever we travel.

PHOTO OF YOUR CAT

It could happen—your cat could get lost while you're on the road. Bring along a clear photo of her, so you'll be able to make LOST CAT posters.

DON'T LEAVE YOUR CAT UNATTENDED

While on the road in hot weather, if you're traveling alone with your cat and have to stop for fuel or to use the rest room, take your cat in with you. I'm not kidding. Bring her carrier in the service station with you because the inside of the car will turn into a oven *fast*. I know you hate to have to subject your cat to the usually awful conditions of a service station rest room, but maybe it'll give her a new appreciation for her pristinely maintained litter box at home. I have a client whose cat was stolen from the car while she was in the gas station rest room. Since hearing that, I never leave my pets alone in the car.

Air Travel

The thought of placing my cat in the cargo hold of the plane is frightening. Fortunately, many airlines allow your cat to travel under your seat. She'll be classified as *baggage* but so what? You can make it up to her later. The cat must be in an airline-approved carrier, though. You can either use a plastic carrier (make sure it states that it's airline-approved) or a soft-sided one such as the Sherpa bag. Airlines have strict regulations about pet travel, so you have to call well in advance. Very often there's a fee to have your cat travel onboard with you. Make your reservation for your pet at the time you book your own ticket because there's a limit as to how many pets are allowed per flight. Some airlines only permit one pet in the entire cabin.

Find out from the airline what documentation will be needed, such as a health certificate. Don't pack your cat's health papers in the luggage—keep it with you so you'll be able to present it when needed.

Put identification on the carrier and also on your cat. The carrier should have a sign that says LIVE ANIMAL. Even though she'll be with you during the trip, the label is in case some unexpected crisis happens and you get separated. The identification tags on the carrier and on your cat should have your home phone number as well as your destination number.

At home, before you place your cat in the carrier, check it out to be sure it's in good condition. With a plastic carrier, tighten all the bolts. With a soft-sided carrier, check the seams and mesh for any tears and double-check all zippers.

When packing for air travel, look over the section in this book on "Traveling by Car" which lists packing essentials. Although you certainly won't be able to pack as heavily as you would for a road trip, many important items shouldn't be forgotten.

Leaving Your Cat at Home

PET SITTERS

By far, the ideal arrangement for your cat is for her to stay in her own home while you travel. Pet sitters can be a dream come true or the ultimate nightmare if you haven't checked them out carefully.

A pet sitting arrangement can range from having your neighbor come over twice a day to feed your cat and clean the litter or hiring a professional pet sitter, to getting someone to actually move into your home while you're away.

If you have a cat-owning friend who would be willing to come over twice a day, I think this works out well because you know you can trust them and they'll be comfortable with the duties needed. Your cat will probably be more comfortable as well since it'll be someone she's familiar with.

Show your friend where the interactive toys are kept and how you play with your cat. Offer to return this favor whenever your friend needs it, and this could end up being a very convenient arrangement.

A professional pet-sitting service is also an option. Besides caring for your pet, they will get your mail, turn lights on and off, and water plants. If you know of pet owners who've used them, ask for names and opinions on the quality of the services. You can additionally get referrals from your veterinarian. In the back of this book, there's also a national pet-sitting locator number.

Before hiring a professional pet-sitting service, ask them the following questions:

- *How long have you been in business?* You don't want to be one of their first clients.

- *Do you have references?* If they don't provide any, look for another sitter. Be sure to check all references.

- *Are you bonded and insured?* A professional pet sitter should be.

- *What plans do you have in case of bad weather?* (As a safeguard, give a nearby neighbor an extra key just in case.) Find out what kind of vehicle they have and what their bad weather contingency plan is. This is where hiring a pet sitter who lives nearby is a good idea.

- *Are you the one who will be making all of the visits?* Some larger services send different sitters depending on who's working that day. The person you interview should be the one who makes the visits.

- *Do you provide a written agreement or contract?* Get everything in writing.

- *What is provided during a visit?* Again, get it in writing.

- *Are you able to administer medication?* This is important if your cat is on prescription medicine. Find out what training the sitter has had and if he or she is capable of making sure your cat gets all necessary medication.

Check out the pet-sitting service thoroughly. After all, you'll be entrusting them with your pets and your home. You should interview the pet sitter in person by having them come to your home. That way you can show them exactly what would need to be done. You can also get a feel for how your cat is reacting to them. If the pet sitter needs to be warned about anything, be sure to inform them. For instance, if your cat bites, has a habit of bolting out the door, etc.

Most pet sitters make one or two visits a day to the home. They charge per visit so be sure you know exactly how many visits you'll need.

Leave the pet sitter all necessary information in case of an emergency. Write the phone number where you can be reached as well as numbers of your neighbors in case the sitter needs immediate help with something. Write your vet's name and number as well. Ask the sitter if they know the location of your veterinarian. Additionally, call the vet clinic and inform them that a sitter will be caring for your cat and provide permission to do any necessary medical treatment. Give the vet your out-of-town number as well. Show the sitter where the cat carrier is in case they need to take your cat to the vet.

If you'll be going out of town for an extended period and you'll be using the pet-sitting service for the first time, one thing I recommend is to do a dry run first. Hire the pet sitter to come for one visit to see how they do. Don't tell them that you're checking them out, just say you'll be arriving home late that evening. Have the pet sitter come in the early evening before you come home from work, for one visit. I tried this method once and based on just that one visit, decided I didn't want them to care for my cats during my two-week trip. Dirty food bowls were left out on the floor (and not even in the area where I instructed her to feed the cats). Also, the window blinds in the front of the house hadn't been closed, although I had specifically requested that.

I now have a pet-sitting service that I trust completely and can rely on, but I had to do my homework to find them.

BOARDING YOUR CAT

Even being in the best boarding facility is stressful for a cat, so if you have a frightened, aggressive or highly territorial cat, she would truly be better off in her own familiar surroundings. Try, try, try to work out a pet-sitting arrangement. If you aren't able to get someone to come to your house, maybe a friend would take your cat in and keep her in one room of their house. For some owners though, the only option is to place their cat in a boarding facility.

Inspect the boarding facility personally. There should be proper ventilation in the boarding room. When you walk in, if the odor makes you feel as if you've stepped into a giant litter box, imagine how horrible it must smell to the cats!

All boarding facilities should require you to show proof of vaccinations. Unfortunately, not all of them do. Any facility that doesn't require your cat to be up-to-date on shots means it's not requiring it of other cats as well. That puts all the cats at risk. Kittens who are not yet fully vaccinated shouldn't be boarded.

Boarding facilities range from simple rows of cages to luxurious multi-tiered individual rooms, complete with televisions. Although it may seem silly at first, the thought of placing your cat in one of these deluxe facilities that look more luxurious than a hotel room, definitely has advantages. The staff often provide more personalized care, the cats have more hiding places, and there are scheduled individual play periods. If you have one of these special boarding facilities in your area, I urge you to check it out. They're surprisingly affordable.

When you bring your cat to the boarding facility, bring her regular food, litter, and medications. Don't bring your cat's litter box, though. It won't fit in the cage and you don't want your cat developing a negative association with it once she gets back home because it reminds her of the boarding facility. Provide your cat with a T-shirt that you've worn as well, for its comforting scent. The Quickdraw McPaw toy is good to bring along as well so the staff can conduct a play session with your cat in such a limited space.

One of the most frightening aspects of being boarded is that cats have no hiding place, so very often they sit hunkered down in of all places, their *litter* box. How stressful for a poor terrified kitty to have to seek refuge there. Bring along a small *high-sided* cat bed (such as an A-frame) if there's room for it in the cage. Make sure the bed is washable, so the staff can clean if it should become soiled. If the cage isn't big enough for a bed, at least place an open paper bag in the cage. You might want to bring a few extra bags in case one gets soiled. Instruct the staff to make sure your cat always has a place to hide.

If your cat becomes too stressed out, a sheet of newspaper can be taped over the front of the cage by one of the staff.

CatwiseClue

Boarding facilities get booked up early for the holidays, so make your reservations well in advance.

Moving to a New Home

From a cat's perspective, it probably doesn't get much worse than this. First, out comes the dreaded carrier, then a car ride, and it's all topped off by the arrival at an unfamiliar location that her owners keep referring to as "Home." *Home? Are you crazy? We left our home hours ago, so turn around and let's head back there. I have birds to watch, mice to keep away, and a nap to take.*

Once again, if cats ruled the world (and I know many people think they already do), you'd never go anywhere, not to work, not on vacation, and certainly not to the vet. A move to a new house? Don't even mention it.

Since moving to a new house is something that most owners will have to do at some point, making it as painless for your cat as possible will also make it a little less painful for you as well.

If you have a cat who goes outdoors, about a week before the move, stop letting her outside. The week before the move is the crunch time for people when their packing becomes more intense, they're sleep deprived, and the stress level rockets off the scale. Your cat, ever the observant one, will sense something is afoot and may choose to lay low for a while by not returning home at night. The last thing you need is to have to spend the day of the move searching outdoors for your kitty. There are many sad cases of owners having to give up and leave their cat because the movers were gone and schedules had to be kept or there'd be no one to let them in at the new location. It's tragic to think about the fear and confusion that the cat must feel when she does head back home and finds no one there for her. Unless a neighbor recognizes her and can capture her, she will go from being a loved family member to a homeless stray. If I'm sounding a bit dramatic, it's because owners often overlook this plan-ahead precaution and their cats *do* disappear before the move. It's worth all the complaining you may have to endure from your cat during the week in order to ensure her safety.

The process of packing is drudgery. For cats, though, it's an intense experience. They often love it, choosing to dive in and out of boxes, thinking you've created this indoor playland just for their amusement— or they hide in fear over the chaos taking place in their once-peaceful territory. Whichever reaction your cat has, precautions have to be taken to be sure she doesn't get packed in a box. HA! HA! you laugh—but it happens. A cat playing in the boxes may decide to take a little nap in one. She burrows down into the linens that you've placed in there. You don't realize that she's in there and you close up the box and into the moving van it goes. Whenever you pack, your cat should be put in a separate room so you'll always know where she is.

The week before your move, get a copy of your cat's medical records from your vet (if you'll be changing vets). If you already have a vet selected in your new location, have them forward your records there. Keep an extra copy of the records with you as well for the trip. Also, the week before the move is a good time to have an ID tag made with your new address and phone number for your cat's collar. You'll put it on your cat the day of the move.

On moving day, have all of the cat's food, medications, etc., in a separate box that will go with you in your vehicle. You don't want to get to the new home and realize you packed the food in some unknown box. The day of the move will be a hectic, stressful time, so either keep your cat confined in one little room or have her boarded for the day. If you have an extra bathroom, put her in there with her litter box, a bowl of water, and a bed. Put a little radio in there and set it to a classical station (cats like that) or even to a talk station to filter out some of the commotion occurring just beyond her door. Place a big sign on the door warning people not to enter.

I also place the cat carrier in the bathroom, so it doesn't get placed in the moving van.

When you get to your new home, your cat should have a little sanctuary room set up for her. An extra bathroom is ideal because less unpacking chaos will occur there as opposed to other rooms that require major unpacking. Set up her litter box, scratching post, a bed, water, and food. Toss a few toys in there as well. If you have an extra bedroom or some other room that you want to use as the sanctuary, set up some of the furniture (even if it's only temporarily where you want it) so she'll have a place to hide. Having the comfort of furniture she's familiar with will be helpful to her. Spray Feliway in the room and set up all of her necessities.

Some cats will make the adjustment in a short time, but others may need a week in the sanctuary room. Don't rush things.

Having your cat in the room also enables you to reinforce those good behaviors such as using the litter box and scratching post.

Take time out from your unpacking to visit and play with your cat. A fifteen-minute play session here or there throughout the day won't wreck your schedule too much, and you'll be providing a world of comfort for your cat. Break open the catnip as well so you and your cat can celebrate your new home in style. Her confinement to the sanctuary room shouldn't be viewed as a jail sentence.

The best way to judge if your cat is ready to be let out of the room is when she resumes normal behavior, i.e., eating, using the litter box, venturing out of the closet, not hiding, etc. Before opening the door, spray Feliway on prominent objects around the house. When you open the door to her room, don't force her to come out. Let her decide at what pace she feels most comfortable. You can leave a few treats scattered just outside the door.

Keep her sanctuary room set up for her because she may choose to go back there if the stress gets to be too much.

If your cat was allowed outdoors in your previous home, this is an excellent opportunity for you to make her an indoor cat. There's a whole new territory right inside the house for her. It's more than enough to keep her busy. The territory outdoors is unfamiliar, and you don't know what other cats are out there who may feel there isn't room enough in the neighborhood for a new cat.

If you're absolutely set on allowing your cat outdoors, wait at least a month so she has a chance to firmly establish comfort in her indoor territory and has fully adjusted to the move. When you do begin letting her out, do it with a leash and harness. After all, there's no connection to this yard for her so you stand a good chance of her running away. Take her out daily for walks *close* to the house so she repeatedly makes the connection. If the weather is nice, sit outside with her on the deck and feed her dinner there so this starts to become her home base. Let her walk in and out of the door so she makes the connection with where the entrance to the home is. She needs to know where to stay while waiting to be let inside. When you allow her to venture farther out in the yard, use a retractable leash (the one for small dogs—it'll be the lightest) so you can still walk with her but she'll feel as if she has more freedom. Do this daily for several weeks. Put some treats in your pocket and when the cat's on the retractable leash, practice calling her by name; when she responds, reward her.

Don't allow your cat outdoors unless she's fully vaccinated, has ID, and is trained to come when called. I know the last one's a stretch for most owners, but it can be done (see chapter 5).

Once again, seriously reconsider making her an indoor cat.

Lost Cat

It does unfortunately happen despite an owner's best efforts. Here are some guidelines in case you are faced with this crisis.

CREATE FLYERS

LOST CAT should be at the top of the flyer. Below that should be a clear picture of your cat. Below the picture include a description, including any unusual or identifying marks. Write the date lost, where the cat was last seen, plus your daytime and evening phone numbers. Offering a reward creates even more incentive. Make it a substantial one so every kid in the neighborhood will go out looking for your cat.

If you have access to a computer, create the flyer using bold, easy-to-read type. If you have to handwrite it, make sure your phone numbers are very clearly readable.

Post the flyers *everywhere* you can: vet clinics, intersections, supermarkets, pet supply stores. Wherever a flyer can be put up, attach yours there.

MAKE THE ROUNDS

Immediately call the local shelter to let them know your cat is lost. Follow that up immediately with an in-person visit to leave a flyer there.

Bring flyers to as many vet clinics as you can. Most vets have a "lost pet" bulletin board. If they don't have room for the flyer, you can at least post the picture with the information written on an index card.

Check in with the police as well.

PLACE ADS

Use your local newspaper to place a "lost cat" notice. Many areas also have small community newspapers—place an ad in that as well. A picture here is very helpful.

INFORM YOUR NEIGHBORS

Go around to the neighbors in your area with your pictures or your flyer. There's a good chance that your scared cat could be hiding in someone's bushes or garage.

If you find your cat, go around and remove all the flyers. Call the shelters, vets, etc., to let the know so they can take down the pictures. That way, people won't still be spending their time looking for your already-found pet. Thank everyone!

If the person who finds your cat refuses the reward, donate money to the local shelter in their name. That way, some other lost kitty may be able to find her home again.

15

And Baby Makes Three . . .
Four . . . Five

What to Do When Your Cat Makes You a Grandparent

It's not exactly the stuff romance novels are made of. Feline mating is a violent and dangerous process. In the presence of a female in heat, any tomcats in the area will fight with each other for the chance to mate with her.

The male paces back and forth nervously, waiting for the signal from the female that it's okay to approach. He then grasps the nape of her neck with his teeth and straddles her. The female arches her back, flips her tail over to one side, and then the tomcat begins thrusting.

Once ejaculation has occurred, the female lets out a scream and struggles to break free of the male's grip. If the male isn't fast enough in terms of retreating, the female attacks him quite aggressively. She then begins rolling, stretching, and genital licking.

The pair may mate again immediately or it may take a while before the female is ready to accept the male again. They may mate many times over the next several hours. As he waits for her to become receptive again he remains on guard to prevent other toms from attempting to claim his female. If other males are present, they may challenge him for a chance to mate with her as well. The result is often a violent fight which ends up with one or more cats getting bitten or slashed. Tomcat fights can result in *very* serious injuries and sometimes even death. If more win a chance to mate with the female, the kittens born to her can have more than one father.

If you're under that worn-out illusion that having your children witness the miracle of birth will be a learning experience—you're missing the boat. The message they should be learning is how to be a responsible pet owner, which means spaying or neutering the cat. Responsibly caring for and loving a pet for many years will be a far more valuable lesson throughout their lives, rather than watching four more kittens come into an already overpopulated pet world.

Why Your Cat Should Be Spayed or Neutered

If you have a mixed-breed cat and you're considering breeding, please think again. I know you love your cat and you think she'll have beautiful kittens, but the truth is, millions of "beautiful" kittens become homeless or are put to death simply because there are too many of them. People end up standing outside of supermarkets with a box full of kittens in a desperate attempt to give them away because homes are hard to come by.

Don't become a backyard breeder. There are enough cats already. Just because you have a purebred cat doesn't mean you can make money by mating her with a male of the same breed. Experienced, reputable breeders are very knowledgeable about breed genetics. Attempting to breed your cat without this knowledge can result in kittens with congenital deformities.

If you believe you'll make money from breeding your cat, you're in for a big surprise. It's an expensive proposition as any breeder will tell you. Good breeders spend a lot of time and money creating a good environment, caring for the adult cats, and raising the kittens. Good breeders are in this because they love the breed and they want to maintain the standard—not to get rich quick.

Even if you hadn't planned on breeding your cat, it can happen "accidentally" if you let your intact cat outdoors. You may have intentions of getting her spayed but she may come home pregnant before you get the chance. And, if you have an intact male cat, don't think you're at an advantage because you won't have kittens to take care of. Instead, you'll be taking care of an injured cat time and time again as he fights with other males. You also have a responsibility as a cat owner to not contribute to overpopulation by letting your intact male roam to randomly mate.

Besides the overpopulation issue, there are medical and behavioral reasons to have your cat spayed or neutered. Spaying prior to a cat's first heat will virtually eliminate the risk of mammary cancer. Neutering your male cat will eliminate the risk of him developing prostate cancer later in life.

The difference between an altered and intact cat is like night and day. Neutering before a cat reaches sexual maturity will virtually eliminate urine spraying and roaming. Even neutering your adult male can greatly reduce those undesirable behaviors. With a female, not spaying her will doom you to endure her endless vocalization and restlessness. It will also attract every tomcat in the neighborhood. I don't know about you, but I'd just as soon not have the local toms urine-spraying the bushes around my front door.

And remember, contrary to what you've probably heard, altering a cat won't make her fat. *Overfeeding* is what leads to obesity.

Male cats are neutered. This surgery involves the removal of the cat's testicles by way of an incision in the scrotum. No sutures are required and post-op care consists of monitoring to make certain the healing incision stays clean and dry. If your cat is allowed outdoors, you may want to keep him inside for several days until he's completely healed.

Female cats are spayed. More involved than neutering, this surgery consists of removing the uterus, tubes and ovaries through an abdominal incision. Your cat will have a few sutures across her shaved tummy which will be removed in about ten days unless absorbable sutures are used.

Your vet will give you specific instructions regarding post-op care. You'll need to monitor the sutures to be sure they stay clean and dry. You also need to monitor to make sure your cat doesn't chew at her sutures. If you regularly bathe your cat, that will have to wait until the sutures are removed.

Limit your cat's activity during the healing process by keeping her indoors and discourage jumping and strenuous activity.

Even though neuter and spay surgeries are probably performed more often than any other procedures, be wary of low cost spay/neuter clinics. A surgery, regardless of how "routine," still involves risk. If you plan on using a low-cost clinic instead of your regular vet, investigate the place carefully. Find out all you can regarding how their procedures are done, what anesthesia is used, are the cats monitored by a surgical assistant during and after the procedure, and not only what kind of sutures are used but how many the vet routinely puts in. I know of one low-cost clinic where the vet was closing spay incisions with only one suture.

If you have confidence in your regular vet, don't go price shopping when it comes to surgery. Your vet has a serious interest in the long-term health of your cat.

Caring for a Mother-to-Be

Well, you may not have planned it, but you might find yourself with a pregnant cat. Maybe you waited just a little too long in deciding when to have her spayed or maybe a pregnant stray found her way into your life.

Gestation in a cat is about sixty-five days. During the first few weeks, you may not be able to detect pregnancy except for an increase in weight.

Some cats experience morning sickness somewhere around the third week of pregnancy. She may vomit and not eat well. This usually only lasts a few days.

If you suspect that your cat may be pregnant, take her to the vet so that if it's confirmed, you can begin prenatal care. Your vet will provide you with a recommended schedule of how many visits you'll need based on your individual cat's health concerns, as well as making recommendations regarding nutritional changes. Don't give any supplements unless advised to do so by your vet. Usually, you'll be instructed to feed a *growth*-formula food due to the extra need for protein and calcium among other nutrients. During the last half of the pregnancy, your vet may advise an increase in the amount of food being fed. That will depend upon your cat's weight and health. You obviously want to avoid creating an overweight cat, which could make her delivery more difficult.

As the cat gets to within about a week or so of delivery, she may need to be fed several smaller meals. Due to her large abdomen, she may not be able to eat her regular meal-size ration. Also at this time, you'll probably make another visit to the vet for a final prenatal exam. You'll also be given instructions on how to prepare for delivery, what to expect, and newborn kitten care.

Preparing for the Big Day

About a week before delivery, the cat will appear restless and you may notice an increase in the amount of grooming she does to her abdomen and genitals. She may begin scratching in clothes piles or digging around in closets as she prepares a nest.

Despite the most elaborate accommodations you may create for the cat to give birth, she'll prefer someplace dark, quiet, and warm. Take a sturdy cardboard box, cut an opening in one side of it and then line it with clean newspaper. You may want to use a box with a lid to offer a nervous queen more privacy yet you'll be able to have easy access to clean it and monitor the activities inside. The box should be tall enough so the cat can stand up and move around.

Place the food and water bowls near the box. The litter box should be within easy reach as well, but not too close.

Don't allow your cat outdoors toward the end of her pregnancy because she may go into labor and deliver her kittens in someone's garage. It's a good idea to keep her in the room you've selected for delivery, so she doesn't go off and choose a different location in the house.

About a day before she's ready to deliver, the cat's temperature drops two or three degrees. If you're experienced at taking your cat's temp and she's comfortable with having it done, you can try taking a reading. If you're at all in doubt, don't do it—just help her get comfortable and leave her alone.

Your cat will, in most cases, deliver her kittens just fine without human interference. You can help a longhaired cat out by trimming the hair (or have the vet do it) around her nipples and the area beneath her tail. Additionally, have a few supplies at hand just in case assistance is needed:

your vet's phone number (and emergency after-hours number)

extra newspaper

clean towels

scissors

antiseptic

dental floss or a spool of thread

infant syringe

Hello, World! (the Delivery)

In the first stage of labor, the cat will pant and begin straining. This can last several hours. She may cry out and almost attempt to bite at her backside. The best thing you can do is give her privacy. She doesn't need the anxiety of having the entire family standing over her. It's not unusual for her to even hiss at you if you get too close. Some cats have been known to eat their kittens if people interfere too much.

In active labor, you may notice a light-colored discharge followed by a darker-colored one. Contractions begin and the first kitten is then usually delivered within thirty minutes. The kitten is surrounded in a membrane that the mother will bite open, then she'll begin licking the kitten's face to clear the nose and mouth to start his breathing. She'll also sever the umbilical cord and roughly lick the kitten all over to stimulate circulation.

Unless another kitten starts coming before the mother can stimulate the kitten's breathing, DON'T INTERFERE. If she doesn't care for the kitten, you can gently tear open the membrane and rub the kitten down with a towel to stimulate breathing. With the dental floss or thread, tie off the umbilical cord about one inch and cut it with the scissors then swab the stump of the cord with antiseptic. Make sure the kitten is breathing before you place him near his mother. If he isn't, use the infant syringe to clear any fluids from the mouth. If he still isn't breathing, hold him securely in your hands and supporting his head, turn him downward and swing him in an arc very gently to clear additional fluid from his nose or mouth. As soon as he's breathing, present him to his mother so she can continue licking him.

Delivery intervals between kittens range from thirty minutes to an hour. A *placenta* for each kitten should be passed after each delivery. The mother instinctively eats the placentas (and sometimes any stillborn kittens as well). If she eats several placentas, it can result in diarrhea so you should remove all of them as well as any stillborn kittens right away. Be sure to count the number of placentas, though, to make sure there is one for every kitten delivered as any retained ones can cause serious infection.

If delivery isn't going well or you're concerned that the mother is having trouble, you'll need to contact your vet. Call immediately if:

- the cat has had strong contractions or is straining for an hour without delivery of a kitten

- the cat appears weak or in pain

- there is vomiting

- a placenta for each kitten isn't delivered

- there's a discharge of fresh blood

- above or below normal temperature

- the cat remains restless

- the kittens continually cry

- you feel anything seems abnormal

(Note: Refer to the medical appendix for information on reproductive and neonatal disorders.)

Once the kittens are born, they'll immediately begin nursing. The first milk, called *colostrum,* is vital because it'll provide the mother's antibodies, which temporarily protect the kittens against disease until their own immune systems begin functioning.

If everything seems to be going well, leave the family alone. Let the mother take care of her kittens without disturbance for the first two weeks, except for any necessary cleaning, feeding the mother, and general monitoring.

If the kittens aren't doing well or the mother is not allowing them to nurse, contact your vet immediately because they'll need to be tube-fed initially. If tube feeding and bottle feeding need to be done, your vet will give you specific instructions.

The next morning after delivery, even if everything went smoothly, contact your vet because an examination of the cat should be performed to be sure there are no retained fetuses. The vet may also check to make sure milk production is adequate and healthy. Bring the kittens along as well so that they won't be separated from their mother.

Newborn kittens are deaf and blind. They locate their mother by scent and perhaps through the vibrations of her purrs. They will spend much time suckling and often develop a preference for a specific nipple.

Many changes happen in the first two weeks. In a couple of days after birth, the umbilical cords fall off. The kittens will double their weight in a week and their eyes and ears will open somewhere around seven to ten days.

The mother remains constantly attentive to her babies. After nursing, she licks them with her warm tongue to stimulate elimination of waste, which she ingests. A cat's devotion to her kittens involves maintaining a clean nest to keep them all safe from predators.

By three weeks of age, you can begin handling the kittens to start their socialization process. Frequent gentle handling by humans can help them grow to become more comfortable and sociable around people. Don't overdo, though, because you can make the mother anxious.

Also at three weeks is when you can begin the weaning process by providing access to solid food. A gradual weaning process is healthiest for both mother and her kittens. By your providing food, the kittens will nurse less and less as each week passes. Remember, it *must* be gradual. Use a kitten formula of either canned or dry that has been softened with warm water. Put a tiny bit of food on your finger and place it on the kitten's lips or under his nose.

Litter box training will pretty much be conducted by the mother. Provide a low litter box for easy access.

At eight weeks of age, the kittens should begin receiving their vaccination series.

Continue your frequent handling and playing with the kittens to help socialize them. They'll also be continuing to develop their skills through littermate playtime.

You may be tempted to start finding homes for the kittens at this stage, but this is still valuable time for them to remain with the mother and their littermates. This time is important for how well they'll interact as adults with other cats. Don't separate the litter until they're at least twelve to fourteen weeks old.

Some of the Important Stages in Kitten Development

THE FIRST TWO WEEKS

- born blind and deaf
- weight at birth will be approximately 3 1/2–4 ounces
- umbilical cords drop off after two to three days
- unable to regulate body temperature
- highly developed sense of smell
- mother stays with kittens virtually around the clock for the first twenty-four hours
- weight will double in the first week
- mother must stimulate each kitten's elimination process by licking

TWO WEEKS–FOUR WEEKS

- eyes and ears open at about ten to fourteen days
- milk teeth start appearing
- at three weeks, the kittens are able to eliminate on their own
- the mother shows her kittens how to cover their waste
- social play begins between weeks three and four
- important socialization time
- righting reflex develops

FOUR WEEKS–EIGHT WEEKS

- able to groom themselves at five weeks
- weaning should be completed by seven weeks
- all baby teeth are in by eight weeks
- continued important socialization time
- play behavior gets rougher as weeks progress

EIGHT WEEKS–FOURTEEN WEEKS

- kittens engage more frequently in object play
- senses will be fully developed by twelve weeks
- adult eye color established around twelve weeks
- adult teeth begin to erupt at fourteen weeks
- adult sleep patterns will begin to develop as weeks progress

SIX MONTHS–TWELVE MONTHS

- kittens reach sexual maturity
- continued growth (but at a slower pace)

Feeding Schedule for Weaned Kittens

Refer to chapter 10, "The Kitty Chef."

Caring for Orphaned Kittens

It may happen that you come across an orphaned kitten or an entire litter. The mother may have gotten killed—or perhaps she rejected her kittens or became ill or unable to nurse due to a mammary infection.

Orphaned kittens, since they don't have the advantage of the mother's body heat, need to be kept warm in an environmental temperature of 85° to 90° F. for their first two weeks of life. By the third week, you can lower the temperature by a few degrees and continue gradually lowering it each week. Your vet may instruct you on how to create a homemade incubator by using a lamp and a cardboard box or whether to use a heating pad on the lowest setting.

Orphaned kittens should be taken to the vet immediately, where you'll be shown how to provide the proper replacement formula using a commercial kitten replacement product. It's a full-time job to feed kittens around the clock. Every two to four hours is usually the schedule in the beginning. Tube feeding (which goes down the esophagus and directly into the stomach) is the preferable method and then changing over to bottle feeding. A kitten replacement formula must be used because ordinary cow's milk lacks the protein and other nutrients kittens need. Feeding has to be done with the kitten in an upright position (the same position he'd be in if nursing from his mother), and if bottle feeding, the kittens must be burped. This is done by holding the kitten up to your shoulder and rubbing his back. You have to be careful not to overfeed because their stomachs are small and the kidneys can't handle an oversupply. Underfeeding is also dangerous, so make certain you have received instructions from the vet and are comfortable with what you need to do. You vet can give you a demonstration on how to hold and feed the kitten as well as how to tell when he's full.

Since your kittens can't eliminate on their own, they'll need your help in stimulating the process. A warm, moist cotton ball can be used to massage the abdomen and anal area to stimulate urination and defecation. This will need to be done after each feeding until they're three weeks old, at which time you'll begin to teach them how to use the litter box. That's done by placing them in the box after meals. Massaging their abdomen with a warm water-moistened finger will help if they need a little extra assistance. Use your fingers to scratch around in the litter to help give them the idea as well. Leave a little of their waste in the litter box to help them make the connection of what the box is for. If any kitten eliminates outside of the litter box, scoop up the waste and place it in the box. The scent will help direct them to the correct place next time.

Keep the kittens clean because they're going to get very sticky and messy during feedings. Use a soft washcloth moistened with warm water (don't immerse kittens in water). They can get chilled easily, so dry immediately with a towel. If needed you can use a hair dryer set on the lowest setting. Keep the dryer far away from the kitten to prevent burning.

Orphaned kittens don't have the protection from the mother's colostrum, so they'll have to be vaccinated at about three or four weeks of age.

Since caring for orphaned kittens is very involved, your best bet is to get all the guidance you can from the veterinarian. Some clinics have technicians who specialize in fostering orphaned kittens and will take them home until they're eating on their own. Some shelters as well have volunteers who are experienced in orphaned care. Call before showing up at a clinic or shelter with orphaned kittens.

A single orphaned kitten who doesn't have the benefit of interacting with littermates may have trouble relating to other cats as he grows. If at all possible, all attempts should be made to locate another nursing mother with a litter. Nursing mothers are very accepting of an orphaned kitten added to the litter. Mothers have even accepted orphans of other species.

Finding Homes for the Kittens

When the kittens reach twelve to fourteen weeks of age, if you aren't planning on keeping them, you'll need to find good homes for them.

Whether this was a planned pregnancy or an accidental random mating, your responsibility extends beyond caring for the kittens until they reach an adoptable age. These precious little lives are totally dependent upon how much effort you place on making certain they get adopted into loving homes.

By taking the easy way out and "getting rid" of them by holding up a sign outside of the supermarket offering free kittens, you have no way of knowing whether they'll get a good home or be sentenced to a horrible life. You should take the time to screen potential adoptive parents. After all, this is a life you've been entrusted with—not a piece of furniture.

Find out if the prospective owners have had pets before. If so, what happened to them? I certainly wouldn't adopt out a kitten to a family with a history of pets being hit by cars. How about any current pets? Do they already have cats? Dogs? Any children? If so, what ages?

Depending upon your views regarding whether a cat should be kept indoors and not declawed, those are issues you'll need to discuss.

You'll want to find out about their lifestyle, how much time they can devote to a cat, and how prepared they are for the responsibility. Do they know what a cat needs?

Come to an agreement regarding vaccinations and spaying or neutering as well. You may agree to cover certain expenses as long as they show proof of compliance. Work all of this out in advance and get it in writing.

Not screening prospective owners by asking questions and checking references can mean a death sentence for the kitten. I have known several people who didn't investigate a prospective owner enough and ended up assuming the kittens were going to good homes—only to discover that they were used as bait to train fighting dogs or were abused. There are truly sick people in this world who answer "free pet" ads in the paper in order to acquire victims for many horrible purposes.

Responsible, caring people don't mind being asked questions concerning their suitability to own a pet. By your thoroughness and concern, the prospective owners know they're getting a kitten that was obviously well cared for and had a healthy start in life.

16
Getting Gray Around the Whiskers

What You Need to Know About Your Geriatric Cat

When is your cat considered old? Well, what kind of life does your cat lead? You can look at the chart in chapter 2 to get a general idea of how a cat's years compare to ours, but as with our life spans, so many factors can have an influence on how accurate those numbers are. An intact, unvaccinated outdoor cat who lives to be four is, in my opinion, an old cat. Compare that to the altered cat kept indoors and vaccinated yearly. At four, that cat is in the prime of his life and may well live another ten or more years. You have a great impact on how well your cat ages by providing him with love, good care, a safe environment, proper nutrition, regular health exams, vaccinations, and having him altered.

Behavior

This is interesting because you may notice that your once short-tempered, untouchable cat has begun to mellow. On the other hand, your sweet-natured, tolerant kitty may now seem irritable.

The cat who used to tear through the house at the speed of light may now restrict his activity to sleeping, stretching, and eating.

The scratching post that was once the center of activity in your home may now be used less frequently. Some cats who in their younger years didn't use posts very much may now regularly seek them out for purposes of stretching and relieving stiff muscles.

Physical Changes

Your cat's weight may begin changing as he enters his golden years. He may appear thin or he may gain weight. Sometimes older cats become obese due to the fact that their calorie intake is the same but their activity level has declined. Others lose muscle tone as they age and seem thin and flabby. You may notice his spine to be more prominent along his back nowadays.

The cat's coat may no longer be as glorious as it once was. He may also not be as fastidious with his grooming.

When you look in your cat's eyes, you may notice they're no longer bright but now have a cloudiness to them.

His gait may be slower, his limbs stiffer, and it may take longer for him to get up from his afternoon nap.

Cold may bother him more now and you might find him curled up by the heating vent or in the sun every chance he gets.

Declining Senses

Some cats suffer a decline in senses with old age. It may be a slight decrease in vision or hearing or it could be as severe as total blindness or deafness.

A cat's sense of smell has a strong influence on his appetite. If your cat has lost interest in food, it may be that he can't smell it as well and so is not interested.

A cat with declining senses is at a severe disadvantage outdoors, so if you haven't already started keeping him inside, you should begin as soon as you feel any of his senses are deteriorating. If you still want him to be able to enjoy the outdoors, on nice days you can bring him out on a leash so he can lounge with you in the sun.

Consult your vet regarding any physical changes or medical symptoms. Don't assume it's just old age—there could be a medical problem that needs to be addressed.

As your cat ages, it's not only important to have him vaccinated and checked regularly, it's essential to do more in-depth troubleshooting. As part of the exam, your vet may recommend routine blood and urine tests. If you start early and do them on a regular basis, you'll be able to catch many problems in their initial stages. You'll also be able to more accurately gauge how fast a problem is progressing. As part of a geriatric profile, your vet may also feel that an ECG and radiograph of the chest be done. Some clinics offer geriatric pet physical "packages" that include various procedures at a reduced fee.

Once my pets turned six, their normal yearly exams began including blood and urine testing. It was through this that we discovered Albie was in the early stages of renal failure long before he began showing symptoms.

Once a cat reaches nine or ten years old, I think it's a good idea to have a checkup every six months instead of just an annual one. You stand a much better chance of catching problems earlier. A year is a long time in a cat's life, and a medical condition can progress a great deal in a matter of months.

Have You Neglected Your Cat's Teeth?

If so, by the time he enters old age, he could be in serious trouble. Periodontal disease can make it painful for your cat to eat. He could even stop eating totally. Should the bacteria enter the bloodstream, it can travel to internal organs and lead to infection.

If you've been faithfully brushing your cat's teeth all these years and having professional cleanings when needed, then your cat probably has nothing more than the usual signs of dental wear and tear. His teeth may not be as white as they once were, but at least they're in good shape with no signs of gingivitis. On the other hand, if you've neglected his teeth, there's a good chance that not only is his breath very unpleasant, but there's probably gum inflammation, loose teeth, and maybe even an abscess or two.

On a regular basis, lift up your cat's upper lip along the side of his mouth and check on the condition of his teeth. Do they look very yellow or even brown? Do the gums look puffy and inflamed? These are signs of gingivitis or periodontal disease (refer to the Medical Appendix for a more specific description). If you aren't comfortable looking in your cat's mouth or if he won't let you, have your veterinarian check him.

Because your cat is getting up there in years, you may be hesitant about putting him under anesthesia for a professional teeth cleaning. The risk of letting periodontal disease advance is more dangerous than the anesthesia. If your vet feels that your cat should have his teeth cleaned, he'll undergo diagnostic tests to determine his anesthesia risk factors.

If you've ever had a toothache or an abscessed tooth, you know how painful it is. Imagine your poor cat enduring a mouth full of sore, infected gums and painful teeth—all at a time in his life when he needs to keep his immune system up and maintain a healthy appetite.

If your cat does undergo a professional cleaning, keep up a regular schedule of at-home care. Brush his teeth at least three times a week (see chapter 12 for instructions). If you just can't do it, ask your vet about using an oral hygiene spray.

Making Day-to-Day Life Easier for an Elderly Kitty

There was a time when Albie was the fastest thing on four feet in our house. He made leaps that didn't seem possible and could run through our obstacle course of furniture without losing any speed. These days, though, his main activity is napping on the bed in the sun. His leaps are now carefully planned and limited to low-level elevations. Every once in a while when he's feeling great, he turns into the kittenlike companion I remember from a few years back, but for the most part, he takes life a whole lot slower.

As he has aged, I've had to make some adjustments so that he continues to remain as comfortable as possible. Look around *your* house and make adjustments needed for your own cat, such as:

EASY ACCESS
To enable your cat to still reach those high places he loves, you can use a multi-tiered cat tree so he can make a series of little jumps. If he has trouble even getting up into a chair, you can place a ramp in front of it. You can either make your own or purchase a commercial one. Pawsway

makes a very sturdy adjustable ramp. Available through mail order, their address is listed in the resource guide.

TEMPERATURE TOLERANCE

Drafts, cold floors, and unheated garages or basements can make a cat's aches and pains seem much worse. An elderly cat may also have a reduced tolerance for cold. If your cat sleeps on a bed on the floor, line it with a fleece pad. To protect him from drafts, use a high-sided round bed. If your cat seeks out the warmest spots in the house, you may want to use a heated pet bed. There are several versions available; some are electric heating pads and some use a microwavable heating unit. Many mail-order companies sell these beds.

LITTER BOX

Your aging cat may not have the greatest bladder control now, especially if he's diabetic or in renal failure. Provide additional litter boxes, so that he doesn't have a long way to go when the need arises. There should be at least one litter box on every floor. If the box is usually in the basement or garage, it may be too difficult for him to negotiate stairs. He may also not want to go out into the cold. Cats who don't use litter boxes and are used to doing their eliminating outdoors, should have litter boxes made available indoors now.

Check on how well your cat can get in and out of the box. It may be time to switch to low-sided boxes. Monitor his litter box habits very carefully now. If you notice a change in urine output or if he eliminates outside of the box, a trip to the vet is needed. Constipation is also a common occurrence in elderly cats. If you notice your cat having difficulty with stool elimination or if he hasn't had a bowel movement recently, he needs to be checked.

FOOD AND WATER

If your cat has difficulty getting around, move his food and water closer to his bed. If he drinks a lot of water now (maybe as a result of a medical condition), provide a bowl in each of his favorite locations. Some cats have the opposite problem, and they don't drink enough water. Always have fresh clean water available. Don't let it get stale, and make sure you clean the bowl daily. If your cat appears dehydrated or you don't think he's drinking enough, consult your vet. Dehydration can be checked by gently lifting the loose skin on the cat's back (at the shoulders). If it doesn't spring back into position right away, he's probably dehydrated.

Don't allow your cat to become obese, which is a danger as he gets less active. An obese cat is more prone to diabetes. Arthritis will be more intolerable as well if he's carrying around extra weight on those sore joints.

Keeping weight *on* the cat may be a problem for some owners. Have your vet do a thorough checkup. If his lack of appetite is caused by fading senses, ask your vet about ways to make the food more enticing. If you're feeding dry food, you may be able to mix a little canned food in as well, which has more of an aroma. Warming the food slightly will also release more of an aroma. Ask your vet about what would be best for your cat's specific condition.

If you've always fed your cat on a schedule, you may find that his stomach can't handle his normal-size meal now. Feeding smaller meals more frequently may be more comfortable.

As for changing his diet, unless your vet recommends it due to a specific health concern, there's no need to switch to a "senior" food (which is usually easier to chew and has less protein and more fiber). If he's having trouble chewing, it may be due to periodontal disease, so have that checked before assuming he needs a softer food.

GROOMING

Your cat may have been a stunner in his prime, but now grooming may be low on his list of priorities. Maintain a regular schedule of brushing to keep his coat in good shape. The massage of the brush will also probably feel especially good. If your cat has sensitive skin, has become bony, or his hair has become thin, switch to a soft brush. You may need to re-evaluate the grooming tools you've used in the past.

Use your grooming sessions as a chance to do a health check as well, especially when it comes to detecting any lumps or bumps.

OTHER PETS IN THE HOUSE

Even though all the pets in your home may be the best of buddies, watch for signs of increasing irritation on the part of your elderly cat. Also, make sure his companions aren't bullying the once "king of the house" now that he's moving a bit slower.

Should you get your cat a new kitten? I'd think long and hard before doing this. A playful "in your face" kitten may not be what your elderly cat had in mind for his golden years.

At a time when he is least able to cope with the added stress and confusion, a kitten may cause your cat to display some behavior problems, such as litter box avoidance.

You also don't want a playful little kitten to have to endure the constant rejection from a cantankerous old feline.

Some elderly cats do great when a kitten is introduced. I've seen it put the sparkle back in the eyes of an aging kitty. I've also seen it cause constant tension and create a stressful last few years for the cat.

Use your judgment, based on what your cat seems to need. If he appears bored and has lost interest in life, playtime with *you* may be all he needs. He may not be able to do the incredible leaps that were once his trademark in his youth, but I'll bet he still has a few good moves left.

PLAYTIME AND EXERCISE

If you don't have interactive toys (shame on you), go out and get some right this minute. Earlier in this book I discussed how playtime and hunting are *mental* exercises as well as *physical*. So no matter how limited he is physically, he'll still enjoy the success of a victorious hunt thanks to your interactive playtime skills. Though he may not be able to move as fast, some form of physical exercise is extremely beneficial. Certainly you don't want him to overdo and risk pain or injury, but a customized play session tailored to his specific health state will do wonders.

The Kitty Tease and Quickdraw McPaw are good choices for cats with limited mobility, because they're extremely enticing even with just a little bit of movement.

Don't forget the catnip when it comes to your older cat. What a great Sunday afternoon treat.

BE TOLERANT

He's been a wonderful cat all these years, so be tolerant of fumbled attempts at jumping on the table that result in something being knocked over. Be tolerant as well of the occasional litter box mishaps (but don't neglect having him checked by the vet). Tell him he's beautiful even though he no longer grooms himself and is unaware of the food on his chin. Just discreetly wipe his face so he doesn't get embarrassed in front of the other pets. Don't be insulted if he doesn't come when you call him or if he acts irritated when his nap is disturbed. Finally, if the mice in your home feel a little safer these days, don't let on to your cat.

If you're having concerns about the quality of your cat's life and need guidance on issues such as euthanasia, talk to your vet (see chapter 17).

17
Legacy of Love

The Goodbye We're Never Prepared to Say

We gently call it "putting the pet to sleep." As a pet owner, it's the hardest decision you'll ever make. We always hope that should we have to face this situation, we'll simply know *when it's time*—that our cat will give us a clear signal that she's in pain or her quality of life has badly deteriorated.

For many owners there's no clear-cut signal from the cat. Depending upon the relationship with your pet, not every owner uses the same guideline. Some watch for a lack of appetite, feeling that as long as she's eating, she still has a will to live. Other owners gauge it by their cat's inability to move around or decline in litter box habits. And of course, no owner ever wants to see their pet in pain. Every day you'll find yourself studying your cat, looking in her eyes, almost willing her to give you the answer. Is she in too much pain? Just when you think that she is, doubt will creep into your mind and you'll second-guess yourself every day. Some owners don't want their pet to experience any discomfort, so they choose to euthanize in the earlier stages of terminal disease.

For some owners, unfortunately, *money* is also a major factor when deciding whether *it's time*. The cost of long-term care is beyond the budget of some families. With the advancements in veterinary medicine, the cost of a break-through life-extending procedure could be out of reach financially. Every responsible pet owner wishes they could spare no expense in doing everything possible to prolong the life of their beloved pet, but in reality, for many that's just not possible.

Your ability to provide long-term care for an ill cat is also a major consideration. Some owners aren't able to medicate their cat, give injections, or perform other necessary nursing duties.

For most owners, there is never a clear sign. You can never know *for sure*. You do the very best that you can for your cat and make your decision based on her condition, spirit, your abilities, the guidance of the veterinarian, and your endless soul-searching. You can seek advice from friends, family, other pet owners in similar situations, veterinarians, but when it comes down to it—the decision is truly yours.

Euthanasia is that last act of love that an owner gives to a beloved but suffering pet. Humanely ending a pet's pain by allowing her to leave this world in peace and with dignity is a truly unselfish act of love.

EUTHANASIA

Once you've made the decision, there are other difficult questions that need to be addressed. Do you plan on being there with your cat? What are your options in dealing with the remains? What is right for one owner doesn't mean it's right for another. Take time to talk with your veterinarian and discuss the options.

Call ahead to the veterinarian's office and make the appointment. Inform the receptionist of the purpose for the appointment, so that you don't have to sit in the waiting room. When you get to the hospital you'll immediately be brought into the privacy of an exam room. If you don't feel that you can remain with your cat, inform the receptionist when you call. Don't feel that you have to be there through the process if you're not comfortable with that. It's a personal decision, and there's no right or wrong. I've accompanied many owners to the hospital during these times and some were unable to watch their pets die. Those owners didn't love their pets any less than the owners who stayed. The goal is to keep the cat calm and make this time as peaceful for her as possible.

When I worked at an animal hospital, I had to be present for the euthanizing of many homeless animals who had been brought to us from the shelter due to severe injuries or illness. Many of the animals had probably never been loved, cared for or even touched. I would hold each one, telling them they were loved. I would also give thanks to the animals for having graced our world with their spirits. Ironically, the process of dying was probably the most peaceful moment of their brief, lonely lives.

The euthanasia procedure is itself, very quick. The euthanizing solution is basically an overdose of an anesthetic, so the procedure does very much resemble putting the pet to *sleep*. If your cat normally gets very stressed or agitated when at the vet, a sedative can be administered before the procedure to calm her. After the sedative, the vet will clip the fur on the cat's foreleg to make the vein more visible. The solution is administered by injection. Your vet will explain to you that sometimes animals may vocalize a bit, but it's not due to experiencing pain. The only pain will be the initial stick of the needle. The cat will immediately become unconscious and in a matter of seconds, a peaceful death will occur.

The vet will ask you afterward if you'd like a few minutes alone. Don't be embarrassed about needing a brief moment alone with your cat after the euthanasia. It's an overwhelming experience and you need time to collect yourself. It can also be helpful to see your cat resting peacefully, especially if she'd been in a lot of pain.

Some veterinarians will come to your home to perform the euthanasia. If your cat gets upset at the vet clinic, or if you'd rather she spend her last moments in the familiar surroundings of her home, discuss this option with your vet.

Another important decision you'll have to make is in terms of the arrangements for your cat's remains. Discuss the options with your vet beforehand. There are full-service pet cemeteries who offer everything from individual burials to cremation (in most cases, this can be arranged through your vet). Depending upon the laws in your local area, you may want to bury your cat on your property.

Coping with Grief

Almost anyone who has ever shared life with a pet will understand the sense of loss you feel. Be prepared though for the people who will inevitably say, "It's only a *cat*" and won't be able to relate to the depth of your pain. Even if your cat had been a member of your family for twenty years, there will always be those people who don't understand the deep connection between humans and their cherished pets. My advice is to surround yourself with the friends and family who *do* understand.

Until you actually experience the loss, you don't know how you're going to react. I've known owners who were shocked at how deeply they grieved. The emotions experienced over the loss of a pet can equal those for the loss of a human.

Don't try to rush the grieving process. Your cat was a beloved member of the family, a cherished friend, a constant companion who gave unconditional love. It will take time to heal, but believe me, healing does indeed happen. Eventually, you'll be able to think of the memories without them being so raw and overpowering. In time, those memories will bring warm feelings and smiles as you fondly remember that very special friend.

If you feel unable to cope or just need a sympathetic ear, there are various pet loss support lines available. I've listed some in the back of this book. Many veterinary universities offer this service.

There are also several books available on coping with pet loss. You'll find books for your children as well as for yourself.

HELPING YOUR CHILDREN

One thing that disturbs me when it comes to how some parents help their older children (over the age of five) through this process is when they immediately get a "replacement" pet. Instead of teaching children that pets are merely disposable and easily replaceable, we should be helping them through this difficult time without trivializing the value of an animal's life.

If your children are old enough to understand, offer clear, honest explanations of what has happened to the pet. Don't go into graphic detail but don't say things such as "the cat ran away" or "the cat went to sleep." Don't tell a child that the cat was sick or injured and died without going on to explain that not all sickness and injury result in death.

Having children plan a memorial for the pet also can help them deal with their grief and any unanswered questions. Provide support for your children and explain that crying and grief are normal. For a lot of children, this will be their first experience with loss and death.

When Your Cat Dies Suddenly

It's difficult enough to prepare ourselves for euthanizing an old or terminally ill pet—the thought of dealing with a sudden death can be unbearable. No one wants to think about it, but sudden, unexpected deaths happen. Cats slip out the door and get hit by cars, attacked by dogs, or killed by cruel people. Cats also fall out of windows. When the death is unexpected, you experience shock, denial, and anger. You may find yourself blaming the people you hold responsible (the vet, the driver of the car, yourself). In the case of negligence, seek advice and take the correct course of action. In a highly emotional state, taking matters into your own hands will only make a tragedy even more of one. Speak to a lawyer if you feel legal action is warranted.

Sometimes pets die accidentally, and it's not anybody's fault. As careful as you try to be, the cat may bolt out the door when a visitor comes in. She may run out in the road and get hit by a car. It's a horrible accident and you may blame yourself more than anyone else involved, but even accidents happen to the most watchful, careful people.

Helping Your Surviving Pets Deal with Loss

The family members who often get overlooked when a death occurs in the family are the other pets. They experience the loss and mourn the absence of their companions. In fact, it's even more difficult for them because they're confused by *your* behavior. Seeing their owner grieving, crying, and not interacting with them as usual can create anxiety and even depression.

Don't overlook your pets during this crisis. They need you. For more information on depression, see chapter 7.

Should You Get Another Pet?

This is another one of those personal decisions that only you can answer. If you've dealt with the loss of your pet and feel ready to open your heart again, there will certainly be a pet out there in need of a loving home.

When is the right time to get another pet? Only you can answer that. My advice, though, is don't try to replace the cat who died. Searching for another cat with the same looks or personality isn't fair to the memory of your beloved cat and it certainly isn't fair to the new cat. The newcomer will never be able to live up to your expectations as you compare her to the loving companion you had for so many years.

If you have pets at home, make sure they've dealt with the loss before trying to introduce another pet. If they're still in crisis, they're likely to be more hostile toward any new addition.

Providing for a Cat in the Event of Your Death

Even though in your eyes, your cat is a bona fide member of the family, in the eyes of the legal system, she's merely personal property. As much as she may be far more deserving than any of your relatives, you can't leave your estate to your cat. That doesn't mean you can't provide for her—in fact, you should. Although we don't think of our pets in terms of outliving us, it can and does happen.

You can leave your cat and money to care for her to someone as specified in your will. Because of the chance that the person chosen could take advantage of this situation, it obviously needs to be someone you *truly trust*. Talk it over with that person and be sure you're both comfortable with this, then discuss it with your lawyer. It has to be arranged so the person will be able to immediately get possession of the cat after your death without having to wait for the will to be read.

Also discuss with your lawyer how to set it up so someone will be able to legally come in and care for your cat in case you're hospitalized. Once all the legal aspects have been taken care of, you should take the time to make sure your cat's emotional needs will be met as well. Sit down and write out instructions for the person who would be caring for your cat. Besides the usual things such as what kind of food, how much to feed, how often, litter preferences, vet's name, etc., include the more personal things. What games does your cat like? How does she like to be petted? Is she afraid of certain things? Does she love to sit in the window all day? How do you groom her? Write down all the things that will not only help the new owner but will also help your cat make a less traumatic transition.

You can either give the letter to the person to keep or you can store it with your cat's supplies. Make sure that the person knows where the letter is. Periodically update the information as needed.

18

Emergencies and First Aid

Keeping Your Cool in a Medical Crisis

I've included this chapter on first aid, handling emergencies, and how to stock a general first aid kit, but keep in mind that the *most important* part of emergency care is getting the cat to the vet immediately. Unfortunately, situations may arise where treatment in seconds is crucial (for example: a cat who isn't breathing or is choking), and how you handle the crisis could mean the difference between life and death.

Being able to act immediately when your cat has been injured, poisoned, or becomes ill may save his life and reduce the amount of pain and suffering he must endure.

The single most important thing you can do to prepare for emergency situations is to *plan ahead.* Now, I know that as you sit there with your cute little kitten in your lap, the last thing you want to think about is the possibility of him being poisoned, hit by a car, or attacked by a dog—but it does happen. Having a plan will mean that you won't waste precious seconds.

First and foremost, know where to take your cat for emergency treatment *after hours.* If there isn't a pet emergency clinic in your area, ask your vet what the emergency procedure is. If there is an emergency clinic in your town, make sure you know how to get there. Take a drive and map out the shortest route. Make sure all family members know how to get there. Most emergency clinics are only open in the evening, so be sure you know their hours.

The plan should also include having a first-aid kit and being familiar with all of the contents.

Keep an assembled cat carrier on hand. Many owners dismantle the carrier for storage, which makes it too time-consuming to use in emergencies. I keep at least one carrier out with a towel in it and my cats use it as an extra place for midday naps.

A cat in pain is scared and often reacts defensively. Your sweet, docile cat when severely injured may bite or scratch when you attempt to help him. Always have a blanket on hand for protection.

Being familiar with your cat's temperature, pulse, and respiration under normal conditions will help you to evaluate his condition during illness or in a crisis.

FIRST-AID KIT

Nothing replaces immediate medical care from a veterinarian, but having an organized first-aid kit can make a difference when it comes down to *seconds* in a life-threatening situation. A well-stocked kit and having the knowledge of emergency procedures can enable you to prevent further damage or blood loss while you transport your cat to the hospital.

Familiarize family members with first-aid procedures and locate your kit in a convenient place. Besides having a first-aid kit, keep a hot water bottle, heating pad, blanket, towels, and a flat board.

Your veterinarian's phone number and that of the nearest emergency clinic should be posted near the phone. You should also post the number of the ASPCA Animal Poison Control Center (see section on "Poisoning").

You can purchase equipped first-aid kits or you can stock your own. I prefer to stock my own, using things that my vet recommends and can instruct me on.

For a container, a fishing tackle box works great. All of the contents can be neatly organized when the box is open and everything is instantly displayed so you don't have to go digging around in search of smaller items. Keep your first-aid kit well supplied, and replenish items before they run low. Check expiration dates and replace unused medicines before they get old.

The following is a general list of first-aid contents. Check with your veterinarian concerning use of specific items if you're unsure of anything.

First-Aid Kit Contents

- flashlight (always have fresh batteries on hand)
- rectal thermometer
- plastic droppers or syringes (for liquid medications)
- blunt-nosed tweezers
- blunt-nosed scissors
- measuring spoons
- plastic measuring cup
- Ace bandage
- small box of cotton swabs
- small box of cotton balls
- roll of 1-inch adhesive tape
- 3-inch-by-3-inch gauze pads
- 1-inch-wide rolled gauze
- 2-inch-wide rolled gauze
- tongue depressors
- triple antibiotic ointment
- bottle of plain eyewash solution
- small jar of water-based jelly (not petroleum jelly)
- small bottle of 3% hydrogen peroxide
- small bottle of Kaopectate or Imodium
- small bottle of milk of magnesia
- diphenhydramine (such as Benadryl) for allergic reactions
- diluted Betadine (1 part Betadine to 10 parts water)
- small bottle of rubbing alcohol
- tube of plain eye ointment (not to be given without consulting with the vet because of questions regarding corneal damage and cortisones)
- activated charcoal
- bulb syringe
- pressure bandage (a handkerchief will do)
- Nutrical
- hair ball prevention paste

HANDLING AN EMERGENCY

1. Obviously, the most important thing is to get to the veterinarian or emergency clinic immediately.

2. To prevent further injury, remove the *cause* if at all possible.

3. Make sure the cat is able to breathe. Watch for rise and fall of the chest. Put your cheek near his nose to feel for air. Clear airways of any obstructions, blood, or fluid.

4. Check for pulse.

5. If you know how, give artificial respiration if cat has a pulse. Give CPR if there's no pulse.

6. Control bleeding.

7. Move the cat as little as possible because the extent of his injury is unknown. When you must move him, support his body to prevent causing further damage and pain. Use whatever you have available for support, such as a blanket, towel, jacket, board, box.

8. If the cat appears to be unable to swallow or is nonresponsive, position his head lower than his body to prevent aspiration of fluids.

9. Cover the cat to keep him warm.

10. Don't panic. I know this is easier said than done, but you need to stay calm enough to assess the situation, provide appropriate immediate care, and *safely* transport the cat to the hospital.

Picking Up and Restraining a Cat

How you pick up and restrain a cat greatly depends on how calm, frightened, or aggressive he is and what type of injury he has sustained. Here are some general guidelines:

HOW TO PICK UP A CAT

These instructions are for a cat who isn't severely injured. If you suspect any fractures, extreme care must be taken to avoid further injury or pain. If your cat isn't frightened and is used to being held, you can pick him up in your usual manner to place him in his carrier.

When dealing with a sick or injured cat, you need to use caution to avoid being scratched or bitten. Carrying your cat in your arms could make you vulnerable to being scratched in the face. Remember that an injured, sick, or nervous cat is unpredictable.

If your cat isn't used to being held, approach him from *above*. Don't go face to face with him because he might react defensively. In a reassuring tone, calmly talk to your cat. Let him first get used to your physical contact by gently petting his head and rubbing his chin. Slide one hand under his chest so that his lower body weight is resting on your forearm. Snuggle the cat close in toward your body to immobilize his hind legs. Gently but securely, grasp his front legs with your fingers. Your other hand can either cradle his chin or if it keeps him calm, you can gently place your hand over his eyes and ears. Carefully place the cat in his carrier. If you don't have a carrier on hand, use whatever you have that will ensure safe transport. In an emergency, even a pillowcase will work.

HANDLING AN AGGRESSIVE CAT

An injured animal is confused and frightened. He doesn't know the reason for his pain, he just knows that he hurts. If at all mobile, his tendency will be to escape. In this crisis situation he most likely won't recognize you or understand that you're trying to help him. You stand a good chance of being scratched or bitten, so take precautions to protect your face, hands, and arms. An injured cat may lash out at your face as you lean in to assess his injuries, so proper restraint is crucial. Most people don't have thick leather or suede gloves handy, but in case you do, use them to protect your hands.

With a cat who may be potentially aggressive, you can grasp him by the scruff of the neck and lift him into the carrier. Offset some of the weight by holding his back legs with your other hand. This also prevents him from thrashing around.

A frightened, aggressive cat can usually be handled more easily if you cover him with a blanket or thick towel. Give him a minute and he'll relax a bit because he'll feel hidden. Gently gather up the cat and towel, tucking the rest of the towel underneath. Don't let your guard down, though, because a cat under these conditions is still very dangerous. Once you've picked him up, place him in his carrier or in a box. If you don't have a carrier or box and are transporting him in a blanket, make sure his head is exposed enough for him to breathe in order to prevent suffocation.

If your cat is too dangerous to pick up inside the blanket, drop a box over top of him. Slightly lifting up one corner, slide a flat piece of cardboard underneath. You can now safely transport the cat.

When in a crisis situation, you'll have to use your judgment on how best to handle and transport the cat based on his condition and what you have available. The most important thing is getting to the veterinary hospital quickly, safely, and without causing injury to yourself or the cat.

If attempting to transport the cat is causing too much stress, he may become too exhausted, which could cause shock. Contact your veterinarian or local emergency clinic for instructions. They may be able to send someone to help.

Respiratory Distress

Foreign objects in the nose, mouth, throat, or bronchi can obstruct breathing, as can wounds to the chest, diaphragm, or the collapse of a lung.

Signs to look for that may indicate respiratory distress: pale or blue mucous membranes (check your cat's gums): gasping, open-mouth breathing; shallow breathing; short, rapid breaths; labored breathing using abdominal muscles; unconsciousness.

If the respiratory distress is caused by choking and you can see the object, try to remove it, using blunt-nosed tweezers or your fingers. If the obstruction is farther down the throat, place your cat on his side and position the heel of your hand right behind the last rib. Firmly push at a slightly upward angle three or four times to dislodge the object. Don't be too forceful or you'll break his ribs. If you can't free the obstruction, get the cat to the vet immediately.

If the respiratory distress isn't caused by choking, it may be due to injury or illness. Get your cat to the vet immediately.

Artificial Respiration

If the cat isn't breathing *but has a heartbeat,* artificial respiration is needed. **Do not attempt this on a cat who is breathing on his own.**

- Remove the cat's collar.

- Open the mouth and pull the tongue outward to prevent it from blocking the throat and so you can check for a foreign body.

- Clear the mouth of any excess saliva or mucous. If there's vomitus in the mouth or if the cat was underwater, suspend him upside down by the hips and gently swing his body a couple of times to remove the liquid.

- Lay the cat on his right side with the body slightly higher than his head. The head and neck should be straight to ensure an open air passageway.

- With his tongue pulled forward, place your mouth over his nose only (don't cover his mouth). Blow air into his nostrils for approximately 3 seconds. You should see the chest expand. Excess air will escape through the mouth. Every two seconds repeat the procedure until the cat begins breathing on his own.

CPR (Cardiopulmonary Resuscitation)

If the cat *has no heartbeat* and *isn't breathing*, CPR must be performed. If the cat *does* have a heartbeat but there's no respiration, then artificial respiration should be performed. **Don't attempt CPR on a cat who is breathing**. If it's at all possible to get to the nearest animal hospital, do so, because CPR is difficult to perform. If you're too far from the nearest hospital, then you'll have to perform the procedure yourself.

- Lay the cat on his right side.

- Continue doing artificial respiration in rhythm with CPR.

- With one hand, place your thumb on the cat's sternum, and your fingers on the opposite side so that your palm is cupping his chest.

- Compress the chest firmly but gently. CPR must be performed gently or the cat's ribs may be broken. The rate is one compression per second. Perform five compressions then administer a breath of artificial respiration without stopping the rhythm of the heart massage.

- Always observe the cat for signs of life and every few minutes check for pulse and spontaneous breathing.

- Stop immediately once you feel a heartbeat.

- Another method of administering CPR is to place one hand on each side of the cat's chest, just behind the elbows. Using both hands, compress the chest five times then perform artificial respiration one time before repeating the chest compression.

- If you've been performing CPR for thirty minutes, it's extremely doubtful that the cat will be revived.

Choking

The symptoms may include: coughing, pawing at the mouth, drooling, difficulty breathing, bulging eyes, unconsciousness.

If your cat is calm enough, attempt to look into his mouth in order to check for a foreign object. You may have to wrap him in a towel for restraint. If possible, remove it, using blunt-nosed tweezers or your fingers. With a struggling or panicked cat, don't attempt to remove the object because you could send it deeper into his throat. As long as the cat is not having breathing trouble, just get to the vet immediately. If the cat is unable to breathe, you'll have to administer emergency first aid. Lay the cat on his side with his head lower than his body and pull out the tongue. Place one hand below the sternum, just behind the last rib. Use your other hand to brace the cat by placing it along his back. With the heel of the hand below the sternum, give four quick upward thrusts (press *in* and *up*). Your thrusts should be forceful but not so hard as to break a rib. Immediately check the cat's mouth to see if you've dislodged the object. If unsuccessful, repeat with four more quick thrusts. If you can't dislodge the object, get to the veterinarian, performing artificial respiration in the meantime.

Controlling Bleeding

APPLYING PRESSURE

Place a sterile or clean gauze pad over the wound and apply even pressure. You can wrap a gauze bandage over the wound but observe the cat's limb for signs of swelling, which could indicate possible circulation impairment. If that happens, loosen the bandage.

If the gauze pad gets soaked with blood, *leave it in place* and just add another one over top. To remove the gauze may disturb any potential clotting.

Don't apply peroxide to the wound, or it'll become harder to control the bleeding. Once the bleeding stops, don't wipe the wound because you risk disturbing the clots and causing the flow to resume.

Another technique to try if direct pressure isn't working is to firmly press the artery located on the inside of the foreleg (in the armpit) or the inside thigh of the hind leg (at the groin). This may help inhibit the blood loss from a limb while an assistant attempts to pressure bandage.

TOURNIQUET

The application of a tourniquet is to be used as a last resort to control life-threatening bleeding to a limb when attempts at pressure bandaging have failed. Irreversible damage and the loss of the extremity can result from a tourniquet that has been left on too long or put on too tightly. Don't apply a tourniquet to any part of the body other than a leg or the tail.

Make a tourniquet by looping a piece of gauze, at least one inch wide, around the limb, a couple of inches above the wound (the tourniquet goes between the heart and the wound). Tie the gauze once (don't make a knot), place a stick or pencil on top then tie one more time. Twist the pencil slowly until bleeding has been controlled. *IMPORTANT: the tourniquet must be loosened every five minutes (for one minute) to allow blood to flow to the limb.*

It's crucial that you get to the nearest vet immediately to prevent permanent damage to the limb.

Shock

Shock occurs when blood pressure falls, causing inadequate blood flow to organs and tissues, which results in decreased oxygen. Attempting to compensate for the decreased circulation, the body speeds up the heart, diverts blood flow away from nonvital organs and tries to maintain enough fluid in circulation. Without adequate oxygen, though, the organs have trouble functioning and the heart has an increasingly difficult time pumping.

Shock isn't always easy to recognize or is mistaken for other conditions. If untreated, shock can cause death.

Some common causes of shock include: trauma in general, heat stroke, burns, poisoning, hemorrhaging, serious illness, dehydration (due to diarrhea or vomiting).

SIGNS OF SHOCK INCLUDE:

- a drop in body temperature (the cat may feel cold to the touch)

- shivering

- pale mucous membranes

- weak pulse (often rapid)

- rapid breathing

- weakness

To treat shock: first stop the bleeding, if any, and administer artificial respiration if breathing stops. If the heart stops, proceed with CPR. Position the cat with his head lower than his body but if he wants to sit, don't force him into a position. Keep him calm and let him settle into the position he finds most comfortable. Don't stress the cat because it'll make breathing more difficult.

Wrap the cat in a blanket and seek emergency veterinary care immediately.

Cleaning Wounds

This applies to less serious wounds. Bleeding wounds should have pressure applied (see "Controlling Bleeding") and immediate emergency veterinary care.

A wound that is less serious should still be treated to prevent infection. It's always best to have the vet check any wounds, regardless of how insignificant they may appear to you.

For home treatment of minor wounds, enlist the aid of an assistant, if possible, to help hold and calm the cat. First, make sure your hands have been washed and that any equipment you'll use is clean. The hair around the wound should be clipped. The easiest way is to put a dab of K-Y jelly or antibiotic ointment on the wound itself prior to clipping and flush it out afterward. This helps collect hair and keeps it from sticking down in the wound. Then, using scissors, *carefully* clip the hair around the edges of the wound. If you don't have any K-Y jelly or ointment, just be very careful and hold the ends of the hair with your fingers as you clip. Next, with a clean, damp gauze pad, cleanse the edges of the wound. Using clean water, flush the wound to remove dirt and debris. If there is trapped debris in the wound, use a clean, wet cotton swab.

Using a gauze pad, you can clean the wound with diluted Betadine. Be sure the Betadine is diluted because strong iodine actually kills cells. Use the gauze pad to dab the wound only once then replace with a fresh one. Don't contaminate the Betadine solution or the wound by reusing the same pad. If you don't have Betadine and plan to use hydrogen peroxide, dilute it with water and use it only once to wash the wound. Peroxide can damage the exposed tissue, so be very cautious.

After the wound has been cleaned, you can apply an antibiotic ointment.

Keeping a bandage on a cat is often tricky, so if the wound needs to be covered to keep it clean, tape it carefully. Make sure the bandage stays clean and dry; change it daily, or more often, if needed.

Always check with your vet to see whether a particular wound should remain bandaged. Some wounds heal faster when left uncovered, and any that are draining pus should be left open to the air.

Fractures

You may notice your cat walking on three legs, unable to put any pressure on the fourth leg. If he doesn't hold it up, it may just drag uselessly. Another sign might be an unusual angle to the leg.

Fractures to the spinal column will cause an inability for the cat to use his legs if the spinal cord is damaged.

Don't waste time trying to splint or treat fractures yourself. In the case of a compound fracture (breaking through the skin), cover the area with a sterile cloth and get the cat to the vet. Don't attempt to push the bone back under the skin.

Be very careful not to move the cat more than needed for safe transport. Using a box that has been padded with towels will be most comfortable.

Heatstroke

Cats are unable to tolerate high temperatures as well as humans do. Heatstroke can happen in minutes if a cat is left in a parked car. Even leaving the windows cracked won't lower the temperature enough. A car parked in the shade will still turn into an oven in a matter of a few brief minutes. Heatstroke is also a risk for cats confined to carriers in hot weather, restricted to sunny decks, porches, or yards without shade or access to water. Cats confined to rooms without air conditioning or any ventilation during hot weather can also suffer heatstroke. Short-nosed breeds such as Persians are especially vulnerable to heatstroke, as are older, overweight, or asthmatic cats. Overexertion on hot days or fever can also cause heatstroke.

Cats can't perspire the way humans do. They must attempt to cool their body temperature through evaporation by rapid breathing and licking their fur. Heat-affected cats drool a lot and lick their coats to spread the saliva in an attempt to cool themselves. As the temperature of the air increases, the cat's system of cooling through evaporation doesn't function sufficiently enough.

With heatstroke, the cat begins panting. The color of the mucous membranes and the tongue turn bright red. Saliva becomes very thick and the cat starts drooling and often vomits.

Left unchecked, the cat becomes weak, unsteady, and may have diarrhea. The mucous membranes then become pale or gray, and the cat collapses into a coma or may even die.

Treatment: remove the cat to a cooler environment immediately. If his body temperature has reached 106° F., wet the cat down with cool (not cold) water and then place him under a fan—this encourages evaporation, which results in cooling. Don't immerse the cat in cold water, because the skin will begin to cool too quickly. Feeling the cold, the vessels to the skin will constrict and blood flow is directed internally. As a result, the core body temperature won't start to drop as rapidly. Provide cool water for him to drink. Massage his skin and legs to regain normal circulation. Take the cat's rectal temperature every five minutes. Once the temperature goes below 103° F., you can cease wetting him down. Because the cat's system is so unsteady, you want to make sure you don't cool him down too much, risking hypothermia.

Get the cat to the veterinarian as soon as possible to check for any internal complications and to provide additional supportive treatment. Very often, a cat suffering from hyperthermia goes into shock.

Observe your cat for several days afterward because not all complications from heatstroke may be immediately apparent. Hemorrhagic diarrhea (due to cell death) and renal failure can appear hours or even days later.

Preventing Heatstroke

- Don't leave your cat in a parked car, even in shaded areas.
- When traveling with your cat in warm weather, make sure he's in a well-ventilated carrier. Don't put the carrier on the side of the car that will get the sun.
- Keep your longhaired cat well groomed to prevent mats, which make it harder for the skin to stay cool.
- Always provide access to fresh drinking water. In warm weather, check the water supply more often.
- Keep a close eye on susceptible cats such as Persians, Himalayans, and also asthmatic and elderly cats.
- For an outdoor cat, provide adequate shade areas and plenty of fresh water.
- Remember, if the air temperature is uncomfortable to you, it's also uncomfortable to your cat.

Hypothermia

Hypothermia can occur when there's a fall in body temperature. This can be caused by exposure to cold, getting wet, shock, after anesthesia, or illness; newborn kittens are also at risk.

Signs include: a rectal temperature below 100° F., being cold to the touch, shivering, depression, stiffness, dilated pupils, and anxiety. Without treatment, the cat will collapse and go into a coma.

Treatment: Wrap the cat in a blanket or towel and dry him off if he's wet. Don't use a hair dryer to warm the cat because you risk causing burns. Fill a hot water bottle with *warm* water and wrap it in a towel before putting it next to the cat's skin. If you use a heating pad it must be set on *low* and place a towel between the pad and the cat's body. To avoid shock, the rewarming process must be slow. Check the cat's rectal temperature every ten minutes. Continue using the warm water-filled bottle until the cat's temperature reaches 100° F.

Hypothermia predisposes a cat to low blood sugar. When he begins moving around again, give a little honey to raise his blood sugar level.

Take the cat to the vet for followup treatment.

If you're unable to get your cat's temperature back to normal within forty-five minutes, get medical attention.

If hypothermia occurs in a kitten, place him under your clothing and use your own body heat to warm him. Don't place him on a heating pad or attempt to feed him. Get him to the vet for immediate medical attention.

Frostbite

This is caused when a cat is exposed to extreme cold. The ears, tail, and feet are the places most usually affected. As circulation is impaired, tissue damage results. At first, the skin will look pale. As thawing occurs, the skin becomes red, swollen, and hot. Later, peeling sometimes occurs. The skin will also be *extremely painful* if touched, so use caution when handling a cat suffering frostbite.

Treatment: Move the cat to a warm area. Either immerse the area in warm (never hot) water or apply warm moist packs until the area appears flushed. **DON'T rub or massage the areas, because you risk causing further damage.** Apply an antibiotic ointment and seek immediate veterinary attention.

Oral antibiotics may have to be given to prevent infection, and your vet may also prescribe a pain reliever.

Frostbitten areas later become more susceptible to cold.

Prevent frostbite by keeping your cat indoors during very cold weather. If you're feeding outdoor strays, provide access to dry shelter.

Burns

Burns can be a particular hazard for cats should they walk across stoves, get too close to a burner, or are splattered with hot oil or boiling water while being underfoot during meal preparation. The paw pads are the most commonly burned areas due to the cat walking on a hot surface (whether that be a hot stove or hot pavement).

For superficial burns, apply a clean, cold water-soaked cloth over the area for about thirty minutes to relieve the pain. Then, gently pat the area dry. Clip the hair away from the burn. Make sure the burn stays clean and dry. Watch for signs of blistering. **NEVER use ice** because it will damage the tissues underneath. Don't apply butter or ointments. Take your cat to the vet in case further treatment is needed.

Second-degree burns often cause blistering, swelling, and usually some oozing. The skin will be very red. Apply a clean, cold water-soaked cloth over the burn. Then very gently pat the area dry. Don't rub. Put sterile gauze lightly over the area, being careful to not touch any blisters. Get to the vet right away.

Third-degree burns are the most serious. Underlying tissues are destroyed. The skin will appear charred or it may even look white. The cat will probably be in shock. Soak a clean cloth in cold water and very gently place it over the burn. Gently put a dry cloth over the wet dressing and get immediate emergency veterinary care. Don't waste time trying to administer any treatment at home. Getting to the vet right away is crucial.

CHEMICAL BURNS
Chemicals that splash on the cat's body or in his eyes can result in serious injury. A cat can even make the situation worse by attempting to remove the chemical from his coat by licking. Fast action on your part is critical to prevent further damage.

For burns to the skin, if you don't know what type of chemical it is, flush the area with clear water. If you have rubber gloves, use them because some chemicals can actually eat through the skin. If you know that the chemical is an *acid* (such as bleach), flush the area with a solution of baking soda and water (1 teaspoon baking soda in one pint of water). Wash alkalis (such as drain cleaner) with a solution of equal parts vinegar and water. If you are at all in doubt, just use clear water. If you have the container, read the label for additional instructions concerning what to put on the burn, then get to the vet right away.

For chemicals splashed in the eyes, place the cat on his side, hold the eyelids open and flush the eyes with lukewarm water. You can also use saline solution. You may need to wrap the cat in a towel for restraint. If only one eye is affected, tilt the cat's head back and rinse *away* from the unaffected eye. Use sterile gauze over the eyes and rush to the vet.

ELECTRIC SHOCK AND ELECTRICAL BURNS
Usually caused by chewing on electrical cords, contact with downed power lines or by lightning.

Never touch a cat if he's in contact with an exposed wire. Involuntary muscle contractions may prevent him from releasing his grip on the wire. Turn the current off at the control panel, then use a wooden broomstick or yardstick to push the cat away from the wire. The cat may be unconscious or in shock. If he isn't breathing, administer artificial respiration. If the cat is in shock, keep him warm. Get to the vet immediately.

Electric shock can cause cardiac arrest. It can also cause pulmonary edema, which is a buildup of fluid in the lungs. Signs of pulmonary edema include: breathing difficulty, open mouth breathing, preferring to sit or stand instead of lying down. Emergency medical care is needed. Even if your cat appears to have recovered, he needs to be checked by the vet. Pulmonary edema doesn't happen right away.

You may not actually catch your cat chewing on an electrical cord but you might notice signs of electrical burns. The usual places are the corners of the mouth and on the tongue. Any inflammation in these areas, redness, blistering, or gray appearance are strong indications of electrical burns. If you notice any of these signs, seek immediate medical attention. Also, check all the cords in your home to locate the one that has been damaged.

Refer to chapter 3 for information on prevention of electrical burns.

Poisoning

Many products we use every day are poisonous to cats. Very often, these products are easily within a cat's reach. For example, have you left cleaning agents out on the counter? What about pill bottles? Remember that antifreeze leak in the driveway? Do you know which plants are toxic to your cat? Are containers of kerosene, paint, pesticides, etc., safely sealed without drips running down the sides? Even if a cat doesn't intend on ingesting a substance, he'll use his tongue to clean it off his fur. So even though cats may be less at risk than dogs for ingesting poisons due to the fact that they don't gulp food, being fastidious groomers still puts them in danger. If the substance is toxic, it will only take a small amount to poison him.

Outdoor cats are more at risk than indoor cats. They're in danger of coming in contact with chemicals and solvents improperly stored in garages, fertilizers, pesticides, sidewalk salt, gasoline, intentional poisoning, and antifreeze, to name just a few. Antifreeze, for instance, is so toxic that less than a teaspoon can be fatal.

All too often we unintentionally poison our own cats by using too many products or inappropriate products on them. In an effort to kill fleas we sometimes overdo by using too many preparations at once or we don't read caution labels. We also give medicines (such as aspirin) without knowing the dangerous and deadly side effects.

Signs of poisoning: Depending upon the poison, signs can range from anxiety and convulsions to depression and coma. You may notice excessive drooling, weakness, a strange odor to the breath or on the body, vomiting, breathing difficulty, bright red color to the mouth (sign of carbon monoxide poisoning).

Cats are in danger of ingesting rodent poisons or the poisoned rodents themselves. Many rodent poisons are anticoagulants, which can cause hemorrhaging. Signs may include: blood in vomit and stool, pale mucous membranes, nosebleeds, skin bruising. When you bring your cat to the vet, if possible, bring a sample of the bloody stool or vomitus.

If you suspect that your cat has been poisoned, try to identify the substance. Read the label for instructions or locate chewed leaves on plants. For help, call your local poison control center. There is also The ASPCA Animal Poison Control Center, which is available twenty-four hours a day, seven days a week. The consultation fee is about thirty dollars. Call (900) 680-0000 (the fee will be charged to your phone bill) or (800) 548-2423 (if you'd rather have the fee charged to a major credit card).

CHEMICAL POISONING

For first aid, whether to induce vomiting depends on the type of poison ingested. An acid or alkali poison such as drain cleaners and solvents will cause more damage, burning the esophagus, throat, and mouth as it comes back up. If the cat vomits kerosene back up, it will also cause additional burns. Check with your vet and poison control center, but here are the general guidelines for first aid:

- for *acids*: give a dose of milk of magnesia (1 teaspoon per 5 pounds of cat)

- for *alkalis*: mix equal parts water and vinegar and give up to 4 teaspoons

Once the acid, alkali or kerosene poison is in the cat's stomach, your only course of action is to dilute it to reduce the amount of damage.

Milk of Magnesia, Kaopectate, or regular milk given orally (by syringe) will help coat the intestines.

For *noncorrosive* poisoning (antifreeze, perfume, pills), you can induce vomiting. You need to do it before the substance gets into the cat's system. Don't attempt this if the cat is convulsing or is unconscious.

- *to induce vomiting:* Give ½ to 1 teaspoon syrup of ipecac (dose is about 1 teaspoon per 10 pounds). Repeat only once after twenty minutes if cat hasn't vomited. An alternative to syrup of ipecac is to administer 1 teaspoon of hydrogen peroxide. This can be repeated in ten minutes if the cat hasn't vomited, but don't exceed 3 teaspoons.

If you don't know what kind of poison was ingested or no antidote is indicated, diluting the poison is the safest route. You can purchase activated charcoal as a liquid. There is also a paste form available that comes in a tube. Follow dosing instructions on the label. Activated charcoal helps to prevent absorption of the poison. Don't confuse activated charcoal with the charcoal used for grilling—they're not the same. Activated charcoal is purchased at a pharmacy. Don't give activated charcoal if you've given syrup of ipecac, because they neutralize each other. Even if your cat has vomited, don't give the activated charcoal if you've already given syrup of ipecac.

You can also use Milk of Magnesia or Kaopectate (1 teaspoon per 5 pounds) to coat the intestines and dilute the poison. If you don't have either of those products, then just use regular milk. You can feed the cat as much milk as possible but do it gradually.

NO MATTER WHAT KIND OF POISON, GET IMMEDIATE VETERINARY CARE. Bring the bottle of poison with you. If the cat has vomited, bring a sample of the vomitus. During transport to the hospital, keep the cat warm, watch for signs of shock, and keep his head lower than his body to allow drainage of fluids or vomitus.

POISONS ABSORBED THROUGH THE SKIN

Organophosphate flea or fly spray can be absorbed through the skin and cause metabolic disease in addition to external burning. See section on "Chemical Burns."

Some Poisonous Household Substances

acetaminophen
   (such as Tylenol)
antifreeze
aspirin
bath oil
bleach
brake fluid
cosmetics
deodorant

detergents
disinfectant cleansers
drain cleaner
fertilizer
floor polish
furniture polish
gasoline
hair coloring
ibuprofen

insecticides
kerosene
laxatives
mothballs
nail polish
nail polish remover
paint
paint remover
perfume

plants
prescription medicine
rodenticides
shampoo
shaving lotion
shoe polish
suntan lotion
turpentine
weed killer

POISONING FROM PLANTS

An indoor cat with not a lot to do to keep himself occupied, may nibble on houseplants. Some cats just do occasional munching, while others leave nothing but mangled stems sticking out of the soil. Depending on the plant, even a few nibbles can be very toxic. Some, like the *dieffenbachia* (also known as dumb cane), cause intense burning and swelling of the mouth and throat, creating difficulty in breathing. Some plants, including the dieffenbachia, will cause burning and further damage again if you attempt to induce vomiting.

I've included a partial list of poisonous plants on p. 331, but there are so many out there. If your cat shows any interest in plants, remove all that are dangerous.

Signs of plant poisoning: Depending on the type of plant ingested, there may be excessive salivation, vomiting, bloody diarrhea, breathing difficulty, fever, abdominal pain, depression, collapse, trembling, irregular heartbeat, mouth and throat ulcers. Things can quickly deteriorate, leading to convulsions, coma, cardiac arrest, and death.

Treatment for plant poisoning depends on the type of plant. If you can identify the plant, contact your veterinarian and local poison control center for instructions. If you are instructed to induce vomiting, refer to the previous section on "Chemical Poisoning."

Administering milk will coat and soothe the intestines and will also dilute poisons. If you haven't given syrup of ipecac to induce vomiting, you can give activated charcoal (follow dosing instructions on the label). Don't administer activated charcoal if you already administered syrup of ipecac because they inactivate each other.

Get the cat to the vet immediately. Keep him warm and watch for signs of shock.

Falls from Windows

Any time your cat falls from the window, however low to the ground it is, get him to the vet for an examination. Even if you don't see any visible signs of injury, he may have sustained internal damage.

Preventing falls: Check all screens to be sure they're secure and not in need of repair. Don't trust a cat with a partially opened, unscreened window, no matter how slight the opening or how big the cat. Don't allow cats out on balconies, even if there are railings. Just because your cat hasn't jumped on top of the railing yet, doesn't mean he won't.

Insect Stings

Cats, with their fascination for anything that moves, can easily end up on the receiving end of a bee sting. Bees, wasps, hornets, and yellow jackets can inflict a painful sting. Stings to the face or mouth can cause dangerous swelling as air passageways may become blocked. Swelling around the throat can result in suffocation.

Aside from the pain and dangerous swelling, some cats, like humans, can have an allergic reaction to insect stings. If swelling persists or the cat shows any signs of breathing difficulty, drooling, seizures, or vomiting, seek emergency medical care.

Treatment: Remove the stinger with tweezers. Apply a thin paste of baking soda mixed with water to relieve itching. Use ice packs or a cold compress to reduce swelling and relieve pain. If you use an ice pack, wrap a small towel around it before placing it next to the cat's skin. Observe the cat for signs of shock. Ask your vet about the use of a cortisone cream to relieve itching if the cat is very bothered by it.

For a sting inside of the mouth, seek immediate medical attention so the vet can observe your cat for breathing difficulty.

Irritating, Toxic, or Poisonous Plants (Indoor and Outdoor)

For the most part, your cat probably won't stand around outdoors and gnaw on your shrubs, but if it looks as if he's interested, you'll have to take precautions. An indoor cat on the other hand, is more likely to nibble on your houseplants.

almond
amaryllis
angel's trumpet
apple seeds
apricot
arrowhead fern
asparagus fern
autumn crocus
avocado
azalea
baby's breath
balsam pear
beech
belladonna
bird of paradise
bittersweet woody
black locust
Boston ivy
box
buckeye
buttercup
cacti
caladium

calla lily
castor bean
cherry
China berry
Chinese evergreen
Christmas trees
chrysanthemum
coral plant
coriaria
creeping Charlie
creeping fig
crown of thorns
daffodil
daisy
datura
day lily
delphinium
dieffenbachia
Easter lily
elderberry
elephant ears
English ivy
English yew

fox glove
geranium
golden chain
ground cherry
hibiscus
holly
honeysuckle
hyacinth
hydrangea
impatiens
Indian rubber plant
iris
ivy
jack-in-the-pulpit
Japanese yew
jasmine
Jerusalem cherry
kalanchoe
larkspur
laurel
lily of the valley
lords and ladies
majesty
malanga
marijuana
mistletoe
moonweed
morning glory
mother-in-law
mushroom
narcissus
needlepoint ivy

nephthytis
nettle
nightshade
Norfolk pine
nutmeg
nux vomica
oleander
onion
ornamental yew
peach
periwinkle
philodendron
poinsettia
poison hemlock
pokeweed
potato
pothos
rhododendron
rhubarb leaves
schefflera
skunk cabbage
spinach
sweet pea
tobacco
tulip
Virginia creeper
water hemlock
weeping fig
western yew
wisteria
yucca

If your cat is prone to being stung, keep Benadryl on hand—or better yet, keep your cat indoors.

Ticks

See chapter 13.

Spiders

Brown Recluse, tarantulas, and Black Widow spiders are severely dangerous. The site of the bite may be extremely painful. The cat may develop a fever, have difficulty breathing, and go into shock. Some spider bites will lead into necrosis or abscesses without having acute signs. Get immediate emergency care. If you actually see your cat get bitten, take him right to the vet.

Drowning

Although a cat is able to swim a short distance, drowning often occurs when he's unable to climb up and out of the water. For instance, cats drown in swimming pools because they can't reach the ledge. If you have a pool and there's a possibility that your pets may get near it, install some kind of a ramp so an animal who accidentally falls in will be able to safely climb out.

First aid for drowning involves: getting water out of the cat's lungs. Hold the cat upside down by the hips and gently swing his body for about ten to twenty seconds or until no more water comes out. Lay the cat on his right side and begin administering mouth-to-nose resuscitation. If the heart has stopped, perform CPR.

When the cat is breathing on his own, take him immediately to the vet for medical care. He may be in shock, so keep him warm.

If the cat was in cold water, wrap him in a blanket and turn the heater up in your car as you transport him to the vet.

Dehydration

Dehydration is the loss of body fluids and often the loss of electrolytes (minerals). Causes of dehydration include: illness, fever, prolonged diarrhea, prolonged vomiting.

You can test for dehydration by gently pulling up on the skin of the upper back. It should snap right back. If the skin falls back into position slowly or stays up in a peak, then the cat is dehydrated. The gums are also another indicator of dehydration. Normally wet, when dehydrated they will look dry and feel tacky.

Treatment: Prompt veterinary care is needed. IV fluid therapy will be administered to replenish fluids and restore electrolyte balance.

Medical Appendix

Listed in this appendix are many of the disorders cats may acquire. Some are very common and others are rare, but being an alert, informed owner can make a big difference in how quickly symptoms get noticed and diagnosed and how fast a cat's pain and suffering will be relieved. The problem could be minor or it could be life-threatening. Your familiarity with your cat and how he normally looks, acts, feels, or sounds enables you to suspect trouble because he just "isn't his usual self." Cats' lives have been saved because of hunches like those.

The purpose of this book is neither to be a complete medical reference nor is it meant to replace the personalized care of your veterinarian. If you'd like to read in more detail about all the disorders that can affect cats, I urge you to add a veterinary medical reference book, such as *The Cornell Book of Cats* (Villard Books), to your home library.

Internal and External Disorders

INTERNAL PARASITES

Tapeworms

These worms live in the intestines and are probably the most common of the internal parasites in adult cats.

Tapeworms require an intermediate host during the larval stage before transmission to the cat. Fleas and lice are common tapeworm hosts and based on the cat's fastidious grooming behavior, it's very likely that at least one flea harboring immature tapeworms will be ingested.

Cats can also acquire tapeworms by eating raw meat or raw freshwater fish. Outdoor cats who routinely hunt can also be exposed through their prey.

The tapeworm attaches itself to the intestinal wall by way of suckers and hooks on the head. The body is comprised of segments, each one containing eggs. These segments break off and pass out of the body in the cat's feces. The segments, which are about a quarter-inch in length, can wriggle by themselves when freshly separated from the worm. You may notice one or two moving segments clinging to the hair around your cat's anus. As the segments dry, they resemble grains of rice. You may also find these dried tapeworm segments on your cat's bedding.

If you notice tapeworm segments, the vet will administer a deworming pill or injection specifically for tapeworms.

If there are tapeworms *in* your cat, it most likely means there are also fleas *on* your cat. Combine the deworming with a comprehensive flea control program to avoid a reappearance of the parasite. Even if you don't see little tapeworm segments on the cat or in the environment, if he has a significant flea problem, there's a chance that he also has tapeworms.

Roundworms

Probably the most common worm found in kittens and puppies. Roundworm larvae are transmitted to nursing kittens by way of the mother's milk. Kittens with roundworms develop a characteristic pot belly appearance while the rest of the body remains thin.

Cats acquire roundworms by coming in contact with egg-contaminated soil. Roundworm eggs are very hard and can withstand conditions in the soil for a long time, until an unsuspecting host comes along.

Roundworms, which grow from four to five inches long, live in the cat's stomach and intestine. You may notice a roundworm in the cat's feces or in vomitus. Roundworms resemble spaghetti (not a pleasant comparison, I know, but it's unfortunately accurate). Symptoms include diarrhea, weight loss, appearance of worms in vomitus or feces, pot belly, lethargy.

As part of the normal vaccination schedule, your vet will routinely deworm your young kitten. Deworming of kittens is generally done in two stages three weeks apart. The deworming medication is taken orally and is very safe for kittens.

Roundworms are rare in adult cats.

If you've adopted a stray cat, in addition to having him tested for diseases and vaccinated, he should also be checked for worms.

Hookworms

Hookworms are more common in dogs than in cats. These thin worms attach to the intestinal wall to feed. Hookworms are relatively small, ranging in length from a quarter- to a half-inch.

Transmission occurs through contact with feces or soil containing the larvae. For kittens, hookworms can be potentially fatal. Transmission doesn't occur in utero. Signs of hookworm can include: diarrhea, weight loss, weakness. Hookworm infection can lead to anemia.

Diagnosis is made by microscopic examination of a stool sample.

Deworming medications are used to treat hookworm. After treatment, the stool should be rechecked.

Heartworm

Heartworm is a disease more commonly associated with dogs. Even though it's not as common in cats, there have been cases so it's important to keep your cat protected.

Heartworm is spread by mosquitoes carrying the larvae. Once the mosquito bites the cat, it injects the larvae from its saliva. When the larvae mature into worms, they move through the circulatory system and eventually travel to the heart or lungs. Signs of heartworm can include: vomiting, cough, loss of weight, anemia. As the disease progresses, it leads to breathing difficulty. Diagnosis is confirmed through blood tests and radiographs.

There is a monthly heartworm preventative that can be administered. Discuss this option with your vet. If your cat goes outdoors and you live in a high-risk area (any climate where a mosquito might pass by), it's a good idea to provide as much protection as you can. Cats living in warm climates may need to remain on heartworm preventative year round. In colder climates the preventative should be given just before the start of mosquito season and continued until the season is well over.

As of this writing, there is no approved treatment for feline heartworm disease.

Toxoplasmosis

Toxoplasmosis can cause birth defects and should be a concern for pregnant women. Both cats and humans can infect young in utero. If you're pregnant or suspect that you might be, another family member should take over litter box responsibilities. Refer to chapter 8 for specific instructions.

Caused by the protozoan parasite *toxoplasma gondii,* toxoplasmosis is acquired by cats ingesting infected prey or coming in contact with contaminated soil. For cats, contaminated soil is dangerous because of their fastidious grooming habits. Paws that touch the soil eventually get licked by the cat's tongue.

People as well as cats are more at risk of acquiring toxoplasmosis by eating raw or undercooked meat that contains the parasite. People who use the same cutting board for preparing raw meat and then raw vegetables are putting themselves at a great risk.

Cats can carry the parasite and remain asymptomatic. If symptoms are present they may include: fever, poor appetite, weight loss, cough, lethargy, diarrhea, enlarged lymph nodes, irregular breathing. Asymptomatic cats can still shed the disease through their feces.

Tests can indicate whether your cat has been exposed to the parasite. If the test result is positive and the cat is in good health, it means he has developed an immunity and most likely isn't a carrier. The presence of oocysts (egg spores) in the feces, though, means that the cat is shedding infective organisms. Humans can also be tested to determine if they carry the organism.

Note: It takes forty-eight hours for the oocysts to become infective once the cat has defecated. Promptly removing stools from the litter box will greatly reduce the risk of infection. If you must handle litter box duties yourself and you're pregnant, invest in a box of disposable gloves and be certain to wash your hands immediately afterward. You should also wear gardening gloves whenever working outdoors.

If you test your cat and find that he hasn't been exposed to the organism and also hasn't built up an immunity, keep him indoors for the duration of your pregnancy. That way, everybody stays safe.

Treatment involves antibiotic therapy.

Tips for Preventing Toxoplasmosis

- Have your cat tested.
- Take care of any fly problems, because they can carry egg spores from infected feces and contaminate food.
- Don't eat raw or undercooked meat and don't feed any to your pets.
- Don't use the same cutting board to cut vegetables that you also use to prepare raw meat.
- Bleach cutting boards and clean all work surfaces with disinfectants.
- Wash your hands *often!* Wash them immediately after handling raw meat, cleaning the litter box, or gardening. Instruct children on hand-washing importance.
- Immediately remove feces from litter box. Sift the litter at least twice a day and completely change the litter and disinfect the box once a week (for more on litter box cleaning, refer to chapter 8).
- Keep a box of disposable gloves near the litter box for all family members to use when cleaning.
- Keep your backyard sandbox covered and don't allow children to play in public sandboxes or in any friend's boxes that are left exposed. Stray cats may have used them for defecation.
- Wash homegrown vegetables because outdoor cats may have used the soil in the garden.
- Wear gloves whenever you do any outside work.
- Keep your cat indoors.

Coccidia

A highly contagious intestinal parasite that mostly affects kittens, coccidia can attack adult cats as well. Transmission occurs through contact with contaminated feces. Signs of infection include: weight loss, dehydration, and mucous-coated diarrhea that often contains blood.

Stressful situations such as malnutrition, overcrowding, unsanitary conditions can cause lower resistance and often lead to coccidiosis. Cats can be reinfected by coming into contact with their own feces, so keeping the litter box very clean is important. Diagnosis is based on microscopic examination of a stool sample. Sometimes coccidia won't be seen under the microscope, so the vet treats the cat based on symptoms.

Treatment involves the use of deworming drugs. Controlling the diarrhea as well as coccidiosis is important to prevent dangerous dehydration.

Giardia

A protozoan parasite that lives in the cat's small intestine, the cyst stage of giardia gets carried out of the body in the cat's feces, making it infective to any animal that comes in contact with the stool. Beside oral contact with infected feces, giardia can be transmitted by ingestion of contaminated water.

A cat may not show active symptoms of giardiasis but can still shed infective organisms. Signs of giardiasis include: diarrhea, which is often yellow in color.

Diagnosis is made by microscopic examination of a stool sample, and treatment includes antibiotics.

Signs of Skin and Coat Problems

- scratching
- crusts and scabs
- mats
- hair loss
- broken-off hairs
- inflammation
- odor to the skin
- pimples or pustules
- rash
- excessive shedding
- appearance of black or white specks in the fur
- appearance of anything that look like insects
- lumps
- lesions
- change in skin color
- dandruff

SKIN DISORDERS

A cat's skin is very sensitive and can be more prone to allergic reactions and injury than ours. Skin problems can show up at any stage in life, and often a condition stays hidden from the owner until there's a loss of hair or overgrooming by the cat is observed. Disorders can range from parasitism, allergies, stress, nutritional imbalances, bacterial infection, injury, burns, exposure, tumors, and the list goes on.

Regular grooming, control of parasites such as fleas, routine checking by the owner, and prompt veterinary treatment when needed will help keep the largest organ of your cat's body in good shape.

EXTERNAL PARASITES

Fleas and Ticks
These little pests deserve a chapter of their own. Refer to chapter 13.

Lice
Lice are rarely found on cats. When infestation does occur, it's usually seen in malnourished, debilitated cats living in unsanitary conditions.

Lice appear as pale-colored wingless insects. Their eggs, called *nits,* become attached to hairs. The nits look similar to dandruff, only they aren't easily brushed away. Nits resemble white sand.

Mats on the cat's coat should be clipped away because lice are commonly found beneath them. They can also be found around the ears, head, neck, and genitals.

Treatment includes bathing the cat, followed by an insecticidal dip used for fleas. NOTE: Because a louse-infested cat is probably very debilitated, extreme caution must be used when deciding on appropriate treatment. Consult your veterinarian before treating an infested cat.

Treatment for the environment consists of vacuuming, washing all pet bedding, and thoroughly cleansing all areas where the cat has been.

Flies

Maggots
Various types of blowflies lay their eggs in open wounds, dead flesh, and soiled or matted hair. Cats most at risk are those with neglected wounds, badly soiled or matted hair, urine- or feces-soaked fur.

The eggs hatch into larvae within eight to seventy-two hours. It takes two to nineteen days for the larvae to grow into full-size maggots. Full-size maggots produce a saliva enzyme that damages the cat's skin, causing ulcers that appear like punched out holes. There is also an accompanying odor to maggot infestation. Left untreated, the cat can go into shock and die from the excreted toxins.

Treatment by your vet involves clipping the soiled hair, removal of the maggots, and cleansing the infected areas. A non-alcohol pyrethrin shampoo is used to kill any trace of remaining maggots.

Infected wounds are treated with a topical antibiotic. Oral antibiotics may be prescribed as well.

Cuterebra

Adult *cuterebra* flies lay their eggs near rodent or rabbit burrows. Cats who come in contact with the infested soil are then at risk of becoming unexpected hosts. This is more commonly seen in kittens than in adult cats.

The larvae penetrate the skin and form a nodule with a breathing hole opening. The larvae remain in the skin for about one month, then drop to the ground. Occasionally, a grown larva can be seen moving around in the open cyst.

Veterinary treatment consists of clipping the hair and carefully removing each larva (sometimes there are multiple wound sites) with forceps. Don't ever attempt to remove the larva yourself because if it ruptures, the cat could go into shock.

After removal, the wound is cleansed and oral antibiotics are given.

Mites

Resembling spiders, but microscopic in size, mites live on the skin of the cat. The *mange* caused by the various types of mites can range from patches of hair loss to sores that develop secondary infections.

Demodectic Mange

This form of mange is more commonly found in dogs. The *demodex* mite resides normally on the animal's skin and usually only causes a localized dermatitis. You may notice areas of hair loss and pus-filled lesions on the skin, generally around the head and neck.

With generalized demodicosis, lesions, thinning hair, or actual hair loss can occur over much of the body. Cats suffering from generalized demodicosis often have a suppressed immune system due to a separate medical condition (such as feline leukemia, diabetes mellitus, chronic respiratory infection).

Diagnosis is made by taking skin scrapings for identification under a microscope. The treatment for localized demodicosis involves the application of a topical agent. Your vet may also recommend the use of an antibacterial shampoo.

Generalized demodicosis is treated by the vet with repeated baths in prescription shampoo and the application of mite-killing dips.

Treatment continues for about three weeks after the last skin scraping shows up negative.

Cheyletiella Mange (Walking Dandruff)
The *cheyletiella* mite causes a large amount of scaly buildup on the skin that resembles dandruff.

Cheyletiellosis is not common in cats, but is very contagious and can be transmitted to humans.

Diagnosis is confirmed through physical examination and skin scrapings. Treatment by your vet includes weekly application of an insecticidal shampoo and dip. Treatment continues for two weeks after the cat is considered cured.

The environment must also be treated and involves the use of flea control products such as sprays and foggers.

Feline Scabies
This is an uncommon skin disease in cats that is very contagious. The mites spend their entire life cycle on the host animal and can't live more than a few days off the cat. Females lay their eggs just under the cat's skin.

Feline scabies causes intense itching and as a result of constant scratching, the skin becomes very raw. There is often hair loss, thick gray to yellow crusty scabs, and in more severe cases, a thickening of the skin.

Diagnosis is made by skin scrapings and treatment includes clipping the hair and gentle bathing to loosen the crusts. Lime sulphur dips are used weekly. Therapy continues for two weeks beyond cure.

The itching can be treated with soothing cortisone ointments or sprays.

Ear Mites
A common problem in cats, ear mites are covered in this chapter under "Ear Disorders."

Skin Allergies
An allergic reaction, also called a *hypersensitivity*, can be as a result of exposure to certain substances through the lungs (such as dust or pollen). There are also food allergies that result from eating a particular food that causes a hypersensitive reaction in the digestive tract. Substances absorbed through the skin can cause allergic reactions (such as flea shampoos or sprays). Insect bites and stings can also cause hypersensitivity. Certain medicines and even vaccines can result in an allergic reaction.

Cats tend to have more skin and intestinal tract allergies than humans. We have more difficulty with allergies affecting our air passages.

Flea-Bite Hypersensitivity
This is the most common hypersensitivity in cats. It may only take one flea to cause a reaction, resulting in severe itching, patchy hair loss, raw skin, and even infection.

In severe cases, the cat may need antibiotics to treat infection. In some cases, oral or injectable cortisone is used to relieve the itching reaction to allow the sores time to heal. Antihistamines may also be given.

For cats with flea allergy dermatitis, products such as Frontline or Advantage are extremely helpful, because many of the fleas won't even get the chance to bite the cat.

If your cat has a strong allergic reaction to fleas, you may want to use both Program (the product taken internally or by injection) in combination with either Advantage or Frontline.

Feline Miliary Dermatitis

This general skin condition is due to various allergens, such as fleas, mites, lice, certain drugs, and even food. The name comes from the millet seed appearance of the tiny crusty bumps that break out around the head and neck, and along the back and tail of the cat. Itching may or may not occur. Bald patches due to excessive scratching may appear.

Treatment involves identifying the allergen. This is easier if fleas or mites are present but more difficult if food or inhalant hypersensitivity is suspected. Veterinary treatment depends on the type of allergen involved.

Contact Hypersensitivity

The result of coming in direct contact with a substance or chemical, contact hypersensitivity can even be caused by the use of a plastic food bowl. The areas on the cat most likely to be affected are where hair is the thinnest, such as the abdomen, ears, nose, chin, and paw pads.

Symptoms include hair loss, inflamed skin, itchiness, and small bumps.

Flea control products (such as shampoos, sprays, or powders) can cause all-over allergic skin reactions. Reactions to the insecticide in flea collars affect the skin around the neck.

Treatment involves identification of allergen and avoidance of further exposure, if possible. Bathing is important if the allergen is still present. Oral or topical corticosteroids may be prescribed to relieve itching but limited or non-exposure to the allergen is the best therapy.

Inhalant Allergy (Atopy)

This is caused by inhalation of allergens such as house dust, pollen, and molds. Depending on the allergen, reactions may or may not occur seasonally and can vary in symptoms.

Signs can include miliary dermatitis, itching around the face and neck, and itchy lesions on the head that cause hair loss.

Diagnosis is made through intradermal skin testing.

The best treatment is, of course, elimination of the allergen. Antihistamines or corticosteroids may be administered.

Food Hypersensitivity

A cat can become allergic to certain foods despite the fact that he may have eaten that particular food for years. Common food allergens include beef, pork, dairy, fish, wheat, and corn.

Signs can include: an itchy rash around the head, hair loss, and possible skin sores due to scratching. Common food allergic reactions include gastrointestinal problems such as vomiting and diarrhea.

Treatment consists of long-term hypoallergenic dietary management.

FUNGAL INFECTIONS

Ringworm

Despite the name, ringworm is not a worm but a fungal disease. One of the most common skin problems of cats, ringworm invades the hair follicle.

Transmission occurs by contact with the organism in soil or through contact with another infected animal. It can also be transmitted by contact with the infected hairs of an animal, for example, the hairs on a pet's bedding. Ringworm is highly contagious and can be transmitted to humans.

The name, ringworm, comes from the appearance of the skin lesion. A red ring outlines a circular patch of scaly skin and broken-off hairs. Very often on cats, the lesions will appear as crusty skin with patchy hair loss that resembles stubble. Ringworm can be found anywhere on the body but is seen most frequently on the ears, face, and tail.

Sometimes diagnosis of ringworm can be made using a special ultraviolet light known as a *wood's light*. The infected hair will glow a yellowish green. Only certain types of ringworm will fluoresce, so a negative wood's lamp inspection doesn't rule out that diagnosis. Also, microscopic examination of the cat's hairs or fungal cultures are used for diagnosis.

Treatment involves clipping the infected hair, which is most important in longhaired cats. For localized ringworm, cleansing the area is done with an iodine-based solution, then a topical antifungal cream or ointment is applied. You'll be instructed to reapply the cream once or twice daily for at least a month.

A more extensive case of ringworm requires the application of an antifungal dip on a weekly basis. Your vet may also prescribe an antifungal drug to be given orally. There's a vaccine available now for use in treating and preventing ringworm, although there are few set guidelines on when and when not to use it.

Treating the environment is essential to stop the spread of ringworm. Discard pet bedding or wash in bleach, and clean all grooming supplies in diluted bleach. A thorough vacuuming of the home should be done right away and repeated twice weekly to remove infected pet hairs. Be sure to throw away the vacuum bag. Thoroughly clean all areas that the cat frequents and use diluted bleach on counters and nonwood floors.

When treating your cat for ringworm, wear disposable latex gloves and wash your hands afterward.

BACTERIAL INFECTIONS

Abscesses

An abscess is a localized pus filled pocket of infection in the skin. Unfortunately, abscesses are common occurrences in the cat world due to the bites and scratches resulting from fights. If you have an outdoor cat (especially a male), there's an excellent chance that at some point he'll develop an abscess. Actually, you'll be lucky if he develops only one in his life. Realistically, you'll probably be making numerous trips to the vet for treatment of several abscesses over the course of your outdoor cat's lifetime.

The inside of a cat's mouth is a breeding ground for all kinds of ugly bacteria. What happens is that a puncture wound caused by sharp teeth or claws quickly seals over on the surface, trapping the bacteria beneath. All too often, your outdoor cat comes home and you don't even know that he has been in a fight because the puncture wound is small and also disguised by fur. What's happening under his skin, though, is that his immune system is working to fend off the bacteria. It isn't until you notice a painful lump on your cat or the skin feels hot that you're aware of a problem. You may even see your cat limping. Sometimes the abscess ruptures, draining a white or reddish pus, accompanied by an odor.

Abscesses can occur anywhere on the body, but they're most often located around the face, neck, legs, and the base of the tail. The face, neck, and legs are prime targets for an opponent during a fight. The base of the tail may get tagged by the attacker's claw or tooth as the victim attempts retreat.

For abscesses that haven't drained, in addition to giving antibiotics, the veterinarian will lance it to allow the pus to escape. Some abscesses require surgery so a drain can be inserted. The drain allows the pus to drip out. The wound is also periodically flushed with an antiseptic solution to keep it open and clean. The goal is to have the wound heal from the inside out so the same problem doesn't recur with the skin sealing in the bacteria. The drain is later removed by the doctor (though in some cases, an impatient cat does it for himself).

Neutering your cat isn't a guarantee that he won't get in any more fights, but there's an excellent chance that the frequency will be lessened. Neutering reduces his inclination to roam, thus limiting his exposure to other male cats.

If you notice any puncture wounds, feel a lump or sense a hot area on the skin, get medical care immediately. The sooner a cat fight wound is treated, the better. It could save your cat a tremendous amount of pain and avoid a lengthy recovery time.

If you have an outdoor cat whom you suspect comes in contact with other cats or who is known for fighting, check him over every day to be sure there are no wounds. Even though cats are notorious groomers, if you see your cat licking one particular area repeatedly, it could be that he's nursing a fight wound. Another sign might be when your normally affectionate cat suddenly cries or becomes agitated when you touch a certain part of his body.

Feline Acne

A fairly common skin condition, acne appears as tiny blackheads or pimples on the chin after hair follicles become clogged. In more severe cases, the pimples drain pus, and the chin and bottom lip become swollen. The cause of acne is believed to be lack of grooming to the chin so dirt and oil accumulate. Cats who eat from plastic bowls may also be more prone to this condition due to the fact that plastic is more difficult to keep as clean as ceramic, glass, or stainless steel. Sleeping on the hard ground may also contribute to the development of acne.

Mild feline acne, where there are just blackheads, can be treated by gentle cleansing with a warm washcloth and a little benzoyl peroxide soap. Scrubbing can worse the condition, so care must be taken to not clean too vigorously. More serious acne requires veterinary treatment. After cleansing, you'll be given a benzoyl peroxide gel to apply to the affected area. Antibiotics may also be prescribed.

Some cats get recurring acne, and the cleansing and benzoyl peroxide gel treatment must be continued indefinitely.

Stud Tail

Caused by overproduction by the sebaceous glands, this disease is seen more in intact males.

With this disorder, the tail appears dirty and greasy. There is also an accompanying odor. As you look closely you'll see the skin near the base of the tail covered in brown waxy debris. Dirt and dust are easily attracted to the oily part of the tail. In more serious cases, the hair follicles get inflamed and the condition becomes painful to the cat.

Treatment for stud tail involves washing the tail in a medically prescribed shampoo on a regular basis. Antibiotics or even surgery may be required if there's inflammation. Neutering the intact cat is also recommended.

Folliculitis

This inflammation of the hair follicles can occur on its own or be the result of another condition, such as feline acne or flea-bite hypersensitivity.

A deeper and more severe condition involving the hair follicles is called *furunculosis*.

Veterinary treatment includes cleansing and then administering topical and oral antibiotics.

Impetigo

Occurring in newborn kittens, impetico results in pustules and crusts developing on the skin. It's believed to be caused by the mother's mouth as she repeatedly moves her kittens.

Antibiotic treatment is administered for about a week.

Alopecia

Alopecia means baldness and can be complete or partial. There are many causes of alopecia.

Excessive grooming due to a behavior problem can cause baldness. This condition is known as *psychogenic alopecia* and is a displacement activity that causes a stressed cat to overgroom.

Alopecia can also result from a hypersensitivity reaction (for instance, fleas or other parasites), infections, or nutritional deficiencies.

Endocrine alopecia, also known as *feline symmetrical alopecia,* is thought to be the result of a sex hormone deficiency because it's seen in neutered and spayed cats. Thinning of the hair is located in the genital area, abdomen, and inner thighs. Treatment for *endocrine alopecia* involves the use of hormone therapy, which can cause serious side effects (depending on which hormone is involved).

Treatment of alopecia is based on the underlying cause. Cats with psychogenic alopecia usually respond well to behavioral therapy in conjunction with anti-anxiety medication.

RODENT ULCER

This is not a condition caused by rodents. The rodent ulcer lesions can develop in cats of all ages. They're found most often on the upper lip but occasionally are seen on the lower lip as well. The lesions appear as thick ulcerated areas that don't necessarily cause itching or pain.

Rodent ulcer lesions can potentially be precancerous. They start out as shiny pink lesions. As they advance, they become deeper in color and ulcerate.

Prompt veterinary care is required. If caught early, treatment involves the use of oral or injectable cortisone and antibiotics. In cases that don't respond to cortisone, surgery may be necessary.

The cause of rodent ulcer is not definitely known and may be allergy-related.

SOLAR DERMATITIS

A chronic inflammation of the skin due to repeated exposure to ultraviolet (sun) light, solar dermatitis occurs in white cats. Symptoms include redness of the skin, scaly, crusty skin, or lesions (especially the ear flaps). Solar dermatitis can develop into cancer if not treated.

Treatment depends on the specifics of the case. Medication may be prescribed for mild cases but for severe solar dermatitis, surgery may be needed. Damaged ear flaps may require surgery.

Keeping your cat indoors during the strongest hours of sunlight is the best way to avoid the damaging effects of ultraviolet rays. Cats who love to lounge in the sun for long periods are especially at risk.

Your vet may recommend the use of a sunblock to cover areas such as the ears. Don't apply one without consulting your vet first because you need to make certain it'll be safe if ingested.

CYSTS, TUMORS, AND GROWTHS

Any lump found on your cat should be immediately checked by the veterinarian. Don't assume that a bump under the skin is benign (noncancerous) just because it doesn't seem to be bothering your cat.

Tumors can occur anywhere on the cat's body, from the head to between the toes.

Cancerous tumors are discussed under "Cancer" in this chapter.

RESPIRATORY SYSTEM DISORDERS

Upper respiratory infections can range from being similar to what would be a mild cold in humans to a life-threatening condition. Many of the initial symptoms are so similar (such as sneezing, nasal discharge, runny eyes) that you might postpone taking the cat to the vet, thinking it's just a case of the

Signs of Respiratory Problems

- coughing
- sneezing
- wheezing
- noisy or moist-sounding breathing
- labored breathing
- rapid breathing
- shallow breathing
- open-mouth breathing
- panting
- discharge from eyes and/or nose
- excessive meowing or crying
- loss of voice
- pale or bluish mucous membranes
- hunched posture
- head held in an extended position
- retching
- fever
- rapid pulse
- loss of appetite

sniffles. Don't play "wait and see" with any suspected upper respiratory infection.

Laryngitis

This is an inflammation of the voice box (larynx). Vocal straining from meowing, howling, or chronic coughing is the most common cause of laryngitis. It can also be a symptom of allergies, respiratory infection, or in rare cases, a tumor.

Seek veterinary attention to determine if the cause is medical or behavioral (laryngitis due to constant meowing may be behavioral in origin). Treatment depends on the specific diagnosis.

Asthma

A cat with chronic asthma may have a dry, hacking cough and wheeze a lot. He often sounds as if he's gagging. As he struggles to breathe, you may notice him sitting with his head extended, trying to take in enough air. In acute cases, the cat may go into respiratory distress as he fights for oxygen.

Asthma can be aggravated by exposure to dust, pollen, grass, litter dust, cigarette smoke, flea sprays, hair sprays, perfume, cleaning sprays and deodorizers, and air/carpet fresheners.

Immediate veterinary treatment is needed. Oxygen therapy may have to be administered along with a bronchodilator. Acute asthma is a very scary thing for a cat (just as it is for humans), so his stress level will be elevated. Try to use minimal restraint as you transport him to the vet. Stress can be a deadly accomplice to an asthma attack.

For chronic asthma, maintenance medication can be prescribed. Avoidance of the irritant (if known) is crucial. Many times the specific irritant that triggers attacks is difficult to pinpoint. You can reduce the chances of an attack by using dust-free litter, avoiding household sprays and carpet cleaners, hair sprays, and other common allergens.

Upper Respiratory Infection

Cats generally become infected through direct contact with another cat. Signs may include conjunctivitis, sneezing, discharge from nose and eyes. The discharge may change from clear to yellowish green as infection worsens. You may notice open-mouth breathing.

Chronic upper respiratory infections can be especially hazardous for short-nosed breeds such as Persians and Himalayans.

Upper respiratory infection is really a broad term. There are two main viral groups that produce most of the upper respiratory infections in cats—the *calicivirus* group and the *herpes* virus group. In addition to the viral component, secondary bacterial infections can also occur.

Treatment involves medications to relieve symptoms and administration of antibiotics. Making sure the cat continues to eat and drink is important, since very often his decreased sense of smell causes appetite decline. If the cat is dehydrated due to the fact that he's not eating or drinking, fluid therapy will be administered either intravenously or subcutaneously.

Pneumonia

This lung inflammation and infection can be a secondary condition to a respiratory illness as the weakened immune system can't fight off the bacteria. It can also be a result of aspirating mucous, fluids, food, or medication. Aspiration can occur during force-feeding, vomiting, seizures, or while the cat is under anesthesia. This is where you must be very careful when you medicate your cat with a liquid or are instructed to force-feed. Cats are very susceptible to aspiration pneumonia. Be sure you get detailed instructions from your vet to avoid aspiration pneumonia.

Symptoms of pneumonia can include: noisy, wet-sounding breathing, fever, coughing, lethargy, and respiratory distress of varying degrees. Diagnosis for pneumonia is made through examination, radiographs, and lab tests. Treatment is based on the primary cause. Antibiotics will be prescribed.

Pulmonary Edema

A secondary condition that can result from conditions such as asthma, pneumonia, heart failure, injury to the chest, or poisoning. It can also occur as a result of an electric shock or a severe allergic reaction.

Pulmonary edema refers to fluid in the actual tissues of the lungs. Signs can include: breathing difficulty, wheezing, and open-mouth breathing.

Veterinary treatment is immediately needed. Once the diagnosis is made, oxygen therapy is used. Diuretics are also administered to pull the excess fluid out of the lungs. Further treatment depends on the primary cause.

Pleural Effusion

This is fluid accumulation in the chest surrounding the lungs, making breathing difficult due to the inability of the lungs to expand properly.

The fluid accumulation can be due to disease such as the wet form of *feline infectious peritonitis* (FIP), which causes a buildup of thick, sticky pus in the chest. Other causes of fluid can include heart failure, liver disease, tumors, or heartworms.

Signs include breathing difficulty and open-mouth breathing. The cat may be unable to lie down and remains seated with his head far forward in an attempt to gasp air. As breathing becomes more difficult, the cat's lips and gums may turn gray or blue, indicating oxygen deprivation.

Emergency veterinary attention is needed. The fluid will be drained from the chest cavity by way of aspiration. Further treatment depends on the primary cause, but the prognosis is often not very optimistic.

Pneumothorax

Air in the chest cavity can be the result of a blow to the chest. This can happen when a cat falls from a tree or window, or sustains an open chest injury (as a result of a blow from an object or from being hit by a car). It can also occur in some chronic lung diseases. Air leaks from the lungs into the chest. This creates less room for the lungs to sufficiently expand, causing respiratory distress.

Signs of pneumothorax begin as shallow, rapid breathing. As the condition worsens the cat begins abdominal breathing and mucous membranes turn blue. Emergency procedures by your veterinarian are needed to remove the accumulated air in the chest and then treat the injury.

URINARY SYSTEM DISORDERS

Lower Urinary Tract Diseases

Lower urinary tract refers to the bladder and urethra. The bladder is the sac that holds the urine. The urethra is the tube extending from the bladder in which the urine travels to exit the body. LUTD (lower urinary tract disease) is actually a broad term, covering the various urinary diseases.

Feline Lower Urinary Tract Disease

FLUTD used to be referred to as *Feline Urologic Syndrome* (FUS). It's a general description that refers to problems connected with the lower urinary tract, including cystitis and obstructions (stones or plugs).

Signs of Urinary Problems

- increased or decreased urination
- voiding outside of litter box
- frequent trips to the litter box
- crying or straining upon urination
- voiding only small amounts of urine
- inability to urinate
- blood in urine
- change in urine color
- change in urine odor
- incontinence
- frequent licking of penis or vulva
- painful abdomen
- distended abdomen
- loss of appetite
- weight loss
- depression
- restlessness
- irritability
- ammonia odor to the breath
- vomiting
- excessive meowing or crying

FLUTD occurs at any age. Both male and female cats are affected, though the long narrow urethra in the male cat increases the chances of urinary obstruction.

Many of my clients have reported that the only way they knew that their cats were experiencing urinary problems was because they were urinating in the bathtubs or in sinks. Blood-tinged urine was visible against the light-colored tubs. Those owners were very lucky that their cats gave them such definite signs. You may not be so lucky and that's why it's important to be very familiar with your cat's normal litter box habits.

One cause of obstructions with FLUTD is the development of *uroliths* (crystals that harden to stones) in the urinary tract. For many years the crystals that developed were *struvite*. They're comprised of magnesium ammonium phosphate. The urine pH is claimed to influence the formation of these crystals. Pet food companies responded by creating diets that maintain a more acidic urine pH, and limiting the amount of magnesium helped in controlling the formation of struvite crystals. Unfortunately, though, the acidic urine that helps prevent struvite crystals may contribute to other problems. For instance, a diet that promotes an acidic urine wouldn't be indicated for a cat with *calcium oxalate* crystals (which are being diagnosed with increasing frequency these days). Therefore, it's important that each case be individually diagnosed by your vet. Don't assume that one of your cats has the same urinary problem as the other just because of similar symptoms.

Male cats are more predisposed to developing a urethral plug. This soft, sandy material, composed of crystal fragments and mucous, accumulates in the urethra. If not treated, this material will actually "plug" the opening of the penis. The cat then becomes *blocked* as urine continues to build up in the bladder. THIS IS AN EMERGENCY, AND DEATH WILL RESULT IF NOT IMMEDIATELY TREATED. On appearance, your cat may repeatedly lick his penis. You may also be able to feel his distended abdomen. Lethargy and dehydration will soon result. Don't delay in getting veterinary help. This blockage can cause death within a few hours. Don't assume the cat is constipated and waste valuable time attempting to administer a laxative.

Treatment involves first relieving the bladder. The vet may insert a needle through the skin and into the bladder to withdraw the urine into a syringe. Sometimes a plug can manually be removed under mild anesthesia. In most cases, a catheter is then inserted temporarily to keep the urethra open and free of obstruction. Recurrent cases sometimes require a surgery called *perineal urethrostomy*. The narrow part of the urethra (at the penis) is removed and a wider opening is created. This surgery isn't always successful and is considered a last resort. The use of prescription diets has *greatly* reduced the need for this surgery.

Long-term treatment for FLUTD involves dietary management with a specific prescription food, based on the individual condition. Make sure the cat's water intake is adequate and don't let him become obese. Exercise is also important. Stress may additionally play a role in recurrences, so keep an eye on changes in the environment that could cause your cat to worry.

Providing clean, easily accessible litter boxes is essential to helping prevent FLUTD. If the box is too dirty or too difficult to get to, the cat may void too infrequently. This can predispose him to FLUTD.

PREVENTING FLUTD

- Feed your cat a high-quality, premium diet. If your vet prescribes a specific diet for your cat, stay on it and don't supplement with table scraps.

- Provide an adequate number of easily accessible litter boxes.

- Keep the litter boxes clean.

- Supply fresh, clean water. Wash the bowl every day before refilling. If your cat eats dry food exclusively, monitor his water intake to make sure he's getting enough.

- Encourage exercise through interactive play.

- Limit the cat's exposure to stress.

- Monitor litter box habits on a daily basis so you'll be familiar with each cat's routine.

- Take the cat to the vet at the first sign of potential urinary problems.

Incontinence

Various diseases can cause incontinence (involuntary voiding of urine). Injuries to the spinal cord can also result in the inability to control the bladder muscle.

Treatment is based on the underlying cause. Drug therapy is sometimes helpful in regaining bladder control.

Kidney Diseases

The *upper* urinary tract refers to the kidneys and the *ureters,* which are the two tubes that lead from the kidneys to the bladder. One of the jobs of the kidneys is to filter the blood, removing wastes. Without this function, wastes would build up in the body to a toxic level.

Since the kidneys are the filtration system for the blood, infections, diseases, and poisons can adversely affect and damage the kidneys themselves.

With reduced kidney function, no matter what the cause, fluid therapy is administered to replace lost electrolytes, correct dehydration, and serve the function of dialysis. Dietary changes are also recommended. The prescription

Signs of Potential Kidney Problems

- increase or decrease in normal water consumption
- increase or decrease in normal urine output
- blood in urine
- halitosis
- vomiting
- diarrhea
- sensitivity or pain in back, near kidney (cat may have a hunched posture)

- weight loss and anorexia
- dull haircoat
- excessive shedding
- fever
- lethargy
- joint pain
- tongue discoloration
- mouth ulcers

diet will be lower in protein and phosphorus, which reduces the workload on the kidneys.

Pyelonephritis

This is most often the result of a bladder infection that travels up into the kidneys. It can also be caused by an advanced infection elsewhere in the body (such as periodontal disease). If the pyelonephritis is *acute,* you may see signs such as bloody urine, fever, vomiting. Due to the kidneys being painful, the cat may develop a hunched posture.

If the infection is *chronic,* weight loss and listlessness may be evident. At this point, the cat will already be in kidney failure.

Successful treatment is dependent upon early diagnosis. Fluid therapy may be administered. Antibiotics are usually prescribed, along with specific dietary management.

Kidney Failure

The filtering components of the kidneys are called *nephrons.* There are thousands and thousands of these. When a large amount of nephrons become damaged or flat-out destroyed, it results in renal (kidney) failure.

Kidney failure can be *acute,* resulting from such things as poisoning, trauma, or blockage in the lower urinary tract.

Chronic kidney failure can occur due to disease (such as *feline infectious peritonitis* or *feline leukemia*), infection, hypertension, age, prolonged exposure to toxins, cancer, or long-term use of certain medications.

A cat is in *chronic* kidney failure when about 70 percent of the kidney has been destroyed. Usually, the first visible sign that the cat is in kidney failure is increased urination. There will also be an increase in water consumption. Accidents outside of the litter box may occur due to the increased volume of urine produced. Chronic renal failure can cause anemia.

As the kidneys continue to deteriorate, waste products that are no longer able to be filtered out, remain in the bloodstream and in the body's tissues. This is called *uremia*. If left untreated, the cat will go into a coma and die of uremic poisoning.

Treatment for *acute* kidney failure involves trying to reverse damage before it permanently destroys the kidney tissues. In *chronic* cases, fluid therapy is used to restore electrolyte (mineral) balance. A low protein/low phosphorous diet will be prescribed to slow the progression of the deterioration. A cat in kidney failure needs fresh, clean water always available. A cat who fails to eat or drink enough water will have to be hospitalized and rehydrated by intravenous fluid therapy.

DIGESTIVE SYSTEM DISORDERS

Vomiting

Vomiting is almost always included in a list of symptoms for just about every disease or disorder.

Due to their self-grooming behavior, cats often vomit as a result of swallowing hair. There are commercial hair ball prevention products that should be

Signs of Digestive Problems

- diarrhea
- constipation
- change in appearance of stool
- blood in stool
- weight gain or loss
- change in appetite
- change in water consumption
- vomiting
- restlessness
- abdominal swelling
- painful abdomen
- swallowing difficulty
- flatulence
- change in hair coat appearance
- halitosis
- appearance of worms in vomitus or feces
- excessive meowing or crying

given to the cat who routinely vomits hair or who grooms very often. Long-haired cats should regularly be given the hair ball prevention.

Another common cause of vomiting is due to eating too fast or overeating. In multicat households, *competitive* eating may develop where one cat tries to eat not only his own food but that of his companion cats' as well. This can be addressed by either feeding the cats in separate locations or by leaving dry food available free-choice.

Cats who nibble on grass or chew on houseplants will usually vomit shortly thereafter. Nibbling on grass is safe, but chewing on houseplants is very dangerous since many are poisonous to cats. For more on this, refer to section on "Poisoning" in the "Emergencies and First Aid" section of this chapter.

Motion sickness can cause vomiting. Often, withholding food before traveling will prevent stomach upset. If the cat still has motion sickness, ask your vet about the use of medication.

If your cat has an occasional episode of vomiting but he otherwise seems healthy and normal, with no other behavior changes, it may just be a mild stomach upset. If he vomits more than one time during that day or evening, withhold food and water for twelve to twenty-four hours in order to give his stomach a rest. Contact your veterinarian for specific instructions. The vet will ask for a description of the vomitus. If he/she determines that a visit isn't needed at this point, you'll be given instructions for home care and whether to administer any medication.

What and *how* a cat vomits can provide possible clues as to the cause. For instance:

Vomiting a foreign object. This is serious because you don't know what damage has already occurred and if any part of the object is still somewhere in the digestive tract. Because of the backward-facing barbs on a cat's tongue, foreign objects that he may lick or chew are often doomed to be ingested. String, ribbon, rubber bands and yarn are especially difficult for a cat to avoid swallowing. Anytime a foreign object is vomited, consult your veterinarian because a radiograph may need to be taken in order to be sure no damage or blockage has occurred.

Vomiting worms. Roundworms (they resemble spaghetti) may be vomited if the infestation is serious. Virtually all kittens have roundworms, and so you may see one in the vomitus. Your veterinarian will need to deworm your cat.

Vomiting feces. This could indicate an obstruction or injury. Immediate medical attention is required.

Projectile vomiting. Possible causes include obstruction or tumor. Get immediate veterinary attention.

Vomiting several times per week. If no hair balls are present and the vomiting isn't related to meals, kidney or liver disease could be the cause. Vomiting also occurs with inflammatory bowel disease, pancreatitis, and chronic gastritis.

Your veterinarian needs to do a complete exam, including blood tests and radiographs.

Obviously, if the cat shows any signs of illness, vomits up anything suspicious, or there's blood or feces in the vomitus, immediate medical attention is required.

Gastritis

This inflammation of the stomach lining can be caused by any number of irritants. *Acute* gastritis may be the result of ingesting a poison, spoiled food, plants, or a medication that irritates the stomach lining. Vomiting is the common sign of gastritis. The cat may also have diarrhea.

Treatment involves identifying the irritant. If the cat has ingested a poison, refer to the section on "Poisoning" in the "Emergencies and First Aid" section of this chapter. Mild gastritis (due to perhaps eating some garbage) can be treated by withholding food and water for twenty-four hours to allow the stomach to rest. Allow the cat to lick ice cubes if thirsty. After twenty-four hours, introduce small amounts of bland food such as Hill's Feline d/d or CNM's EN Formula.

Chronic gastritis can be the result of long-term drug therapy, chronic hair balls, ingestion of foreign objects. *Chronic* gastritis can also be secondary to another underlying disorder such as pancreatitis, renal failure, heartworm, liver disease, or diabetes. Some chronic gastritis cases have been attributed to *helicobacter*—one of the contributory agents of gastric ulcers.

Treatment of *chronic* gastritis involves identifying the underlying cause. Your veterinarian will perform numerous diagnostic tests. Dietary changes may need to be made based on the primary disorder. *Chronic* gastritis usually requires the use of a low-fiber, easily digestible food. Treatment may involve antibiotics and gastric protectants.

Diarrhea

Diarrhea is another one of those symptoms that can be connected to various underlying diseases and disorders. The odor, color, and consistency of the diarrhea may produce some clues as to the possible underlying cause.

Dietary changes can give a cat a case of diarrhea, which is why all adjustments should be done gradually to avoid intestinal upset. Overfeeding is another common reason cats develop diarrhea.

A change in water can cause diarrhea. Carrying an extra supply when traveling is always a good idea.

Outdoor cats run the risk of developing diarrhea by ingesting prey, eating garbage, or rotting foods as well as poisons.

Most kittens, once they are weaned, become lactose intolerant. *Lactase*, which is the enzyme needed to digest the milk sugar, lactose, is no longer present once the kitten begins eating solid food. This is why adult cats often develop a case of diarrhea after being fed a bowl of milk.

Food allergies can make specific ingredients difficult for your cat to digest. Feeding table scraps is especially dangerous and can result in a case of diarrhea.

Diet isn't the only thing that can cause diarrhea. Stress can play a role as well. When a cat goes to the veterinarian, is boarded in a kennel, or experiences any major upheaval in his life, he may experience a mild or even severe case of diarrhea.

Diarrhea that lasts longer than a day can result in dehydration. Left unchecked, this can cause shock.

A cat with diarrhea should be checked by the vet if:

- it lasts longer than a day;

- it's accompanied by vomiting, fever, or lethargy;

- the diarrhea contains blood or mucous;

- there is a putrid odor;

- there is an unusual color to the stool (normal color is brown);

- you suspect that the cat may have ingested a toxic substance.

Stool Appearance

Brown   normal

Tarry black   digested blood, possible bleeding in the upper portion of the digestive tract

Fresh, red blood   bleeding in the lower portion of the digestive tract

Green or yellow   undigested, having gone through the digestive tract too fast

Very light   possible liver disease

Gray, foul-smelling   undigested

Very watery   irritation in the digestive tract, lack of absorption

Oily-looking stool   malabsorption

Soft, non-formed stool of normal color   possible overfeeding, change in diet or food of lower quality, parasites

Treatment of diarrhea: a mild case of diarrhea that has no other accompanying signs may be treated at home upon the advice of your vet. Withhold food for twenty-four hours. Provide ice cubes for the cat to lick. After twenty-four hours you can introduce small amounts of a bland, non-irritating diet such as Hill's Feline d/d or CNM's EN Formula.

Constipation

This results when stools are retained in the colon, causing them to become hard, dry, and difficult to pass. Constipation can have many causes, such as hair balls, obstructions, dietary factors, or certain diseases.

Cats on the average have at least one stool per day. The cats who have bowel movements only every couple of days are the ones inclined to become constipated.

Owners can often miss the fact that their cat is constipated in a kind of "out of sight, out of mind" way. With diarrhea, the cat often misses the litter box, so you're left with the evidence on the middle of the carpet. Even if the cat does go in the box, with diarrhea it's very apparent that the stool is abnormal. With constipation, though, an owner may easily lose track of the last time the cat had a bowel movement. It may not be until you actually see the cat straining to defecate or you finally notice the rock-hard fecal balls left in the litter that you're aware of the problem.

Chronic constipation is commonly the result of hair balls. Longhaired breeds are more prone to this, as are the shorthaired cats who live with them, due to allogrooming. You may notice that the cat not only vomits hair balls but you may see hair in the stool. The use of a hair ball prevention product is recommended in that case.

A diet with an inadequate amount of fiber can cause constipation. Cats who don't drink enough water will often have difficulty passing stools as well.

Megacolon is a condition where the colon becomes enlarged and is unable to contract sufficiently to evacuate the stool (see section on "Megacolon").

Stress is another psychological factor that can cause a cat to become constipated. A change in the cat's routine, a move to a new house, new baby, being left in the care of others, etc., can all upset a cat's normal routine. Often, when there's a move to a new environment it's not uncommon for the cat to not have a bowel movement for a couple of days. During any family upheavals or potentially stressful times, be extra aware of your cat's litter box habits and notify your vet if the cat goes longer than two days without a bowel movement.

Serious constipation can cause *fecal impaction*. Treatment for this requires veterinary attention. The vet will give a laxative orally as well as administering an enema. Commercially available enemas should never be used. They're extremely harmful to cats. Never attempt to give an enema to the cat yourself. This is best left up to the veterinarian. Severe cases may require hospitalization and the administration of several enemas.

Treatment for constipation depends on the underlying cause and the severity of the condition. Mild cases can be treated with veterinary laxatives and the addition of higher fiber foods. Bran added to canned foods is an excellent bulk-producing agent to help keep the stool soft and more easily passable. There must be sufficient water present for the bran to work so it should only be added to canned food. A little canned pumpkin is an excellent source of fiber as well. In addition, make sure clean, fresh water is always available. Cats with *chronic* constipation often need to be on high fiber diets indefinitely.

Keeping your cat active and at a good weight will help prevent constipation as well. Incorporate regularly scheduled interactive playtime with your cat.

Inflammatory Bowel Disease

This is actually the broad name that refers to the several gastrointestinal disorders. IBD can be broken down into:

gastritis   affecting the stomach

colitis   affecting the large intestine

enteritis   affecting the small intestine

enterocolitis   affecting both the small and large intestine

Depending upon the specific condition, different types of inflammatory cells set up residence in the mucousa of the intestines. Definitive diagnosis as to which specific disease has infiltrated the digestive tract requires endoscopy or biopsy. Endoscopy is performed with a thin fiber optic tube called an endoscope that can be placed in the digestive tract.

Treatment for IBD may include the use of corticosteroids and immunosuppressive drugs to reduce inflammation. Dietary management is crucial in treating IBD. An increase in fiber is often of help in many cases.

Malabsorption

Inflammatory bowel disease, pancreatic disease, and liver disease are just some of the underlying conditions that cause the failure of food to be absorbed in the small intestine.

Signs of malabsorption include an oily-looking stool with a rancid odor (due to the presence of undigested fat). The cat will appear thin yet have an increased appetite.

Treatment involves the use of a prescription diet and medications to improve digestion. Your veterinarian may prescribe a vitamin supplement for the cat.

Megacolon

Megacolon occurs when a section of the large intestine (colon) enlarges and balloons out, causing feces to become lodged there instead of traveling down to the rectum. The longer the waste remains trapped, the more water is resorbed, resulting in rock-hard feces. The cat then becomes constipated.

Megacolon is believed to be caused by prolonged or chronic constipation. This is something that owners of cats who suffer from repeated bouts of hair ball-caused constipation need to be aware of. Other causes include tumors or complications from pelvic fractures. It can also be congenital, as is often seen in Manx cats.

Treatment involves determining the underlying cause (not always possible), removing the fecal impaction, correcting dehydration (usually by laxatives and warm-water enemas). Long-term care involves treating for constipation by feeding prescription food and administering a feline laxative or stool softener. Your vet will instruct you on exactly what kind to use. In some cases, surgery is performed to remove the ballooned section of colon.

Flatulence

The passing of gas can be related to eating a diet high in fiber. It can also be a problem for cats who are fed diets containing beans or highly fermentable vegetables such as cabbage, cauliflower, and broccoli. Additionally, milk can cause gas (as well as diarrhea). Cats who gulp their food and swallow a lot of air can end of being a bit gassy.

Flatulence accompanied by an abnormal stool can be a symptom of a more serious underlying medical condition.

Don't give your cat any commercial anti-gas medication intended for humans. Consult your veterinarian to determine the primary cause. He/she may then make dietary changes. Medication can be given after meals to ease the problem. For cats who gulp their meals, leaving food available free-choice may alleviate the need to eat so much so fast.

Impacted Anal Glands

There are two sacs located on either side of the anus at about five o'clock and seven o'clock. The purpose of these sacs is to mark the cat's stool with a very malodorous secretion to help identify that particular cat and his territory.

The contents of the anal glands are normally emptied upon defecation. The secretions can vary from being thin and liquid to thick and creamy. Color can range from brown to yellow. The odor, of course, is always unmistakable.

Cats usually don't experience much difficulty with impaction of the anal glands but if it does happen, they can be manually expressed by your veterinarian. If it becomes an ongoing problem, your vet can show you how to express them yourself (it's not difficult, just not one of the more pleasant aspects of being a pet owner).

The most common sign of anal gland problems is "scooting." You'll notice your cat dragging his rump along the carpet in an effort to express the contents of the glands.

If you notice a particular odor coming from the cat's rear end, it may indicate an anal gland problem. Sometimes, you may notice the odor on the cat's *breath* due to his licking the anal glands. This is a sign that they may need manual emptying.

Anal glands can also become infected or abscessed. Signs include: swelling on either side of the anus, frequent scooting, pain. Blood or pus may be visible in the secretions. Seek veterinary attention immediately for treatment. For infection, the glands will be expressed and an antibiotic will be injected into them. Oral antibiotics will be prescribed as well. You may be instructed to use moist warm compresses at home. An abscess will be lanced and drained. The wound must heal from the inside out so it will have to remain open to allow drainage. This is done usually through flushing diluted Betadine two or three times a day. An oral antibiotic is administered as well.

Hepatic Lipidosis (HL)

This is a common disorder of cats, when fat accumulates in the liver cells. Hepatic lipidosis is usually due to an underlying primary cause, such as kidney disease, starvation, obesity, or diabetes. Hepatic lipidosis may result from any disease process that stops a cat from eating—the reason being that as the body begins to break down fat, fat and by-products begin to accumulate in the liver. Since cats lack certain enzymes that are important for complete fat metabolism, the fat stays in the liver. *Idiopathic* hepatic lipidosis refers to cases where no underlying cause can be identified.

When fat accumulates in the liver, the organ becomes enlarged and turns yellow. As liver failure progresses, jaundice becomes visible.

Treatment involves fluid therapy and nutritional support. In cases of anorexia, force-feeding or the administration of a stomach tube are needed. After the cat begins eating on his own, a prescription diet will be required long-term.

Pancreatitis

The pancreas has two main jobs: It produces insulin for metabolization of blood sugar, and it produces pancreatic enzymes used for digestion. *Diabetes mellitus* (sugar diabetes) is a common disorder in cats that results from an insufficiency in insulin production.

What causes pancreatitis is not definitely known. It's suspected that it might be due to enzymes flowing back from the small intestine and back through the pancreatic duct. Initially, while in the pancreas the digestive enzymes are inactive until they enter the small intestine. Therefore, a backflow of activated enzymes (along with intestinal bacteria) that re-enters the pancreas can create an inflammation.

In the cat, signs of pancreatitis may not be very visible. Abdominal pain or vomiting won't always be present. The only symptom may be anorexia.

Diagnosis involves blood tests to determine pancreatic enzyme levels along with performing diagnostic imaging procedures.

Treatment varies, based on case severity.

Obesity

Refer to chapter 10, "The Kitty Chef."

Signs of Musculoskeletal System Problems

- lameness
- reluctance to move
- pain
- limited range of motion
- constipation
- weight loss
- sensitivity to being touched

- flaky skin
- greasy hair coat
- fishy odor to the coat
- fever
- loss of appetite
- loose teeth
- curvature of the back
- stiffness upon rising

MUSCULOSKELETAL SYSTEM DISORDERS

Arthritis

There are different kinds of arthritis. *Osteoarthritis,* the most common form, is also known as *degenerative joint disease.* What happens with this disease is that the cartilage layer on the surface of the joint deteriorates. It mostly occurs as a result of aging but can also develop as a result of an injury to the joint surface.

Lameness is the most common sign and is made worse by cold damp weather or after strenuous activity. The cat may also appear stiff upon getting up after sleeping.

Polyarthritis is an inflammatory disease that may be connected to one or more viral infections.

Hip dysplasia is not common in cats. It refers to a shallow ball and socket hip joint, which results in degenerative problems.

Treatment depends on the type and severity of arthritis and underlying causes. Surgery may be required. Keeping your cat warm will also lessen pain, since arthritis is aggravated by cold and damp conditions.

Unfortunately, aspirin and Tylenol—commonly used for arthritis in humans—are toxic to cats. If your cat is uncomfortable, consult your vet regarding possible pain medication.

Preventing your older cat from being obese will lessen the pain associated with arthritis by reducing the weight load on joints.

Parathyroid Diseases

The four parathyroid glands, located in the neck (at the thyroid), secrete *parathyroid hormone.* This hormone helps maintain proper blood calcium and phosphorus levels. Calcium is one of the most important minerals in the body. If the amount of calcium in the blood falls or the amount of phosphorus gets too high, the parathyroid glands release parathyroid hormone (PTH) to raise the calcium level. They do this by pulling it from the bones. The consequences of this can lead to a thinning of the bones. The more brittle they become, the more at risk of fractures the cat becomes.

Successful treatment depends on early diagnosis. Treatment includes calcium supplementation and dietary changes.

Nutritional Secondary Hyperparathyroidism

This is caused by a diet too high in meat and low in calcium. This is where homemade diets can be dangerous. Good-quality commercial cat food is nutritionally balanced to provide the right amount of meat and minerals. Demineralization of the bone can result from feeding an all-vegetable diet as well.

This disease is seen more in kittens who are on all-meat diets, which doesn't allow for their extra calcium requirements to promote bone growth and development.

Symptoms in kittens appear as a reluctance to move, lameness, and bowed legs. Limping may also be seen due to possible fractures. In adult cats, the thinning of the bones causes brittleness and high risk of fractures. The teeth also become loose. Left unchecked, curvature of the back develops and can lead to a collapsing of the pelvis.

Treatment involves correcting the diet to address the kitten or adult cat's nutritional needs and administering calcium supplementation. A cat with fractures should be confined to a cage to allow healing and to prevent additional fractures.

If diagnosed early, prognosis is good. If the disease has progressed to where the bones have become deformed, recovery is very doubtful.

Renal Secondary Hyperparathyroidism

Due to kidney disease, which creates a high level of phosphorus, the parathyroid glands secrete an excessive amount of parathyroid hormone to raise the calcium level. As with *nutritional secondary hyperparathyroidism,* calcium is pulled from the bones, causing thinning and demineralization. The prognosis is usually guarded.

Steatitis

Also known as *yellow fat disease,* it's caused by a vitamin E deficiency. Cats fed excessive amounts of unsaturated fatty acids end up with vitamin E being destroyed. The result is a painful inflammation in the body fat. The fat turns yellow and becomes very hard.

Red meat tuna has high levels of unsaturated fatty acids, and a cat eating sufficient quantities will develop this extremely painful disease. An ongoing diet consisting of fish in general will commonly lead to steatitis if not properly supplemented with vitamin E. Straight canned tuna intended for humans is the most dangerous of all because it isn't supplemented with vitamin E.

Initial signs include a greasy hair coat and flaky skin. The hair coat may develop a fish odor as well. As the disease progresses, the cat becomes reluctant to move or be handled. Even petting becomes too painful. The cat runs a fever and has a poor appetite.

Diagnosis is based on the dietary history and will be confirmed by taking a biopsy of the fat.

Treatment involves dietary correction by switching to a well-balanced food and supplementing with vitamin E.

Prevent this disease in the first place by never feeding any tuna to your cat, even if it's in commercial cat food. Especially avoid canned tuna intended for humans. Tuna, having such a strong taste and odor, can cause a cat to become addicted to its flavor. Once you start feeding it to your cat, you may find him rejecting his other more balanced food.

If you want to feed fish-flavored cat food to your cat, limit it to very occasionally and avoid tuna all together.

Vitamin Overdosing

Excessive amounts of fat soluble vitamins (A, D, E, K) in the body beyond what is needed, can adversely affect the cat's normal growth, development, and health. Good-quality commercial foods are formulated to be nutritionally complete and well balanced to meet a cat's needs. Supplementing with additional vitamins and minerals can cause disorders such as bone problems, deformities, lameness, and pain.

Vitamin A is stored in the liver, so excess amounts don't wash out of the body in the urine. Overdosing this vitamin either through supplements or diet (of liver, milk products, carrots) can result in severe neck and back pain and joint swelling. As the disorder progresses, the cat develops very limited range of motion in the neck. Other signs can include constipation, weight loss, and sensitivity to being touched.

If diagnosed early, dietary correction (and discontinuation of any supplementation) may reverse symptoms. If allowed to progress, the symptoms are irreversible.

ENDOCRINE SYSTEM DISORDERS

Hypothyroidism

The thyroid gland, located in the neck, is responsible for maintaining the body's metabolism. The thyroid produces two major hormones, tri-iodothronine (T3) and thyroxine (T4). When the gland fails to manufacture sufficient

- change in appetite
- change in weight
- lethargy
- low body temperature
- restlessness
- increased or decreased water consumption
- increased or decreased urination
- behavior change
- change in bowels

amounts of these hormones, hypothyroidism (underactive thyroid) results. Though extremely rare in cats, it can, however, be the result of surgical removal or destruction of the thyroid gland in treating for *hyperthyroidism.*

Hyperthyroidism

Excessive amounts of the thyroid hormones tri-iodothronine and thyroxine result in *hyperthyroidism* (overactive thyroid). It's a disease more commonly seen in aging cats (the average is about twelve years of age). Hyperthyroidism can lead to a form of *cardiomyopathy* (heart disease).

Signs of this disease include: restlessness, increased appetite, weight loss (despite an increased appetite), rapid heart rate, dull hair coat, vomiting, increased water consumption, and increased urination. A behavior change you may notice is increased activity and, in some cases, aggression. Also, as the excessive hormone level increases the workload on the heart, the cat may develop *cardiomyopathy.*

Diagnosis is based on blood tests to determine levels of T3 and T4.

Treatment for hyperthyroidism may include antithyroid drug therapy, surgical removal of the gland, or the administration of radioactive iodine. The choice of treatment is based on your cat's specific condition, whether heart disease is present and if there's a veterinary specialist in your area who performs radiation therapy. The thought of radioactive iodine may sound scary to you but is, in many cases, the best treatment because it doesn't require any anesthesia and usually only one dose is needed to bring the thyroid back to producing normal levels of hormones. The downside to treating with radioactive iodine is that the cat will have to be quarantined for about a week or two. Cost is also a consideration for some owners. Surgery is an option if radiation therapy isn't available where you live.

The drug *methimazole* sometimes is used to control hyperthyroidism. This requires you to pill your cat daily for the rest of his life. Additionally, some cats may suffer side effects from the drug, including vomiting, loss of appetite, or lethargy.

Diabetes Mellitus

Diabetes mellitus occurs when there is an inadequate amount of insulin production by the pancreas. Insulin, which is secreted into the circulatory system, enables the body's cells to metabolize sugar into energy. Without insulin, the sugar levels in the blood become elevated. The excess sugar is eliminated by way of the kidneys, because it can only be excreted in urine. This means there will be increased urination and thirst. Testing the cat's urine will reveal the presence of sugar. Because the cells in the body aren't able to utilize the glucose (sugar) in the blood, the cat becomes lethargic. He also will begin losing weight despite having a large appetite.

Diabetes can be found in cats of any age but is seen more frequently after the age of six. Obesity puts a cat at great risk as well. Cats on long-term corticosteroid or progestin therapy should be routinely tested for diabetes.

When the body can't metabolize sugar, it begins using its own tissues for energy. This results in the presence of *ketones* (acid) in the blood. If the disease has progressed this far, an acetone odor may be detected on the cat's breath. As the condition worsens, breathing becomes more difficult and eventually the cat goes into a diabetic coma.

Diagnosing diabetes is done by testing for the presence of sugar and ketones in blood and urine.

Treatment depends on the severity of the condition. In cases of dehydration and electrolyte imbalance, fluid therapy will be administered. Insulin injections will be started and monitored, and the cat will remain hospitalized until the correct dosage has been established.

Before the cat is discharged, you'll be given instructions on how to administer insulin injections under the skin. The cat will need to be monitored carefully because dosage adjustments may have to be made. You'll have to return to the vet on a regular basis for a while. Dietary instructions will also be explained to you.

In some cases insulin injections aren't used, and instead, diabetes is controlled through dietary management and oral drugs. Not every cat is a candidate for this, though.

If your cat is obese, you'll be instructed to put him on a calorie-restricted diet to better control his diabetes. The diet change needs to be *very gradual,* so follow your veterinarian's instructions carefully. High-fiber diets help control glucose levels in the blood in addition to aiding in weight reduction. The timing of feedings will need to coincide with insulin injections. The cat's day-to-day meals need to be consistent because insulin requirements vary, depending on the diet.

Home care of a diabetic cat can be done relatively easily as long as you

Signs of Heart Trouble

- weakness
- coughing
- lethargy
- abnormal pulse
- irregular heart rhythm
- pale or bluish mucous membranes
- breathing difficulty
- cold limbs

- swollen abdominal cavity
- vomiting
- fainting
- heart murmurs
- crying
- lameness or paralysis
- head tilt
- loss of appetite

follow instructions and are committed. You'll also need to bring the cat back to the veterinarian regularly to test blood glucose levels.

CIRCULATORY SYSTEM DISORDERS

Cardiomyopathy

Cardiomyopathies are diseases that affect the heart muscle, making it unable to function efficiently.

Dilated cardiomyopathy occurs when the heart muscle stretches, becoming thin, weak, and unable to effectively contract. The chambers of the heart enlarge and fill with too much blood. Dilated cardiomyopathy is seen more commonly in cats middle-aged and older.

A deficiency of the amino acid *taurine* has been discovered as one of the major causes of dilated cardiomyopathy. Since that connection was made in the 1980s, cat-food manufacturers have supplemented their products with taurine. As a result, dilated cardiomyopathy is now rarely seen. This is one very important reason to feed your cat a good-quality *cat* food and never *dog* food. Dog food isn't supplemented with taurine.

Signs of dilated cardiomyopathy can come on relatively quickly (over a matter of days) and can include breathing difficulty, loss of appetite, noticeable weight loss, weakness, erratic pulse, and lethargy. As breathing becomes more difficult, the cat may sit with his neck extended in an attempt to get enough air.

With *hypertrophic* cardiomyopathy, the walls of the left ventricle thicken, decreasing the size of the ventricular chamber. The amount of blood pumped in and out of the heart decreases.

Hypertrophic cardiomyopathy isn't related to taurine deficiency. One of the causes is high blood pressure as a result of hyperthyroidism or renal failure. Signs can include loss of appetite, decreased activity, and respiratory distress. Sudden death may occur.

Diagnosing cardiomyopathy (and more specifically, which type) requires electrocardiogram, ultrasound, radiographs, and blood chemistries.

Treatment for cardiomyopathy starts with easing the workload on the heart. Depending on the specific condition, therapy may include the use of diuretics (to correct fluid retention), digitalis drugs, and other medications that improve the heart function. Most of the medicines are the same ones used for human heart disease. These drugs can be very toxic, so close veterinary monitoring is required.

A sodium-restricted diet almost always is prescribed. Treatment for *dilated* cardiomyopathy may also include taurine supplements.

Arrhythmia

Arrhythmias are changes in the normal heartbeat rhythm. There can be many causes of arrhythmias, including electrolyte imbalance, stress, heart disease, certain drugs, fever, hypothermia, and exposure to toxins. Arrhythmias may result in sudden death.

Cats with severe ongoing diarrhea or vomiting, diabetes or kidney disease may develop *hypokalemia* (low serum potassium), which can result in an arrhythmia. Hyperthyroid cats may develop a fast heart rate (known as *tachycardia*), as can cats with cardiomyopathy or one under stress. A slower than normal heart rate is called *bradycardia*, which can occur due to many conditions—among them, hypothermia.

Treatment is based on the underlying primary condition.

Heart Murmur

Heart murmurs occur when the normal flow of blood is disturbed as it travels through the heart. With a stethoscope, instead of hearing the normal *lub dub*, you hear abnormal sounds.

Murmurs are graded on a scale of 1 to 6 (6 being the most serious). They can be caused by many things, including congenital birth defects or heart disease. Many cats who are otherwise healthy can have a murmur. Less serious murmurs that don't appear to be connected to any underlying condition are graded and monitored during each veterinary exam.

Heartworm

Refer to the section on "Internal Parasites" in this chapter.

Anemia

Anemia refers to an inadequate number of red blood cells, which are the oxygen carriers for the body's tissues.

Anemia can be caused by blood loss due to hemorrhaging and also parasite infestation or poisoning. A severe coccidia, or hookworm, infestation can result in a large amount of blood loss. Bloodsucking external parasites such as fleas can inflict an alarming amount of damage to a cat's blood supply. Flea-infested kittens are especially vulnerable to becoming anemic, as are weaker, older cats.

Diseases that interfere with bone marrow production or cause destruction of cells can result in anemia (such as *feline leukemia* and *feline infectious anemia*). Abnormal reactions to certain toxins and drugs can also lead to anemia.

Signs of anemia include pale mucous membranes, weakness, lethargy, loss of appetite, and decreased tolerance to cold.

Treatment is based on the primary cause. With severe anemia, blood transfusions are performed.

Arterial Thromboembolism

A blood clot in the artery, arterial thromboembolism causes the flow of blood to become obstructed to that artery. Causes can include trauma (such as an injury to the heart), cardiomyopathy, or heart disease.

Signs depend on the area of the body affected. The cat may appear lame or even experience paralysis in the legs. The legs may also be cold to the touch.

This is an extremely painful condition, and affected cats may vocalize incessantly. Treatment is often unsuccessful.

Signs of Nervous System Disorders

- restlessness
- weakness
- loss of balance
- abnormal eye movements
- fixed pupils
- irregular breathing
- semiconsciousness or unconsciousness
- slow heart rate
- seizures
- skin twitching
- tail lashing or biting
- sudden aggression
- vomiting
- head tilt
- paralysis of any body part (including tail)
- incontinence

NERVOUS SYSTEM DISORDERS

Head Injuries

This commonly occurs as a result of the cat being struck by an automobile. Other causes include falling from a tree or a window, or being hit with an object.

The brain is protected by a surrounding layer of fluid and then encased in the skull. Even with all the cushioning and protection, a major blow to the head will fracture the skull and possibly cause injury to the brain. A brain injury can also occur without a fracture to the skull.

After a head injury, brain swelling can occur, which creates pressure on the brain. This is an emergency because if not treated, it will lead to brain damage and death.

Any time your cat sustains a blow to the head, however minor, he should be examined by the vet. If you aren't sure if he suffered a blow to the head but he seems weak, his gait is strange, he's dazed, or his eye movements appear abnormal or fixed, seek immediate medical care.

Years ago when I worked as a veterinary technician, I was always amazed at how many people would call on the phone to say that their cat had just been hit by a car and they'd go on to say that the cat seemed dazed but was otherwise okay. The owners were just wondering if a vet exam was *really* necessary. I couldn't imagine not having my little *eight-pound* cat examined for possible internal injuries or concussion after being struck by a *3500-pound* vehicle.

Increased pressure on the brain occurs in the first twenty-four hours after the injury. Depending upon the severity of the injury, the swelling may be *mild, moderate,* or *severe.* Even mild pressure is a serious condition and needs immediate veterinary attention. Any delay can result in irreversible brain damage or death.

Epilepsy

A recurrent seizure disorder can be brought on by many causes, such as trauma, tumor, exposure to toxins, kidney failure, or hypoglycemia.

A seizure results from an abnormal pattern of brain activity. Seizures are more common in dogs than in cats.

Epilepsy becomes a catchall term in veterinary medicine for seizures due to an undiagnosed cause. For example, seizures caused by renal failure shouldn't be classified as epilepsy; in this case, correction of the underlying cause should control the seizures. The drugs *phenobarbitol* or *valium* would be of no use long-term.

The area of the brain affected will determine the type and severity of a seizure. A seizure can be as insignificant as staring off into space for a few seconds or as major as a grand mal.

Prior to a seizure, the cat may appear restless. Once a grand mal seizure begins, the cat falls onto his side and becomes very stiff while exhibiting jerking movements of the limbs. He may chew or experience facial twitching. Urination, defecation, or vomiting are also very likely during a seizure. Cover your cat with a towel and keep him safe from thrashing against dangerous objects. Keep the room quiet and dark so you don't stimulate another seizure. Any seizure that lasts more than a few minutes requires immediate veterinary care to prevent brain damage. When the seizure passes, the cat may appear disoriented.

Veterinary care involves diagnosing and treating the primary cause. The seizures themselves can be controlled through medication.

Feline Hyperesthesia Syndrome

This is a disorder that mostly affects young cats under five years of age but can still be seen in older cats as well. Described by vets as a neurotransmitter malfunction, feline hyperesthesia syndrome is similar to the panic attacks that humans experience. This disorder appears more commonly in Siamese, Burmese, Himalayan, and Abyssinian breeds.

The majority of cats with feline hyperesthesia syndrome groom excessively, sometimes to the point of mutilation. Skin twitching and tail lashing is also exhibited, followed by sudden bursts of activity, darting around wildly. This behavior can range from mild skin twitching to actual seizures. Some cats become aggressive during these episodes and attack companion pets or even their owners. Cats under stress seem to be more at risk.

Diagnosis is done through an MRI performed by a specialist. Physiologic conditions such as spinal problems, epilepsy, and skin conditions must be ruled out.

This disorder is usually controlled by medication.

Peripheral Vestibular Dysfunction

The vestibular system is responsible for detecting certain types of head movement and reacting to maintain balance.

The *labyrinth* is a bony part of the ear that's crucial for equilibrium. Should it become inflamed or broken, peripheral vestibular dysfunction will occur. Infections of the middle or inner ear can also cause this condition.

Symptoms include loss of balance, circling, head-tilt, vomiting, and abnormally rapid eye movements (nystagmus).

Treatment is based on the underlying cause.

Early medical attention is required to prevent progression of the disease, which could lead to permanent damage.

Spinal-Cord Injuries

These are caused most commonly by falls and being hit by automobiles.

A cat who is unable to stand or walk may have sustained spinal cord injury and should be transported very carefully to the vet. Transfer him to a flat board or onto a blanket (carry it as a stretcher) to prevent doing further damage.

A cat's tail is very vulnerable to being run over, which can cause spinal-cord separation as the cat tries to escape. This leads to tail paralysis, nerve damage, and loss of bladder and rectal function. Even if a cat seems fine otherwise but his tail hangs limp, immediate veterinary attention is required to assess damage to the bladder (which may be permanent or temporary).

Treatment of spinal-cord injuries depends on whether it has been severed. For bruising, medications are administered to reduce swelling. If the spinal cord has been severed, the cat will be paralyzed.

Spina Bifida

Common in the Manx cat, this birth defect is a malformation of the bones in the lower back. These cats run the risk of not having properly formed sacral and coccygeal (tail) vertebrae. Severely affected cats may have a weakness in hind leg movement or difficulty urinating and defecating. These cats should be monitored for constipation.

REPRODUCTIVE AND NEONATAL DISORDERS

Vaginitis

Vaginitis is a vaginal inflammation and infection. There is often a discharge with vaginitis. If left untreated, the infection may spread up into the bladder.

Signs of Reproductive System Problems

- abnormal heat cycles
- vaginal discharge (other than normal heat)
- discharge from penis
- undescended testicles
- swollen or irritated testicles or penis
- swollen or inflamed vulva
- foul odor
- tenderness or pain
- unretracted penis
- frequent licking of penis or vulva
- swollen, tender, or red breasts
- lumps
- fever
- vomiting
- reluctance to nurse
- restlessness
- lethargy
- loss of appetite
- increased water intake
- increased urination

The sign you'll most commonly see will be the cat continually licking at her vulva.

Treatment usually involves the use of topical medication.

Mammary Tumors

These are relatively common in cats. Mammary tumors are mostly found in females but males can develop them as well.

Mammary tumors that are *malignant* (cancerous) are mostly found in older cats. Treatment involves mastectomy. The cat must be rechecked on a regular basis, because recurrence is quite common.

The risk of mammary tumors can be virtually eliminated by spaying prior to the first heat cycle.

Cystic Endometrial Hyperplasia

The tissues of the uterine wall (endometrium) thicken and develop cysts. This occurs in cats that cycle repeatedly without mating. The follicles of the ovaries produce an abnormally high level of estrogen, which leads to the formation of these cysts. The cat may show no signs of illness.

The best treatment for cystic endometrial hyperplasia is spaying.

Metritis

This infection of intact cats causes the uterine lining to become inflamed. It's usually caused by unsanitary conditions when the cat is giving birth or by trauma to the birth canal during parturition.

Signs of *acute* metritis can include fever, vaginal discharge, poor appetite, and lethargy. *Acute* metritis can be fatal if not treated.

Signs of *chronic* metritis are harder to detect because there are usually no outward signs other than an aborted pregnancy or the inability to become pregnant at all. Another possible sign might include an inability to gain weight. An astute owner may suspect that the cat just isn't feeling right.

This is a serious infection. Treatment involves the use of antibiotics. Kittens may need to be hand-raised.

Pyometra

This life-threatening infection causes the uterus to fill up with pus. There are two forms of this infection: *open* and *closed.*

With *open* pyometra, the large amount of pus becomes visible as a discharge. With *closed* pyometra, the pus accumulates in the uterus without discharging, creating a very toxic situation for the cat.

Signs of pyometra can include: a firm, distended abdomen; loss of appetite; discharge (with *open* pyometra only); increased water intake and increased urination; and vomiting (*closed* pyometra).

This is a life-threatening condition. Veterinary attention is needed immediately. The treatment for pyometra is surgery (hysterectomy).

False Pregnancy

More commonly seen in dogs, false pregnancies can occur in cats whose eggs weren't fertilized during ovulation.

The usual sign is that the cat will begin displaying nesting behavior. Some cats may even have some degree of mammary development.

There is no veterinary treatment required for this specific condition, but have the cat examined to rule out the possibility that there was actually an aborted pregnancy.

A cat who repeatedly exhibits false pregnancy behavior should be spayed.

Mastitis

Mastitis is an infection of the mammary glands (it can affect one or more of the glands) caused by a bacterial infection. A wound or scratch to the breast can introduce bacteria into the gland. The kittens' nails can even cause a scratch as they nurse. The milk from the infected glands is toxic and can infect the nursing kittens.

Signs of mastitis include breasts that are swollen, hot, tender, or red. The cat may have a fever and lose her appetite. The milk may or may not appear normal. The nursing kittens should be removed immediately and hand-raised with kitten milk-replacement formula.

Treatment involves the administration of antibiotics. Cool moist compresses should be applied to the breast several times a day. Don't use warm compresses because that will increase blood flow which in turn, stimulates the gland to continue producing milk. Make sure the compresses are *cool*. In the case of an abscess, a drainage tube may need to be inserted surgically.

Depending on the specific case, the kittens may need to be on antibiotics as well.

Your veterinarian will provide instructions on the procedure for drying up the mother's milk should that be necessary.

Affected glands may become hard or firm as scar tissue replaces normal mammary tissue; this can reduce milk production with future litters.

Eclampsia (Milk Fever)

Due to the calcium demand during nursing, a cat with a low serum calcium level can develop eclampsia. This is more apt to happen when the mother cat has a large litter.

Eclampsia results in muscle spasms. Initially, the signs are rapid breathing, restlessness, pale mucous membranes, uncoordinated gait, and dangerously high fever. The muscles in the face tighten, exposing the teeth. Eventually the cat goes into full body muscle spasms, and finally, paralysis.

Eclampsia is an emergency. The cat needs to be taken to the hospital immediately for calcium replacement therapy (given by IV). Feed the kittens using a milk replacement formula.

Once the cat has recovered from the emergency, she'll be given vitamin/mineral supplements but the kittens shouldn't be allowed to continue nursing.

Kitten Mortality Complex

A broad term that refers to the various neonatal infections and diseases as well as other influences (such as low birth weight) that can cause death in kittens.

The first two weeks of life are the riskiest for newborns. Of the fatalities that occur, they mostly happen within this time frame.

The newborns have such an uphill battle. Kittens are at risk of diseases transmitted from the queen in utero. Congenital defects also can affect the mortality rate. Another factor is that kittens are unable to regulate their body temperature, so if the area in which they're kept isn't warm enough it can lead to hypothermia. Low blood sugar and dehydration are additional dangers at this young age. Poor sanitary conditions will also put kittens at risk of disease. Then there are the possibilities of injuries sustained during birth, lack of milk production from the mother cat, as well as the chance that she may not provide adequate care and attention. Not every would-be mom reads the manual on what her kittens will need. Some cats can even reject their own kittens.

Inadequate milk production is a common cause of kitten mortality. This can be due to the size of the litter or as a result of the mother being fed a poor-quality diet.

Fading Kitten Syndrome

This disease is believed to be transmitted to the kittens as they pass through the birth canal. Initially after birth, all will seem fine: The mother is healthy and the kittens are nursing; then within a week or two, one or more kittens die. If the disease appears in older kittens of at least three weeks of age, it won't be fatal.

Symptoms include: a yellowish diarrhea, excessive crying, vomiting, refusal to eat, and breathing difficulty.

Contact your veterinarian immediately. Treatment depends on age of the kittens and severity of the symptoms.

Hernia

A hernia is a hole in the abdominal wall. This appears as a little protrusion on the cat's underside. The bulge may be soft and able to be temporarily pushed back. If the protrusion can't be pushed back or appears as a hard, painful, swollen area, it needs immediate attention because blood supply to the tissue may be cut off. Umbilical hernias are the most commonly seen.

Umbilical hernias, if they don't recede on their own within the first six months, can be surgically repaired. This is commonly done during the spay or neuter surgery. If you are planning on leaving your cat intact, the umbilical hernia surgery will have to be done by the time the cat is six months old.

If you feel any type of lump on your kitten's belly, have it examined by the veterinarian.

Birth-Related Infections

Umbilical Infection
The kitten's navel may look inflamed with pus drainage. Clipping the umbilical cord too close to the abdomen can lead to this kind of infection. Unsanitary conditions can put a kitten at risk of umbilical infection as well.

If the cord was severed too close to the abdomen, cleanse the area and apply an antibiotic ointment such as Neosporin. Don't allow the mother to lick the kitten in that area because she could make the condition worse. If you're in doubt about how to properly care for the area, consult your vet. If an infection has already taken hold, contact your veterinarian because more specific treatment is needed.

Toxic Milk Syndrome
Breast infections such as *mastitis* cause the milk of the mother to become toxic to her kittens. Commercial milk replacement that has not been properly prepared or has turned bad may also be toxic. Signs of toxic milk syndrome can include excessive kitten vocalization, diarrhea, or a bloated stomach. *Septicemia* can result from toxic milk syndrome.

Treatment involves removing the kittens from the mother. If the mother has an infection, immediate veterinary attention is required and the kittens shouldn't nurse from her again until after you get approval from the vet. Diarrhea and dehydration must be treated, and the kittens will have to be hand-fed. Antibiotics may be administered by injection.

Septicemia
This infection can enter the bloodstream by way of an infected umbilical cord. Bacteria-infected milk can also lead to this condition. This is seen in kittens under two weeks of age.

Signs include: vocalization, distended, bloated stomachs, and difficulty in defecation. It may appear as if the kitten is constipated, but if you look at his bloated abdomen you'll see it has developed a dark red or blue color. As the septicemia gets worse, the kitten will cease nursing, develop a low body temperature, lose weight, and become dehydrated.

Treatment involves determining the underlying primary cause. If it's due to infected milk, the kittens must be removed from the mother and both she and her kittens will need care. Kittens must be treated for diarrhea and dehydration.

Insufficient Milk Supply
If kittens appear hungry, cry excessively, or aren't tended to by the mother (which can occur with first-time mothers), there may be an insufficient supply of milk. Contact your veterinarian for a milk replacement formula.

Paraphimosis (penis that is unable to be retracted)

Normally, when the penis is retracted, it slides back into the sheath. Long hair that sticks to the penis after mating may prevent it from sliding back. The most common cause is when hair collects around the penis and over time forms a ring.

Trimming the long hair around the penis before mating your male cat is recommended to prevent this condition.

To treat, gently slide the *prepuce* (skin) back away from the penis and remove any trapped hairs. Gently hold the penis head and check for hairs caught on the spines. Next, lubricate the penis with a little K-Y jelly or olive oil. Very gently slide the prepuce back over the penis. If the penis still doesn't retract, take the cat to the veterinarian.

Hair caught on the spines of the penis can cause irritation and even infection. If the penis looks irritated, has a discharge or odor, veterinary treatment is required.

Even if the penis can be retracted back into the sheath, if any of the above signs are present or if the cat frequently licks at his penis, veterinary attention is needed.

Cryptorchid Testicles (undescended)

A male cat should have both testicles descended into the scrotum at birth. If one or both fail to descend, they are referred to as *cryptorchid*.

A cat with either one or both cryptorchid testicles should be neutered and not used for breeding. If left undescended, the testicle can develop a tumor.

Male Infertility

Attempting to breed the male cat too often (more than twice a week) can result in a low sperm count. On the other hand, mating too infrequently can lead to a low sperm count as well.

A cat with both undescended testicles may be sterile. If one testicle has descended, he might be fertile but shouldn't be bred.

Age also affects fertility, as does obesity, poor nutrition, and other diseases.

In terms of genetics, male tortoise shell and male calico cats are almost always sterile.

Diagnosis involves determining the underlying cause by way of clinical tests, history taking, and physical examination. Treatment will be based on case specifics.

Female Infertility

Infertility in females can be caused by cysts on the ovaries or abnormal heat cycles (especially as the cat gets older). Abnormal heat cycles can be the result of insufficient daylight (an initiating factor in estrous cycling). Treatment for cysts involves surgical removal. Treatment for abnormal heat cycles is based on the specific cause. If it's due to lack of daylight, increasing the cat's exposure to at least twelve hours of light per day is usually recommended.

INFECTIOUS DISEASES

Viral Diseases

Feline Viral Rhinotracheitis (FVR)

Feline viral rhinotracheitis is produced by a *herpes* virus. It's the most serious of the respiratory diseases of cats and is fatal for kittens. FVR is spread by direct contact with saliva, nasal/eye discharge, or by contact with the litter box or water bowl.

Symptoms start with a fever, progressing to sneezing, coughing and eye and nasal discharge. The eyes become inflamed, which can lead to ulcerations, eventually forcing the eyelids shut. The nose can become totally blocked due to the thick discharge, causing open-mouth breathing. Symptoms can also include stomatitis (mouth ulcers), which makes eating extremely painful, so the cat loses weight. Even if the mouth doesn't become ulcerated, the compromised sense of smell due to congested nasal passages can cause a loss of appetite. Warming the food slightly will help release the aroma, making it more appealing.

Treatment includes antibiotics, topical eye ointments, IV fluids, and nutritional support. The nose and the eyes have to be kept clear of discharge. Use a cotton ball moistened with water to clean the eyes and nose. A little drop of baby oil can be used over chapped areas of the nose.

Severe infections can leave a cat susceptible to recurring colds.

A yearly vaccination will help prevent your cat from developing this disease.

Feline Leukemia Virus (FeLV)

A highly contagious viral disease that grows in bone marrow and spread via secretions, FeLV positive cats have suppressed immune systems that leave them highly susceptible to other diseases and FeLV-potentiated malignancies.

Transmission occurs most often through exchange of infected saliva. Possible transmission may occur as a result of sharing food and water bowls or allogrooming. Sexual contact and bite wounds are definite forms of transmission. Kittens can acquire the disease in the mother's uterus or by nursing on the infected milk.

FeLV may not show up in the blood of an infected cat until a month or more after exposure. Some cats can be carriers without showing active symptoms themselves. Some cats exposed to FeLV may develop an immunity. This is called *transient viremia*, where the virus is in the blood and saliva but the cat's antibodies are able to eliminate it within about eight to sixteen weeks.

Persistent viremia refers to the virus that continues to be present in the cat's blood and saliva after the eight to sixteen week period. Having taken a firm hold of the cat's immune system, the virus causes the body to become susceptible to any number of diseases. This is where FeLV-potentiated diseases become fatal to a cat. There are also cats who develop a *latent infection,* which means that they produce antibodies that eliminate the virus from the blood (and ultimately from the saliva), but it stays in the bone marrow. The majority of cats with *latent infections* eventually become disease-free after months to years. Stress may, however, reactivate the virus prior to the body eliminating it. Latently infected pregnant cats can transmit the virus to fetuses in utero.

Signs of FeLV are rather nonspecific. Initial signs of illness may include: fever, loss of weight, depression, change in bowels, vomiting. The cat may also become anemic, showing pale mucous membranes. Specific signs then change when the other diseases develop as a result of immunosuppression.

Diagnosis of FeLV is done through two types of tests:

- The ELISA test is done in the veterinarian's office. The results become available within about twenty minutes. This test determines if the virus is in the blood or secretions. Cats testing positive with the ELISA test could be in the *transient viremia* stage and may still extinguish the virus. It's for that reason that positive tests should be repeated in twelve to sixteen weeks.

- The IFA (immunofluorescence assay) test is sent to a lab and detects if the virus has progressed to a later stage.

Discrepancies can occur between the ELISA test and the IFA test because they're detecting the virus at different stages. If the ELISA test is being repeated, the IFA should be done again also. Latent infections may not be detectable; some new types of testing may be able to detect the virus.

Treatment involves providing relief for the cat and prolonging life if possible. Antibiotics, vitamin supplements, IV therapy, and anti-cancer drugs are available, but both the owner and the veterinarian must work together on the ethical question of the cat's quality of life. Anti-cancer drugs are very powerful and you have to consider how much the cat should have to endure. In addition, there is the risk of treating a cat who may continue to shed this virus, putting other cats at risk.

Prevention involves testing of any cats before introduction into your household. Ideally, in multicat households, new cats should be tested, quarantined for three months, then retested.

If you had an FeLV-positive cat in the household, disinfect the home, replace all litter boxes, food/water bowls. All remaining cats should be tested and then retested in three months.

If an FeLV-positive cat was recently removed from your single-cat household, disinfect the home, throw out the litter box, food/water bowls, and wait at least one month before bringing in another cat.

There are vaccinations available against FeLV. For kittens, the first vaccination is given at twelve weeks of age and a followup is needed three weeks later. Even adult cats must receive an initial series of two vaccinations spaced three weeks apart. An annual FeLV booster is required.

If your vaccinated cat has been bitten by a cat whom you suspect could be FeLV-positive (i.e., any unknown cat), have him tested because no vaccine is 100 percent foolproof.

Feline Immunodeficiency Virus (FIV)

It's related to the human AIDS virus (HIV), but FIV doesn't produce HIV in humans and HIV will not produce FIV in cats.

FIV was first identified in California in the 1980s. Some studies suggest that FIV may have a role in some non-FeLV lymposarcomas.

FIV is spread mainly through bite wounds, which puts outdoor cats, especially roaming males, at greatest risk. Casual contact is not a main form of transmission.

The immune suppressed conditions caused by FIV can be hard to distinguish from FeLV, such as anemia, infections, and low white blood cell count. Signs of FIV can include various symptoms, depending upon the route of infection. Gingivitis, periodontitis, and stomatitis (mouth ulcers) are relatively common, which leads to inability to eat and eventual emaciation. Skin infections, urinary infections, eye and ear infections, diarrhea, and respiratory infections are also possible. Delayed healing may be an important clue.

There are several stages of FIV. As with HIV, it begins with the acute stage following exposure where the cat develops a fever and enlarged lymph nodes. The cat may then go through a lengthy stage of being an asymptomatic carrier. Following that, there is the stage of ARC (aids related complex) and AIDS.

Diagnosis is based on an ELISA test, which can be performed in the veterinarian's office. The diagnosis should also be confirmed by doing additional tests, such as an IFA (immunofluorescence assay) or a Western Blot Immunoassay. The latter two tests are sent out to a diagnostic lab.

A single positive test only proves that your cat has been exposed to the virus, and so the immune system has issued a response. Therefore, have two tests performed for confirmation. If possible, retest in three to four months.

Kittens may test positive for FIV until four to six months due to maternal antibodies. Positive tests in cats under six months of age are of little or no value.

A positive diagnosis of FIV shouldn't mean an immediate death sentence for your cat. FIV-positive cats (if they're healthy) can live for months and even years. A positive diagnosis does mean, though, that the cat must strictly be an indoor cat and no other new cats can be introduced into the home.

Treatment includes supportive therapy based on the specific infections involved. Treatments used are only for providing relief and controlling the progression of infection. AZT, the human drug, is toxic to cats.

For now, the only way of preventing FIV is to limit your cat's exposure to the virus by keeping him indoors. Since there is currently no vaccine available, the most effective method is nonexposure.

If you do allow your FIV-negative cat outdoors, have him neutered to reduce his inclination to roam and fight. Keep him up-to-date on all of his other vaccinations and have him checked at the first sign of anything awry.

Feline Panleukopenia

Also known as *feline infectious enteritis* or *feline distemper,* this is a highly contagious and serious disease. It can attack a cat at any age and is one of the primary causes of death in kittens.

The disease is spread by direct contact with infected cats or their secretions. An airborne virus, it can be spread by contact with an infected cat's food or water bowl, litter box, bedding, furniture, toys, and even from a human's contaminated hands or clothing.

The feline panleukopenia virus can remain in the environment for more than a year. Thorough cleansing and disinfecting with diluted bleach solution must be done by anyone who handles or treats an infected cat.

Signs of illness vary but can include fever and vomiting. The cat often develops a hunched pose, due to abdominal pain. He may sit with his head hanging over the water bowl. If he is actually able to eat or drink, he often vomits afterward. A yellowish diarrhea develops, sometimes streaked with blood. The cat's coat usually develops a dull appearance. When you handle or pick up the cat, he may cry out due to abdominal pain.

Panleukopenia attacks the cat's white blood cells. As the number of healthy white cells diminish, the body is susceptible to secondary infections.

The earlier you get to the vet when symptoms first appear, the greater the chance of a cat surviving this disease. Treatment includes: antibiotics, IV fluid therapy, and nutritional support.

The best prevention is to vaccinate your cat. A kitten should be vaccinated first at six to eight weeks old and again three weeks later. In high-risk situations a third vaccination should also be administered. An annual booster is required.

In an environment where panleukopenia has been present, thorough cleansing and disinfecting must be done with a solution of bleach and water. Throw out anything in the cat's environment that can't be disinfected.

Feline Infectious Peritonitis (FIP)

Caused by a strain belonging to the *coronavirus* group, FIP is spread by direct contact with secretions. The cats most often infected are under three years old. A few cats who are exposed to the virus may develop only mild respiratory infections but can then become carriers while remaining asymptomatic. For the majority of cats though, FIP if fatal.

The most at risk for FIP are catteries, households with a dense cat population, undernourished cats, kittens, or cats already suffering from another illness.

There are two forms of this disease: *effusive* ("wet") and *noneffusive* ("dry"). Both are fatal. In the wet form, fluid accumulates in the chest or abdomen. You may notice breathing difficulty as the lungs become unable to expand. Fluid that accumulates in the abdomen causes it to become enlarged and painful to the touch. Other signs include: fever, loss of appetite, diarrhea, anemia, vomiting. Jaundice may also develop. Cats with the *effusive* form of FIP don't usually survive more than a couple of months.

The *noneffusive* form of FIP doesn't involve fluid production, but rather, attacks the organs, such as the brain, liver, kidneys, pancreas, and eyes. Signs can include: liver failure, kidney failure, neurologic disease, retinal disease, blindness, pancreatic disease. Cats with *noneffusive* FIP may survive several months.

Diagnosis may be based on clinical signs, blood tests and fluid analysis but the only definitive diagnosis is an organ or tissue biopsy. Most blood tests will only confirm the exposure of the cat to a corona virus—not necessarily FIP. The evidence can be strong enough, though, especially in the case of *effusive* FIP to presume a diagnosis.

Treatment is unfortunately limited to supportive therapy to provide relief: antibiotics and anti-inflammatories. There is no cure.

There's a vaccine available that's administered intranasally and given in two doses, three weeks apart. The cat must be at least sixteen weeks old to receive the vaccine. Some researchers believe that cats are exposed to FIP as very young kittens and then the disease actually occurs later in life. Therefore, they say that vaccination after sixteen weeks of age is of little value. The current vaccine is still very controversial and research is continuing. Many veterinarians believe that household cats aren't in a high risk category and therefore shouldn't be vaccinated at this time. Since medical findings can change rapidly, consult your veterinarian in case advancements have been made since publication of this book.

If your cat is in a high-risk category, make sure his health is maintained through proper nutrition, vet checkups, and vaccinations. Address all health concerns immediately, however minor they may appear (that means fleas, other parasites, the slightest sniffle or sneeze). Keep the area where the cat lives disinfected regularly. Use a solution of a half-cup bleach in a gallon of water to disinfect the environment. In a densely populated cat environment, this is crucial.

Feline Calicivirus (FCV)

It's spread by direct contact with nasal or eye discharge and saliva. It can also be spread by coming into contact with the litter box or water bowl of an infected cat.

Initial symptoms include eye and nasal discharge, fever, and sneezing. As the disease progresses, drooling is seen due to ulceration of the mouth and tongue. The cat stops eating, loses weight, and has more and more breathing difficulty.

Treatment involves the use of antibiotics and anti-inflammatory medications. You can help keep the nose and eyes clear of discharge by using a cotton ball moistened with water or saline solution. A drop of baby oil can be used on chapped portions of the nose.

There is a vaccine available to help protect your cat against FCV.

Rabies

This fatal disease enters the body usually by way of a bite from an infected animal. The virus, which is in the animal's saliva, enters the open wound and travels through the central nervous system to the brain. The incubation period can range from a couple of weeks to several months, depending upon how far the initial bite wound was to the brain and how long it takes for the virus to infiltrate the nervous system—its transport route to the brain.

Rabies takes two forms, *furious* and *paralytic* (also called the "dumb" form). Infected animals may exhibit signs of both. The *paralytic* form represents the time close to death but an animal may not reach that form due to death occurring from seizures during the *furious* stage.

Initially with rabies, the cat may appear nervous, restless, or irritable. He may become sensitive to light and loud noises. He'll seek hiding places and become withdrawn. These symptoms may last a few days before the cat goes into the *furious* stage.

The *furious* form can last anywhere from a day to a week. The cat becomes aggressive, biting at the air or imaginary things. He can suddenly attack and bite any approaching human or animal. Restrained cats will attempt to gnaw through crates or cages. In a short time, the cat develops tremors and muscle twitching, leading into convulsions.

When the *paralytic* stage takes over, it shows up first around the head and neck as the muscles become paralyzed. The image most people associate with rabies is the animal who seems afraid to drink water. It's actually this paralysis that causes an inability to swallow. The cat drools and often paws at his mouth. The paralysis prevents him from fully closing his lower jaw so his tongue can be seen hanging out. This partial paralysis soon gives way to complete paralysis. The cat collapses, and death follows soon after.

The only true diagnosis is through microscopic examination of brain tissue which is done by way of necropsy. Treatment is not available.

If your *unvaccinated* cat has been bitten by a rabid animal, it will most likely be recommended that he be put down or placed in quarantine for at least six months. If your cat has been vaccinated and is bitten by a rabid animal, he will be given an additional booster vaccination and placed under observation.

Prevention comes down to making sure you have your cat vaccinated against rabies. Kittens can be vaccinated starting at three months of age. A booster is given one year from that date. Then, depending upon the type of vaccine and your state's law, boosters are administered yearly or every three years.

When it comes to animal bites, all wounds should be immediately cleansed with soap and water. If you have any questions or concerns about a bite that your cat received, consult your veterinarian.

Bacterial Diseases

Feline Infectious Anemia

Caused by an organism called *hemobartonella felis*, which attaches to the red blood cell surface of cats, feline infectious anemia results in anemia.

It's believed that this disease more commonly affects male cats ranging from one to three years of age.

It's presumed that blood-sucking parasites and insects such as fleas may pass the contaminated blood to a healthy cat after biting an infected one. Kittens can be infected in utero if the mother is infected.

Signs can include pale gums and mucous membranes, and vomiting. If the disease progresses slowly, significant weight loss may be noticeable. An *acute* case may not show weight loss but rather sudden weakness, fever, loss of appetite, and the skin will appear jaundiced due to the breakdown of red blood cells.

Diagnosis is made by microscopic examination of blood smears. More than one sample may need to be taken because there's a period when the parasite isn't visible in the blood.

Antibiotic treatment in addition to other medication is usually administered for several weeks. Extreme cases may require blood transfusions. Provided that the anemia isn't too far advanced, treatment is often successful; however, the parasite may never be completely eliminated from the body, and the disease may recur following stress.

Flea and parasite control should also be part of the comprehensive program to reduce the cat's exposure to feline infectious anemia.

Bordetella Bronchiseptica (FeBb)

Once known primarily as causing *kennel cough* in dogs, FeBb is now recognized as a possible respiratory pathogen which can cause similar signs in cats. Upper respiratory infections resulting from FeBb can lead to pneumonia.

Signs can include fever, loss of appetite, listlessness, runny eyes, coughing, nasal discharge, sneezing, and increased lung sounds. Although coughing is a common sign in dogs, it may or may not appear in cats.

It's believed the transmission primarily occurs through oronasal exposure to secretions and excretions of infected cats.

Bordetella alone can't be diagnosed based on physical examination or clinical signs due to the similarity of signs associated with other respiratory pathogens. Culture swabs must be taken and sent to the laboratory.

Cats who have clinically recovered from FeBb can continue to shed the organism for about nineteen weeks.

Affected cats are treated with antibiotics.

A vaccine for FeBb is available. Cats in high-risk environments (such as boarding facilities, catteries, shelters, cat shows, multicat households) should be vaccinated. If you have a cat in a low-risk environment, speak to your vet about whether the FeBb vaccine should be a part of the yearly routine.

The vaccine is given intranasally.

Salmonellosis

A bacterial infection caused by a type of salmonella (there are many). Cats more often seem to be asymptomatic carriers and appear relatively resistant to salmonella. The cats most susceptible are the ones under stress, living in unsanitary or overcrowded conditions, malnourished, or already weakened by illness. Bacteria is shed in the feces of carrier animals.

Cats can acquire salmonella by ingesting raw food, rodent or bird feces, and also by canned food that has been contaminated.

Signs of salmonellosis include fever, loss of appetite, abdominal pain, dehydration, diarrhea, and vomiting. There are some cases, though, where no sign of diarrhea is exhibited.

Diagnosis is made by examination, fecal cultures, and blood tests. This infection is difficult to diagnose. Treatment involves fluid therapy to correct dehydration. Antibiotics may also be used.

To help prevent salmonellosis, never feed your cat raw or undercooked meat. If your cat is an outdoor hunter, he's at a greater risk of contracting this bacterial infection. If you choose not to confine him indoors, make sure his immune system stays in peak condition through premium nutrition, booster vaccinations (there is no salmonella vaccine), regular vet checks and keeping his environment sanitary. Finally, don't let your cat ingest captured prey.

Cat Scratch Disease

I've decided to include cat scratch disease in this chapter, because so many people don't understand exactly what it is. They only know that it's connected somehow to cats.

This disease is one that affects humans. Cats can be asymptomatic carriers. Cat scratch disease is usually self-limiting and consists of a red sore at the location of the bite or scratch. An enlargement of the lymph nodes closest to the wound may develop, usually lasting several weeks or even months. In most cases, the lymph nodes then return to normal size. In a few cases, cat scratch disease results in a more severe condition, including fever, fatigue, headache, and loss of appetite. For immunosuppressed humans, the disease can become life-threatening.

Always clean and disinfect any scratch or bite you receive from a cat, however minor. This disease is more apt to occur when scratched by a stray cat rather than a known pet. Consult your doctor if you have any questions about a cat-related wound.

Instruct children on the proper and gentle handling of cats, so hopefully they will avoid getting scratched in the first place.

Feline Chlamydiosis

Also known as *feline pneumonitis*, it's a respiratory infection that can range from mild to very severe and is spread through direct contact.

Symptoms include conjunctivitis, which causes redness and discharge from the eyes. Sneezing, loss of appetite, coughing, and breathing difficulty are also signs.

Treatment includes the use of oral and ophthalmic antibiotics. Cats usually recover from this disease, although recurrence is common.

There is a vaccine available to help protect your cat from this disease, which may or may not be included in routine vaccinations.

Fungal Diseases

Histoplasmosis

This disease is caused by a soil fungus. Transmission occurs through inhalation. Histoplasmosis is rarely found in cats. Young cats are more susceptible.

Symptoms can include: respiratory difficulty, fever, weakness, loss of appetite, and diarrhea.

Diagnosis is made by doing a culture and then treatment involves the use of long-term antifungal medication. The prognosis, though, is usually not very good.

Aspergillosis

Signs of infection by this fungus, which is found in soil and decaying debris, usually include respiratory and digestive disorders.

Cats already infected with panleukopenia seem to be the most susceptible to aspergillosis.

Antifungal drugs are part of the therapy used to treat this disease. Prognosis is guarded.

Cryptococcosis

A common fungal infection of cats, it's found in bird droppings and is usually acquired by way of inhalation.

The infection usually results in respiratory illness with signs such as sneezing, thick nasal discharge, coughing, breathing difficulty, and weight loss. Hard growths may develop across the nose.

Diagnosis is made by sending samples to the lab for culturing. There is also a blood test available for diagnosing cryptococcosis.

Antifungal drugs are used to treat this disease. In some cases, surgery may also be necessary.

Ringworm
Refer to section on "Skin Disorders."

DISORDERS OF THE MOUTH

Retained Deciduous Teeth

Kittens have twenty-six deciduous (baby) teeth, which eventually get replaced by adult teeth. The transition begins at about three months of age and is usually completed by the time the kitten reaches seven months.

Occasionally, one or more of the baby teeth don't come out and as the adult teeth emerge they get pushed out of proper alignment. When you look in the kitten's mouth you'll notice two sets of teeth. If left alone, this leads to a badly aligned bite and rapid progression of dental disease.

Treatment consists of pulling the retained baby teeth.

Halitosis

This isn't the primary problem but rather, a symptom of another condition, and finding the cause is crucial. You can't just treat this as a simple case of bad breath.

Gingivitis, periodontal disease, certain infectious diseases, or urinary problems can cause halitosis. A strange mouth odor can also be a sign of poisoning. Diabetes may also produce a characteristic odor due to acetone. Anytime you notice a strange or foul odor to your cat's breath, have him checked by the vet so the primary cause can be accurately diagnosed.

Signs of Mouth or Throat Problems

- inflammation of lips or gums
- change in appearance of tongue
- receding gums
- yellow or brown deposits on teeth
- halitosis

- loss of appetite
- excessive drooling
- pawing at mouth or face
- swelling on the face or neck
- ungroomed hair coat
- difficulty in swallowing

Following a regular program of cleaning your cat's teeth will help prevent gingivitis, which can cause bad breath. Refer to chapter 12 to learn how to care for your cat's teeth.

Gingivitis and Periodontitis

Gingivitis, a common problem for all pets, refers to the inflammation of the gums. Gingivitis begins when the bacterial film known as *plaque* coats the tooth. The invisible plaque is caused by the growing bacteria in food that gets trapped between the teeth. *Calculus* or *tartar* forms as the soft plaque mineralizes into a hard substance. No longer invisible, calculus appears yellow or brown on the teeth.

Signs of gingivitis: a thin red line on the gums. It'll almost look as if someone outlined your cat's gums with a red pen. As the disease progresses, you may notice bad breath. As the infection worsens, the inflamed gums form pus pockets and your cat may begin drooling.

Periodontitis refers to the inflammation to the periodontal membrane around the tooth. At this stage teeth may be loose, roots abscessed, and gums receded. The infection may have spread to the bone. Eating and chewing become too painful for the cat.

Left untreated, the infection in the bones can become life-threatening as it spreads to the cat's organs.

Scaling and polishing of your cat's teeth should be done by your veterinarian as often as needed. At that time, loose teeth will need to be extracted. The whole procedure is done under anesthesia, so your cat doesn't feel any pain.

For instructions on caring for your cat's teeth, including brushing, dental rinses, and tartar-reducing foods, refer to chapter 12.

Excessive Drooling

Salivary glands secrete saliva, a fluid that aids in digestion of food. Drooling is more commonly associated with dogs, but a cat might drool when given oral medicine. You also may notice drooling during displays of affection as he seems to get so carried away with his joy. Cats often drool when sprayed with flea control products if they lick their fur afterward.

Excessive drooling can be a sign of many health problems as well. Dental disease can cause drooling, as can foreign bodies caught in the mouth or throat. Drooling can be a sign of poisoning. Heat stroke is another possible cause. Runny noses, watery eyes, or sneezing that accompany drooling can indicate a respiratory infection.

Stomatitis (sore or ulcerated mouth)

Periodontal disease can cause inflammation and ulcers of the mouth. The cat will have a strong mouth odor, puffy red gums, and a dark brownish saliva. This condition is also known as *trench mouth*.

Stomatitis can also be connected to certain respiratory diseases, as well as FeLV, FIV, and renal disease, among others.

Symptoms include pawing at the mouth, inflamed mouth, drooling, inability to eat, and head shaking.

Treatment involves diagnosing the primary cause, cleaning the mouth, treating the ulcers, pulling loose teeth, and placing the cat on appropriate antibiotics. An at-home oral hygiene program will be prescribed, and the cat must stay on a very soft diet while the mouth heals.

EYE DISORDERS

Conjunctivitis

This is an inflammation of the lining of the eyelid and sometimes the bulbar conjunctiva as well. One or both eyes can be affected. There is usually a discharge that may be clear and watery or thick and puslike. The eyes will be red or inflamed. Sometimes edema will be present. The cat may blink often and paw at his eyes. They may even appear to be swollen shut. Crusts may form on the eyelids.

Conjunctivitis can be caused by an irritant such as dust, dirt or some type of allergen. A clear watery discharge may indicate a viral upper respiratory disease or allergies. If the discharge is thick and changes color, it could suggest a secondary bacterial infection.

There are several causes of conjunctivitis. Specific treatment will depend on the underlying cause. Eye drops or ointments will be prescribed and if there are crusts on the eyes, warm soaks will be administered.

Signs of Eye Problems

- bleeding from or around the eye
- squinting
- rapid blinking
- unusual movement of the eye
- eye discharge
- pawing or scratching at eye
- appearance of third eyelid
- swelling in or around the eye
- pain
- fixed pupils
- one pupil of different size
- opaque film covering the eye
- bloodshot eyes
- irritated, red, or inflamed conjunctiva
- crusting over eye
- sunken or protruding eyeball
- eyelid drooping
- tearing

If your cat is squinting or appears to have conjunctivitis, don't administer any previously prescribed medicine until you've seen the vet. If a corneal ulcer is present, using the wrong ointment or drops can cause more serious injury.

Some cats sabotage recovery by continually scratching or rubbing at the eyes. If this is the case, your veterinarian will recommend the use of an Elizabethan collar to prevent him from gaining access to the eyes.

Appearance of the Third Eyelid

Injury or illness can cause the third eyelid to become visible. If only one eye is involved, it's most likely an infection or injury to the eye itself. If the membrane is visible over both eyes, illness may be the cause.

Have your cat seen by the veterinarian for a complete exam to determine the cause of the third eyelid appearance and begin appropriate treatment.

Haws Syndrome

This is a relatively common condition in cats that results in a protrusion of the third eyelid. Its cause is unknown and may be associated with self-limiting diarrhea. The condition is temporary, lasting anywhere from one to two months. Treatment may include topical medication. If diarrhea is present, that must be treated as well.

Horner's Syndrome

A constant partial appearance of the third eyelid, Horner's syndrome is due to the loss of nerve stimulation of the muscle that keeps it retracted. In addition to third eyelid protrusion, symptoms may include: small pupil, retracted eye, and lid droop.

Horner's syndrome is a sign of a neurologic problem. Causes can include injury to the neck or upper spinal column, along with middle ear infection. Treatment is based on primary cause.

Blocked Tear Ducts

Normally, excess tears drain into the tear duct, which leads into the nose. If the normal tear drainage system becomes blocked, the tears spill out over the eyelid and run down the face, causing the hair to become stained. A cat with a chronic clear discharge not accompanied by redness to the eye, may have blocked tear ducts.

There are several causes for the tear ducts to become blocked. It can be the result of the sharp turns that the drainage system has to take in short-nosed, flat-faced breeds such as Persians and Himalayans. It can also be caused by injury, thick secretions, infections (especially chronic ones), or tumors. Even dirt or litter can cause the blockage.

To check for adequate drainage, the veterinarian will use *fluorescein*, an ophthalmic dye in the eye. Under a special light, the dye should be apparent at the nostril opening if the drainage system is functioning. Sometimes only one side is blocked.

Treatment depends on the underlying cause. Infections are treated with antibiotic therapy. Reduction of inflammation by using ophthalmic steroid drops may open the ducts. Flushing the ducts with saline is often done to loosen whatever is causing the plug. This procedure is often performed under an anesthetic.

Corneal Ulcers

Usually caused by an injury, they can also be the result of a secondary infection. Eye injury due to a cat fight is a common cause of corneal ulcers. Inadequate tear production that results in dry eyes can also cause ulcers.

The ulcer may be large enough to be visible to you or it may be too small to see with the naked eye. Early treatment is crucial to preventing a more serious condition. To find small ulcers, the veterinarian will stain the eye with fluorescein, an ophthalmic dye. The eye is then rinsed and under a special light, any ulcers will retain traces of the dye.

If your cat is squinting, don't assume it's conjunctivitis and place any previously prescribed medicine in his eye. Certain medications can cause very serious injury to the eye when ulcers are present.

Keratitis

An inflammation of the cornea that can affect one or both eyes. Signs include: appearance of the third eyelid, squinting, discharge, sensitivity to light. The cat may also paw at his eye. This inflammation is painful to the cat. If left untreated, the cat may suffer permanent loss of vision.

Keratitis can be the result of a traumatic injury or *entropian* lesion (where the eyelid rolls inward and the lashes irritate the cornea). Many infectious agents can also be the cause.

A veterinarian should be seen immediately. Antibiotics are usually prescribed. To reduce pain, a topical ointment will also be administered.

Glaucoma

This is increased fluid pressure inside the eyeball itself. Glaucoma in cats is usually secondary, caused by things such as injury, infection, cataracts, or tumors. The fluid builds up because something scars over or blocks drainage.

As fluid pressure increases, the eye gets larger, harder and begins to bulge. It is a painful process. Glaucoma can affect one or both eyes. Other symptoms may include dilated pupils and squinting, increased appearance of vascular structures in the sclera (red eye).

Left untreated, retinal damage occurs and the cat could lose vision.

Eye pressure can be measured by the vet, using an instrument that is placed over the eye's surface.

Hospitalization and possible surgery are required for acute cases of glaucoma to relieve pressure. In severe cases, removal of the eye is necessary. Chronic glaucoma may be treated with topical and oral medication.

Cataracts

An opacity of the lens that gives it a milky appearance, cataracts can develop as a result of injury or infection. Not just a condition of old age, cats can develop cataracts at any time. Diabetic cats may develop them as they age.

Depending upon the cause of the cataract, surgery can be performed if needed. Following surgery, vision may be somewhat diminished so the cat will have to be kept indoors.

Nuclear Sclerosis

A common eye disorder that occurs with aging. As the cat gets older the lens continues to grow, pushing toward the center of the eye, creating a buildup of cells. This results in a grayish or bluish haze. This condition, normal to the aging process, doesn't seem to obstruct vision. No treatment is usually needed. This condition is not the same as cataracts.

Uveitis

Inflammation of the inner eye that's commonly seen in connection with various infectious diseases in cats, such as *feline leukemia* or *feline infectious peritonitis*. It can also be the result of physical trauma. With uveitis, the eye becomes increasingly soft.

Symptoms include: red, watery eyes, squinting, constricted pupils, and sensitivity to light. This condition is very painful.

Veterinary care includes diagnosis and treatment of the primary illness or cause, along with medication to reduce inflammation and relieve discomfort.

Left untreated, uveitis can lead to blindness.

Blindness

Numerous disorders can cause blindness as can injury. If you suspect that your cat is going blind or is blind, contact your veterinarian to determine the cause.

If your cat is blind or has diminished vision, he must never be allowed outdoors. Kept indoors, a blind cat can do well as long as his environment remains consistent. Refrain from rearranging furniture and keep his food, water, bed, and litter box in the places he's familiar with.

DISORDERS OF THE NOSE

Infections

A nasal infection can be the result of respiratory disease, injury, or the presence of a foreign object. Signs usually include: nasal discharge, sneezing,

Signs of Nasal Problems

- sneezing
- discharge
- crusting
- bleeding
- pawing at face
- breathing difficulty

- open-mouth breathing
- swelling
- lumps or tumors
- severe dental/oral infections
- decreased appetite
- change in nasal appearance

breathing difficulty, noisy or wet sounding breathing, and loss of appetite. You may notice open-mouth breathing as the cat's nose becomes more congested.

A nasal discharge that is yellow or puslike indicates a bacterial infection.

After diagnosing the specific condition, appropriate antibiotics will be given. A decongestant may also be prescribed. Helping your cat to breathe comfortably is of the utmost importance, so gently wipe any discharge or crusts from the nose with a moistened cotton ball. You can also use a drop of baby oil on the nose to keep it from becoming chapped. Your vet may recommend the use of a vaporizer.

IMPORTANT NOTE: Cats who can't smell usually become anorexic.

Sinusitis

Symptoms can include sneezing and a white or yellow nasal discharge which may or may not contain blood. Sinus infections can be a secondary result of an allergy, respiratory infection, injury, or fungal infection. A tooth abscess can also lead to sinusitis.

The underlying cause must be treated. Antibiotics will be prescribed and in extreme cases, surgery may need to be performed to allow drainage.

DISORDERS OF THE EAR

Otitis

Cats can develop inflammation of the outer ear (*otitis externa*) from bacteria, wax accumulation, ear mites, or infected wounds.

Symptoms include inflammation, scratching or pawing at ears, odor, appearance of exudate, head shaking, or ear flaps held at an unusual angle.

Treatment involves cleansing the ear (see chapter 12 for instructions on how to keep the ears clean) and the application of a topical antibiotic medication.

Signs of Ear Problems

- scratching or pawing at ears
- head tilt
- discharge
- swelling of pinnae (ear flaps)
- bleeding
- odor
- appearance of gritty black material in ears
- excessive wax
- inflammation in or around ears
- crusting
- hair loss around ears
- lumps on or inside the ear
- abnormal ear movements

Middle ear (*otitis media*) inflammation can be caused by parasites, bacteria, fungi, or foreign bodies.

Symptoms include head tilt and lack of balance.

Treatment may include the use of antibiotics or antifungal medication. In some cases, surgery may be required.

Inner ear infections (*otitis interna*) are extremely serious and can result in irreversible damage and even death. Signs can include hearing loss, vomiting, loss of coordination and balance, circling, and abnormal eye movements. Treatment may include the use of antibiotics or antifungal medication.

Deafness

Deafness can be caused by a variety of things, including: injury, infection, aging, obstructions, tumors, poisons, and certain drugs. It can also be congenital. White cats with blue eyes are often deaf. In odd-eyed white cats, the deafness occurs on the side with the blue eye.

If your aging cat is going deaf or has already become totally deaf, avoid startling him. You can announce your arrival or intentions to handle him through the vibrations of your footsteps. When approaching a deaf cat who is sleeping, make your footsteps heavier so he'll feel the vibrations. If the cat is awake and his attention is focused elsewhere, slowly come into his visual field. Don't just come up behind a deaf cat and pick him up.

If you suspect deafness, have your cat examined by the veterinarian to check for infections, injuries, or obstructions.

Ear Mites

The most common cause of ear problems in cats, these microscopic parasites feed off skin tissue. They live and breed in the ear canal, causing itching and irritation, but they can also travel to other parts of the body.

Ear mites are extremely contagious to other pets, so if one pet has an infestation, there's a good chance that his companions will have them as well.

Left untreated, ear-mite infestation can cause serious trouble as the ear canal becomes irritated and raw.

The most common sign of ear-mite infestation is constant scratching and repeated head shaking. The cat may also hold his ears at an unusual angle. When you examine the ears you'll find dry, dark, crumbly brown debris, resembling coffee grinds. During violent head shaking or scratching you may notice some of the debris expelled out onto the hair coat.

Ear mites are actually white in color. The brown debris in the ear is the digested material and wax.

A confirmed diagnosis of ear-mite infestation is made by taking a sample of the debris in the ears for examination under the microscope. There, you're able to see the tiny mites moving all around. One look at the numerous mites under the microscope and it's easy to understand how itchy and irritating they must be for the cat.

Veterinary treatment involves careful and gentle cleaning of the ears. It has to be done gently because the ears will be very irritated and raw. After cleaning, you'll notice how red and inflamed the ear canals are. Cleaning is important for the miticide to be effective so the mites won't be able to hide in the accumulated debris.

Follow the instructions concerning length of time for treatment because ear mites have a three-week life cycle. If treatment is stopped too early, infestation will reappear.

There are several ear-mite treatment products available. Specific dosage instructions may vary, depending on the product. Some medications require refrigeration, so ask your vet if you're not sure.

Your vet may administer an injection of *ivermectin* instead of or as a supplement to topical treatment.

During ear mite treatment, keep the nails trimmed on your cat's hind feet to reduce scratching-related damage to the ears and surrounding area.

Hematoma

When a cat violently shakes his head, a blood vessel can break, causing a bulging pocket of accumulated blood in the ear flap. Such severe head shaking and scratching can be the result of ear mite infestation or an ear infection. Surgery is often required to prevent a recurrence, otherwise the pocket that was formed from the blood clot will fill up with fluid again.

Other causes of a hematoma can include cat fights and trauma to the head.

Sunburned Ears

To prevent this condition, limit the cat's access to the outdoors, especially on sunny days. When the cat does go outdoors, apply a sunblock to the ears.

Check with your veterinarian on which one is safe for cats. Check the ears regularly and seek immediate attention for any signs of sunburn or ulcers. This can develop into skin cancer.

Frostbite
The tips of the ears are especially susceptible to frostbite. This subject is covered in chapter 18, "Emergencies and First Aid."

CANCER
Cancer can develop anywhere in the body: the skin, in the mouth, lymph nodes, blood cells, or any internal organ.

Since many cancers aren't outwardly detectable, anytime your cat displays symptoms of not feeling well, consult your veterinarian.

Neoplasia is a word you'll commonly hear in connection to tumors. It refers to a tumor that continues to grow (a neoplasm).

Tumors are divided into two categories: *benign* and *malignant.* A benign tumor generally grows slower, doesn't spread to other areas of the body, and is very often able to be surgically removed if necessary. A tumor that's diagnosed as malignant, is cancerous, grows rapidly, has an irregular shape and spreads to other parts of the body. Surgery may or may not be successful in removing a malignant tumor.

Treatment for malignant tumors depends on the specific case. One rule does apply to all cancers, though: early detection provides a greater chance of successful cure.

Different types of treatment include:

surgery (sometimes used with other therapies)

chemotherapy (anticancer drugs)

Signs of Cancer

- lumps or bumps
- swelling
- growths on the skin
- weight loss
- loss of appetite
- nonhealing wounds

- weakness
- depression
- lethargy
- anemia
- coughing
- breathing difficulty
- chronic diarrhea

radiation therapy (sometimes used with chemotherapy or surgery)

cryosurgery (freezing the tissue)

hyperthermia therapy (heating the tissue to a very high temperature; sometimes used with other therapies)

immunotherapy (natural and chemical immune boosting agents; sometimes used with other therapies)

Each treatment has advantages and disadvantages. Tumors that have spread or are in difficult-to-reach locations may need a therapy such as radiation. It's not unusual to employ a combination of treatments to control and hopefully eliminate the cancer.

Cancer is, unfortunately, relatively common in cats.

Resource Guide

AAFCO

American Association of Feed Control Officials
Georgia Department of Agriculture
Capital Square
Atlanta, GA 30334-9004
send a SASE for information

Veterinary Organizations

The Academy of Veterinary Homeopathy
751 N.E. 168th Street
North Miami Beach, FL 33162-2427
(305-652-1590)
(fax: 305-653-3337)

American Association of Feline Practitioners
2701 San Pedro N.E.
Suite 7
Albuquerque, NM 87110
(505-888-2424)

American Holistic Veterinary Medical Association
2214 Old Emmorton Road
Bel Air, MD 21015
(410-569-0795)
(fax: 410-569-2346)
E-mail: ahvma@compuserve.com

American Veterinary Medical Association
1931 North Meacham Road
Schaumburg, IL 60173-4360
(847-925-8070)
www.avma.org

International Veterinary
Acupuncture Society
P.O. Box 1478
Longmont, CO 80502-1478
(303-682-1167)
(fax: 303-682-1168)
E-mail: ivasoffice@aol.com

Product Manufacturers

Bayer Corp.
P.O. Box 390
Shawnee Mission, KS 66201
(800-633-3796)
Advantage

Cat Dancer Products Inc.
6145 Green Valley Road
Neenah, WI 54956
(800-844-6369)
www.catdancer.com
Cat Dancer, Cat Charmer

Cats With An Attitude
P.O. Box 88019
Phoenix, AZ 85080-8019
(602-580-8573)
WhiskerWare—an oval bowl with whisker dips

Claworks
1821 N.W. 65th Street
Seattle, WA 98117
Quickdraw McPaw

Colora Mill Outlet
P.O. Box 74
Colora, MD 21917
(410-658-8111)
Various-sized cat trees

Cosmic Pet Products
133 South Burhans Blvd.
Hagerstown, MD 21740
(888-226-7642)
*Cosmic Cat Scratching Post, Cosmic Cat Catnip,
    Incline Scratching Post, various cat toys*

Doskocil Manufacturing Co.
P.O. Box 1246
Arlington, TX 76004-1246
(817-467-5116)
Double Door Deluxe kennel

Farnam Companies/Veterinary Products Laboratories
301 W. Osborn Road
Phoenix, AZ 85013
(800-234-2269 or 602-285-1660)
Feliway

Fat Cat, Inc.
73 Troy Avenue
Colchester, VT 05446-3120
(800-799-MEOW)
www.fatcats.com
Kitty Hoots Crackler

Fe-Lines Inc.
2924 Sixth Avenue
Fort Worth, TX 76110
(888-697-2873)
Sticky Paws

Felix Company
3623 Fremont Avenue N.
Seattle, WA 98103
(206-547-0042)
Felix Katnip Tree Scratching Post

Flexi-Mat Corporation
2244 S. Western
Chicago, IL 60608
(800-338-7392)
Cat Napper Window Perch

The Galkie Company
P.O. Box 20
Harrogate, TN 37752
(800-82-KITTY)
Kitty Tease

Go Cat
3248 Mulliken Road
Charlotte, MI 48813
(517-543-7519)
Da Bird

Great China International, Inc.
2045 California Avenue
Suite 106
Corona, CA 91719
(909-272-9750)
Kitty Tunnel

Kong Company
16191-D Table Mountain Parkway
Golden, CO 80403-1641
(303-216-2626)
www.kongcompany.com
Kitty Kong, Zoom Groom

Merial
2100 Ronson Road
Iselin, NJ 08830-3077
(888-637-4255)
Frontline Top Spot

Miracle Groom
36 Magnolia Avenue, Suite A
San Anselmo, CA 94960
(800-575-3515)
Miracle Groom Waterless Bath

Novartis
P.O. Box 26402
Greensboro, NC 27404-6402
(800-332-2761)
Program

Our Pet's
Virtu Co.
1300 East Street
Fairport Harbor, OH 44077-5573
(800-565-2695)
www.virtupets.com
*Play-n-Treat, Push-n-Roll, Zig-n-Zag,
Play-n-Squeak*

Pet Care With Love, Inc.
P.O. Box 764
Glenview, IL 60025-0764
(800-441-1765)
PawsWay Ramp

Pets 'n People, Inc.
27520 Hawthorne Blvd.
Rolling Hills Estates, CA 90274
(310-544-7125)
*Nature's Miracle Stain & Odor Remover, Nature's
   Miracle Urine Odor Source Locator*

Safe Living/Smart Products
4500 140th Avenue North
Suite 220
Clearwater, FL 33762
(727-507-0707)
www.safeliving.com
Safe Living Electronic Smart Cord

Sherpa's Pet Trading Company
135 E. 55th Street
New York, NY 10022
(800-743-7723)
www.SherpaPet.com
soft-sided cat carrier

Valore Inc.
2 Grove Street
Cos Cob, CT 06807
(800-597-4541)
Grannick's Bitter Apple

Veterinary Ventures
844 Bell Street
Reno, NV 89503
(800-805-7532)
Drinkwell Pet Fountain

VRx Pharmaceuticals
1656 W. 240th Street
Harbor City, CA 90710
(800-969-7387)
C.E.T. Forte Chews

Zoo West Distributors
919 E. Valencia Avenue
Burbank, CA 91501
(888-966-9378)
Pet Alert Sign

Mail-Order Catalogs

Cats, Cats, & More Cats
190 Route 17M
P.O. Box 270
Monroe, NY 10950
(800-708-2287)

Drs. Foster & Smith, Inc.
P.O. Box 100
Rhinelander, WI 54501-0100
(800-826-7206)

K-V Vet Supply
P.O. Box 245
David City, NE 68632
(800-423-8211)

Pedigrees
1989 Transit Way
Brockport, NY 14420-0905
(800-548-4786)

R.C. Steele
P.O. Box 910
Brockport, NY 14420-0910
(800-872-3773)

Magazines

Cat Fancy
Subscription Service Department
P.O. Box 52864
Boulder, CO 80322-2864
(fax: 303-604-7455)
In addition to Cat Fancy, *which is available at news-*
stands and by subscription, they publish Cats USA
and Kittens USA, *two annuals that are available*
at newsstands, as well as a popular cat series.

Cats magazine
Subscribers Services
P.O. Box 56886
Boulder, CO 80322-6886

I Love Cats
457 Seventh Avenue
New York, NY 10123
(212-244-2351)

Pet Life
1400 Two Tandy Center
Fort Worth, TX 76102
(800-767-9377)

Your Cat magazine
1716 Locust Street
Des Moines, IA 50309
(800-642-7333)

Hotlines

ASPCA National Animal Poison Control Center
(800-548-2423 for credit card calls)
(900-680-0000 charged to your phone bill)
There is a consultation fee which can be charged
to a major credit card or automatically charged to
your phone bill, depending upon which of the
above numbers you call. The consultation fee is
about $30.

Dr. Louis J. Camuti Memorial Feline Consultation
and Diagnostic Service
Cornell Feline Health Center
Cornell University
(800-548-8937)
M, W, F 9:00 A.M.–12:00 P.M. and
2:00 P.M.–4:00 P.M.

Florida Pet Loss Support Hotline
University of Florida at Gainesville
(352-392-4700, ext. 4080)
You pay the long-distance phone charge.

Ohio State University Pet Loss Support Hotline
(614-292-1823)
Staffed M, W, F 6:30 P.M.–9:30 P.M.
You pay the long-distance phone charge.

Pet Loss Support Hotline
University of California at Davis
(530-752-4200)
Staffed M–F 6:30 P.M.–9:30 P.M. Pacific time
You pay the long-distance phone charge.

Tufts University Pet Loss Support Hotline
(508-839-7966)
Staffed M–F 6:00 P.M.–9:00 P.M. Eastern Time

Insurance Companies

Pet Assure
10 S. Morris Street
Dover, NJ 07801
(888-789-7387)
(fax: 973-442-7547)
www.petassure.com
A discount membership that offers a 25-percent discount with participating vets and 10-percent discount with certain mail-order companies. They offer a family plan.

Petshealth Insurance Agency
(800-799-5852)
Available in all but a few states.

Veterinary Pet Insurance Co.
4175 E. La Palma
Suite 100
Anaheim, CA 92807
(800-872-7387)
www.petinsurance.com
Available in all but a few states.

Pet-Sitter Organizations

National Association of Professional Pet Sitters
1030 15th Street N.W.
Suite 870
Washington, D.C. 20005
(referral network: 800-296-7387)
www.petsitters.com

Pet Sitters International
418 East King Street
King, NC 27021-9163
(pet sitter locator line: 800-268-7487)
www.petsit.com

Registry Organizations

American Association of Cat Enthusiasts (AACE)
P.O. Box 213
Pine Brook, NJ 07058
(973-335-6717)
(fax: 973-334-5834)
www.aaceinc.org

American Cat Association (ACA)
8101 Katherine Avenue
Panorama City, CA 91402
(818-781-5656)

American Cat Fanciers Association (ACFA)
P.O. Box 203
Point Lookout, MO 65726
(417-334-5430)
www.acfacat.com

Canadian Cat Association (CCA)
220 Advance Blvd.
Suite 101
Brampton, Ontario, CANADA L6T 4J5
(905-459-1481)

Cat Fanciers' Association (CFA)
P.O. Box 1005
Manasquan, NJ 08736
(908-528-9797)
www.cfainc.org

Cat Fanciers Federation (CFF)
P.O. Box 661
Gratis, OH 45330
(937-787-9009)
www.cffinc.org

The International Cat Association (TICA)
P.O. Box 2684
Harlingen, TX 78551
(956-428-8046)

Index

pills, administering, 77–78
plants:
    poisonous, 43, 60, 129, 329,
        331
    potted, using as litter box, 181
play, 103–23
    aggression during, 143
    aging and, 303
    behavior modification and, 112–
        114
    biting and scratching during,
        140–41
    bubble blowing and laser glow-
        ing, 107–8
    catnip and, 114–16
    defining, 104–5
    fighting vs., 120–21
    interactive, 105–7, 108, 110,
        111, 112–14
    in multicat households, 111
    nocturnal, 137–38
    and taking photographs of your
        cat, 121–23
    time for, 109–11
    toys in, see toys
playful body posture, 35
pleural effusion, 350
pneumonia, 350
pneumonitis, 387
pneumothorax, 351
poisons, 43, 326–30, 388
    household substances, 326–27,
        329
    plants, 43, 60, 129, 329, 331
polyarthritis, 363
predatory aggression, 148
pregnancy, feline:
    caring for pregnant cat, 288–
        289
    false, 375
pregnant women, and cats, 4, 160
    preparing your cat for the baby's
        arrival, 236–39
product manufacturers, resource
    guide for, 399–401
Program, 259

protein, 199–200
pulmonary edema, 350
pulse, how to take, 76
purebred cats, 7
purr, 29
pyelonephritis, 354
pyometra, 374

Quickdraw McPaw, 107, 239

rabies, 384–85
radiographs, 71
registry organizations, 403
relationships, 223–40
    bringing a second cat into the
        home, 223–27, 303
    children, 5, 239–40
    easing tension in multicat
        households, 227–30
    guests and other strangers,
        234
    introducing a dog to your cat,
        230–34
    new baby, 236–39
    new spouse, 234–36
renal secondary hyperparathy-
    roidism, 364
reproductive system disorders,
    373–79
    infertility, 378–79
    signs of, 373
rescue groups, 11
resource guide, 399–403
respiratory distress, 316
respiratory rate, 24, 76–77
respiratory system disorders, 348–
    351
ribbon and string, 41–42
    stringed toys, 109, 120
ringworm, 19, 344–45
rodent ulcer, 347
roundworms, 336
rubber bands, 41–42
rubbing, 33

safety:
    home, 4–5, 39–63
    outdoors, 50–51
    toys and, 109, 120
salmonellosis, 386
"save our pet" signs, 63
scabies, feline, 342
scent marking, 31–33, 54
    spraying, 6, 32–33, 54, 55, 162,
        163, 169–70, 171–80
scratching, 27, 33, 88, 89, 183–
    194
    cat scratch disease and, 386–
        387
    declawing and, 168, 184–85
    horizontal, 192
    need for, 184
    plastic nail caps and, 192–93
    in play, 140–41
scratching pads, 192
scratching posts, 4, 89–90, 150,
    185–91, 192
    choosing of, 186–87
    location of, 189
    making your own, 187–88
    replacing of, 193–94
    training your cat to use, 189–
        192
sebaceous (oil) glands, 32, 251,
    346
seizures, 371–72
septicemia, 377
shedding, 242
shelters, 5–6, 10–11
shock, 319–20
sinusitis, 394–95
sitters, pet, 276–78, 403
skin, 19
skin disorders, 340
    acne, 251, 346
    allergies, 342–44
    feline miliary dermatitis, 343
    flea-bite hypersensitiviy, 258,
        342–43
    solar dermatitis, 347–48
skunk encounters, 256